UNITED STATES ECONOMIC
MEASURES AGAINST CUBA

UNITED STATES ECONOMIC MEASURES AGAINST CUBA

Proceedings in the United Nations and International Law Issues

Introduction by Richard Falk

EDITED AND WITH COMMENTARY BY MICHAEL KRINSKY AND DAVID GOLOVE

ALETHEIA PRESS
NORTHAMPTON, MASSACHUSETTS

Aletheia Press
P.O. Box 1178
Northampton, Massachusetts 01061

Manufactured in the United States of America

Library of Congress Cataloging-in-Publication Data

United States economic measures against Cuba : proceedings in the
    United Nations and international law issues / edited and with
    commentary by Michael Krinsky and David Golove ; introduction
    by Richard Falk.
            p.   cm.
    ISBN 1-880831-02-3 (lib. bdg. : alk. paper) : $55.00.—ISBN 1-
880831-01-5 (pbk. : alk. paper) : $20.00
    1. Sanctions (International law) 2. Economic sanctions, Ameri-
can—Cuba. I. Krinsky, Michael. II. Golove, David.
JX1246.U54 1993
337.7291073—dc20   92-43229
                                                           CIP

SUMMARY OF CONTENTS

PREFACE xvii

ACKNOWLEDGMENTS xxiii

INTRODUCTION BY RICHARD FALK 1

PART I: PROCEEDINGS IN THE UNITED NATIONS
          GENERAL ASSEMBLY 13

PART II: SCOPE OF UNITED STATES ECONOMIC
          MEASURES 85

PRINCIPAL FEATURES OF THE UNITED STATES ECONOMIC
MEASURES AGAINST CUBA 86

RECENT UNITED STATES EFFORTS TO INTERFERE WITH
THIRD COUNTRY TRADE AND INVESTMENTS 97

CHRONOLOGY OF UNITED STATES LEGAL MEASURES 107

ECONOMIC CONTEXT FOR THE CURRENT UNITED STATES MEASURES 127

PART III: UNITED STATES PROGRAM AND PURPOSES:
          1989-1992 135

THE NEW RATIONALE: PROMOTION OF REPRESENTATIVE
DEMOCRACY AND A MARKET ECONOMY 136

INTENSIFICATION OF UNITED STATES ECONOMIC MEASURES 163

ALTERNATIVE APPROACHES TO UNITED STATES-CUBA RELATIONS 169

PRESIDENT FIDEL CASTRO ON DEMOCRACY IN CUBA 180

PART IV: MEASURES AFFECTING THIRD COUNTRIES:
           THE INTERNATIONAL LAW ISSUES 185

EUROPEAN COMMUNITY AND CANADIAN OBJECTIONS 188

ORGANIZATION OF AMERICAN STATES 212

UNITED STATES LEGAL POSITION 218

PART V: ECONOMIC COERCION AND FREE TRADE IN
           INTERNATIONAL LAW 233

INTERNATIONAL INSTRUMENTS 235

UNITED NATIONS RESOLUTIONS ON THE USE OF ECONOMIC COERCION
BY DEVELOPED COUNTRIES AGAINST DEVELOPING COUNTRIES 242

1989 UNITED NATIONS GROUP OF LEGAL EXPERTS AND THE
INTERNATIONAL COURT OF JUSTICE 246

TRADITIONAL UNITED STATES POSITION ON ECONOMIC COERCION 257

THE EMERGING UNITED STATES POSITION AND ITS INTERNATIONAL
RECEPTION: ECONOMIC COERCION TO PROMOTE DEMOCRATIC CHANGE 274

NOTE ON THE UNITED STATES' RELIANCE ON THE 1975 OAS
RESOLUTION ON CUBA 301

NOTE ON NATIONALIZATION OF UNITED STATES-OWNED PROPERTY 309

NOTE ON UNITED STATES ALLEGATIONS OF CUBAN HUMAN
RIGHTS VIOLATIONS 312

FREE TRADE: GATT AND THE NEW INTERNATIONAL
ECONOMIC ORDER 319

APPENDIX: ADDITIONAL GENERAL ASSEMBLY
            MATERIALS 333

CONTENTS

PREFACE xvii

ACKNOWLEDGMENTS xxiii

INTRODUCTION BY RICHARD FALK 1

PART I: PROCEEDINGS IN THE UNITED NATIONS
           GENERAL ASSEMBLY 13

Forty-Sixth Session (1991)

CUBA'S REQUEST FOR CONSIDERATION OF ITEM TITLED
"NECESSITY OF ENDING THE ECONOMIC, COMMERCIAL
AND FINANCIAL EMBARGO IMPOSED BY THE UNITED
STATES OF AMERICA AGAINST CUBA" 18

UNITED STATES RESPONSE TO THE CUBAN INITIATIVE 20

CUBA'S SPECIFICATION OF THE EXTRATERRITORIAL
REACH OF THE UNITED STATES MEASURES 20

UNITED STATES COMMUNICATIONS WITH
MEMBER STATES 26

CUBA'S MEMORANDUM ON THE LEGALITY OF THE
UNITED STATES MEASURES 29

CUBA'S REQUEST TO DEFER FURTHER CONSIDERATION
OF THE AGENDA ITEM 35

UNITED STATES COMMENT ON THE DECISION
TO DEFER 36

Forty-Seventh Session (1992)

CUBA'S RESPONSE TO UNITED STATES RESTRICTIONS
ON THIRD-COUNTRY SHIPPING 38

CUBA'S RESPONSE TO THE CUBAN DEMOCRACY ACT
OF 1992 44

UNITED STATES "TALKING POINTS," FALL 1992 49

CUBA'S REVISED DRAFT RESOLUTION 51

GENERAL ASSEMBLY DEBATE, NOVEMBER 24, 1992 52

TALLY OF THE VOTE, NOVEMBER 24, 1992 83

PART II: SCOPE OF UNITED STATES ECONOMIC
MEASURES 85

PRINCIPAL FEATURES OF THE UNITED STATES ECONOMIC
MEASURES AGAINST CUBA 86

BILATERAL ASPECTS 86

PROHIBITIONS AFFECTING THIRD COUNTRIES 89

STATUTORY AUTHORITY FOR ADMINISTRATIVE
MEASURES 92

LEGISLATIVE MEASURES AFFECTING TRADE
WITH CUBA 94

RECENT UNITED STATES EFFORTS TO INTERFERE WITH
THIRD COUNTRY TRADE AND INVESTMENTS 97

THIRD-COUNTRY TRADE WITH NO UNITED
STATES NEXUS 97

THIRD-COUNTRY SUBSIDIARIES OF UNITED STATES
CORPORATIONS 100

UNITED STATES-ORIGIN PARTS 102

CUBAN NICKEL 104

NATIONALIZATION CLAIMS 104

PAST PRACTICES 106

CHRONOLOGY OF UNITED STATES LEGAL MEASURES 107

ECONOMIC CONTEXT FOR THE CURRENT UNITED
STATES MEASURES 127

ANDREW ZIMBALIST, THE COST OF THE UNITED STATES
EMBARGO AND ITS EXTRATERRITORIAL APPLICATION
TO THE CUBAN ECONOMY 127

PART III: UNITED STATES PROGRAM AND PURPOSES:
1989-1992 135

THE NEW RATIONALE: PROMOTION OF REPRESENTATIVE
DEMOCRACY AND A MARKET ECONOMY 136

ROBERT S. GELBARD, PRINCIPAL DEPUTY ASSISTANT
SECRETARY OF STATE FOR INTER-AMERICAN AFFAIRS,
APRIL 8, 1992 137

CUBAN DEMOCRACY ACT OF 1992 147

NOTE ON PASSAGE OF THE CUBAN DEMOCRACY ACT 155

NOTE COMPARING UNITED STATES POLICY
TOWARD CHINA 156

NOTE ON PREVIOUS EXPLANATIONS OF UNITED
STATES POLICY 158

INTENSIFICATION OF UNITED STATES ECONOMIC MEASURES 163

REPORT TO CONGRESS, 1988 163

NOTE ON RECENT EFFORTS TO ISOLATE CUBA 166

Alternative Approaches to United States-Cuba Relations 169

    Robert S. McNamara, January 21, 1992 169

    Representative Dave Nagle (D-Iowa), April 2, 1992 171

    Prof. Jorge I. Dominguez, April 2, 1992 175

    Dr. Richard Lesher, President, Chamber of
    Commerce, May 9, 1992 178

    Pastors for Peace, May 1992 180

Statements of President Fidel Castro on Democracy in Cuba 180

    Speech at the First Ibero-American
    Summit, July 16, 1991 181

    Press Conference at the Summit Conference
    of the Group of Three, October 23, 1991 182

Part IV: Measures Affecting Third Countries:
          The International Law Issues 185

European Community and Canadian Objections 188

    Démarches and Other Communications, 1990-1992 188

    United Kingdom and Canadian Blocking
    Orders, 1992 195

    Note on the General Agreement on
    Tariffs and Trade 199

    European Community's 1982 Legal Comments
    on the Extraterritorial Issues Presented
    by United States Economic Measures
    Against the U.S.S.R. 200

Organization of American States 212

    1975 OAS Resolution 214

STATE DEPARTMENT RESPONSE TO THE OAS
RESOLUTION 214

AMENDMENT TO COMMERCE DEPARTMENT REGULATIONS
IN RESPONSE TO THE OAS RESOLUTION 215

WILLIAM D. RODGERS, ASSISTANT SECRETARY OF STATE
FOR INTER-AMERICAN AFFAIRS, SEPTEMBER 23, 1975 216

UNITED STATES LEGAL POSITION 218

NOTE ON THE STATE DEPARTMENT AND THE AMERICAN
LAW INSTITUTE'S RESTATEMENT OF THE FOREIGN
RELATIONS LAW OF THE UNITED STATES 218

KENNETH W. DAM, DEPUTY SECRETARY OF STATE,
EXTRATERRITORIALITY AND CONFLICTS OF
JURISDICTION, APRIL 15, 1983 224

JOHN R. STEVENSON, LEGAL ADVISER TO THE STATE
DEPARTMENT, EXTRATERRITORIALITY IN CANADIAN-
UNITED STATES RELATIONS, OCTOBER 12, 1970 230

PART V: ECONOMIC COERCION AND FREE TRADE IN
INTERNATIONAL LAW 233

INTERNATIONAL INSTRUMENTS 235

CHARTER OF THE ORGANIZATION OF
AMERICAN STATES 235

CHARTER OF THE UNITED NATIONS 236

UNITED NATION'S DECLARATION ON PRINCIPLES
OF INTERNATIONAL LAW CONCERNING FRIENDLY
RELATIONS AND CO-OPERATION AMONG STATES
IN ACCORDANCE WITH THE CHARTER OF THE
UNITED NATIONS 238

UNITED NATIONS RESOLUTIONS ON THE USE OF ECONOMIC
COERCION BY DEVELOPED COUNTRIES AGAINST
DEVELOPING COUNTRIES 242

NOTE ON THE HISTORY OF THE GENERAL ASSEMBLY
RESOLUTIONS 242

UNITED NATIONS CONFERENCE ON TRADE AND
DEVELOPMENT, RESOLUTION 152 (VI), JULY 2, 1983
REJECTION OF COERCIVE ECONOMIC MEASURES 244

GENERAL ASSEMBLY RESOLUTION 210 (XLVI),
DECEMBER 20, 1991 ECONOMIC MEASURES AS
A MEANS OF POLITICAL AND ECONOMIC COERCION
AGAINST DEVELOPING COUNTRIES 245

1989 UNITED NATIONS GROUP OF LEGAL EXPERTS AND THE
INTERNATIONAL COURT OF JUSTICE 246

NOTE ON THE EXPERTS' VIEWS AND THE NICARAGUA
OPINION 246

REPORT OF THE SECRETARY-GENERAL, OCTOBER 10, 1989
ECONOMIC MEASURES AS A MEANS OF POLITICAL AND
ECONOMIC COERCION AGAINST DEVELOPING COUNTRIES 249

CASE CONCERNING MILITARY AND PARAMILITARY
ACTIVITIES IN AND AGAINST NICARAGUA
(NICARAGUA V. UNITED STATES OF AMERICA)
(MERITS) 253

TRADITIONAL UNITED STATES POSITION ON ECONOMIC COERCION 257

The Declaration on Friendly Relations 257

NOTE ON THE UNITED STATES POSITION 257

1966 SPECIAL COMMITTEE ON PRINCIPLES OF
INTERNATIONAL LAW CONCERNING FRIENDLY
RELATIONS AND CO-OPERATION AMONG STATES 258

Opinions of the Office of the Legal Adviser to the
State Department 263

NOTE ON THE STATE DEPARTMENT'S VIEW OF THE
NONINTERVENTION PRINCIPLE 263

GEORGE H. ALDRICH, ACTING LEGAL ADVISER,
OCTOBER 25, 1974 265

DAVID H. SMALL, ASSISTANT LEGAL ADVISER FOR
NEAR EASTERN AND SOUTH ASIAN AFFAIRS,
NOVEMBER 12, 1976 268

*United States Justification for Its Economic Sanctions
against Argentina* 270

NOTE ON THE UNITED STATES VIEW OF ECONOMIC
COERCION UNDER THE OAS CHARTER 270

EXPLANATION OF UNITED STATES VOTE ON RESOLUTION
234 (XVII-0/82) OF THE INTER-AMERICAN ECONOMIC
AND SOCIAL COUNCIL, OCTOBER 22, 1982 273

THE EMERGING UNITED STATES POSITION AND ITS
INTERNATIONAL RECEPTION: ECONOMIC COERCION TO
PROMOTE DEMOCRATIC CHANGE 274

*International Court of Justice's Consideration of
Intervention to Promote Democracy* 274

NOTE ON THE REJECTION OF THE REAGAN AND
BUSH DOCTRINES BY THE INTERNATIONAL
COURT OF JUSTICE 274

CASE CONCERNING MILITARY AND PARLIAMENTARY
ACTIVITIES IN AND AGAINST NICARAGUA (NICARAGUA V.
UNITED STATES OF AMERICA) (MERITS) 276

*International Reception Given United States Economic
Sanctions against Panama* 285

NOTE ON REJECTION OF ECONOMIC COERCION BY
THE LATIN AMERICAN ECONOMIC SYSTEM 285

DECISION NUMBER 271 OF THE LATIN AMERICAN
ECONOMIC SYSTEM, MARCH 29, 1988 286

*Views of the American States on Promotion of
Democracy in the Western Hemisphere* 287

NOTE ON OAS RESOLUTION 1080 287

OAS GENERAL ASSEMBLY RESOLUTION 1080,
JUNE 5, 1991 289

STATEMENT OF THE MEXICAN REPRESENTATIVE
FOLLOWING ADOPTION OF OAS RESOLUTION 1080,
JUNE 5, 1991 290

GUADALAJARA DECLARATION, JULY 19, 1991 291

NOTE ON THE COUP IN HAITI AND OAS MEASURES
UNDER RESOLUTION 1080 293

RESOLUTION OF THE MINISTERS OF FOREIGN AFFAIRS
OF THE OAS 1/91, OCTOBER 2, 1991 SUPPORT TO THE
DEMOCRATIC GOVERNMENT OF HAITI 295

NOTE ON THE DECLARATION OF THE PRESIDENTS OF
MEXICO, COLOMBIA AND VENEZUELA AND THE
DECLARATIONS OF THE RIO GROUP ON RELATIONS
WITH CUBA AND THE HAITIAN COUP 297

NOTE ON THE UNITED STATES' RELIANCE ON THE 1975 OAS
RESOLUTION ON CUBA 301

RESOLUTION I OF THE NINTH MEETING OF
CONSULTATION OF MINISTERS OF FOREIGN
AFFAIRS, AUGUST 10, 1964...304

FINAL ACT OF THE SIXTEENTH MEETING OF
CONSULTATION OF MINISTERS OF FOREIGN
AFFAIRS, JULY 29, 1975 305

CLOSING SPEECH BY THE MINISTER OF FOREIGN
RELATIONS OF COSTA RICA AND PRESIDENT OF
THE SIXTEENTH MEETING OF CONSULTATION
OF THE MINISTERS OF FOREIGN AFFAIRS,
JULY 29, 1975 306

NOTE ON NATIONALIZATION OF UNITED STATES-OWNED PROPERTY 309

NOTE ON UNITED STATES ALLEGATIONS OF CUBAN HUMAN
RIGHTS VIOLATIONS 312

FREE TRADE: GATT AND THE NEW INTERNATIONAL
ECONOMIC ORDER 319

NOTE ON ECONOMIC EMBARGOES UNDER GATT 319

GENERAL AGREEMENT ON TARIFFS AND TRADE 322

GATT: THIRTY-EIGHTH SESSION AT MINISTERIAL
LEVEL, MINISTERIAL DECLARATION,
NOVEMBER 29, 1982 324

NOTE ON THE NEW INTERNATIONAL
ECONOMIC ORDER 325

CHARTER OF ECONOMIC RIGHTS AND
DUTIES OF STATES 327

APPENDIX: ADDITIONAL GENERAL ASSEMBLY
              MATERIALS 333

A1. RESOLUTION OF THE LATIN AMERICAN
PARLIAMENT 333

A2. STATEMENTS BY RELIGIOUS BODIES 334

Regional Committee of the Christian Peace
Conference in Latin America and the Caribbean 334

O.A. Romero Study and Solidarity Group......................... 335

Bishop of the Methodist Church of Cuba 335

Methodist Church of Cuba 336

Council of Methodist Churches in Latin America
and the Caribbean.. 336

Dr. Martin Luther King, Jr. Memorial Centre 338

Cuban Ecumenical Council 338

A3. STATEMENT BY CUBAN AMBASSADOR ALARCÓN
BEFORE THE GENERAL COMMITTEE, SEPTEMBER 18, 1991 339

A4. THE FIRST MEETING OF THE GENERAL COMMITTEE,
SEPTEMBER 18, 1991 343

A5. ADDITIONAL UNITED STATES COMMUNICATIONS WITH
MEMBER STATES, FALL 1991 344

A6. CUBA'S DRAFT RESOLUTION, FORTY-SIXTH
SESSION 346

A7. AMBASSADOR ALARCÓN'S ADDRESS TO THE GENERAL
ASSEMBLY PLENARY MEETING, NOVEMBER 13, 1991 347

A8. GENERAL ASSEMBLY PLENARY MEETING,
NOVEMBER 13, 1991 355

A9. SUMMARY OF PRESS CONFERENCE HELD BY
AMBASSADOR ALARCÓN, NOVEMBER 14, 1992 355

A10. CUBA'S INITIAL RESPONSE TO UNITED STATES
RESTRICTIONS ON THIRD-COUNTRY SHIPPING,
APRIL 27, 1992 363

A11. CUBA'S DRAFT RESOLUTION, FORTY-SEVENTH SESSION 365

A12. ADDITIONAL REMARKS AT THE GENERAL
ASSEMBLY PLENARY MEETING, NOVEMBER 24, 1992 366

PREFACE

The hope of this volume is to facilitate consideration of the United States economic embargo against Cuba in the light of international law. Although more than three decades old, there is new reason to subject the United States effort to legal scrutiny, and a new urgency.

Notwithstanding the end of the cold war, the United States has intensified its economic pressure against Cuba and, by the State Department's own estimate, has helped bring that nation close to economic collapse. The cold war concerns once cited by the United States as its reasons for pushing Cuba to the economic brink and, if possible, beyond—Cuba's strategic alliance with the Soviet Union and its support for armed insurgencies in third countries—are gone. In their place, the United States advances a radically different rationale, the promotion of political democracy and a market economy in Cuba.

No international body has approved such a venture in economic coercion, and none of the United States' traditional allies has joined in it. Moreover, the United States has withdrawn from the accommodation it reached in the mid-seventies with Western and Latin American countries wishing to pursue their own trade policies toward Cuba. The United States' renewed prohibition against foreign subsidiary trade with Cuba and its renewed sanctions against third-country vessels that trade in Cuban ports, as well as other measures and threats against third-country interests, have brought the United States into sharp conflict with virtually the entire international community, including its closest allies.

Cuba and others have long asserted that the United States' true and unchanging goal is to restore its pre-revolution control over the island. They cite in support the United States' decision to intensify sanctions even though the traditional national security rationales no longer obtain. Some identify the animating force behind United States policy to be the Cuban exile community in Miami, which they view as pursuing similar ambitions. But even accepting the United States' current explanation for its policies, weighty and perhaps dispositive questions are posed. Are economic measures of the scope and intensity mounted by the United States permissible under international law when they are undertaken for the purpose of transforming the internal political and economic system of a sovereign state? What limits does international law place on United States efforts to secure third-country compliance with its embargo policies?

We do not seek to answer these and related questions of international law in this volume. We do seek to provide information and documentary materials necessary for their consideration. While directed to the legality *vel non* of the United States effort, our exposition of the United States measures—their current scope and historic evolution, their present and past rationales, their basis in international law and their international reception—should prove helpful to a policy evaluation as well.

Our point of departure is the recent proceedings at the United Nations. The General Assembly's adoption of a resolution condemning aspects of the United States embargo is a development of substantial significance. The General Assembly debate, moreover, helps frame the pertinent legal issues. In Part I, we reprint with explanatory commentary substantially all the material from the General Assembly proceedings.

In Parts II and III we provide a full exposition of the United States measures. We then turn in Parts IV and V to the legal issues which emerged from the General Assembly proceedings as central to their consideration.

In Part II we detail the current United States prohibitions in both their bilateral and multilateral aspects, trace the President's statutory authority for imposing such measures, and provide a chronology of their evolution since the Cuban revolution in 1959. We also summarize a series of incidents spanning the years of the Bush administration in which the United States reportedly went beyond the scope of its published administrative regulations to disrupt third-country trade and investment with Cuba. We conclude Part II with Professor Andrew Zimbalist's economic study of Cuba's special vulnerability as it seeks to establish new international trade and financial links in the wake of the Eastern bloc's collapse.

In Part III we examine changes in the United States program and policies during the period 1989 through 1992. We note the ways in which the Bush administration and Congress alike sought to intensify United States economic pressure on Cuba, and we delineate the shift in rationale from traditional security and foreign policy concerns to the promotion of democracy and a market economy. We reprint at length the Bush administration's explanation of its policies and the text of Congress' recent initiative (the Cuban Democracy Act of 1992), contrast the previous explanations offered by the United States for its economic campaign against Cuba, and provide a sampling of alternative views advanced in the United States domestic policy debate about Cuba.

In the General Assembly proceedings, the international community condemned the United States for the extraterritorial reach of its economic measures. This is a controversy with many antecedents in the United States embargo programs against Cuba and other countries. In Part IV we first set out the European Community's legal objections to the Cuban Democracy Act of 1992, which brought that controversy to a head. We then contrast the sharply divergent international law theories of national jurisdiction historically advocated by the United States, on the one hand, and by Western Europe, Canada, and Latin America on the other.

In Part V we come to the overriding legal issue of economic coercion. In the General Assembly debate, Cuba charged that the United States economic measures, designed to coerce changes in Cuba's political and economic institutions, violated the fundamental international law principles of nonintervention and the sovereign equality of states. The United States asserted that every state has the unfettered discretion under international law to determine its own trade relations and so the nonintervention principle is inapposite. Since the Cuban draft resolution was directed principally to the extraterritoriality issue, the General Assembly debate on economic coercion was inconclusive. Nonetheless, the historic rift between the Northern industrialized states and the states of the Southern tier on the scope and meaning of the nonintervention principle was discernible. The General Assembly may well take up the issue again when it returns to the United States economic measures at its next session in fall 1993.

We begin our exposition of the economic coercion issue with the great post–World War II international instruments upon which Cuba relies, setting out their text in pertinent part and providing a variety of historical materials on the meaning of their edicts against intervention. We set out the traditional United States position that trade relations are within the scope of a sovereign's discretion. We trace the divergence and ultimate confrontation between the Northern industrialized countries and the countries of the Southern tier on the legal implications of the nonintervention principle for the use of coercive economic measures and we suggest the importance of the issue in North-South relations.

We then treat at length the United States position which emerged during the Reagan and Bush administrations and its international reception to date: that whatever the constraints of the nonintervention principle otherwise might be, the use of coercive measures as well as other forms of pressure to promote democratic reforms is legitimate. Our inquiry focuses on the cases of Nicaragua, Panama, and Haiti, for these are defining conflicts in recent North-South relations and carry broad doctrinal implications.

The case of Haiti is of particular moment and receives special attention. All of the states of the Western hemisphere, with the support of the United Nations General Assembly, have joined in the use of economic coercion to achieve the reinstatement of the elected Aristide government. Additionally, they have established by unanimous consent more general procedures for the collective defense of the democratic governments of the hemisphere. Yet most of Latin America and the Caribbean remains dedicated to the nonintervention principle. Concern with military coups against newly or only episodically democratic governments and concern with historic patterns of pressure and intervention from the North vie in their legal doctrine.

The documents provided here illustrate the effort by Latin American and Caribbean states to reconcile these competing concerns. They suggest an attempt to differentiate between collective measures to defend existing democracies such as in the case of the Organization of American States' Haiti sanctions and unilateral measures to coerce democratic changes in existing regimes. This is particularly evident in the positions these states have taken on the United States economic measures against Cuba.

Other issues emerged in the General Assembly proceedings, albeit as secondary themes, and we treat these as well in Part V—Cuba's nationalization of United States-owned property in 1959 and 1960, United States allegations of human rights violations by Cuba, and Cuba's reliance on free trade principles.

Our method throughout has been to mix primary documentary sources with our own extended exposition of the United States measures and relevant developments in international law and practice. Much of the documentary material has not been readily accessible before.

This volume, we trust, may profitably be read cover to cover. Since we contemplate it also serving those without that interest or inclination, however, we have sought to make each of the volume's five sections coherent without reference to the other sections. For example, the reader can turn directly to Parts IV and V for an exposition of the international law issues that emerged from the General Assembly proceedings, and skip the primary documentary materials from the General Assembly proceedings set out in Part I.

We commend to the reader the valuable introduction to this volume contributed by Professor Richard Falk of Princeton University. In a wide-ranging, substantive discussion, Professor Falk sets the United States economic measures in the broad sweep of post–World War II developments in international law and relations as well as in the historic dynamic of United States-Cuban relations. He argues their illegality under contemporary international law, with its central commitment to respect each sovereign's choice of political and economic systems and its understanding of the link between nonintervention as a norm and maintenance of international peace and security. Professor Falk also explains why the United States economic campaign against Cuba is a test of whether the United States can pursue a foreign policy that is consistent with international law, particularly in its relations with small, neighboring states in the South.

Our interest in the issues addressed here grows out of our legal practice. Our law firm has represented governments and individuals confronted with United States embargoes, most notably but not exclusively the government of Cuba. Our work on this volume, which is independent of that representation, was supported by a generous grant from the John D. and Catherine T. MacArthur Foundation.

This volume appears at what could be a decisive moment, with the change in United States administrations, the end of cold war concerns and rationales, and passage of the General Assembly resolution. We believe that now, more than ever, consideration of the international law issues we seek to elucidate is essential.

Michael Krinsky and David Golove
New York, New York
January 21, 1993

ACKNOWLEDGMENTS

Publication of this book was made possible by a generous grant from the John D. and Catherine T. MacArthur Foundation, which is gratefully acknowledged.

Richard Falk, Albert G. Milbank Professor of International Law and Practice, Princeton University, was instrumental in the realization of this project of the North American chapter of the Lelio Basso Foundation for the Rights and Liberation of Peoples (Rome), which he chairs. We wish to acknowledge as well the Lelio Basso Foundation in Rome for the encouragement it provided to its North American chapter and to thank for their assistance and enthusiasm Sara Di Grazia, Howard Friel and Jason Dirks of Aletheia Press, June Garson, Kezia Gleckman Hayman, Kimberly Stanton, Professor Andrew Zimbalist, and our law partners whose welcomed forbearance was essential.

We dedicate this volume to our spouses, Ann and Susan, and to our children, Joshua, Sam, Laura, and an eagerly awaited but yet to arrive son.

INTRODUCTION

Richard Falk

This volume is being published as a project of the North American chapter of the Lelio Basso International Foundation for the Rights and Liberation of Peoples (Rome), an independent educational organization concerned with issues of human rights, democracy, and intervention. A particular concern of the Basso Foundation has been the use of interventionary tactics by the countries of the industrialized North as a way of exerting control over the countries of the developing South in the postcolonial era.

We of the North American chapter are proud to publish this volume. The materials collected here represent the first systematic attempt to offer interested readers a balanced and scholarly account of the use of economic sanctions against Cuba: their evolution, their scope, and their problematic character under international law. In highlighting the pertinent issues of international law, making available inaccessible documentary materials, and providing interpretive and explanatory editorial guidance, this volume makes a significant contribution to a critical understanding of official U.S. policy toward Cuba, especially as assessed from the perspective of international law.

The editors of this collection, Michael Krinsky and David Golove, have contributed extensive commentary based on their knowledge and experience in the area of economic sanctions and international law. Both editors are associated with the New York law firm Rabinowitz, Boudin, Standard, Krinsky, and Lieberman, an organization having wide-ranging experience representing states seeking to cope with the impact of U.S. economic sanctions. For example, the firm represented the government of Chile during the Allende period, the Central Bank of Iran during the hostage crisis when Iranian assets were frozen, as well as the government of Cuba since 1960. These same American lawyers have also represented the Aristide government of Haiti, as well as various United States citizens seeking to vindicate their constitutional rights in the face of restraints imposed by the sanctions policy of the U.S. government.

Publication of these materials at this time seems especially appropriate in light of recent dramatic and divergent developments. In one direction, there has been a further tightening and extension of sanctions by way of the Cuban Democracy Act of 1992 (the so-called Torricelli Bill), a legislative step that had broad bipartisan support in the U.S. Congress, was encouraged by the Bush administration, and was backed by Bill Clinton during the presidential campaign. In another direction, an unprecedented condemnation of the extraterritorial aspects of U.S. economic sanctions against Cuba took place in the form of United Nations General Assembly Resolution 47/19, which was passed on November 24, 1992, by a one-sided fifty-nine to three vote (with seventy-one abstentions), and which also enjoyed the overt support of official organs of the European Community, such significant Latin American countries as Mexico, Brazil, and Venezuela, and normally reliable Western states such as Canada, France, Spain, and New Zealand.

The vote was even more one-sided than it appeared, as other important U.S. allies, including the United Kingdom, have expressed their strong objections to the extraterritorial aspects of the U.S. sanctions but abstained in the U.N. setting, presumably to avoid straining relations with the United States. But the policy divergence is clear and significant. The main countries of Western Europe seek normal economic relations with Cuba and have recently provided Cuba with some economic assistance—not, to be sure, in amounts that offset the loss of Soviet aid, but it is nonetheless symbolically revealing and underscores the vindictiveness of the U.S. approach.

Such commitments to normal economic relations with Cuba do not necessarily imply approval of Cuba's internal policies, nor do they imply a reluctance to complain about Cuban internal policies in appropriate forums if deemed to violate international human rights standards. What is implied, however, is respect for Cuba's sovereign rights, including its right of self-determination. To deny these rights is to violate international legal prohibitions on intervention in internal affairs and to deny small states the benefit of equal rights under international law.

This U.N. initiative is especially impressive in light of current U.S. influence within the Organization. The resolution challenges directly the extensive sanctioning efforts of the United States that seek to minimize non–U.S. trading relations with Cuba entered into from foreign territories. In this regard, the U.S. sanctions policy is not only being challenged from the perspective of the sovereign rights of other countries, but it is having the effect of revealing how diplomatically isolated the United States has become in regard to its Cuba policy. The implications of the U.N. resolution are twofold: first, that virtually every country other than the United States favors normal economic relations with Cuba as a matter of national policy, and second, that these countries formally object to the U.S. effort to entangle their relations with Cuba in a hostile sanctions web. The present volume includes primary materials that frame this controversy between the U.S. government and the organized international community over respective legal rights and duties.

Of course, the issues at stake are broader and deeper than the questioning of those aspects of the U.S. embargo that attach punitive measures intended to shape the trading policies of third countries and the overseas activities of subsidiaries of U.S. corporations. The fundamenal issue of law and policy is whether it is ever appropriate to use economic coercion on a unilateral basis as a way of destabilizing the governing process of another country. Cuba has diplomatic relations with virtually the entire world at this point. In this crucial respect, the questions posed by these sanctions against Cuba are dramatically different from the legal and political assessment of sanctions against South Africa during the latter stages of apartheid, against Iraq since its invasion of Kuwait, and against Haiti since the military coup against Aristide. In the first two cases, the sanctions policy enjoys the formal collective backing of the United Nations, and in the Haitian case that of the Organization of American States.

This matter of collective imposition is not a mere technicality. It suggests that reliance on economic coercion is a general community policy justified by some serious violation of fundamenal international law on the part of the target country, and not merely the projection of power by the strong in relation to the weak. Even such a collective foundation, when it exists, is no more than a necessary condition. It does not by itself ensure the legality of sanctions or their moral appropriateness. Increasingly, collective sanctions are facing criticism and legal challenge in a number of settings. For instance, the maintenance of U.N. sanctions against Iraq since the cease-fire in the Gulf War has been widely criticized on humanitarian grounds as increasing the suffering of the Iraqi civilian population while no longer serving any legitimate international purpose. Indeed, several independent assessments have concluded that continuing sanctions against Iraq have had a counterproductive impact on their alleged goal of putting pressure on the Iraqi government and especially on its notorious leader, Saddam Hussein. In these circumstances, sanctions seem to have created in Iraq a mood of siege, giving Saddam and the Baath party the opportunity to present Iraq and its people as embattled victims of a vindictive international order, being crudely manipulated by the United States.

Nevertheless, without such a collective process of imposition a sanctions policy is without doubt more legally and politically dubious. The case of Cuba is exemplary. Here is a small, poor, and vulnerable country located close to an aggressive superpower. Cuba has been continuously subjected to more than thirty years of economic sanctions in one form or another, with justifications shifting as circumstances change. For much of this period the main official justification relied upon in Washington was the degree to which Cuba provided the Soviet Union with a vehicle for hemispheric penetration.[1] But more recently, with the end of the cold war and the collapse of the Soviet Union, the emphasis has been shifted to Cuba's internal political life, its alleged violations of human rights, and its denial of political democracy.[2] Such contentions seem arbitrary, especially considering the willingness of the U.S. government to look the other way in recent years in cases of far worse abuses of human rights on the part of other countries in the region such as Guatemala, El Salvador, and Honduras. Even ideological factors do not suffice as explanation, given the willingness of the United States to overlook the far worse human rights record of the Peoples Republic of China.

The answers to the question "Why Cuba?" seem painfully obvious from an objective viewpoint: first of all, the existence of a well-organized anti-Castro exile community in the United States that has used its financial and political influence effectively, second, an anti-Marxist animus in Washington that regards Cuba as ripe for destabilzation in light of the withdrawal of Soviet support and the collapse of world communism, and third, the geopolitical legacy of Monroe Doctrine–era diplomacy that regards Central America and the entire Caribbean as falling within a U.S. sphere of influence. Understanding these pressures helps to explain why the U.S. government would persist with, and more astonishingly extend further, a policy that was controversial and legally and morally dubious during the height of the cold war.

From another perspective, the U.S. government, from the outset of the Castro era, has been asserting its historical claims to control the political destinies of the hemisphere, and especially the countries situated nearby. In the language of geopolitics, Cuba—since the beginning of its existence as an independent country in the aftermath of the Spanish-American War (1898)—has had the gross misfortune to fall squarely within a U.S. sphere of influence, and as such has experienced severe economic exploitation reinforced by periodic interventions, including several carried out before 1959 when the supposed apprehension about hemispheric penetration by an alien ideology took hold.

---

1. For a careful exposition, see David Baldwin, *Economic Statecraft* 176-180 (1985).

2. See the U.S. position taken during the U.N. General Assembly debate in 1992 preceding the adoption of Resolution 47/19.

Any country in this Caribbean/Central American region during the last several decades that has repudiated U.S. primacy has quickly become a target of intervention, including Guatemala (1954), the Dominican Republic (1965), Nicaragua (1980s), Grenada (1983), and Panama (1989), to mention the most obvious instances.

Cuba was, of course, subjected to a direct military intervention under U.S. guidance—the Bay of Pigs invasion of 1961—but withstood the challenge. Cuba's successful defense of its territory raised the stakes for the White House, because this suggested the possibility that a small Caribbean country might successfully defy the will of Washington and pursue its own independent path in foreign and domestic policy. The longevity of Castro's Cuba has been, and remains, a thorn in the side of the U.S. government. The anticapitalist orientation of Castro's Cuba (as with the other "enemies" of the U.S. government in the region since 1945) helped cause the original interventionary reflex in Washington. Critics of this interventionary diplomacy have all along insisted that official contentions based on cold war arguments and hemispheric security were largely window dressing, and that the main motivation for the policy was the threat to traditional patterns of U.S. political and economic dominance, which was rooted in market relations and profitable investment opportunities. The persisting presence on Cuban territory, throughout this entire period, of a U.S. naval base at Guantanamo Bay, acquired from Spain in the aftermath of the Spanish-American War, is indicative of the extent to which Cuban-American relations remain under a colonial shadow.

The anti-Cuban sanctions policy is also a test of whether the United States can pursue a foreign policy that is consistent with international law, particularly in its relations with small, neighboring states in the South. This century has been notable, in part, for the attempt to establish the rule of law in relations among sovereign states, especially its legal condemnation of aggressive force. Leading countries agreed on this foundational legal principle, thereby removing war from the realm of sovereign discretion, in the Pact of Paris (also known as the Kellogg-Briand Pact), concluded in 1928. This norm of behavior, flaunted by the Axis Powers of Germany, Italy, and Japan during the 1930s in the lead-up to World War II, served as the main rationale for warfare relied upon by the victorious Allied Powers, led by the United States and the Soviet Union.

This experience of large-scale destructive war, culminating in the atomic attacks on Hiroshima and Nagasaki, had three principal effects relevant to the struggle to suppress aggressive war: (a) the punishment of surviving German and Japanese civilian and military leaders as individuals accountable for their failure to uphold the prohibition on aggressive war and therefore guilty of crimes against peace, a process given form in the Nuremberg Judgment and given an enduring legal reality in the substance of the Nuremberg Principles as drafted by the International Law Commission of the United Nations in 1950; (b) the embodiment of the prohibition on aggressive force (that is, all force that is not a legitimate exercise of self-defense against a prior armed attack) as a cardinal element of the United Nations Charter, a document that is regarded as the organic law of the international society of sovereign states; and (c) the so-called "lesson of Munich," named after the diplomacy of appeasement pursued by the European democracies in response to the militarism of Hitler's Germany, and climaxed by the sacrifice of Czechoslovakia to Hitler's aggressive appetites at Munich in 1938 on the mistaken premise that through appeasement Germany's claims could be satisified and a costly war avoided.

In retrospect, appeasement was discredited and the political and moral lesson learned was the importance of resisting the aggression of expansionist states early, rather than later. The lesson of Munich guided early cold war thinking in the West, leading to the Truman Doctrine, which committed the United States to the defense of Greece and Turkey in 1947 as a way of deterring the alleged threat of Soviet aggression. This policy was then generalized in terms of the strategic doctrines of containment and deterrence, and supposedly put to a decisive test during the defense of South Korea in response to an armed attack in 1950 by North Korea, a communist country regarded as incapable of acting without prior approval from the Kremlin. These developments, each complex and susceptible to varying lines of interpretation, strongly underscore the attempt on the part of the world community to reinforce and make effective the prohibition on aggressive force.

But the record remains mixed and problematic, especially in regard to the behavior of the United States. Although formally championing all three policy-related effects of World War II described above, the United States has made a series of self-serving exceptions over the years. First of all, it insists on defining for itself what constitutes aggression and what constitutes self-defense, and has relied upon an elastic conception of defensive force that includes repeated recourse to interventionary diplomacy in its relations with the Third World. Further, the U.S. government has refused to accept the authority of the United Nations or even the World Court when its own use of force is being questioned, as was the case in the 1986 decision of the World Court that found illegal the principal U.S. efforts to destabilize the Sandinista government of Nicaragua. In addition, the U.S. government has maintained and relied upon the covert operations capabilities of the C.I.A. to project its power in a manner designed to distort the constitutional processes of other countries and evade the prohibition on aggression. The U.S. government refuses to limit its discretion to make use of covert operations as an instrument of foreign policy or even to make public the occasions on which such force is used.

And finally, policymakers and leaders in the United States, backed by the academic establishment, have embraced an approach to other countries based on what can be described as the "realist consensus," namely, treating law and morality as irrelevant in the relations among sovereign states and especially in the shaping of the foreign policy of a superpower. George Kennan and Dean Acheson, the architects of cold war thinking, were articulate advocates of realism, as were such later luminaries as Henry Kissinger and Zbigniew Brzezinski. Realism also found its way into academic circles, including the domain of international law. Many leading jurists have either accepted at face value U.S. rationalizations for recourse to force in the implementation of its foreign policy, or have argued that a superpower cannot be expected to restrict its freedom of action in pursuit of national interests out of deference to international law.[3] A clear endorsement of such realism is to be found in Thomas Franck's qualified support for the refusal of the U.S. government to respect the authority of the World Court in relation to its direct and indirect reliance on force against Nicaragua during the 1980s.[4]

The evolution of U.S. foreign policy in the more than three decades since the triumph of the Cuban revolution is a textbook instance of the gap between the abstractions of contemporary international law and the concrete realities of geopolitics. Cuba has had the double misfortune of having its revolutionary experience interpreted by the U.S. government and a largely compliant news media, without confirming evidence, as being part of the Soviet expansionist challenge and thereby subject to the broader teachings of the lessons of Munich. The whole interaction has been one long series of self-fulfilling prophesies enacted at Cuba's expense. Initially, U.S. leaders insisted that Cuba under Castro was dangerous because it was a Soviet outpost in the hemisphere, thereby effectively denying Cuba's leaders any choice, and, ironically, driving Cuba into a condition of security and economic dependence on Moscow by mounting a variety of interventionary operations (overt and covert) and embarking on a policy of unrelenting economic warfare against this poor and vulnerable country.

As might have been expected under such circumstances, neither Havana nor Moscow were consistently prudent in response, as highlighted by the Soviet attempt to deploy nuclear missiles on Cuban territory. This deployment led to the Cuban Missile Crisis in 1962, the closest call to World War III throughout the entire cold war. The failure of the

3. For an elaborate exercise in legal rationalization, see John Norton Moore, *The Secret War in Central America: Sandinista Assault on World Order* (1987).

4. Professor Franck's defense of realism is to be found in his book, *Judging the World Court* (1986); the position is more generally argued in Franck, *Nation Against Nation: What Happened to the U.N. Dream and What the U.S. Can Do About It* (1985).

military intervention at the Bay of Pigs and the near disaster of the Cuban Missile Crisis a year later convinced both superpowers that it was futile and unacceptably risky to determine the destiny of Cuba by military means. These unsuccessful military gambles on both sides induced the shift to economic warfare. As is well known, the United States mounted as much pressure as it could over the years, while the Soviet Union acted to offset some of this pressure by providing Cuba with massive economic assistance, including purchasing a large share of Cuban sugar at subsidized prices and supplying most of Cuba's petroleum needs. Thus, during this period Cuba was decisively cast in its historical role as pawn in the superpower rivalry because neither the United States nor the Soviet Union would back down or move toward a posture of respect for Cuba as a sovereign state entitled to pursue its own independent destiny within the limits of international law. The U.S. government has never been able to accept the reality of Castro's Cuba, while the Soviet government was willing to go to great lengths to keep an ideological ally from collapsing under pressures exerted by its rival. As in many other instances of cold war confrontation, the outcome was a stalemate from the perspective of the two superpowers, but the Third World country bore the burden.

One does not have to accept the conspiratorial explanation of John F. Kennedy's assassination—depicted, for instance, in Oliver Stone's film *JFK*—to be convinced that no U.S. President has enjoyed the domestic freedom of action to normalize relations with Cuba at any point along the way. The Cuban lobby as concentrated in Miami has been strong, focused, and influential, and has been backed by powerful, right-wing elements in the Washington security establishment, including the C.I.A. and Pentagon. Its supporters also include capitalist interests that remain committed to restoring Cuba to its pre-Castro status as an American tourist playground and foreign investors' paradise, virtually without government regulation and serious taxes on business operations. In this regard, it is not difficult to grasp the bipartisan continuity and the realist character of U.S. foreign policy toward Cuba, despite normalizing initiatives from Havana at various points and the failure of economic warfare to destabilize Castro or even to weaken the Cuban commitment to revolutionary solidarity, as expressed by its role in southern African countries during the 1970s and early 1980s.

Against this background of frustration and continuing domestic pressure, it becomes more understandable why the end of the cold war has brought about an intensification, rather than an abandonment, of anti-Castro policies. Expectations in Washington have moved from the realm of symbolism to the realm of substance. With the withdrawal of Soviet diplomatic and economic support, the Castro government seems finally vulnerable. After all, if the Sandinistas could be driven from power, why not Castro? The effort to extend sanctions extraterritorially, even at the expense of friction with allies and in opposition to the espousal of a free-trade outlook, should be interpreted as part of this escalated effort to tighten the screws, thereby denying Cuba the benefit, to the extent possible short of an actual blockade, of economic relations with third countries.

But an appreciation of the factors that have held U.S. foreign policy toward Cuba rigid for all these years should not be allowed to obscure its illegal character. The illegality of training and financing of Cuban exiles for a military expedition of the sort that eventuated in the Bay of Pigs should be self-evident, as is the reliance on C.I.A. maneuvers of various kinds, including well-documented efforts to assassinate Castro (even enlisting Mafia operatives as contract killers) or to undermine the Cuban constitutional order by various disruptive tactics—for example, the secret infiltration of an engine-destroying chemical into the Cuban fuel supply at one point during the 1960s to wreck the public transportation system. Less legally clear is recourse to economic warfare in the form of unilateral trade sanctions. On the one side is the U.S. claim that countries are free to trade or not with partners of their choice and retain their discretion to abandon preferential policies of aid. Opposing this is the clear extension of the prohibition on military force by way of legal norms to encompass economic coercion.

A fundamenal legal document in this regard is the Declaration on the Inadmissibility of Intervention in the Domestic Affairs of States and the Protection of their Independence and Sovereignty, United Nations General Assembly Resolution 2131 (XX), adopted with the affirmative votes of both Cuba and the United States by a count of 109 in favor, none opposed, and a single abstention, on December 21, 1965. In the preamble of G.A. Res. 2131, emphasis is placed on a comprehensive view of the duty of nonintervention as previously established by a long line of prior legal instruments, including several in the inter-American setting, and as extending to all forms of coercion intended to alter the policies or governing process of a target country.

The resolution puts appropriate stress on the equality of states—whether large or small, rich or poor, strong or weak—in relation to legal rights and duties of states, and affirms as one of the principal duties respect for rights of self-determination expressed in terms of the "conviction that all peoples have an inalienable right to complete freedom, the exercise of their sovereignty and the integrity of their national territory, and that, by virtue of that right, they freely determine their political status and freely pursue their economic, social and cultural development." In the operative provisions, the intent of the document is made more specific. In numbered paragraph 2 the text reads, "No State may use or encourage the use of economic, political or any other type of measures to coerce another State in order to obtain from it the subordination of the exercise of its sovereign rights or to secure advantages of any kind."

Other provisions of G.A. Res. 2131 reinforce this central commitment to respect the choice of political and economic systems and to the link between the obligation to respect nonintervention as a norm and the maintenance of international peace and security. As the materials in this volume make clear, the intention and effects of U.S. trade sanctions against Cuba have been flagrantly interventionary in these regards at all stages.

The U.S. government has offered a variety of quasi-legal arguments in support of its sanctions policies. These arguments have been fashioned in response to changes in the international situation, especially the dramatic shift brought about by the end of the cold war. Initially, the United States relied mainly on the argument that its economic embargo of trade with Cuba was designed to limit Cuba's capacity to export revolution to the hemisphere, and to retaliate for allegedly confiscatory Cuban expropriations of U.S.-owned property in Cuba. Later, the justification was overtly interventionary: to disrupt Castro's capacity to govern; to discredit the Cuban experience as a positive model of people-centered development that, if successful, might exert an influence on other states in the region; and to increase the costs to the Soviet Union of providing Cuba with neutralizing economic assistance.

Now is certainly an opportune moment to reconsider official U.S. policy toward Cuba. The November 1992 U.N. resolution, being so widely supported and imposing on the Secretary-General a duty to report on the extent of compliance at the next session of the General Assembly, creates new political pressure and offers a pretext to Washington to change its policies toward Cuba. New presidential leadership in the White House may also be helpful in breaking with the past. True, the Clinton presidential campaign seemed to go out of its way to endorse the Torricelli approach—the latest congressional enactment—but no binding commitment was made and the U.N. resolution has introduced a new fact into the policy-making process.

If the new leadership in the White House could be persuaded to drop the extraterritorial aspects of sanctions, then the self-defeating character of the overall policy would be exposed. In an era when economic relations with China are being actively promoted and relations with Vietnam are being gradually normalized, it would seem more anachronistic than ever for the United States to continue to regard its close neighbor Cuba as posing some sort of lethal threat to U.S. interests and values. Many officials may dislike Castro or disapprove of Cuba's human rights record, but such attitudes do not provide any legal justification for economic warfare. A primary purpose of this book is to document this absence of legal justification.

If the U.S. government remains captive to its anti-Cuba policies there are other avenues of action available. Some have recently suggested that the U.N. General Assembly should seek an advisory opinion from the World Court in the Hague, but such a possibility, even if it could be acted upon, which is unlikely, would be of only limited utility. At best, the outcome would only be "advisory." Further, the Court is not allowed to use its advisory jurisdiction to pronounce upon bilateral disputes between countries, and hence could not be expected to address the core commitment of the U.S. government to economic warfare. And finally, in the course of its decision in the *Nicaragua* case the Court seems to suggest in reference to Nicaraguan objections to a U.S. economic embargo (without extraterritorial features) that such policies did not violate customary international law.

In the end it will probably require pressure from U.S. citizens to induce the White House to change U.S. policy toward Cuba. Our hope is that this volume will encourage this process by documenting the extent to which economic warfare collides with international law and with the opportunities for peaceful and equitable international relations among sovereign states in the post–cold war world.

PART I

PROCEEDINGS IN THE UNITED NATIONS GENERAL ASSEMBLY

Over the course of two sessions in 1991 and 1992, the General Assembly, at Cuba's request, considered an agenda item titled "Necessity of ending the economic, commercial and financial embargo imposed by the United States of America against Cuba." We reprint in this volume substantially all the material from the General Assembly proceedings, from Cuba's request to include the item on the General Assembly's agenda to the General Assembly's vote on Cuba's draft resolution. In this Part I, we set out the principal Cuban and United States documents framing the issues, the verbatim transcript of the culminating debate at the General Assembly's November 24, 1992 plenary meeting, the resolution adopted by the General Assembly, and the tally of the vote. We set out the balance of the materials in an appendix at the end of the book.

In its several presentations on the item, Cuba placed substantial reliance on international law. It contended that in their extraterritorial aspects the United States measures exceeded the bounds of national jurisdiction. Cuba further contended that, in both their bilateral and multilateral aspects, the United States measures constituted unlawful economic coercion and violated the principles of nonintervention and the sovereign equality of states. The goal of the United States measures, Cuba repeatedly asserted, was to impose a political and economic order more to the liking and benefit of the United States.

The United States maintained that its economic measures with respect to Cuba were not an appropriate subject for United Nations consideration since they concerned only bilateral relations and were predicated on a sovereign's right to choose the governments with which it wishes to have commercial and political relations. In explaining why it chose not to trade with Cuba, the United States initially cited Cuban support for insurgencies in third countries, but after the political settlement in El Salvador, no longer made reference to that concern. It also cited Cuba's lack of democratic institutions, its repression of dissent, and the Cuban nationalization of United States-owned property in 1959 and 1960. The United States' somewhat abbreviated discussion of the reasons for its economic measures are supplemented in Part III of this volume, where we set out the United States' contemporaneous and historic explanations at length.

On November 13, 1991 Cuba's Ambassador addressed a plenary meeting of the General Assembly, and, after arguing Cuba's position, requested that the General Assembly defer further consideration of the item until its next session. As Cuba requested, the General Assembly took up the issue again at its forty-seventh session in November 1992. In the interim, the Congress of the United States had enacted the Cuban Democracy Act of 1992, and President Bush signed the measure into law on October 23, 1992. This legislation significantly expanded the impact of the United States economic measures on third-country relations with Cuba.

On November 24, 1992 the General Assembly, in a plenary meeting, debated and then approved a Cuban draft resolution expressing the General Assembly's concern with measures "whose extraterritorial effects affect the sovereignty of other States" and, citing the obligation under international law to refrain from such measures, called for their repeal. The resolution also reaffirmed the principles of the sovereign equality of states and nonintervention enshrined in the Charter of the United Nations and other international instruments.

The General Assembly instructed the Secretary-General to prepare a report on the resolution's implementation for its consideration during the next session. The General Assembly also placed the United States embargo on the next session's provisional agenda.

There was substantial participation in the debate leading to the adoption of the resolution. In addition to Cuba and the United States, twenty-nine member states addressed the General Assembly. The United Kingdom spoke on behalf of the European Community;[1] Indonesia spoke on behalf of the conference of non-aligned countries.[2]

[1] The European Community members are Belgium, Denmark, France, Greece, Ireland, Italy, France, Luxembourg, The Netherlands, Portugal, Spain, and the United Kingdom.

[2] The members of the non-aligned conference are: Afghanistan, Algeria, Angola, Bahamas, Bahrain, Bangladesh, Barbados, Belize, Benin, Bhutan, Bolivia, Botswana, Brunei Darussalam, Burundi, Burkina Faso, Cambodia, Cameroon, Cape Verde, Central African Republic, Chad, Chile, Colombia, Comoros, Congo, Cote D'Ivoire, Cuba, Cyprus, DPR of Korea, Djibouti, Ecuador, Egypt, Equatorial Guinea, Ethiopia, Gabon, Gambia, Ghana, Grenada, Guatemala, Guinea, Guinea-Bissau, Guyana, India,

The Cuban Ambassador delivered a lengthy address devoted to the twin themes Cuba had developed over the course of the General Assembly proceedings—the United States assertion of extraterritorial jurisdiction over third-country trade with Cuba, and the United States effort to coerce Cuba with respect to its internal affairs. The United States representative spoke briefly, insisting once again that the embargo was "essentially a bilateral issue." In delineating the "good reasons" for the United States' choosing "not to trade with Cuba," the United States representative gave new prominence to the 1960 nationalization of United States-owned property and repeated as well the United States charge of "human rights abuses and lack of democracy in Cuba." No member state with the arguable exception of Argentina defended United States policy on its merits.

Condemnation of the extraterritorial reach of the United States measures was uniform, strongly stated, and punctuated with frequent references to the Cuban Democracy Act of 1992. Those voicing support for the draft resolution maintained that the United States had exceeded its national jurisdiction under international law. Many also asserted that the United States measures affecting third countries violated the international law principle of nonintervention, since the United States was seeking to coerce third countries into modifying their sovereign decision to maintain trade relations with Cuba. Ten members of the European Community abstained but criticized the extraterritorial reach of the United States measures, and the other two E.C. members, France and Spain, voted in favor of the draft resolution. Almost without exception, member states coupled explanations of their decision to abstain with rejection of the United States assertion of extraterritorial jurisdiction.

The Cuban draft resolution placed principal emphasis on the extraterritoriality issue, and member states differed on whether the resolution required the General Assembly to take a position on Cuba's charge that the United States measures constituted unlawful intervention in Cuba's internal affairs. Some member states, such as Canada, New Zealand, and Venezuela, considered it possible to vote for the Cuban draft resolution without implying a position on the latter question, but others did not. Those disagreeing with the Cuban position, or believing

---

Indonesia, Islamic Republic of Iran, Iraq, Jamaica, Jordan, Kenya, Kuwait, Lao People's Republic, Lebanon, Lesotho, Liberia, Libyan Arab Jamahiriya, Madagascar, Malawi, Malaysia, Maldives, Mali, Malta, Mauritania, Mauritius, Mongolia, Morocco, Mozambique, Myanmar, Namibia, Nepal, Nicaragua, Niger, Nigeria, Oman, Pakistan, Palestine, Panama, Papua New Guinea, Peru, Philippines, Qatar, Rwanda, Saint Lucia, Sao Tome & Principe, Saudi Arabia, Senegal, Seychelles, Sierra Leone, Singapore, Somalia, Sri Lanka, Sudan, Suriname, Swaziland, Syrian Arab Republic, Togo, Trinidad & Tobago, Tunisia, Uganda, United Arab Emirates, United Republic of Tanzania, Uzbekistan, Vanuatu, Venezuela, Vietnam, Yemen, Yugoslavia, Zaire, Zambia, Zimbabwe.

it not wise for the General Assembly to take up the question at this juncture, abstained. Others who voted for the resolution expressed their concurrence with the Cuban view. It may be that the General Assembly will address the nonintervention issue in a more conclusive manner when, in accordance with the resolution, it considers the United States measures again at its next session in 1993.

Even though the Cuban draft resolution did not force the nonintervention issue to any conclusion, the General Assembly debate did suggest a difference of opinion drawn largely along a North-South divide. In essence, member states drawn from Latin America, Africa, and Asia agreed with the Cuban position that important—even fundamental— principles of the modern international legal order were at stake. Speaking on behalf of the conference of non-aligned countries, Indonesia relied on the principles of nonintervention and the sovereign equality of states in calling for an end to the United States economic measures.[3] Several members of the non-aligned conference delivered individual statements emphatically concluding that the United States economic measures violated those principles, with Tanzania and Vietnam giving notably full statements.

Brazil, Ecuador, and Mexico, as well as others, stopped short of expressly condemning the United States bilateral economic measures but called for the United States and Cuba to negotiate, in the words of Brazil, "pending problems in accordance with international law." In the sometimes restrained language of diplomacy, this formula communicated rejection of the United States position that it may pursue in its unfettered sovereign discretion whatever economic relations with Cuba it chooses, and suggested that, to the contrary, the United States must act within the confines of the nonintervention principle.

The Russian Federation expressed adherence to the view that economic coercion was improper from a legal viewpoint even if meant to promote democracy and respect for human rights. Pointedly, the Russian Federation also reaffirmed its intention of maintaining normal commercial relations with Cuba. The Russian Federation nonetheless abstained, explaining its view that bilateral negotiations rather than international debate held the best hope for resolution of United States-Cuban differences.

---

[3] The Tenth Conference of Heads of State or Government of Non-Aligned Countries, held in Jakarta in September 1992, had adopted the following statement as part of its final document (NAC 10/Doc.2/Rev.1, September 5, 1992):

[The Heads of State or Government] urged the Government of the United States to cease its unneighbourly acts against Cuba and to terminate the series of economic, commercial and financial measures and actions imposed upon that country for over three decades, which have inflicted enormous material losses and economic damage. They called for an end to the violation of Cuba's territorial waters and air space, and to hostile radio and television broadcasts which are

The twelve members of the European Community, through the United Kingdom, expressed agreement with the United States position that, save for their impact on third countries, the United States measures against Cuba are "primarily a bilateral matter for the Governments of the United States and Cuba." In an apparent departure from the traditional Latin American position, Venezuela suggested that bilateral relations between states, including their commercial manifestations, were not an appropriate subject of international concern. In a somewhat elliptical statement, Argentina indicated a different approach, suggesting that Cuba's failure to recognize democratic rights may be a consideration weighty enough to override the normally applicable constraints against the use of economic coercion.

The member states considering the United States measures to be in conflict with the nonintervention principle implicitly rejected the position of Argentina. Some, such as Mexico and Ecuador, expressly adverted to the relationship of economic coercion and democratic, or human, rights but to the opposite effect, suggesting that respect for the principles of nonintervention would best promote democratic reforms.

The debate in all its aspects revolved almost exclusively around issues of international law. Those member states from the Southern tier to support the Cuban draft resolution were particularly firm in insisting upon the central role of legal principles in establishing appropriate international relations. Almost all those to speak suggested that the end of the cold war cast United States-Cuban relations in a new light.

From the combination of these varying opinions on the import of the Cuban draft resolution and the underlying issues, as well as other views and interests perhaps not given expression in the debate, there emerged a vote of fifty-nine in favor of the Cuban draft resolution and three opposed (Israel, Romania, and the United States) with seventy-one abstentions. Among the Western powers, Canada, France, and Spain voted for the resolution, as did New Zealand. Japan joined the other major industrial powers in abstaining. Of the former Eastern bloc countries, only Ukraine voted in favor. Brazil, Chile, Colombia, Ecuador, Mexico, Uruguay, and Venezuela voted for the resolution; Argentina, Bolivia, the Central American states, Paraguay, and Peru abstained. China, India, Indonesia, Iran, Iraq, Malaysia, and Pakistan voted for the resolution, as did most of the African continent. Of the seventy-three members of the non-aligned conference to vote, forty-seven voted in favor of the draft resolution and twenty-six abstained.

---

inconsistent with international law, and to restore the Guantanamo base to Cuban sovereignty. In this regard, they further called upon the United States to resolve its differences with Cuba through negotiations on the basis of equality and mutual respect.

CUBA'S REQUEST FOR CONSIDERATION OF ITEM TITLED
"NECESSITY OF ENDING THE ECONOMIC, COMMERCIAL
AND FINANCIAL EMBARGO IMPOSED BY THE
UNITED STATES OF AMERICA AGAINST CUBA"

[Cuba supported its request for inclusion of the United States embargo on the agenda of the General Assembly's forty-sixth session with an explanatory memorandum (A/46/193, August 19, 1991), which follows. Cuba asserted that the United States economic measures were an "integral element" of its thirty-year long "aggressive policy" toward Cuba, and described the profound impact which those measures have had on Cuba due to the "decisive weight of the United States in the world economy." Cuba also distributed in support a resolution of the Latin American Parliament calling for an end "to the economic and trade blockade" of Cuba (A/46/193, Add. 1, August 27, 1991) and resolutions by international and Cuban religious bodies to the same effect (A/46/193/Adds. 2-6, September 12, 1991), which are reproduced in the appendix (A1 and A2).]

For more than 30 years the Government of the United States has been pursuing an aggressive policy against Cuba with the declared aim of imposing on it the political, social and economic order which the United States authorities consider most fitting. This policy has included direct military intervention, the threat of nuclear annihilation, the instigation and carrying out of countless acts of sabotage and plans to assassinate Cuban leaders, all of which has been officially recognized by successive United States Administrations and documented in detail in the United States Congressional Record.*

An essential element of this policy is the economic, commercial and financial embargo which the United States has imposed and applied against Cuba throughout the above-mentioned period and which is now being intensified and expanded.

The United States embargo has caused Cuba substantial material losses and has obliged it to make extraordinary efforts to change its economic relations, which in the past were entirely dependent on the United States market. This has entailed intensive readaptation of the structure of production, consumption and services to different types of technology, equipment, raw materials and consumer goods from other countries, in many cases obtained at short notice, all of which has caused enormous economic and social damage and hardship.

The discriminatory measures against Cuba in the world of finance—the ban on the use of the United States dollar, the denial of access to the United States banking system and the boycott imposed on it in

---

*With regard to attempts to assassinate President Fidel Castro, see Senate Select Committee to Study Governmental Operations With Respect to Intelligence Activities, Alleged Assassination Plots Involving Foreign Leaders, Interim Report, S. Rep. No. 465, 94th Cong., 1st Sess. (1975).

international financial and credit institutions—have been a major additional obstacle for Cuba's international economic—and especially commercial—relations, and have limited even more the possibilities of external financing of the Cuban economy.

The United States Government has also tried to compel third countries to apply such a policy against Cuba, even seeking to impose its own discriminatory legislation beyond the confines of its national jurisdiction, thereby violating the sovereignty of other States. In its most recent legislative session, the United States Congress to that end adopted new measures which clearly are unlawful and violate international principles and norms.

It should be emphasized that the embargo continues to include a total prohibition on Cuba's acquisition of foodstuffs, medicine and medical supplies and equipment of United States origin. This criminal practice, applied totally and systematically for three decades, has caused and still causes appreciable additional harm to the Cuban people. Because of the inhuman character of this practice, a proposed amendment was even put forward at the beginning of this year in the United States Congress itself. This amendment, which would permit a humanitarian exception for the export of medicine and certain medical equipment, has already encountered strong opposition from governing circles in Washington.

Although the far-reaching changes carried out in Cuba during this period have enabled the people to achieve incomparably higher living standards in terms of social progress—as seen in the notable achievements in such fields as health, education, food, employment, housing and social protection for the entire population—these results have obviously been achieved through the people's efforts and sacrifices, which have been unjustly and excessively compounded by the embargo.

At the present stage in international relations, when an attempt is being made to restructure them on the basis of cooperation and reduction of tension, it is particularly unjust, anachronistic and irrational to maintain and even intensify against Cuba a policy based on the most flagrant violation of the norms of coexistence among States, as set forth in the Charter and various General Assembly resolutions.

The United States Government is virtually alone in continuing to apply this policy against Cuba. The vast majority of those States which, in the past, joined in the embargo have gradually adjusted their position and today maintain normal relations with Cuba.

However, the decisive weight of the United States in the world economy and its renewed efforts to perpetuate and extend this policy have transformed the economic embargo into a serious obstacle for the independence and development of Cuba, causing continuing material damage and harm to the Cuban people.

The United States embargo against Cuba constitutes a flagrant violation of the principles of sovereign equality of States and nonintervention in their internal affairs, and is a constant source of tension that impairs the normal development of international relations.

Consequently, the Government of the Republic of Cuba deems it necessary for this question to be considered as a matter of priority by the General Assembly at its forty-sixth session, so that decisions may be taken which will help to end this unjust and illegal situation.

UNITED STATES RESPONSE TO THE CUBAN INITIATIVE

[On August 21, 1991 the United States Department of State responded to the Cuban request in a brief statement released by its press office.]

Q.: What is the U.S. position on Cuban Perm Rep Ricardo Alarcón's request that the UN General Assembly during the upcoming sessions discuss an end to "the economic, commercial and financial blockade" of Cuba by the United States?

A.: The U.S. embargo of Cuba is not an appropriate issue for discussion at the UN. Every government has a right and responsibility to choose the governments with which it wishes to have commercial and political relations. The United States does not have full diplomatic or commercial relations with Cuba in response to Cuba's policies of internal repression and support for insurgency abroad.

Ambassador Alarcón is mistaken in calling the embargo a "blockade." A blockade implies that the United States is taking action to prevent other countries from trading with Cuba. That is clearly not the case.

The purpose of the embargo is not to dictate to Cuba, as Amb. Alarcón claims but a reflection of our policy regarding Cuba's record of internal repression and support for insurgency abroad. We seek to limit the flow of hard currency that can be used by the Cuban government to support insurgencies and to repress its own people.

CUBA'S SPECIFICATION OF THE EXTRATERRITORIAL
REACH OF THE UNITED STATES MEASURES

[On September 11, 1991 the Cuban Ambassador replied to the United States position that its "embargo" of Cuba is a question of bilateral relations not appropriate for discussion at the United Nations (A/46/193/Add.7, September 13, 1991). He specified twelve ways in which the United States systematically seeks "to obstruct and prevent other countries from developing trade relations with Cuba." These measures, in Cuba's view, constitute a "blockade," not simply an "embargo" of trade between United States nationals and Cuba. In addition, the Cuban Ambassador reiterated Cuba's contention that, in both their bilateral and multilateral aspects, the United States measures have the illicit objective of imposing on Cuba "a political, social and economic system which the United States authorities consider to be more acceptable." The Cuban bill of particulars was prepared before the United States extended the reach of its economic measures with passage of the Cuban Democracy Act in October, 1992.]

On 21 August last, the Department of State of the United States of America announced the official position of the United States Government on our request for the inclusion in the agenda of the General Assembly of an item on the "Necessity of ending the economic, commercial and financial embargo imposed by the United States of America against Cuba."

In a statement issued on that day, the above-mentioned Department stated: "The United States embargo of Cuba is not an appropriate issue for discussion at the United Nations. Every Government has a right and a responsibility to choose the Governments with which it wishes to have commercial and political relations." With reference to the letter which I addressed to you on 16 August last (A/46/193), the statement goes on to say: "Ambassador Alarcón is mistaken in calling the embargo a blockade. A blockade implies that the United States is taking action to prevent other countries from trading with Cuba. That is clearly not the case."

I wish, however, to draw briefly to your attention some of the current provisions of United States law which the Department of State purposely omitted in its statement and which clearly show that legislative action and other measures have been taken to obstruct and prevent other countries from developing trading relations with Cuba, thereby unquestionably implementing a policy of blockade. As an example that illustrates the nature of the blockade imposed by the United States of America against our country, I also attach a list of commercial transactions with third country companies, through which Cuba sought to obtain medical equipment and products, which were interrupted or simply canceled as a result of the embargo and pressure from the Government of the United States of America. [The referenced document is omitted.—EDS.]

In its official statement the United States Government contradicts United States law and actions, and it is inconsistent when it adverts to the right of the Government to choose the Governments with which it wishes to have commercial and political relations. Maybe it has not realized that the other members of the international community also have that right and that it is therefore up to them, not to the United States of America, to decide whether to have this type of relations with our country?

As stated in the explanatory memorandum requesting the inclusion of this item, the blockade imposed by the United States is an essential element of that country's aggressive policy against Cuba the declared objective of which is to impose on Cuba a political, social and economic system which the United States authorities consider to be more acceptable.

Consideration of this matter by the General Assembly is appropriate and is inherently justified by the principles and purposes upon which the United Nations is based.

In view of the relevance of the attached documents (see annex) and of this letter to the consideration of the inclusion of the item, I should be grateful if you would circulate them among all Member States as documents of the General Assembly.

(Signed)
Ricardo Alarcón de Quesada
Ambassador
Permanent Representative

Annex

The United States recently has stated that "the basic goal of [its trade and financial] sanctions is to isolate Cuba economically and deprive it of United States dollars" (The United States Department of the Treasury, Office of Foreign Assets Control, *Cuba: What You Need to Know About the U.S. Embargo* (June 20, 1991)). Consistent with this goal, the United States has gone well beyond suspending commerce between its own citizens and Cuba to seek the most sweeping extraterritorial application of its embargo laws. In doing so, it has exceeded the confines of its national jurisdiction under international law and has violated the sovereignty of other States.

Summarized below are the major respects in which the United States seeks extraterritorial application of its embargo laws against Cuba.

1. The United States prohibits a corporation or other business entity organized under the laws of a third country and located and doing business in that country from exporting to Cuba products manufactured wholly in that third country, but which incorporate any United States component part or material. This is so irrespective of whether the component part or material has been completely transformed in the new product. Exceptions are possible only upon application by the third-country company demonstrating that the United States-origin component parts or materials constitute 20 percent or less of the value of the product (*Source:* 15 Code of Federal Regulations § 774.1; 15 Code of Federal Regulations § 785.1).

2. The United States prohibits nationals of third countries from re-exporting United States origin goods to Cuba unless their re-exportation is specifically approved by the United States Department of Commerce. It is the policy and practice of the United States Commerce Department to deny approval. It makes no difference whether or not the third-country national originally obtained the goods for resale or how long the third-country national has owned the goods (*Source:* 15 Code of Federal Regulations § 774.1).

3. The re-exportation restrictions apply equally to United States technical data, that is, information in any form, tangible or intangible, which can be used in the design, production or manufacture of products. Under the applicable restrictions, a third-country national may not re-export to Cuba technical data that originally was exported from the United States. Moreover, in many instances third-country nationals may not export products manufactured wholly in the third country and containing no United States components or materials simply because the products were produced by use of United States-origin technical data (*Source:* 15 Code of Federal Regulations § 779.1; 15 Code of Federal Regulations § 779.8; 15 Code of Federal Regulations § 779.4).

4. The United States asserts the power to extend the embargo to corporations and other business entities organized under the laws of third countries and located and doing business in those countries simply because they are owned or controlled by United States corporations or persons. A third-country company, moreover, may be found to be "controlled" by a United States entity and hence subject to the embargo even when the United States ownership interest in the company is a minority share. The concept of "control" is applied flexibly and leaves the United States Government wide discretion in its enforcement.

Current United States Government policy is to permit third-country companies owned or controlled by United States entities to engage in import and export transactions with Cuban nationals. A wide range of commercial transactions are still prohibited, however, including investments by the third-country company in Cuba, financing Cuban commercial activities, joint ventures with Cuban companies and other normal commercial transactions.

Furthermore, even the import and export transactions that are permitted are subject to strict limitations. The third-country company must apply to the United States Treasury Department for a license to enter into these transactions. In order to obtain a license, the third-country company must demonstrate that it operates independently of the head office in the type of transactions for which the license is sought; that no officer or employee of the head office has had or will have any involvement whatsoever in the licensed transaction; that the transaction will not involve United States dollar accounts or dollar financing; and that any financing or extension of credit by the third-country company will comply with the Treasury Department's strict limitations. The United States Government has acknowledged that these restrictions prevent many third-country companies from seeking licenses.

In addition, this exception for third-country companies, limited as it is, has no application to branches of United States companies which are operating and licensed to do business in third countries. The embargo prohibitions continue to apply to them in full. The exception only applies to companies which are separately incorporated in a third country (*Source:* 31 Code of Federal Regulations § 515.559; 31 Code of Federal Regulations § 515.329; Testimony before United States Congress of Director of the Office of Foreign Assets Control Newcomb, 2 August 1989).

5. The United States extends the embargo to third country corporations and other business entities located and doing business in those countries if there is even a minority participation by Cuban nationals. Even as little as 25 percent ownership by Cuban nationals may be sufficient to subject the third-country company to the embargo. Such companies are considered "Cuban nationals" for all purposes and hence may not have any financial or commercial dealings with the United States or United States nationals. Any property the company may have in the United States will be frozen (*Source:* 31 Code of Federal Regulations § 515.302).

6. The United States prohibits third-country banks from maintaining United States dollar-denominated accounts for Cuba or Cuban nationals. It also prohibits any use of United States currency or United States dollar-denominated accounts in transactions between third-country nationals and Cuban nationals (*Source:* United States State Department, Background Briefing to Latin American Embassies, 12 July 1963; Deputy Secretary of the Treasury Robert Carswell, Conference on the Internationalization of the Capital Markets, March 1981; Comptroller General's Report to the Congress of the United States, 14 November 1980).

7. The United States bars the importation of goods manufactured in a third country by a company organized under the laws of that country which are made of or derived even in part from any article which is a growth, produce or manufacture of Cuba. It makes no difference whether the Cuban article incorporated in the third-country product is only a raw material used in manufacturing the product, is found only in trace amounts or has been thoroughly transformed in the process of manufacture (*Source:* 31 Code of Federal Regulations § 515.204).

8. The United States bars the importation of all goods which originally were the growth, produce or manufacture of Cuba regardless of

whether the present owner is a third-country national, there is no current Cuban interest in the goods and no matter how long they have been owned by the third-country national (*Source:* 31 Code of Federal Regulations § 515.204).

9. The United States, by administrative fiat, has declared that literally hundreds of corporations and other business entities organized under the laws of third countries and located and doing business in those countries are "specially designated" nationals of Cuba. Upon the issuance of such a declaration, all of the prohibitions of the embargo applicable to Cuban nationals automatically apply to the "specially designated" entity, and hence no United States national may have any commercial or financial dealings with the designated entity and all of its property located in the United States is frozen. The ground for designation, unsupported by any judicial findings, is that the designated company has acted on behalf of the Government of Cuba or is owned or controlled directly or indirectly by the Government of Cuba.

The United States on occasion has withdrawn a designation in response to the protest of the affected third-country company or its government, effectively conceding it acted erroneously. The purpose of the United States nonetheless was achieved, as the threat of being designated has had a coercive impact upon these and other companies, dissuading some from dealing with Cuba for fear of being designated (*Source:* 31 Code of Federal Regulations § 515.306).

10. United States law requires United States representatives to the principal international financial institutions to oppose the granting of any loans or other financial support to Cuba. The affected international financial institutions include the Inter-American Bank, the International Bank for Reconstruction and Development, the International Development Association and the International Monetary Fund (*Source:* 22 United States Code § 283r; 22 United States Code § 284j; 22 U.S.C. § 286aa).

11. The United States Senate recently approved measures that would extend the extraterritorial reach of the embargo even further. These initiatives are meant to have a coercive impact on the policies of third countries whether or not they are enacted into law at this time. One such measure would reverse the current practice of permitting the foreign subsidiaries of United States companies to engage in limited export-import transactions with Cuba. Other measures target specific countries that are Cuba's current economic partners. They would require those countries to cease all direct or indirect assistance to Cuba or face reprisals, such as exclusion from significant United States trade and financial programmes and the United States blocking support from international financial institutions. The coercive effect of these pending measures is heightened by the past practice of the United States—

relaxed only in the face of international protest—of prohibiting United States-owned third-country subsidiaries from engaging in trade with Cuba, of denying economic assistance to any country which itself furnished assistance to Cuba and of denying assistance to any country which permitted its vessels and aircraft to transport goods to or from Cuba (*Source:* Senate Bill No. 1435, §§ 517, 902 and 2007, adopted 26 July 1991; 22 United States Code §§ 2730 (a) (1974)).

12. In addition to the measures enacted or proposed to be enacted into United States law, a United States policy aimed to pressure third-country Governments and companies to sever ties with Cuba or face the consequences has been documented by research and press accounts published in the United States, Cuba and other countries (*Source:* "Cuba Woos Capitalists Feebly, Driven by Need Instead of Desire," *The Wall Street Journal,* 11 September 1991, p. A13).

UNITED STATES COMMUNICATIONS WITH MEMBER STATES

[On September 18, 1991 the Cuban Ambassador urged the General Assembly's General Committee to recommend inclusion of the requested item on the General Assembly's agenda (A/BUR/46/SR.1, September 24, 1991). The General Committee agreed, and the General Assembly subsequently adopted its recommendation. An unofficial transcript of Ambassador Alarcón's speech to the General Committee and an official United Nations summary of the remarks by the United States representative in response (A/BUR/46/SR.1, September 24, 1991) are set out in the appendix (A3 and A4).

In the weeks following the General Committee's decision, the United States pursued discussions with member states both at the United Nations and in the capitals in opposition to the Cuban initiative. As part of this effort, the United States summarized its principal points in the informal documents reproduced below and in similar documents reproduced in the appendix (A5). In essence, the United States maintained that its measures against Cuba represent a legitimate exercise of its sovereign right under international law "to choose to have relations with whom it wishes to have relations" and, in any event, are justified "because the Government of Cuba supports insurgency abroad, engages in internal repression and lacks democratic institutions."

In his remarks to the General Assembly on November 13, 1991, the Cuban Ambassador took note of these documents and in particular of portions which he contended were a "clear and direct threat" of retaliation by the United States against member states if they were to support the Cuban initiative.]

I.

As you know, the Cuban delegation at this year's UN General Assembly has inscribed a new issue on the agenda: "The necessity of ending the economic, commercial, and financial embargo imposed by the United States of America against Cuba."

The Cuban initiative is totally unacceptable. The U.S. embargo is consistent with international law. Furthermore, the U.S. relationship with Cuba is not an appropriate issue for discussion at the UN. Every government is free to choose with whom it wishes to have relations.

The Cuban initiative is designed to resurrect old superpower antagonisms at a time when a new spirit of international cooperation has taken root in the UN.

The United States does not have full diplomatic or commercial relations with Cuba because the Government of Cuba supports insurgency abroad, engages in internal repression and lacks democratic institutions.

The embargo was established in an effort to influence Cuban behavior. We seek to limit the flow of hard currency which can be used by the Cuban government to support insurgency in El Salvador and to repress its own people.

The United States supports peaceful democratic change in Cuba. It is the Cuban people who should decide the future of Cuba.

President Bush said last May that if Cuba held free and fair elections, under international supervision, respected human rights and ended support for insurgencies, relations with the United States could improve significantly.

Cuba's recent Fourth Party Congress failed to make any significant reforms in either the economic or political spheres. Reports from Havana (diplomats and general contacts) indicate that the government's refusal to address Cuba's problems with real reforms has left the Cuban public pessimistic about Cuba's future.

In recent weeks, Cuban authorities have stepped up repression of dissident activity. Twelve activists who signed a document urging free elections were arrested prior to the Party Congress, and are being charged with making "clandestine publications" and "abetting crimes."

Despite successful efforts to remain a member of the UN Human Rights Commission, Cuba has continued to flaunt UNHRC actions, refusing to cooperate with that organization's special envoy.

We understand concern over the humanitarian problems of the Cuban people. This concern might be best directed at attempting to persuade the Government of Cuba to end the oppressive policies which are the principal cause of the Cuban people's hardships and suffering.

On October 23-24 the Presidents of Mexico, Colombia and Venezuela met with Cuban President Castro in Cozumel, Mexico. Castro once again passed up the opportunity to seek a democratic transition in Cuba. Instead, he condemned the United States and said he was "extraordinarily satisfied" with the way communism had worked in Cuba.

In view of your relations with them, we would appreciate your going to the Cubans in an effort to have the resolution withdrawn. The Cubans should understand that their insistence that you support them threatens your good relationship with the U.S. The American Congress and people will be watching this important issue very carefully.

We do not wish to see a bitter fight develop over this agenda item. We will not, however, shy away from defending our legitimate interests. At any rate, a debate on the issue will only increase tensions and will not result in the U.S. lifting the embargo.

II.

[The first eleven paragraphs of this document, which are omitted here, are identical to the first eleven paragraphs of the preceding document.]

We understand your interest in regional solidarity and your hope that by cooperating with Cuba you can help steer the Castro Government towards democracy. If Cuba were sincere, however, about improving relations with its neighbors it would not put its friends in the awkward position of squaring off against the U.S. in an international forum.

On October 23-24 the Presidents of Mexico, Colombia and Venezuela met with Cuban President Castro in Cozumel, Mexico. Castro once again passed up the opportunity to seek a democratic transition in Cuba. Instead, he condemned the United States and said he was "extraordinarily satisfied" with the way communism had worked in Cuba.

We urge you to instruct your ambassador in Havana and/or your UN Permrep to approach the Cubans in an effort to have the resolution withdrawn. The Cubans should understand that their insistence that you support them threatens your good relationship with the U.S. and could damage their bilateral relations with your government.

We do not wish to see a bitter fight develop over this agenda item. We will not, however, shy away from defending our legitimate interests. At any rate, a debate on the issue will only increase tensions and will not result in the U.S. lifting the embargo.

III.
Embargo Points

The United States does not have full diplomatic or commercial relations with Cuba as a result of Cuba's support for insurgency abroad, policies of internal repression, and lack of democratic institutions.

The U.S. originally imposed the economic embargo in 1962, after Cuba nationalized some $1.8 billion 1962 dollars worth of U.S.-owned property without paying prompt, adequate, and effective compensation, as required under international law. There are 5,911 separate

American claims pending against the Government of Cuba. These claims are today valued at over $5 billion, including 6 percent interest per annum.

That embargo has remained in effect in an effort to bring about a change in Cuban behavior at home and abroad. We seek to limit the flow of hard currency that can be used by the Cuban Government to support insurgency in El Salvador and to repress its own people. Cuba has supplied arms, including advanced anti-aircraft missiles, to the FMLN. Cuba has denied a UNHRC envoy access to the Cuban people, in open disregard of a UN mandate.

Cuba's UN Ambassador Ricardo Alarcón is mistaken in calling the embargo a "blockade." The U.S. is not blocking other countries' trade with Cuba. The U.S., as a sovereign country, may determine with what countries it will have financial and commercial relations. This is consistent with international law.

Embargo regulations allow for licensing of humanitarian donations to private institutions in Cuba. Items under this provision may include food, medicine and medical supplies, clothes, educational materials and other goods which are required to meet basic human needs. For example, church members in the U.S. may send medicines to Cuba to be distributed by their correspondent church. Kosher food shipments to the Jewish community in Havana are licensed every Passover.

Embargo regulations allow Cuba to purchase directly from the United States any medicines unavailable elsewhere.

Embargo regulations also allow for the U.S. Treasury to license trade with Cuba by foreign subsidiaries of U.S. companies if the U.S.-origin content is less than 20 percent and there is no U.S. financing involved. In recent years, the bulk of licensed U.S. foreign subsidiary exports has been agricultural commodities. The Administration opposes legislation calling for an end to licensed U.S. subsidiary trade with Cuba because it would have a negative impact on our allies.

Cuba is likely to seek to persuade fellow Latins to help replace lost trade and aid from the U.S.S.R. and Eastern Europe. Some Latins believe that by integrating Cuba into the Latin American community, violence can be avoided. The best way to avoid violence in Cuba is for the current Government to make a firm commitment to a peaceful and democratic transition. Aid to Cuba now will bolster the Castro regime and the continuation of the one-party socialist system.

CUBA'S MEMORANDUM ON THE LEGALITY
OF THE UNITED STATES MEASURES

[On October 25, 1991 the Cuban representative circulated a document (A/46/599, October 25, 1991) responding to the arguments made by the United States. He reviewed international law to support Cuba's contention that, by seeking the extraterritorial application of its economic measures, "the United States has exceeded the confines of its national jurisdiction under international law and has violated the sovereignty of other states as well as that of Cuba." The Cuban representative likewise reviewed international law to support Cuba's contention that the United States measures constituted an illegal effort to coerce Cuba "into adopting an economic and political system more to the liking and advantage of the United States."]

A few days ago, after the General Assembly had unanimously approved the inclusion in the agenda of the forty-sixth session of the supplementary item entitled "Necessity of ending the economic, commercial and financial embargo imposed by the United States of America against Cuba"—now agenda item 142—the Government of the United States engaged in a series of intense *démarches* with other countries in an effort to ensure rejection of the just demand of Cuba that it put an end to that illegal, inhuman and immoral policy.

One of the most unusual arguments marshalled by the United States Government in the course of those *démarches* is its repeated claim that the United Nations General Assembly is not an appropriate forum for consideration of the question referred to in agenda item 142. It further maintains that the United States will regard any consideration of that item by the General Assembly as interference in its internal affairs, thus wrongly assuming the role of the aggrieved party, whereas it is not a bit upset by its own attempt to impose its wishes on others through force and coercion. But it reaches the height of hypocrisy—or perhaps it lets its imagination run riot—when it asserts that the criminal policy of imposing on the Cuban people the social, economic and political system that is to Washington's taste, is in conformity with international law. That assertion may be presumed to mean that the United States Government regards its policy decisions as having force of law for the rest of the world. In any case, nothing could be more ludicrous.

The document annexed to this letter contains a summary of the factors indicating that the economic, commercial and financial embargo imposed by the United States of America against Cuba constitutes a gross violation of the Charter of the United Nations and of international law. Consequently, I would be grateful if you could have this letter and its annex circulated as a document of the General Assembly under agenda item 142.

> (Signed)
> Carlos Zamora Rodriguez
> Ambassador
> Alternate Permanent
> Representative

Annex

The United States has boasted of the economic injury caused to Cuba by its preventing any commercial, tourist or financial relations "with the country that, by reason of geography and history otherwise would be its major trading partner" (*President's Report to Congress on Measures to Enforce Restrictions*, p. 5 (1989)). Not content with exercising even this extraordinarily coercive power, the United States has sought to impose the most extensive extraterritorial application of its embargo against Cuba.

The major respects in which such extraterritoriality is applied have been detailed in document A/46/193/Add.7 of 12 September 1991. The present document demonstrates that by imposing the embargo extraterritorially, the United States is acting in violation of settled principles of international law.

It bears emphasis at the outset that, by its assertions of extraterritorial jurisdiction, the United States is seeking the economic isolation of Cuba which it cannot achieve through the voluntary cooperation of third countries. The Member States of the United Nations do not themselves maintain an embargo against Cuba. Nor has any international or regional organization authorized an embargo, the Organization of American States having withdrawn its sanctions against Cuba—adopted under United States pressure in 1964—more than 15 years ago.

By nonetheless vigorously seeking the extraterritorial application of its embargo, the United States has exceeded the confines of its national jurisdiction under international law and has violated the sovereignty of other States as well as that of Cuba. This is so even without reference to the illicit purpose to coerce Cuba into adopting an economic and political system more to the liking of the United States. That the purpose of the United States itself is unlawful makes the United States' excessive claim of international jurisdiction even more objectionable.

The Member States of the United Nations repeatedly have rejected the claim of the United States of extraterritorial jurisdiction for its embargo laws on grounds fully applicable to the Cuban embargo—although this has not deterred the United States from forcefully pursuing the latter. Thus, the European Community rejected the United States position when, in 1982, the United States imposed an embargo which, though limited in the range of goods covered, was similar in its extraterritorial reach to the Cuban embargo. The United States acted in supposed response to the embargoed country's alleged interference in the internal affairs of another State. The Council of Ministers of the European Communities delivered a note advising the United States that "the European Community considers the United States' measures contrary to international law," and also submitted comments from the Commission of the European Communities, concluding that:

> The United States measures, as they apply in the present case, are unacceptable under international law because of their extraterritorial aspects. They seek to regulate companies not of United States nationality in respect of their conduct outside the United States and particularly the handling of property and technical data of these companies not within the United States.

(Note of the Council of Ministers Of the European Communities and Comments of the Commission of the European Communities (1982), reprinted in A.V. Lowe, ed. *Extraterritorial Jurisdiction, An Annotated Collection of Legal Materials* 197 (1983)).

That United States origin goods or technical data might be involved was of no consequence, since "goods and technology do not have any nationality and there are no known rules under international law for using goods or technology situated abroad as a basis for establishing jurisdiction over the persons controlling them." The United States embargo therefore "clearly infringes the principle of territoriality," which "is a fundamental notion of international law." (Comments of the Commission of the European Communities (1982)).

The courts of several nations have condemned the United States' assertion of extraterritorial jurisdiction on these grounds. (*See, e.g., American President Lines v. China Mutual Trading Co.,* 1953 A.M.C. 1510, 1526 (1953) (Hong Kong Sup. Ct.); *Moens v. Ahlers North German Lloyd,* 30 R.W. 360 (1966) (Tribunal of Commerce Antwerp).

The international community likewise has rejected the United States position that it can impose its embargo on companies organized under the laws of a third country and doing business there on the ground that they are owned or controlled by United States nationals. This position abrogates the clear sovereignty of the country under whose law the corporation was created and where it maintains its principal office, and thus cannot be sustained under international law. The International Court of Justice squarely ruled to that effect in *Barcelona Traction, Light and Power Co., Ltd. (Belgium v. Spain),* 1970, I.C.J. Rep. 1, 3.

The position of various Latin American countries on this point is well known, and the vigorous protests of these States led in the 1970s to a limited relaxation of the United States policy towards third-country companies trading with Cuba. Other countries in the Western Hemisphere and Europe have long objected to United States efforts to impose the Cuban embargo upon native corporations on account of United States participation in their ownership. The European Community, in its 1982 protest, was also categorical on the point, and all the courts with occasion to consider the matter have rejected the United States position as incompatible with international law. (*See*, for example, *Compagnie européenne des petroles S.A.* v. *Senor Nederland B.V.* (District Court, The Hague, 1982), *reprinted in* 22 *International Legal Materials* 66.) So unrelenting has been the United States assertion of jurisdiction on this basis that no less than 18 countries, including many of the main trading partners of the United States, have felt compelled to protect their sovereign jurisdictions by the adoption of legislation authorizing their executives to order companies established under their laws to disregard United States embargo directives.

Notwithstanding the clear and emphatic consensus of the international community on this issue, the United States continues to assert—and to exercise—jurisdiction over third-country companies simply because they are substantially owned or controlled by United States companies. The United States prohibits these third-country companies from engaging in a wide range of transactions with Cuba, including making investments in Cuba, financing Cuban trade activities or entering into joint ventures with Cuban companies. The United States also requires these third-country companies to seek United States Treasury Department licenses in order to engage in import-export transactions with Cuba and prohibits any use of United States dollar accounts even in those export-import transactions it licenses. Moreover, the United States prohibits the foreign branches of United States companies from engaging in *any* trade with Cuba.

The United States assertion of world-wide jurisdiction over dollar denominated bank accounts and dollar denominated trade is perhaps the most extreme of the United States' assertions of extraterritorial jurisdiction, as well as among the most insidious, given the prevalent use of the United States dollar in international trade. In its embargo against Cuba, the United States has purported to prohibit foreign banks wholly owned by foreign nationals and operating entirely on foreign soil from maintaining dollar denominated accounts for Cuba or conducting dollar denominated trade transactions involving Cuba—even when the source of the dollar credits has nothing to do with the United States, United States nationals or United States-origin goods.

When the United States first attempted to impose this prohibition on Latin American banks in the 1960s, diplomatic protests ensued. So clearly lacking in legal authority is this position that the United States, expressly anticipating its rejection by the international community, sought in other more recent embargo programmes only to restrain dollar transactions by foreign branches of United States banks. Even that far more limited claim, however, was rejected as incompatible with the sovereignty of the host country. (*See Libyan Arab Foreign Bank v. Bankers Trust Co.,* 1 Lloyd's L. Rep. 59 (1988); *Libyan Arab Foreign Bank v. Manufacturers Hanover Trust Co.(No. 2),* 1 Lloyd's L. Rep. 608 (1989)).

Nonetheless, the threat of the United States imposing its will by freezing unrelated assets of the foreign banks in the United States has been a potent as well as unlawful weapon in the continuing efforts of the United States to disrupt the commercial and financial relations of Cuba with third countries.

The attempt by the United States to secure extraterritorial compliance, lacking jurisdictional foundation, also is objectionable because it seeks to compel third-country participation in an embargo pursued for an unlawful purpose: coercing Cuba into adopting an economic and political system more to the liking and advantage of the United States. As stated in the Declaration on Principles of International Law concerning Friendly Relations and Cooperation among States in accordance with the Charter of the United Nations, adopted in 1970 by the General Assembly without dissent:

> No State or group of States has the right to intervene, directly or indirectly, for any reason whatever, in the internal or external affairs of any other State. Consequently, armed intervention and all other forms of interference or attempted threats against the personality of the State or against its political, economic and cultural elements, are in violation of international law.
>
> No State may use or encourage the use of economic, political or any other type of measures to coerce another State in order to obtain from it the subordination of the exercise of its sovereign rights and to secure from it advantages of any kind. . . .

The same clear prohibition, which emanates from the Charter of the United Nations and is universally acknowledged to have attained the status of binding international law, has been repeated and reaffirmed in numerous other resolutions of the General Assembly, and in other international instruments such as, for example, the Vienna Convention on the Law of Treaties, the General Agreement on Tariffs and Trade and the Charter of the Organization of American States.

It cannot be doubted that the intensity and comprehensive character of the United States embargo amounts to economic coercion. Nor can it be doubted from the historical record or from the United States' unabashed explanations for continuing its embargo today that the purpose of its unparalleled economic coercion against Cuba is "the subordination of the exercise of its sovereign rights and to secure from it advantages."

The embargo, both in its direct and in its extraterritorial respects, also violates the treaty obligations of the United States. The General Agreement on Tariffs and Trade, to which both the United States and Cuba are parties, prohibits a country from imposing a trade embargo except "when necessary for the protection of its essential Security interests." Neither now nor ever has it been possible credibly to claim that Cuba poses a threat to the national security of the United States.

Thus, both because of its extraterritorial scope and its underlying purpose to coerce Cuba into abandoning the economic and political system it has freely chosen, the United States embargo violates the most basic principles of the United Nations and of international law. Notwithstanding some assessments currently in vogue about the positive implications of the new international situation for universal respect of the Charter of the United Nations and international law, the United States, in flagrant violation of the latter and far from withdrawing from its illegal conduct, has continued to intensify and expand its embargo against Cuba.

CUBA'S REQUEST TO DEFER FURTHER
CONSIDERATION OF THE AGENDA ITEM

[On November 11, 1991 Cuba introduced a draft resolution (A\46\L.20) for the General Assembly's consideration in connection with Agenda Item No. 142, which is reproduced in the appendix (A6). It declared that the United States economic measures contradict "the principles embodied in the Charter of the United Nations and international law" and called for their "immediate end."

Two days later Ambassador Alarcón addressed the General Assembly in a plenary meeting. He stressed the extraterritorial applications of the United States measures and provided numerous examples of United States' interference with trade between Cuba and third-country companies. Ambassador Alarcón sought to demonstrate "the total falsehood of the U.S. allegations that this item is restricted to a bilateral difference between the two countries" and further, "that this blockade is an international problem and that its consideration by the General Assembly is entirely legitimate."

Ambassador Alarcón also rejected attempts "to explain the blockade as a result of the cold war and the confrontation that prevailed between the two formerly antagonistic blocks." Rather, he asserted, the United States' "economic warfare" against Cuba is part of its century-old effort to prevent Cuba from achieving "its full and definitive independence."

Ambassador Alarcón proposed that the General Assembly defer further consideration of the agenda item and the Cuban draft resolution until the next session of the General Assembly, to be held in fall 1992. In explanation, he cited a United States "campaign of intimidation, threats and pressures" against member states and concluded that "in these circumstances, the Assembly would find it difficult to objectively consider the draft resolution before it and to allow each and everyone to assume, in all freedom and without fear of reprisal, the most appropriate position."

Without objection and without further debate, the General Assembly deferred further consideration of the item to its forty-seventh session, inscribed the item on the provisional agenda for that session, and carried over the Cuban draft resolution.

Ambassador Alarcón's address and the General Assembly's action on item 142 (A/46/PV. 46, November 15, 1991) are reproduced in the appendix (A7 and A8).]

UNITED STATES COMMENT ON THE DECISION TO DEFER

[The United States Mission to the United Nations issued a press release (USUN 90-(91), November 13, 1991), observing that Cuba had been unsuccessful in generating substantial support for its position. The United States restated its position that the agenda item "deals with an essentially internal decision" of the United States as to the conduct of its "bilateral trade," which "is first and foremost a question of national sovereignty" and thus inappropriate for consideration by the General Assembly. The United States denied that its embargo measures are applied extraterritorially. In addition, it cited a number of reasons for its trade policy with Cuba, including Cuba's expropriation without compensation of U.S.-owned property in 1959-60 and its view that "since coming to power in 1959, the Cuban Government has supported efforts to subvert democratically-elected governments in neighboring countries and has trained terrorists from the world over." It added further that Cuba "oppresses its own people."

The United States' press release is set out below. Materials from Cuba's press conference, held after the Cuban Ambassador's remarks to the General Assembly, are reproduced in the appendix (A9).]

For Immediate Release
Press Release USUN 90-(91)
November 13, 1991

Note to Correspondents
Cuban Draft Resolution on The United States Trade Embargo

It is noteworthy that Cuban efforts to generate support for their draft on this subject were unsuccessful, and that the Cubans themselves decided not to put their resolution to a vote in the General Assembly.

The United States *would have preferred not to speak out* on the Cuban item because it deals with an *essentially internal decision* not appropriate for consideration in this body. My delegation did not oppose its inscription because the Government of the United States has long been committed to the principle of liberal inscription. Nevertheless, we believe that the resolution proposed by the Cuban delegation constitutes interference in the internal affairs of the United States.

Bilateral trade is first and foremost a question of national sovereignty. Governments make decisions to initiate trade, to end trade, to adjust the terms of trade, to suspend trade and to restore trade based on national interest. Is it the role of this body to tell a country, any country, where its national interests lie? Should the General Assembly begin the practice of instructing countries that are not now trading with one another to begin doing so? If such a resolution were adopted it would create a dangerous precedent, a precedent that could be invoked at a later time against any country.

The Cuban Delegation recently circulated a document on the so-called "extra-territoriality" of the U.S. Trade Embargo against Cuba. Some delegations are concerned over Cuban claims in that document that countries that refuse to cooperate with the embargo could be subject to U.S. retribution, that the embargo prohibits trade between Cuba and companies located in third countries. Such claims are false.

Embargo regulations specifically provide that subsidiaries of U.S. firms located in foreign countries may be licensed by the U.S. Department of the Treasury to trade with Cuba. In fact, recent press reports have indicated that applications for such trade have tripled since last year, representing sales of about 500 million U.S. dollars to Cuba. This trade appears, in part, to be taking the place of the declining Cuban trade with Eastern Europe. Cuba's economic difficulties are primarily due to its inefficient economic system, and are compounded by the recent reduction in foreign assistance, chiefly from Eastern Europe, on which its economy had been dependent.

Most of the measures the Cubans refer to in their document refer to U.S. legislative proposals which never became law. It is unfortunate that in the interest of truth they did not draw this distinction themselves.

The United States chooses not to trade with Cuba for good reasons. The Government of Cuba expropriated millions of dollars in private property belonging to U.S. individuals and has refused to make reasonable restitution. The U.S. embargo is therefore a response to the unreasonable and illegal behaviour of the Cuban Government.

Unfortunately, the behaviour of the Cuban Government has not become more reasonable with the passage of time.

Since coming to power in 1959, the Cuban Government has supported efforts to subvert democratically-elected governments in neighboring countries and has trained terrorists from the world over.

The Cuban Government oppresses its own people. Hundreds of human rights abuses have been documented by organizations free from political affiliations such as Amnesty International and the Inter-American Commission on Human Rights. In recent weeks, Cuban authorities have stepped up repression of dissident activity. Just last month twelve activists who signed a document urging free elections were arrested and are charged with making "clandestine publications" and "abetting crime."

Within the United Nations, the Cuban Government continues to flout the UN Human Rights Commission. The Cuban Government has persecuted many of those who spoke to or cooperated with the Commission Working Group which visited Cuba. It also refuses to cooperate with the special envoy of the UN Human Rights Commission.

The Government of Cuba is fully aware of what it can do to bring about an improvement in bilateral relations with the United States and a change in our trade policy. As President Bush said in May: "If Cuba holds fully free and fair elections, under international supervision, respects human rights, and stops subverting its neighbors we can expect relations between our two countries to improve significantly."

CUBA'S RESPONSE TO UNITED STATES
RESTRICTIONS ON THIRD-COUNTRY SHIPPING

[On April 18, 1992 President Bush issued a directive closing United States ports to third-country vessels carrying goods or passengers to or from Cuba or carrying goods in which Cuba or Cuban nationals have an interest. At the same time, he endorsed legislation pending in Congress, the Cuban Democracy Act of 1992, to intensify still further the United States economic measures. Among other provisions, the bill provided for a ban on any third-country vessel loading or unloading freight in the United States for 180 days after its departure from a Cuban port it had entered to trade in goods or services.

Within days Cuba denounced President Bush's actions in a document distributed to the General Assembly (A/47/179, April 27, 1992), reproduced in the appendix (A10). In August Cuba distributed a fuller document, reproduced below, analyzing these shipping restrictions under international law (A/47/400, August 26, 1992). Cuba argued that they were punitive measures designed to coerce third-countries "into abandoning their sovereign decision to maintain normal trade relations with another country" and hence violated the principle of nonintervention. Cuba also argued that the new restrictions violated the rights of both the third countries and Cuba under specific provisions of the General Agreement on Tariffs and Trade (GATT) guaranteeing freedom of navigation and the free transit of goods, and violated as well general principles of free trade and commerce. Cuba pointed out that President Bush had acted over the known objections of the European Community and others, and that the new measures reinstated in substantial part the restrictions withdrawn by the

United States in 1975 to comply with the Organization of American States' decision permitting each member state to determine its own trade relations with Cuba.]

I have the honour to enclose herewith a recent study by a group of legal and economic experts entitled "Recent measures by the United States of America to reinforce the illegal economic, commercial and financial blockade against Cuba."

During consideration of item 142 of the agenda of the forty-sixth session of the General Assembly, entitled "Necessity of ending the economic, commercial and financial embargo imposed by the United States of America against Cuba," we had the opportunity to provide details of the many ways in which the above-mentioned embargo is extraterritorial in nature and goes beyond the limits of the national jurisdiction of the United States under international law, and also violates the sovereignty of other States as well as that of Cuba (A/46/193/Add.7 of 13 September 1991 and A/46/599 of 25 October 1991).

This recent measure by the United States Government is a significant addition to the list of actions taken by that country against Cuba which exceed its national jurisdiction. Like previous measures that were extraterritorial in nature, this latest attempt to damage bilateral commercial relations with Cuba also violates the cardinal principle of non-interference in the internal affairs of States, to the detriment both of third countries and of Cuba.

Consequently, I should be grateful if you would have this letter and its annex published and distributed as a document of the General Assembly under item 39 of the provisional agenda.

> (*Signed*)
> Carlos Zamora Rodriguez
> Ambassador Extraordinary
> and Plenipotentiary
> Charge d'affaires a.i.

Annex

Recent measures by the United States of America to reinforce the illegal economic, commercial and financial blockade against Cuba.

On 24 April 1992, the United States closed its ports to all third-country vessels "carrying goods or passengers to or from Cuba" (57 Federal Register 15216 (24 April 1992)). By thus disrupting natural shipping routes and driving up freight costs, the United States seeks to discourage Cuba's export of its own products and its import of third-country products.

Not content, the United States extended this new prohibition to third-country vessels carrying goods in which Cuba has any "interest." Cuba is deemed to have an "interest" in goods owned by third-country companies if they are made or derived in whole or in part of any article which is the growth, produce or manufacture of Cuba. Thus, for example, a third-country vessel could not put into a United States port if it was carrying from one third country to another steel products manufactured by a third-country company with trace amounts of Cuban-origin nickel or third-country food products processed with Cuban-origin sugar. With this prohibition, the United States seeks to discourage third-country companies from purchasing Cuban-origin articles for use in the manufacture of their own exports.

To underscore their importance, the President of the United States personally announced these new administrative measures (statement of the President, the White House, Office of the Press Secretary (Kennebunkport, Maine), 18 April 1992). Far from exhibiting any appreciation of the constraints of international law and comity, the United States President brazenly proclaimed the United States intention "to isolate Cuba" until it abandons its internal political institutions in favour of those more to the liking of the United States. In a subsequent statement (letter of 4 June 1992) to Congress, the United States President, with equal disregard for international law and comity, proclaimed that these measures are "meant to discourage countries from increasing trade with Cuba and limit the development of tourism." There is no pretense whatsoever that the closing of United States ports to third-country vessels, or the avowed United States "policy of economic and political isolation" of which it is a part, is in response to any activity of Cuba in the international sphere or is in any way related to the security interests of the United States.

At the same time, the United States President endorsed the legislative initiative to close United States ports to third-country vessels for 180 days after they trade in a Cuban port without regard to the origin or destination of the cargo on board. Thus, for example, a third-country vessel that offloads cargo in Cuba and takes nothing on board could not enter a United States port for 180 days. The same would be true for a third-country vessel that takes on cargo in Havana and delivers it in a third country (testimony of State Department representative David Dworkin, hearings on the Cuban Democracy Act of 1992, H.R. 5322, House Foreign Affairs Committee, 28 May 1992).

The international community has already condemned these actions as being in derogation of third-country rights and interests. In a memorandum circulated in the United States Congress, the European Community wrote of the 18 April administrative measures now in effect:

"These regulations are in conflict with long-standing rules on comity and international shipping and will adversely affect the European Community's trade with the United States."

Referring both to the 18 April administrative measures and the United States President's endorsement of the shipping provision in the Cuban Democracy Act, the European Community wrote further:

"We are concerned at the apparent willingness of the United States Government to endorse passage of a Cuban Democracy Act containing extraterritorial elements which will disrupt the normal business activities of companies and shipping lines based in member States of the European Community. These measures would constitute the second batch of actions (following the Treasury regulations referred to above) which would be aimed at forcing foreign persons outside the proper jurisdiction of the United States to submit to United States law and foreign policy.

"As we have reiterated on countless occasions, such extraterritorial extension of United States jurisdiction is unacceptable as a matter of law and policy ....

"We hope that the United States Administration and Congress will reflect further on the expediency of supporting legislation which has the capacity to cause damage to trade relations at a time when the bilateral and multilateral agenda is already overcharged. Recognition by allied countries of different economic and foreign policy approaches to countries should be a normal result of international discourse between them. Attempts to force one country's agenda on the other can only lead to conflict and to a denial of the principles that the European Community-United States Transatlantic Declaration is designed to underpin."

Earlier, in response to a similar proposal then pending in the United States Congress to close United States ports, the European Community had stressed that the proposal, "which even in war time would be an infringement of the international law on neutral shipping, is completely unacceptable in peace time," (*Démarche*, 18 April 1990), and "would be in conflict with long-standing rules on comity and international law" (*Démarche*, 7 April 1992).

What was said with respect to the United States infringing upon the rights and interests of the European Community is of course equally true with respect to the rights and interests of all the Member States of the United Nations.

Even the United States previously recognized that the shipping measures it has now adopted would violate the rights of third countries. In 1975, the Organization of American States (OAS) lifted its collective sanctions against Cuba and resolved "to leave the State parties to the Rio Treaty free to normalize or conduct in accordance with the national policy and interests of each their relations with the Republic of Cuba at the level and in the form that each State deems advisable" (Final Act of the Sixteenth Meeting of Consultation of Ministers of Foreign Affairs, OAS/Ser.F/II.16, Doc. 9/75 rev.2, 29 July 1975). The United States expressly recognized that "in order to conform" with this action of the OAS it was necessary for it to repeal those aspects of its economic blockade which penalized third-country vessels that trade with Cuba (73 Department of State Bulletin 404 (1975)). Accordingly, "in keeping with this action by the OAS," the United States repealed its long-standing prohibition against the bunkering of third-country vessels engaged in trade with Cuba (40 Federal Register 171, p. 10,508 (3 September 1975)). The measure adopted now is even more extreme than that which, in 1975, the United States acknowledged would violate the rights of third countries in the absence of collective sanctions, since it denies entry to United States ports altogether and not merely bunkering privileges.

As stated in the Declaration on Principles of International Law concerning Friendly Relations and Cooperation among States in accordance with the Charter of the United Nations, adopted in 1970 by the General Assembly without dissent:

"No State or group of States has the right to intervene, directly or indirectly, for any reason whatever, in the internal or external affairs of any other State. Consequently, armed intervention and all other forms of interference or attempted threats against the personality of the State or against its political, economic and cultural elements, are in violation of international law.

"No State may use or encourage the use of economic, political or any other type of measures to coerce another State in order to obtain from it the subordination of the exercise of its sovereign rights and to secure from it advantages of any kind ...."

The same clear prohibition, which emanates from the Charter of the United Nations and is universally acknowledged to have attained the status of binding international law, has been repeated and reaffirmed in numerous other resolutions of the General Assembly, and in other international instruments such as, for example, the Vienna Convention on the Law of Treaties and the Charter of the OAS.

The new measure imposed by the United States violates the rights of third countries to determine their own "external affairs." By disrupting existing shipping routes and increasing the costs of trade with Cuba, the United States attempts—as it frankly concedes—to coerce third countries into abandoning their sovereign decision to maintain normal trade relations with another country.

The new measure is similarly meant to coerce Cuba's sovereign will with respect to its "internal" affairs. It cannot be doubted that the intensity and comprehensive character of the United States embargo, now augmented by this new measure, amounts to economic coercion. Nor can it be doubted from the historical record or from the United States' unabashed explanations for continuing its blockade today that the purpose of this unparalleled economic coercion against Cuba is "the subordination of the exercise of its sovereign rights and to secure from it advantages."

The United States measures are also in flagrant disregard of the principles of free trade and commerce reaffirmed many times by the General Assembly and set forth definitively in the Charter of Economic Rights and Duties of States (Resolution 3281(XXIX)), which provides in relevant part:

"Article 4

"Every State has the right to engage in international trade and other forms of economic cooperation irrespective of any differences in political, economic and social systems. No State shall be subjected to discrimination of any kind based solely on such differences ...."

This provision, as others in the Charter of Economic Rights and Duties of States, applies to the field of international economic relations the fundamental principles of sovereign equality of States, nonintervention and the duty to cooperate, which are the bedrock of the Charter of the United Nations and of international law. It is noteworthy that, while some member States may have expressed reservations with respect to this or other provisions of the Charter of Economic Rights and Duties of States on a variety of grounds, they have nonetheless expressed through the European Community's above-quoted communication their objection to the United States' most recent measure, so extreme and unjustified is its interference with their sovereign decision to maintain normal trade and shipping relations with Cuba.

Moreover, the United States measures patently violate both the rights of third countries and of Cuba to free trade and shipping guaranteed by the General Agreement on Tariffs and Trade, which is fully binding on the United States. Article V of the General Agreement on Tariffs and Trade (GATT) recognizes "the freedom of transit through the territory of each contracting party, via the routes most convenient for international transit" of goods, vessels and other means of transport "to or from the territory of other contracting parties." This right of free transit applies irrespective of the "place of origin, departure, entry, exit or destination, or on any circumstances relating to the ownership of [the] goods." The United States refusal, therefore, to permit third-country vessels to enter United States ports because they are carrying cargo in transit to or from Cuba derogates in the starkest terms from its obligations to the international community under article V.

The right of free transit codified in article V, moreover, has long been recognized as an essential element in the international protection of commerce. As long ago as 1921, the Convention and Statute on Freedom of Transit (the "Barcelona Convention"), upon which article V of GATT was based, required States to permit free transit by rail or waterway for international commerce. The Permanent Court of International Justice affirmed the right of free transit recognized in the Barcelona Convention in its decision in *The Railway Traffic Between Lithuania and Poland Case* (Ser. A/B, No. 42, pp. 108, 120 and 121 (1931)).

The executive order is likewise contrary to fundamental treaty obligations because, in violation of article XI of GATT, it imposes impermissible restrictions upon the importation into the United States of goods from third countries with which the United States has no dispute. Article XI expressly forbids any "prohibitions or restrictions other than duties, taxes or other charges" upon the importation of a product of another contracting State. Yet the United States has imposed a restriction not authorized by article XI, namely, that the imported goods not be shipped to the United States aboard vessels that are also carrying cargo in transit to or from Cuba.

There can be no justification for the United States violation of these treaty rights of transit and commerce. Article XXI relieves a contracting party from its obligations under GATT only to the extent necessary for the "protection of its essential security interests ... in time of war or other emergency in international relations." As noted, the United States no longer even pretends that Cuba threatens its security interests, and the only emergency in international relations is that posed by the United States continuing efforts to intervene in Cuba's internal affairs and deny the rights of third countries to determine their own relations with Cuba.

Thus, this newest measure serves to confirm our prior contention that the United States blockade violates the most basic principles of the United Nations and of international law, and merits the condemnation of the General Assembly.

CUBA'S RESPONSE TO ENACTMENT OF THE CUBAN DEMOCRACY ACT OF 1992

[On October 23, 1992 President Bush signed into law the Cuban Democracy Act of 1992, Title XVII, Pub. L. No. 102-484, §§ 1701, *et seq.*; 106 Stat. 2575, which is reprinted in its entirety in Part III. Cuba responded promptly in the document reproduced below (A/47/654, November 10, 1992). It pointed to the Cuban Democracy Act's extensive statement of purposes as demonstrating that the United States is seeking through its economic measures to dictate Cuba's internal political and economic system. Cuba also condemned the legislation for extending further the extraterritorial reach of the United States economic measures. The legislation prohibits foreign subsidiaries of United States corporations from trading with Cuba and "blacklists" third-country vessels which trade in Cuban ports. Many of the member states that addressed the General Assembly in the November 14, 1992 debate directed their remarks in substantial part to the Cuban Democracy Act.

While the legislation was still pending in Congress, Cuba had distributed copies of communications by the European Community to the State Department and Congress objecting to certain of its features (A/47/272 and A/47/273, June 15, 1992). These and other E.C. communications are set out in Part IV of this volume. In addition, Cuba had distributed expressions of support from a variety of nongovernmental sources (A/47/271, June 15, 1992; A/47/263, June 11, 1992), which are omitted.]

I have the honour to draw your attention to further aggressive measures against Cuba taken recently by the Government of the United States of America. Barely two weeks ago, on 23 October 1992, President George Bush brought into force, as part of the defense appropriations act, the arrogantly entitled "Cuban Democracy Act of 1992" which he signed in Miami amidst considerable electoral fanfare; the Act was also known, while at the legislative stage, as the "Torricelli draft," and was adopted by the United States Congress on 6 October.

This Act, whose aim is further to tighten the economic and financial embargo imposed by the United States of America against Cuba, constitutes a gross and unprecedented violation of the Charter and of international law, as it seeks to subordinate the sovereignty not only of Cuba—which is the main target of the measure—but also of each and every one of the members of the international community to the political decisions taken by Washington, which are presented as purportedly legal measures of an extraterritorial scope.

These further measures by the Government of the United States provide full confirmation for the positions long maintained by Cuba, and which we put before the Organization since the forty-sixth session of the General Assembly, regarding the illegal and immoral policy of blockade and isolation practised against Cuba by the Government of the United States for over three decades.

In view of its relevance to the consideration of this matter by the General Assembly at its current session, I should be grateful if you would circulate this letter and the annex thereto as official documents of the General Assembly under agenda item 39.

(Signed)
Alcibiades Hidalgo Basulto
Ambassador
Permanent Representative of Cuba
to the United Nations

Annex

On 23 October 1992, despite the opposition of many in his own country and the strong objections raised in the international community, President George Bush of the United States signed into law legislation which takes the United States economic, commercial and financial blockade of Cuba to new and still greater extremes. Both an assault on the sovereignty of Cuba and on the sovereignty of third countries, this new United States measure, the so-called "Cuban Democracy Act of 1992," is a grave and open challenge to the international community as a whole.

Even before the passage of this legislation, we demonstrated that the blockade of the United States was in violation of international law because it seeks to coerce Cuba into adopting an economic and political system imposed by the United States. We have always maintained also that the national security and foreign policy concerns advanced by the Unite States for more than 30 years to justify its blockade were pretextual. Now, these pretences are gone and the true motivations of the blockade of the Unites States have been openly and arrogantly revealed.

With a candour that is both astonishing and frightening, the Government of the United States has proclaimed, in this new legislation and in the accompanying statements of President Bush and his State Department, its goal of coercing Cuba, through an ever-intensifying programme of economic strangulation, into abandoning its economic and political system in favour of one dictated by the United States, thus blatantly violating the United Nations Charter and international law as concerns the fundamental rights of Cuba to exercise, without hindrance, its sovereignty, independence, self-determination and its juridical equality as a State.

We had additionally detailed for the General Assembly the many ways in which the United States went well beyond suspending commerce between its own citizens and Cuba to seek the most sweeping extraterritorial application of its economic measures and we have demonstrated that, in doing so, the United States has exceeded the confines of its national jurisdiction under international law, has violated the sovereignty of other States and has violated as well the treaty rights of third countries. (A/46/193/Add. 7, 13 September 1991 and A/46/599, 25 October 1991.)

The new measure of the Government of the United States goes still further in the extraterritorial extension of its own legislation by proclaiming the right of the United States, as a matter of law as well as policy, to intrude on the sovereignty of third countries and to regulate unilaterally international trade and shipping in order to achieve its goal of determining Cuba's political and economic system.

The United States attempt through this most recent blockade measure to, at the same time, determine the political and economic system of another nation (Cuba in this instance), submit all other countries to its legal jurisdiction, and unilaterally regulate international trade and shipping for the purposes of its own political expediency, is a glaring denial of the most fundamental rights of all States under the Charter and international law and of the United Nations itself. As such, it must by firmly rejected by this Organization.

If this growing challenge goes unanswered, the United Nations and the international order premised on the principles that its Charter seeks to preserve will suffer irreparable injury.

Among the many unacceptable features of this new legislation are the following:

1. *United States goals and policy.* As suggested by its title, "Cuban Democracy Act of 1992," the legislation makes no pretence of being premised on United States national security or foreign policy concerns and states the dislike of the Government of the United States of the political and economic system of Cuba as the basis of its policy towards that country. It defines the objective of that policy as the establishment in Cuba of a system to the liking of the government of the United States. It further defines the nature of the policy as that of undertaking United States Government actions to overthrow the existing Cuban system, both through direct bilateral measures and by coercing the cooperation of other States.

Indeed, the legislation prohibits the President of the United States from modifying the ban on third-country companies trading with Cuba or the ban on third-country shipping—both of which it establishes—unless he certifies to the United States Congress that Cuba is "moving toward establishing a free market economic system" and has adopted specified changes in its electoral and political system. The rights and sovereignty of third countries are thus made subordinate to the effort of the United States to dictate the internal political and economic system of Cuba.

2. *Third-country companies trade with Cuba.* The legislation categorically prohibits third-country companies from engaging in any transactions with Cuba if they are owned or controlled by United States nationals. It matters not that the third country's policy or law favours trade with Cuba. Nor does it matter that the companies organized under the laws of the third country, domiciled there, managed by third-country nationals, carry out their business independent of any control or direction by their United States shareholders and wish to engage in transactions with Cuba lacking any nexus whatsoever to the United States. Furthermore, third-country companies are subject to this prohibition even if foreign nationals own as much as 60 percent of the company's stock and United States nationals simply own the balance.

3. *Third-country shipping.* The legislation prohibits third-country vessels from loading or unloading goods in United States ports for 180 days after they have entered Cuban ports for trade in goods or services. This "blacklist" of third-country vessels trading with Cuba applies even though there is no United States or Cuban interest in the vessel and even though there is no cargo on board bound to or from Cuba.

The legislation prohibits third-country vessels from entering United State ports if they are carrying goods or passengers to Cuba or from Cuba. This prohibition prevents third-country ships from taking on bunker fuel or other ships' stores in United States ports, as well as from loading or unloading cargo.

The legislation prohibits the sale of ships' stores of United States origin anywhere in the world to third-country vessels carrying goods or passengers to or from Cuba. Thus, a third-country company without any United States interest, operating in a third-country port, is prohibited by this legislation from servicing third-country vessels with bunker fuel or ships' stores of United States origin.

The legislation closes United States ports to third-country vessels carrying third-country goods from one third country to another if the goods were made in whole or in part from goods of Cuban origin. It matters not that the goods were manufactured in a third country, are owned by a third-country national and are being delivered to a third-country national. If the third-country product contains any product of Cuban origin in any quantity—whether sugar, or tobacco, nickel, or biomedical products—the vessel is barred from entering United States ports, whether its purpose be to load or unload cargo, take on bunker fuel or ship stores or to make repairs. Moreover, the legislation prohibits the sale of bunker fuel or ships' stores of United States origin to those third-country vessels by third-country companies anywhere in the world.

4. *Sanctions against third countries which maintain commercial relations with Cuba.* The legislation declares it to be the policy of the United States "to make clear to other countries that, in determining its relations with them, the United States will take into account their willingness to cooperate" with the sanctions programme of the United States against Cuba. To implement this policy, the President "should encourage the Governments of countries that conduct trade with Cuba to restrict their trade and credit relations." To enable the President to do more than "encourage" third countries in that direction, the legislation authorizes the President to impose "sanctions against countries assisting Cuba." Significantly, the definition of "assistance" to Cuba which would subject third countries to these "sanctions" includes ordinary trade if the United States, in its own unilateral judgement, considers the terms of that trade to be "more favorable than that generally available in the applicable market."

5. *Continued blockade of medicines.* The legislation reconfirms the prohibition of the United States against persons subject to the jurisdiction of the United States selling medicines to Cuba. It goes further, however, in that it even seeks to discourage third countries from providing medical assistance to Cuba.

Humanitarian donations of medicines to the Government of Cuba will make the third country subject to Presidentially imposed sanctions authorized by the legislation. Similarly, sales to the Government of Cuba or even to Cuban non-governmental organizations on terms the United States considers to be more favourable than normally available in the applicable market would make the third country subject to the same sanctions. Only if the United States—not the third country—conducts on-site inspections in Cuba of the medicines' distribution will the third country be immune from such sanctions.

6. *Continued blockade of food.* The legislation reconfirms the prohibition of the United States against any sale of food or foodstuffs to Cuba by persons subject to the jurisdiction of the United States. Although humanitarian donations to non-governmental organizations are permitted, it is evident that only the unimpeded access of Cuba to food and foodstuffs on a commercial basis can have a substantial effect on the welfare of the Cuban population.

Just as the legislation seeks to discourage third-country sales and donations of medicines to Cuba, so does the legislation seek to discourage third-country sales or donations of foods and foodstuffs. Donations of food to the Government of Cuba would make a third country subject to Presidentially imposed sanctions authorized by the legislation. So, too, would sales to the Government of Cuba or to non-governmental organizations on terms the United States considers to be more favourable than generally available in the applicable market.

7. *United States funding of political opposition in Cuba.* This legislation authorizes the President of the United States to provide "assistance" to groups within Cuba opposed to the current political system. This open interference in the internal affairs of a sovereign State is made even more striking by the fact that the United States blockade, at the same time, prohibits United States citizens from providing assistance—whether in the form of donated funds, supplies, training or services—to any Cuban institution, whether governmental or non-governmental. This categorical prohibition applies even to any assistance United States persons might wish to offer Cuba in support of any development project, whether in the cultural, educational, health or other fields.

UNITED STATES "TALKING POINTS," FALL 1992

[As it did during the forty-sixth session of the General Assembly, the United States chose in fall 1992 to communicate its position to member states through informal "Talking Points" which follows. The United States, re-ferring to the Cuban initiative as a "propaganda exercise," reiterated the basic points it had made previously. It also acknowledged the concerns of many member states with the Cuban Democracy Act of 1992 but sug-gested that they could be most usefully addressed through normal diplo-matic channels and warned that Cuba was using that legislation as a pretext for a broader United Nations debate on bilateral aspects of United States-Cuba relations.]

We understand that the Cubans again plan to sponsor a resolution against the U.S. economic embargo of Cuba.

In our view, the UNGA is not the forum, nor is the Cuban resolution the vehicle, to address the bilateral issue of the embargo.

A Cuban propaganda exercise at the United Nations—and that is what their effort is—would do absolutely nothing to resolve any concerns which others may have regarding the Cuban situation. It would, how-ever, create a climate of acrimony and confrontation which is not in any of our interests.

The U.S. has a sovereign right to determine with which countries it will maintain diplomatic and economic relations. The embargo was imposed only after the government of Cuba, in violation of international law, seized U.S. investments—worth 1.8 billion dollars in 1962—with-out compensation.

The embargo is not designed to hurt the Cuban people. The truth is that Cuba is able, and always has been, to buy medicines and other goods from any other country in the world. Embargo regulations allow licensing of humanitarian donations, including medicine and medical supplies, from U.S. sources to nongovernmental organizations in Cuba. In addition, after complying with licensing and verification procedures, the Cuban government can now purchase medicine directly from the U.S.

We understand that some governments may be opposed to certain provisions of the Cuban Democracy Act. We are aware that the Cuban government will try to take advantage of this opposition to manipulate others into supporting its anti-embargo resolution.

Concerns which your government may have about the Cuban De-mocracy Act can be most usefully addressed in normal bilateral channels. That issue is distinct from the embargo per se, and it is inappropriate and unproductive to debate it at the UN.

Cuba uses the Cuban Democracy Act as a pretext. What it really wants is a UN debate on an aspect of bilateral relations with the U.S., and to shift the world's attention away from the Cuban regime's many failures.

Accordingly, to deny the undemocratic and repressive Castro regime the approbation it seeks, and to deny that regime the ability to misuse the UN for its own purposes, we urge you not to support this Cuban initiative.

CUBA'S REVISED DRAFT RESOLUTION

[On November 18, 1992 Cuba tabled a draft resolution (A/47/L.20, November 18, 1992), reproduced in the appendix (A11), which, in a revised form deleting any explicit reference to the United States in its text, was put to a vote on November 24. We set out here the Cuban draft resolution (A/47/L.20/Rev.1, November 23, 1992), adopted by the General Assembly as Resolution 19 (XLVII).]

The General Assembly,

Determined to encourage strict compliance with the purposes and principles enshrined in the Charter of the United Nations,

Reaffirming, among other principles, the sovereign equality of States, nonintervention and non-interference in their internal affairs, freedom of trade and international navigation, which are also enshrined in many international legal instruments,

Concerned by the promulgation and application by Member States of laws and regulations whose extra-territorial effects affect the sovereignty of other States and the legitimate interests of entities or persons under their jurisdiction, and the freedom of trade and navigation,

Having learned of the recent promulgation of measures of that nature aimed at strengthening and extending the economic, commercial and financial embargo against Cuba,

1. *Calls upon* all States to refrain from promulgating and applying laws and measures of the kind referred to in the preamble to this resolution in conformity with their obligations under the Charter of the United Nations and international law, and with the commitments which they have freely entered into in acceding to international legal instruments which, *inter alia,* reaffirm the freedom of trade and navigation;

2. *Urges* States which have such laws or measures to take necessary steps to repeal or invalidate them as soon as possible in accordance with their legal regime;

3. *Requests* the Secretary-General to prepare a report on the implementation of this resolution and to submit it for consideration by the General Assembly at its forty-eighth session;

4. *Decides* to include the item in the provisional agenda of the forty-eighth session.

THE GENERAL ASSEMBLY DEBATE,
NOVEMBER 24, 1992

[We reprint in its entirety the official, verbatim transcript of the General
Assembly debate on the Cuban draft resolution at the plenary meeting
held November 24, 1992 (A/47/PV.70, November 24, 1992). We then set
out the tally of the General Assembly vote, fifty-nine in favor, three opposed (Israel, Romania, and the United States of America), with seventy-
one abstentions.]

The President (interpretation from French): The General Assembly
has before it a draft resolution issued as document A/47/L.20/Rev.1.

I will now call on the representative of Cuba, who will introduce the
draft resolution in the course of his statement.

Mr. Hidalgo Basulto (Cuba) (interpretation from Spanish): A year
ago the delegation of Cuba requested that the General Assembly consider
in plenary session, and as a priority issue, the need to put an end to the
economic, commercial and financial blockade imposed by the Government of the United States against my country. The continuation and
reinforcement of that unjust and unlawful blockade have made its
consideration imperative once again during this session of the General
Assembly.

Cuba would have preferred that the reasons for bringing this item
before the most important body of the United Nations had disappeared;
that we were not facing circumstances equal to, and even more serious
than, those that led the General Assembly quite correctly and legitimately to consider appropriate the discussion of this crucial issue for
the future of my people. Regrettably, that was not to be.

While many, both within and outside of this Hall, may have hoped
that the Government of the United States—in the face of indisputable
evidence of rejection—would take measures to rectify a policy that violates international law, the Charter of this Organization, and many
other legal instruments freely accepted by that country, the reality has
been totally different.

To the amazement of international public opinion and in spite of the
timely complaints and warnings from other States that would be affected
by such decisions, the Administration of President George Bush decided
to apply during this past year a set of new measures geared to reinforcing
the blockade and tightening the siege by which the United States has,
for more than three decades, been attempting to strangle Cuba. That
circumstance renders even more urgent and relevant the debate that
we are now commencing.

During the discussion of this item last year, it was irrefutably demonstrated that what my delegation was placing before the Assembly for
its consideration was neither—as deceptively suggested then—an

internal affair of the United States nor a bilateral issue between that country and Cuba, and thus inappropriate for consideration by the United Nations.

It was, and indeed still is, a policy carried out by the United States in violation of its most basic international obligations and to the detriment of the sovereignty and rights not only of Cuba but of its own citizens and of the international community as a whole. It was impossible for them to deny the obvious: that policy aimed to extend United States jurisdiction extraterritorially so as to compel Cuba and other States, as well as companies and individuals outside the territory of the United States, to comply with Washington's political decisions.

Obviously, that behaviour stemmed from the desire to impose upon the Cuban people a political, social and economic system to the liking of the United States and selected by it and, essentially, to re-establish the domination the United States exerted during the darkest period of our history.

In the opinion of my country, the international community's resumed discussion of the conduct of the most developed country on the planet *vis-a-vis* a small neighbouring nation is not an exercise in rhetoric, and certainly not a propaganda exercise, as has been asserted.

The blockade is the most serious of the diverse forms of aggression that the Government of the United States has been waging against Cuba. It is an unethical, immoral act systematically designed to subject a whole country to hardship and hunger, in flagrant violation of the human, political and social rights of its people.

It is a denial of our right to development, to national self-determination, to the exercise of our sovereignty; it is a breach of the essential norms of co-existence among civilized nations, of the principles of the San Francisco Charter; it is the worst contemporary example of how relations between rich and poor would be in a world designed at the whim of the most powerful.

The web of anti-Cuban legislation woven over the course of 30 years by eight United States Administrations has had a negative effect on my country's economy. As a result of legislation adopted by the United States, all imports and exports between the two countries are forbidden, as are any contracts between citizens of each country or with citizens of third countries residing in Cuba, the provision of services, financial transfers and the flow of scientific or technological information.

Legislation adopted by the United States restricts the freedom of its citizens to travel to my country; it is forbidden for United States planes to land in Cuba, regardless of the country from which they have taken off; illegal limitations are imposed, *inter alia,* on Cuban airlines in their commercial operations, including the use of routes close to the United States. As a result of United States legislation, severe restrictions are imposed on shipping, in violation of the principle of freedom of navigation and, with a dedication worthy of a better cause, there is close scrutiny for the presence of components or raw materials of Cuban origin in goods imported into the United States from third countries.

A listing of all the repressive actions that comprise this policy would be unending.

Even if they were exclusively bilateral, as is also falsely alleged, they would constitute a shameful record of the flouting of the most universal norms of international law, not to mention basic moral considerations.

I can imagine no programmatic or ideological justification for those actions.

In 1776 in his classic *An Inquiry Into the Nature and Causes of the Wealth of Nations,* Adam Smith proposed that "trade serves more to unite than to divide peoples." Even earlier, Baron Charles de Montesquieu had said that trade served to unite nations since its natural effect was to incline towards peace.

From the outset the nature of the United States action has, as my delegation has always maintained, gone far beyond a decision with solely bilateral implications. There have been more than enough laws and examples since the 1960s to demonstrate that a priority objective for the Government of the United States has been to impose its decisions regarding Cuba on third countries.

The consequences of this policy for an underdeveloped country, one with a small amount of land and densely populated, an ex-colony that was until 1959 dependent on the economy of the United States, are truly immeasurable.

Not a single economic or social element of Cuban existence escapes the consequences of the blockade. From the beginning it meant forced reorientation of all the country's trade towards different, more distant markets, the prohibition of access to known, nearby sources of technology and the abrupt severing of traditional financial links.

These are not abstract statements. To replace the United States locomotives used in our sugar industry, and adapt the railroad tracks as a result, Cuba had to invest $480 million. Under the new conditions the cost of the equipment that had to be purchased for sugar cane cultivation is estimated at $2.6 billion. Nine thousand United States tractors, 580 rice harvesters and tens of thousands of other items of agricultural equipment were rendered useless by the blockade. The cost was $100 million dollars. Losses in the nickel industry are at least $400 million, in the electric industry they are $120 million and in motor transport they are almost $100 million.

The blockade has meant losses of at least \$3.8 billion for the tourist industry. Above-average costs for the charter of ships as a result of the United States restrictions add up to at least \$375 million.

Civil aviation, telephone communications, the purchase of medicines and foodstuffs, intellectual property rights, sporting activities, access to technological know-how, access by the population to goods and services, the possibility of establishing two-way cultural communication between the United States and Cuba, and many other areas of our national life have all been affected by the harsh reality of the prohibitions.

Any calculation must of necessity be incomplete, but the most recent studies estimate that the material cost the Cuban people have had to pay over the course of 32 years as a result of the United States blockade is no less that \$38 billion.

The actions taken in the past year by the Government of the United States not only confirm all my statements, but also add a number of elements, certain aspects of which are even more detrimental to the interests of the international community.

Allow me in this regard to review briefly a number of facts and to voice some brief reflections.

Over the whole of the past year the Republican Administration and the United States Congress have been considering and arguing about an initiative regarding the possible ways and means of strengthening the blockade, in the hope that the sudden rupture of Cuba's economic and trade links with the countries of the defunct community of socialist countries would give them an opportunity to achieve the goal of bringing about the collapse of the Cuban economy and of creating internal political pressures in Cuba that would contribute to the achievement of their aims and force my country to accept Washington's dictates. While in the Congress several proposals were taking the form of unified legislation, on 18 April President Bush issued an Executive Order forbidding entry into United States ports of third-country vessels engaged in trade with Cuba. In this context, for example, on 12 September the United States authorities refused entry to Long Beach Bay, California, for repairs, to a freighter flying the Greek flag transporting Chinese rice to Cuba.

The Executive Order also introduced additional restrictions on the dispatch of humanitarian aid packages to Cuba by United States citizens.

In his statement announcing that decision and referring to discussions taking place at the same time in the Congress, President Bush expressed his opposition to the sale of medicines and the donation of foodstuffs to official Cuban institutions. This statement ended with the following declaration (*spoke in English*): "My Administration will continue to press Governments around the world on the need to isolate economically the Castro regime. Together we will bring Cuba to a new era of freedom and democracy." (*spoke in Spanish*) With those words he reiterated the intention to continue to ignore the sovereignty of Cuba and of the rest of the international community, including many of his own allies.

That goal became a reality, in a strange form, when discussions between Congress and the Administration finally gave birth to the legal monstrosity known as the "Cuban Democracy Act of 1992," which Congress passed on 6 October and the President signed on 23 October, exactly 32 days ago. A full description of the legal and political abomination that Act represents would take up more than a volume and would probably require the efforts of many lawyers and specialists in behavioural disorders. A summary of the Act, its objectives and its effects, appears in the annex to document A/47/654, which all delegations have had the opportunity to examine. Out of respect for the intelligence of the Assembly I shall not attempt to repeat here the contents of that summary. However, some comments are essential.

The first thing that comes to mind is the illicit and anti-juridical nature of this so-called law. From its title to its very end, it exudes a total disdain for the basic international obligations of any State—in this case the United States—in a civilized society of nations regulated by universally known and accepted norms, principles and legal instruments. The annex to the above-mentioned document A/47/654 describes *grosso modo* seven different ways in which one or several of the stipulations of that law flagrantly violate fundamental norms of international law.

In brief, those violations have to do with the aims and the nature of the policy *vis-a-vis* Cuba that is shaped by that law; the prohibitions imposed on the subsidiaries of United States corporations in third countries trading with Cuba; the restrictions and reprisals that will be applied against the shipping of third countries trading with Cuba—the above stipulations incorporate the Executive Order to the same ends issued by President Bush on 18 April last—the use of intimidation and sanctions that would, also, by way of reprisal, be imposed against third countries maintaining trade relations with Cuba; the permanent blockade of shipments of medicines and foodstuffs to Cuba; and the financing by the Government of the United States of groups in Cuba opposed to my country's present political system.

If the text is studied with care, it will be found that virtually all the fundamental norms or principles of international law that constitute the pillars of this Organization are undermined. It also contains the formulations of unparalleled cynicism disguised by the cosmetic language typical of the carrot-and-stick mentality that the promoters of this legislation have used to counter their many opponents and to persuade the naive of the alleged generosity and balance of the law. In fact, there is not a single word in that law that is not aimed at the unconditional subordination of the Cuban people.

It can be seen that, in reality, this has been the essence of the policy of the blockade carried out against Cuba. Nevertheless, this new law returns to restrictive actions that were tried in the 1960s and that should be unimaginable 30 years later, in a world where East-West contradictions no longer exist and at a time when the birth of a "new order" is being hailed.

Nonetheless, what truly amazes us and goes well beyond the importance of any of the specific stipulations of the law is the fact that, by approving this law, the United States Congress and President Bush have in fact decided and proclaimed openly that the violation of international law constitutes the law of the United States.

Can the international community meeting in this Organization turn a deaf ear to such a challenge? Would this not suffice to convince the most skeptical person of how serious a mistake it would be to ignore this arrogance without a commensurate response, and of the consequences that would entail?

It is indecent that to achieve the aim of stripping the Cuban people of its fundamental rights this law resorts to coercion through a complex system of restrictions, prohibitions, threats and sanctions, against both foreign Governments, companies and citizens of the United States itself.

In the first case, the intention is to apply the law through the extraterritorial extension of United States jurisdiction, a method favoured of late by the authorities of that country. These attempts have been rejected, quite rightly and on the irrefutable basis of international law, by a number of States, both before and after the promulgation of the law. By way of example, allow me to quote briefly two consecutive paragraphs of the press release issued by the European Community on 8 October—two weeks before the promulgation of the law by President Bush—in which he was encouraged to veto it and prevent its entry into force. The two paragraphs say:

(*spoke in English*)

"The EC has persistently voiced its opposition to the unilateral extension by the U.S. of the reach of trade measures implementing U.S. foreign or national securi y policies.

"During the last two years, the European community has been on record with other nations such as Canada in opposing legislative initiatives to tighten further the U.S. trade embargo upon Cuba. Such actions would have to be applied extraterritorially of the U.S. jurisdiction, in violation of the general principles of international law and the sovereignty of independent nations."

(*spoke in Spanish*)

After an appeal of this nature, can such a challenge by the United States to the international community be justified—as some have suggested—by considerations of internal or electoral policy? My delegation believes there is more to it, and that such disregard for international law is not to be taken as superficial, but rather as a prelude to extremely serious intentions in the face of which the international community must be vigilant.

If any doubt remains that the Government of President Bush acted in full awareness of the positions it adopted *vis-a-vis* its international obligations, I would suggest the reading, in the United States Congressional Record, of the process of discussion and approval of this law and the study of the testimony of eminent lawyers, professors of prestigious universities in the United States and members of the United States Congress itself, who put forward diverse and substantial arguments regarding the flagrant contradictions between this law and international law, the constitutional rights of United States citizens and the economic interests of farmers and businessmen of this country.

I could quote here several of these interesting opinions or the various statements that many Governments have made public regarding this legislation, but I will limit myself to citing one very eloquent testimony. A little over two years ago, on 16 November 1990, President Bush refused to approve the law entitled "Omnibus Export Amendments Act," as he considered that it diminished presidential authority regarding foreign policy. In commenting on section 128 of that law, on the prohibition against United States subsidiaries in third countries from trading with Cuba, in his "Memorandum of Disapproval," he stated, "There would be an extraterritorial application of United States laws that could compel foreign subsidiaries of U.S. companies to choose between violating the laws of the United States or of the host country."

Further comments are unnecessary.

What, then, could we say about this new law regarding Cuba? Its unfitting title, "Cuban Democracy Act of 1992," already announces in capital letters its interventionist aims. It would seem that in speaking of Cuba it does not refer to the sovereign and independent State which I am proud to represent, but to a territory or possession of the United States, such as the state of Massachusetts, or the city of New York, even though, in fact, not even in those territories does Washington attempt to impose its will in such a manner. What it deceptively attempts to assign to the Cuban people is simply a subordinate and second-class nationality, thus openly disclosing the profoundly and inherently interventionist intentions with which United States authorities regard their neighbours to the South.

This law abandons all previous pretexts with which, until not so long ago, they disguised, under the cloak of foreign policy or national security, their one true aim of reimposing on Cuba the yoke from which my people has been free for as long as the blockade imposed by its old oppressor has been in force.

For these reasons many in the United States and elsewhere have rightly compared this law, known in its legislative stage as the Torricelli Amendment, with another of a similar character, the Platt Amendment, that the Government of the United States imposed on the Cuban Constitution of 1901 as a precondition to putting an end to its military occupation of the island, by which it granted itself the prerogative of intervening in Cuba and also stripped my country of part of its territory, which it still illegally occupies in Cuba's Guantanamo Bay. Orville Platt and Robert Torricelli have, for my people, exactly the same value: the equivalent of being historically and legally null and void. Before them, in 1896, Colonial Governor Valeriano Weyler proclaimed a policy of scorched earth and population reconcentration closely akin to the present proposal of the Bush Administration; but it was not able to dash the Cuban people's urgent longing for independence.

But this law has greater scope than Weyler's edicts or Platt's blackmail. When the latter was imposed on it in 1901, Cuba was a subjugated and isolated nation under military occupation by the United States; today Cuba is free and has links with the rest of the world. Thus, to subjugate it anew, the United States would require the cooperation or the acquiescence of the international community. That is precisely what this law seeks to promote by coercive procedures against third parties.

With regard to the element of extraterritoriality that unquestionably characterizes this law, allow me to call to the attention of the General Assembly the fact that the original expression of extraterritoriality in United States legislation regarding the blockade derives from attempts by Washington to decide the political, economic and social structure of Cuba, whose sovereignty it has unceasingly tried to subordinate to United States jurisdiction.

I should add, in this context, that, with regard to Cuba, extraterritoriality is not a recent phenomenon but a characteristic that has been present in the blockade policy since its very beginning and includes the efforts that the Government of the United States has been making for decades to secure the cooperation of other countries with that policy. The difference is that now, by means of a pseudo-legal formula, extraterritoriality is more openly proclaimed and more explicitly extended to those third countries that have links, no matter how legitimate, with Cuba.

The United States blockade against Cuba has always been a policy inspired by genocidal intent and aimed at subjection of the Cuban people through hunger and deliberately provoked deprivation. For many years Cuba was able to mitigate the consequences of that policy through its foreign transactions and the economic and commercial relations that it established with the socialist countries, with which it came to conduct 85 percent of its trade.

With the recent break in those relations, Cuba's entire foreign trade is now exposed to the pernicious effects of the blockade policy pursued by the United States, whose Government constantly persecutes each and every one of my country's commercial operations, obstructs Cuba's access to external sources of financing and tries to block potential involvement of foreign capital in Cuban development projects.

While this immoral, illegal and inhuman policy has not been and will never be capable of bending Cuba's will, it is nonetheless, in the present circumstances, doing severe damage to the economic and social development of the country, to consumption levels and to the general standards of living of the Cuban people.

Particularly harmful is the blockade imposed on foodstuffs and medicines, which forces Cuba to purchase those vital commodities in distant markets at prices that are higher by not less than 30 percent. As was highlighted in the Congress of the United States by more than one participant in the hearings that preceded the adoption of this law, about 90 percent of the goods imported by Cuba from United States subsidiaries in third countries—goods whose import is prohibited by law— were specifically foodstuffs and medicines. As all representatives can imagine, the greatest hardship deriving from this inhuman policy is being suffered by the most vulnerable sectors of the population—the elderly, the ill and the children.

I have here a new list of arguments, a new set of "talking points," by which the Government of the United States is, this year, again, attempting, by deceptive and feeble reasoning, to oppose the General Assembly's consideration of agenda item 39, with which we are dealing today. Once again the Government of the United States has tried to prevent this Organization from complying with its inescapable duty to take a position on the brutal abuse of international law, and of everything that this Organization stands for, that the blockade against Cuba amounts to. We are aware of the representations the United States has made, to that end in a number of capitals, carrying a message that can be summed up in two sentences: "Give us a free hand to subjugate Cuba. Cuba is ours."

I believe it is obvious to all that we Cubans think very differently, and I am certain that the General Assembly and every one of its Member States will refuse to let the fundamental principles uniting us all in this Organization be so grossly violated or replaced by a virtual "law of the jungle."

I shall return to this issue, but, having referred to the blockade on foodstuffs and medicines, I should like to dwell for a moment on one paragraph of the "talking points" I mentioned, in which the Government of the United States attempts to disguise the truth and even to present this shameful aspect of its policy as proof of generosity towards Cuba. I shall not refer to every one of the evasions, half-truths and falsehoods that make up the paragraph.

Document A/47/654 contains information that will enable representatives to draw their own conclusions; I want simply to bring to the attention of this Assembly some brief extracts from the resolution adopted on 12 November of this year by the United States organization called the American Public Health Association regarding the law recently adopted by the Government of the United States against Cuba. Its last preambular paragraph reads as follows:

"Noting that APHA"—that is, the American Public Health Association—"presented testimony on April 2, 1992 before the Committee on Foreign Affairs of the U.S. House of Representatives, and on August 5, 1992 before the Western Hemisphere Subcommittee of the United States Senate Committee on Foreign Relations, urging the Congress to reject this bill as an attempted attack on the health and well-being of an entire population."

Similarly, the resolution states in its first operative paragraph:

"The American Public Health Association urges the new President and Congress to lift this embargo and pass legislation revoking the 'Cuban Democracy Act of 1992' as destructive to both the Cuban and American people."

As can be deduced from the foregoing, that prestigious organization, whose membership consists of more than 50,000 health professionals and community leaders in the United States, disagrees totally with the positions and arguments of its government.

Like the APHA, an increasing number of sectors of international public opinion are beginning to understand that the United States blockade against Cuba constitutes a crime against humanity and a brutal, flagrant, persistent and premeditated violation of the fundamental human rights of the Cuban people.

With regard to the new arguments formulated by the United States delegation, I must acknowledge that, perhaps because they were frightened at the crude way in which the United States threatened other countries last year, their version this year is less absurd. For the rest, with the exception of the logical updating required by an additional year of acts of aggression against Cuba, the new version uses the same fallacious arguments as the preceding one.

I believe that not many will be convinced today by the argument that the item we are now discussing is simply a bilateral issue between Cuba and the United States or that the United Nations and its General Assembly are not the appropriate forum in which to deal with this issue. I regard as truly ineffectual the argument that aims to dissociate the law promulgated by President Bush on 23 October from the blockade that has been imposed by the United States against Cuba for more than 30 years, as if they were different things.

For that reason, I do not consider it necessary to waste time in refuting this case; I shall simply, by quoting another paragraph of his aforementioned statement of 18 April 1992, let President Bush disprove it himself. Perhaps foreseeing some misinterpretation by his subordinates and as if to clarify things, the President of the United States said on that occasion:

"I believe in and I am committed to work with the Congress this session to pass a stronger, more effective 'Cuban Democracy Act,' which tightens the embargo and closes any unintentional loopholes. . . ."

I hope that this version from such an authoritative source leaves no doubt that the "talking points" are wrong.

The "talking points" also say that Cuba is trying to divert world attention from the many failures of its regime. Can it be that they regard as a failure the fact that Cuba has for more than three decades resisted, and in today's unfavourable conditions continues to resist, the brutal assault by the United States? Can it be that they consider it a failure that, in spite of the blockade, no one in Cuba starves or is forsaken—in contrast with the "successful" society of the United States? Can it be that they consider a failure the fact that Cuba has been able to achieve and maintain, up to now, one of the highest levels of health care in the world, in spite of the serious obstacles created by the United States blockade of medicines and foodstuffs? Is it a failure to have achieved a high level of cultural and scientific development, to have built a society based on human solidarity, to have eliminated racial discrimination and eradicated unemployment and illiteracy? Can it be that, because of those considerations, they are trying to return us to subjugation, poverty, hunger, ignorance, and that is why they maintain and do everything in their power to improve the blockade against Cuba? Since I respect the intelligence of this Assembly, even that of the representatives of the United States, I will let each and every one here reply to these questions according to his or her better judgment.

Finally, Cuba is accused of attempting to misuse the United Nations for its own evil ends. Nothing could be more ludicrous. Everyone here and elsewhere is aware of who is attempting to make the United Nations a dependency of its own State Department and to what end.

Now, with respect to this fallacious argumentation of the United States, I would simply like to request the Assembly's opinion on the following questions: Where can a small country that, against the rule of law, is suffering aggression and being strangled by a great Power go but to the United Nations? Can that country be abandoned to the free will of the Power assaulting and strangling it? Would that not be the equivalent of denying this Organization and of giving powerful nations the authority to impose their will upon the weak? Would such an attitude correspond to the legal regime upon which contemporary international relations are based? By answering these questions members will no doubt understand why Cuba has brought this issue before the United Nations, as well as the reasons why the Government of the United States is trying to prevent consideration of agenda item 39 by the General Assembly.

In our case, we have also brought this issue to the United Nations because we believe in its role and in what it represents for the peoples of the world, and also because we trust in international solidarity in the face of injustice being committed by a country as arrogant as it is powerful. We know that millions and tens of millions of honest people worldwide, and in the United States itself, that numerous States, organizations and personalities are calling with increasing vigour for the cessation of this injustice and looking towards this Organization with hope. We know, too, that this effort will not end until lawfulness is restored, as nothing motivates mankind more than the urgency of redressing an injustice.

Before concluding, I would like to point out that my country fully understands that the main responsibility for the present situation regarding the issue we are considering today falls upon the outgoing Administration and that a new one is in the process of being incorporated into the Government of the United States. We also know that this outgoing Administration is the eighth among those that, with some variations, have in essence continued the policy of blockade against Cuba, and that it will leave, in this regard, a heavy legacy.

Several previous opportunities to correct the injustice we are addressing today have been squandered by more than one Administration of the United States. We believe, nevertheless, that the new Administration will also have before it the possibility of rectifying a wrongful policy, and we prefer that it decide not to waste this opportunity. If this proves to be the case, Cuba, in the framework of strict respect for international law, will always be ready to seek the best solutions to controversial issues between our two nations.

To conclude, I would like to introduce the draft resolution contained in document A/47/L.20/Rev.1, which I trust all members have before them and on which my delegation would wish the Assembly to take action today.

I am doing so on behalf of a nation forged in the struggles for its own identity and independence. Our brief but intense history of struggle against two powerful empires has left no doubt in our minds. For our people there is only one way to live. This has been taught to us by the most illustrious personalities in this harsh but unremitting battle of many generations.

One of the founders of our nation, who initiated the first of our wars of independence, in 1868, and who presided over the Republic in Arms, Carlos Manuel de Cespedes—to us Cubans, the "Father of the Motherland"—has taught us, more than a century ago, the Cubans of that time and those today, that "Our motto is and will always be: Independence or Death. Cuba must not only be free, but it cannot be a slave ever again."

Mr. Arria (Venezuela) (interpretation from Spanish): With regard to the draft resolution before us, it is Venezuela's position not to intervene in bilateral relations between States, or the commercial implications deriving from such circumstances. It is quite clearly up to the parties to negotiate and resolve their differences in some other forum, within a bilateral context.

The matter now before the General Assembly is not one such situation. On the contrary, the adoption of legislation by the United States Congress, in approving a law that includes the so-called Torricelli Amendment, has given the situation a basically multilateral dimension, in that it has introduced penalties and restrictions that have a bearing on the sovereign right to free trade to which all the nations of the world are fully entitled.

If legislative bodies in one country were to be allowed to adopt laws of extraterritorial scope, we would then be faced with a questionable and an illegal precedent that might encourage an undesirable and unacceptable tendency on the part of a legislative body in any nation to try and legislate for the entire world. With all due respect for any democratic parliament, we must nevertheless state clearly that such approaches are not compatible with the universal process of democratization of relations between States and are indeed in open contradiction of the United Nations Decade of International Law, which the General Assembly proclaimed in 1989.

Venezuela is committed to the full application of the purposes and principles enshrined in the Charter of the United Nations and of the norms of international law, and, basically, those instruments that have now become sources of law. Here we would highlight General Assembly resolution 2625 (XXV) of 1970, entitled "Declaration on Principles of International Law concerning Friendly Relations and Cooperation among States in accordance with the Charter of the United Nations," which reaffirms the duty of every State to refrain in its international relations from military, political or economic, or any other kind of coercion directed against the political or economic independence of any other State.

The presumption to exercise jurisdictional sovereignty extraterritorially is therefore inadmissible in all its legal, political, economic and moral aspects. Conflicts between two parties are precisely that—between two parties. To presume to involve the entire international community in order to ensure that the interests of one of those parties prevails is totally unacceptable.

My delegation maintains that the draft resolution now before the Assembly does not involve a decision on the political aspects of the bilateral relationship between Cuba and the United States. What we are discussing is the sovereign right of nations that are not involved in a bilateral conflict to trade freely, as is guaranteed by the provisions of the General Agreement on Tariffs and Trade (GATT). We cannot understand how, nor can we agree that, a national law can compel other sovereign States to violate the trade norms laid down in GATT itself.

Venezuela endorses what other countries and groups of countries have said on this issue, to the effect that we must be able to guarantee the rights of all companies that are located in our territory and as a result are subject exclusively to our national legislation and the international commitments entered into by our countries.

My country will vote for the draft resolution, because we have an obligation to protect our jurisdictional sovereignty and our legitimate commercial interests, which would otherwise be damaged by the legislation of another country.

Mr. Montaño (Mexico) (interpretation from Spanish): The item that we are discussing is of special interest to the Government of Mexico, since it relates to fundamental principles of international law.

My country's foreign policy is based on the conviction that respect for the law is the best guarantee of peace and harmony in the coexistence of States. Principles such as sovereign equality, self-determination and non-interference by a State in the internal affairs of others, all of which constantly guide my country's conduct of its international relations, have been elevated to the level of constitutional principles in Mexico.

In our participation in the work of the United Nations we have been committed throughout to strengthening and codifying international law, a task which becomes more pressing at times of uncertainty, such as those we are now experiencing, which arise out of a profound process of world-wide transformation. We are convinced that the new world order of freedom and justice which is being progressively built on the ruins of the old bipolar confrontation must be founded on respect for the sovereignty of States and full observance of international law. This view was expressed from this rostrum by the Minister for Foreign Affairs of Mexico in the general debate at this session of the General Assembly, when he said:

"International law is the binding force that will make it possible to build a true international order at the end of this century. Our Organization must assume with clear vision, dedication and courage world leadership in the defense of international law. Respect for the internal jurisdiction of States is the basis for our civilized and peaceful coexistence." (A/47/PV. 9, pp. 54-55)

Unremitting defence of, and promotion of respect for, international law is not only a recourse of weak countries in the face of the powerful. Nor can international law be an instrument used selectively by the powerful when it serves their interests, to be disregarded thereafter if it comes into conflict with those interests. As we stand on the threshold of a new century, with the end of the division of the world into antagonistic blocs of nations bringing us the opportunity of giving real meaning to the concept of international cooperation, Mexico believes that making international law prevail must be the fundamental commitment of all nations, regardless of their military power or level of economic development.

Among nations, as among individuals, law is an irreplaceable component of democracy, and the rule of law must find daily expression in all aspects of the life of society.

In the sphere of economic cooperation the new conditions of the world economy, characterized by vigorous and progressive interdependence, compel unlimited respect for freedom of trade and navigation, principles that are protected in many instruments of international law. The only exceptions they admit are situations that are clearly defined and regulated in those instruments themselves or in collective security mechanisms.

The countries of Latin America and the Caribbean are making considerable efforts at the domestic level to overcome our underdevelopment, modernize our economic structures and participate more broadly in the world economy. These efforts are complemented by our continued dedication to our aspiration to advance along the road of regional economic complementarity and regional liberalization of trade. Like the efforts of other groups of developing countries, they call for a favourable world environment, which includes full freedom of trade, free of protectionist attitudes and operating within a legal framework of absolute respect for the sovereignty and territorial integrity of States.

The Government of Mexico will always firmly reject any attempt to apply in its territory the legislation of any other State, which would be a violation of international law. In particular, when a country claimed that its legislation applied to Mexico's trade with third countries, my Government described that attitude as a violation of the basic principles of nonintervention. It accordingly categorically rejected the validity of such claims.

The Government of Mexico maintains that a State's decision to establish trading links with another is a full expression of its sovereignty and consequently is not subject to the will of third States. It is for the Government of Mexico, and for it alone, in full exercise of its sovereignty, to decide with whom it will engage in trade relations and the modalities of such relations. Just as Mexico, of its own free will, decides its foreign policy, it has made it perfectly clear that the commercial and trading activities of Mexican corporations or corporations established in our country are governed, and will be governed, exclusively by Mexican legislation.

Those are some of the observations that my delegation deemed it appropriate to contribute to this debate, which we hope will help to emphasize in this forum the pre-eminence of international law and the sovereignty of States over secondary interests or political considerations.

Mr. Sardenberg (Brazil): The consideration of item 39 by the General Assembly this year cannot fail to take into account recent developments that have met with concern in many different countries. In this respect, the Government of Brazil has made public

> "its concern over the promulgation, by the United States Government, on 23 October of this year, of legislation which extends to subsidiaries of American companies located abroad the sanctions applied to companies located within the United States which trade with Cuba. This legislation establishes additional restrictions, such as the ban, for 180 days, on the entry into U.S. ports of vessels which have called at Cuban ports.
>
> "The Brazilian Government is currently evaluating the implications of this legislation, in light of both international law and the interests of Brazilian companies, on the understanding that the relationships of companies located in Brazil with third countries are only regulated by Brazilian legislation, by international agreements to which Brazil is a party and by the decisions of international organizations of which Brazil is a member."

The end of the cold war, the disappearance of East-West confrontation, and the strong trend towards democratization, both within and between nations, have opened the way for a changing international situation with renewed prospects for understanding and international cooperation. This international atmosphere has encouraged negotiated solutions of persistent conflicts, as well as the overcoming of historical divergences. The same should apply in the case of Cuba. A renewed dialogue would facilitate change and help resolve pending problems in accordance with international law.

In this spirit, Brazil stands ready to cooperate so that Cuba can more easily overcome its current difficulties in peace, justice, freedom and democracy. Our objective remains the full reinsertion of Cuba in the Inter-American system. The Brazilian Government believes that an environment of mutual respect and full compliance with international law can help create the necessary conditions for overcoming the current differences affecting the relationship between Cuba and the United States. It is our hope that the deliberations we are undertaking under this item, and on the draft resolution presented by the delegation of Cuba on the necessity of ending the economic, commercial and financial embargo imposed by the United States of America, will also be inspired by this atmosphere, so that mutual understanding and a will to overcome differences may make possible a constructive dialogue.

We have witnessed world-wide phenomena in which ideological, economic, commercial and financial barriers have been removed in favour of shared objectives of peaceful and mutually advantageous coexistence, prosperity, and welfare. It would also be most welcome if in our continent the climate of misunderstanding and confrontation which has characterized the relationship between Cuba and the United States could give way to new forms of understanding and cooperation.

[The President closed the list of speakers with the Assembly's consent.—EDS.]

Mr. Wisnumurti (Indonesia): I deem it a privilege to deliver this statement on behalf of the non-aligned countries.

It is with deep concern that the non-aligned countries have observed the prolonged differences between the United States and Cuba. It is also regrettable that those relationships, which have persisted for over three decades, are now being further extended in the form of an embargo on trade. In this context, we believe that the use of economic sanctions against Cuba can only aggravate the situation. Punitive economic action on such a scale will inflict even greater hardship on the people of Cuba and impede their development aspirations. We therefore believe that such differences, no matter how deep or how intense they may be, should be resolved in accordance with recognized principles of international law and the Charter of the Organization.

At their tenth Summit Meeting, held last September in Jakarta, the Heads of State or Government of the non-aligned countries stated that the attainment of stable peace, common security and social and economic justice must be firmly rooted in the rule of law, the precepts of the Charter, respect for the sovereignty of nations and strict adherence to the principles of non-interference in internal affairs of States, which should not be diluted or abridged. This is of particular importance in the present post–cold war era of transformation in the relations among nations. The Summit also reaffirmed the inadmissibility of the use of force and the assertion by States of claims to exercise extra-territorial rights. In this context, the Summit called on the United States to terminate the economic, commercial and financial measures and actions that have been imposed on Cuba and called for negotiations to resolve their differences on the basis of equality and mutual respect.

The Non-Aligned Movement has always maintained that international relations must be governed by international law and by the principles of the Charter. At this juncture we cannot turn away from those approaches to resolving differences between nations. We remain convinced that rapprochement between the United States and Cuba would contribute to the stability of the region and to the promotion of cooperation, along the lines of what is taking place in other regions.

[The representative from the Democratic People's Republic of Korea spoke next. His remarks are reprinted in Appendix A12.—EDS.]

Mr. Trinh Xuan Lang (Viet Nam): For more than 30 years the economic, commercial and financial embargo imposed on Cuba, which involves prohibition of the provision of foodstuffs, medicines, medical supplies and equipment of United States origin, has inflicted on that country enormous material losses and economic damage. Moreover, the Cuban Democracy Act of 1992, also known as the Torricelli Bill or Torricelli Amendment, which was signed into law last October, makes the economic difficulties even more serious, hinders the peaceful process of economic development in that country and inflicts indiscriminate suffering upon the Cuban people, including the elderly and innocent children. No peace-loving and justice-loving people in the world can accept that arbitrary act, which is completely at variance with the basic norms of international relations and the changing political atmosphere that now prevails on our planet.

Given the profound changes in international relations we have witnessed in the past few years, the post–cold war world we are living in today is characterized by the intensified efforts of the international community to establish a rule of law, by the reduction of tension and by trends towards peace and the peaceful settlement of disputes. Our world today is also characterized by increasing trade and economic cooperation and by the interdependence of nations as a result of the globalization of the world economy.

Respect for the national independence and sovereignty of States, for the right of peoples to self-determination and for equality between them have always been, and must forever remain, among others, the basic principles of international relations. It is on the basis of national sovereignty and self-determination, free from outside interference, that a State has the right to choose for itself the political, social and economic systems suited to its own specific conditions. No country in the world has the right to impose its will on others or to inflict punishment upon them if they are not resigned to bowing to its orders. All countries, big or small, rich or poor, strong or weak, have the equal right to exist, develop and participate on a non-discriminatory basis in world affairs.

In the present international context, as I have mentioned, the unilateral imposition of economic embargo by one country on another has become an obsolete policy. Therefore, the continuation and further strengthening of the embargo against a small and peace-loving country like Cuba has no justification whatsoever and runs counter to the positive trends of our times. The subordination of one country to another country's legislation runs counter to nations' right to self-determination and constitutes a serious violation of the United Nations Charter and of international law, including the laws on freedom of trade and navigation.

In expressing their solidarity with the Government and people of Cuba, the Heads of State or Government of non-aligned countries meeting in Jakarta, Indonesia, last September once again called for cessation of the unneighbourly acts against Cuba and termination of the series of economic, commercial and financial measures and actions imposed upon that country. Many countries, including some of those in Europe and North America, have voiced their concern over and rejection of the so-called Cuban Democracy Act of 1992.

Having been subjected to an economic and trade embargo for many years, the Government and the people of Vietnam fully sympathize with and strongly support the Government and people of Cuba in their legitimate demand for an immediate end to the economic, commercial and financial embargo imposed on them. We support Cuba's call on the international community to extend to that country the necessary cooperation, with a view to helping it mitigate the consequences of this embargo. We strongly believe that the lifting of the embargoes against Cuba and other countries will be a great contribution towards the economic development of those countries and towards promoting peace, international harmony and cooperation.

Mr. Nyakyi (United Republic of Tanzania): Last year, upon the urging of many delegations, including my own, the delegation of Cuba agreed to the deferment of the debate on agenda item 142 in order to permit the continuation of efforts, then under way, to ease the tension in relations between the United States and Cuba and to promote dialogue and a negotiated solution to their differences.

Regrettably, it must now be admitted that we were too optimistic. Not only has a whole year gone by without any visible improvement in the situation, but, as recent developments show, there has, in fact, been a deterioration of the situation. The new United States legislation constitutes unacceptable interference, not only in Cuba's internal affairs, but also in the right of third countries to choose their cooperating partners. By widening, tightening and intensifying the embargo against Cuba the new law amounts to a serious and dangerous escalation of this totally unacceptable pressure against Cuba. This body has a duty to speak out against this flagrant violation of the principles of the Charter of the United Nations and of international law.

My delegation welcomes the statement made by the Permanent Representative of Indonesia, speaking on behalf of the States members of the Non-Aligned Movement. It goes without saying that his statement has the full support of the Tanzanian delegation.

As my delegation understands the situation, this debate is not about the bilateral differences between Cuba and the United States of America. It is not about the different political and economic systems which the two countries have embraced. It is not about their differing reactions to the events of the last three-and-a-half years in Eastern and Central Europe and their repercussions throughout the world. It is about the right of countries, whatever their size, ideological persuasion or level of development, to choose, without interference from any quarter, their partners in international economic and commercial relations. It is about the right of third countries to exercise their freedom to choose whom to do business with. It is about the duty of States, big and small, rich and poor, to respect the principles of the Charter and of international law governing the conduct of relations between States. It is about the duty of the international community, and especially of its principal organ, the United Nations, to secure compliance by all Member States with their obligations under the Charter and numerous resolutions of the General Assembly.

Paragraph 2 of Article 1 of the Charter makes it clear that a fundamental purpose of the United Nations is the development of friendly relations among nations based on respect for the principle of equal rights and self-determination of peoples. The embargo against Cuba is a clear violation of the provisions of this Article. It is also a violation of General Assembly resolution 2131 (XX), which prohibits the use of economic, political and other types of measures to coerce a State in order to secure the subordination of its rights. It is also a contravention of General Assembly resolution 2625 (XXV), which requires States to refrain from military, political, economic and any other form of coercion aimed against the independence or territorial integrity of any State.

It is also a violation of General Assembly resolution 36/103, which enjoins Member States to refrain from measures that would constitute interference or intervention in the internal affairs of other States, including any multilateral or unilateral economic reprisal or blockade as a means of exerting political pressure or coercion against other States. In this connection, it should be noted that this embargo is directed not only against Cuba but also against third countries' rights freely to enter into economic and commercial relations with Cuba. Those countries, big and small, that complain that the embargo constitutes interference with their right to engage in trading relations with Cuba are therefore fully justified.

The last three-and-a-half years have seen fundamental changes in the international arena—changes that hold great promise for a new world order based on the rule of law and, in particular, on the principles of the United Nations Charter. Many intractable conflicts have found solutions in which bitter enemies have become reconciled, and old rivalries have been buried. Sadly, the 30-year old dispute between the United States of America and Cuba is one of the few exceptions, one of the few situations not to have benefited from the new climate of reconciliation, dialogue and accommodation. This is tragic because all the factors favouring a peaceful resolution of the differences are present in the current international environment.

The ending of the cold war, effectively eliminating super-Power rivalry in the Western hemisphere, has removed a major cause of friction between the two countries. In Central America, the replacement of the use of force by negotiations as a means of settling conflicts has removed another major cause of or excuse for friction and suspicion within and between countries of the region and has ushered in a new era that holds the promise of good-neighbourliness and cooperation.

The communique issued by the Heads of State or Government of the Ibero-American States following their meeting in Guadalajara, Mexico, on 18 and 19 July 1991, in which they stated that

"the principles of sovereignty and nonintervention are reaffirmed and recognition is given to each people's right to build freely, in peace, stability and justice, its own political system and institutions." (A/46/317, annex, para. 3)

That is an eloquent expression of the new spirit of understanding and cooperation in the region. The 23 leaders also pledged themselves

"to promote greater democracy and pluralism in international relations, with full respect for the sovereignty, territorial integrity and the political independence of States, as well as the sovereign equality and self-determination of peoples."

The countries of the region deserve all encouragement and support in their efforts to resolve internal and inter-State conflicts and to find new ways of living and cooperating with one another. By accepting Cuba as an equal member of the region, the countries of the Latin American and Caribbean region have proclaimed, as loudly as they can, that Cuba poses no threat to anyone. They have also conceded to

Cuba the right to organize its affairs in accordance with the wishes of the people of Cuba. We in this Assembly should call on all countries in the hemisphere to follow the example of the overwhelming majority of the countries in the region.

[The representative from Iraq spoke next. His remarks are reprinted in Appendix A12.—EDS.]

Mr. Razali (Malaysia): The Malaysian delegation wishes to express its support for the position taken by Indonesia, which spoke in its capacity as Chairman of the Non-Aligned Countries. We share the position taken at the Tenth Summit Conference in Jakarta, in September 1992. We were a party in the taking of that position.

Although this matter can best be settled between the two countries, the right of Cuba to appeal to the United Nations must be respected, especially its concern over the issue of extraterritoriality.

Members of the United Nations are obliged to support fundamental principles of international law. The present climate of international cooperation and peaceful settlement of bilateral and international problems offers ample opportunities for countries in their best traditions to seek solutions to problems.

Inter-State relations are increasingly being directed towards cooperation rather than confrontation. Records of past history should not stand in the way of settling problems between countries. Old adversarial positions are not compatible with the present changed climate for the defusion of disputes and conflicts. In this context we appeal for the issue to be settled on the basis of sovereignty and mutual respect.

Malaysia hopes that the support for the draft resolution at this session of the General Assembly will be a manifestation of the clear wishes of the majority at the United Nations to settle this problem peacefully and amicably. It is the belief of my delegation that should there be a normalization of relations there will be many significant and positive benefits for the region as a whole.

[The representatives from Equatorial Guinea and the Libyan Arab Jamahiriya spoke next. Their remarks are reprinted in Appendix A12.—EDS.]

Mr. Takht-Ravanchi (Islamic Republic of Iran): In the emerging cooperative atmosphere, the international community, spared from bloc rivalries, is aspiring to a new era in inter-State relations based on the principles of justice, full respect for the principles and norms of international law, international cooperation, common prosperity, respect for territorial integrity and the sovereign equality of States, and non-aggression and non-interference in the internal affairs of other States. Clearly, the rule of law in international relations is, more than ever before, in the forefront.

It is quite appropriate to recall here that the programme of activities of the United Nations Decade of International Law rightly calls upon States to act in accordance with international law and the Charter of the United Nations.

The principles of the sovereign equality of States and that of nonintervention and non-interference in the internal affairs of other States are fundamental principles of international law that form the cornerstone of contemporary international relations. Respect for those principles has been incorporated in a number of international instruments, such as the Charter of the United Nations, the Manila Declaration on the Peaceful Settlement of International Disputes, and the Declaration on Principles of International Law concerning Friendly Relations.

Last year, at the forty-sixth session of the General Assembly, the representative of Cuba elaborated on his Government's positions regarding the item under consideration, namely, "The necessity of ending the economic, commercial and financial embargo imposed by the United States of America against Cuba," and on the hardships the Cuban people have been experiencing for the past 30 years. This morning we also heard the statement of the Permanent Representative of Cuba, in which he referred to a new measure aimed at strengthening the embargo against his country.

The Islamic Republic of Iran is cognizant of the difficulties the Cuban nation faces as a result of the embargo. In this regard I should like to quote a paragraph from the final document adopted at the Tenth Summit Meeting of the Movement of the Non-Aligned Countries, at Jakarta, which states that the States members "urged the Government of the United States to cease its unneighbourly acts against Cuba and to terminate the series of economic, commercial and financial actions imposed upon that country for over three decades, which have inflicted enormous material losses and economic damage."

In conclusion, we once again urge all States to abide by their obligations under international law, which is certainly the basic condition for the maintenance of world peace and security. We also wish to extend our support to any step that the General Assembly may wish to take in order to elevate the rule of law in international relations. It is universally admitted that in the case of a conflict between domestic law and international law the latter prevails over the former. Thus, the international community cannot and should not remain silent in cases of enactment of domestic legislation by a given State aimed at imposing a specific political or economic structure upon another State or at undermining the economic or political stability of another State. Undoubtedly, such measures constitute a violation of the generally accepted principle of non-interference and nonintervention in the internal affairs of States.

[The representatives from Yemen, Algeria, and Zimbabwe spoke next. Their remarks are reprinted in Appendix A12.—EDS.]

Mr. Ayala Lasso (Ecuador) (interpretation from Spanish): I wish to recall, in respect of the item under consideration, that on 30 October this year Ecuador's Ministry of Foreign Relations, in keeping with its traditional international policy, reaffirmed the fundamental validity of the rule of law as the basis of peaceful international relations. The Ministry also addressed the principle of the self-determination of peoples, with all the rights and responsibilities it entails, and reiterated its firm support for the strengthening of representative democracy throughout the region.

In addition, Ecuador confirmed its opposition to policies or measures by which any country attempts to prohibit free commerce between sovereign States. It added that Ecuador would maintain its trade relations within the legitimate exercise of its sovereignty.

Ecuador considers that, even though decisions in the conduct of bilateral trade relations fall under the auspices of national sovereignty, there are general obligations enshrined in multilateral treaties, and that there are other, even more important, obligations related to fostering freedom of trade in a climate of cooperation and solidarity. They are among the positive trends in a world which has now left the cold war behind and is seeking to build a more just and constructive future. These obligations must be accepted and respected.

As for the problem that has given rise to the draft resolution before us, my country is of the view that dialogue and agreement between the parties directly involved would be the most appropriate peaceful means of resolving the matter. I hope that this will come about as soon as possible so that, at the same time, in a climate of mutual respect between all States, democracy may flourish more vigorously and the rule of law may grow stronger throughout our hemisphere.

Mr. Watson (United States of America): The Government of Cuba would have us believe that it is a defender of international law and free commerce and navigation. In fact, the Government of Cuba is using these lofty sentiments as a pretext. What it really wants is to involve the international community in one aspect of its bilateral relations with the United States: the United States economic embargo against Cuba.

The United States chooses not to trade with Cuba for good reasons. The Government of Cuba, in violation of international law, expropriated billions of dollars worth of private property belonging to United States individuals, and has refused to make reasonable restitution. The United States embargo—it is not a blockade—is therefore a legitimate response to the unreasonable and illegal behaviour of the Cuban Government. I need not labour here the fact that economic embargoes have been used fairly often by other States throughout the world.

In addition, the United States chooses not to trade with Cuba because of our concerns about human rights abuses and the lack of democracy in Cuba. We believe that the future of Cuba should be determined by the Cuban people and not by a regime imposed upon them.

Cubans should be able to enjoy freedom of speech and association and the basic human rights recognized by this great institution. Unfortunately, the behaviour of the Cuban Government on all of these issues has not become more reasonable with the passage of time. In contrast to the policy of the Cuban Government towards its own population, the United States embargo is not designed to hurt the Cuban people.

The truth is that Cuba is, and always has been, able to purchase goods from any country in the world except the United States and its firms. Moreover, embargo regulations allow the licensing of humanitarian donations, including medicine and medical supplies, from United States sources to non-governmental organizations in Cuba.

In addition, after complying with licensing and verification procedures, even the Cuban Government can now purchase medicine directly from the United States. Licenses for the shipment of millions of dollars' worth of medicines, medical equipment and humanitarian packages have been approved during the current year. This continues—and in some ways it is easier—under the Cuban Democracy Act.

The problems that Cuba faces are due to its refusal to adopt economic and political reforms—not to external conditions. We understand that some Governments are concerned about the Cuban Democracy Act ban on trade by United States subsidiaries. The United States Government believes that these concerns are best addressed through normal bilateral channels, and certainly not in a General Assembly resolution.

Cuba uses the Cuban Democracy Act as a pretext. What it really wants is a debate on its bilateral relations with the United States, as is evidenced by its intemperate statement this morning. This propaganda exercise at the United Nations—and that is what Cuba's effort is— does nothing to resolve any concerns that others may have regarding the Cuban situation.

In our view, the General Assembly is not the forum, nor is the Cuban resolution the vehicle, to address this essentially bilateral issue of the embargo. Accordingly, we urge the Assembly not to support the Cuban draft resolution now before it.

The President (interpretation from French): Having heard the last speaker in the debate on this item, we shall proceed to consider draft resolution A/47/L.20/Rev. 1.

I shall now call on those representatives who wish to explain their votes before the voting.

May I remind delegations that, in accordance with General Assembly decision 34/401, explanations of vote are limited to 10 minutes and should be made by delegations from their seats.

Mr. Mongbe (Benin) (interpretation from French): In a few moments we shall take a decision on draft resolution A/47/L.20/Rev.1 on the necessity of ending the economic, commercial and financial embargo against Cuba, which was submitted under agenda item 39. The fact that this item comes up annually and is debated in plenary meetings demonstrates the importance that the international community attaches to it.

There is a danger of failure to see that this matter has deep ideological roots, but it is a crucial economic issue, which has now assumed very serious humanitarian proportions. The Benin which I represent has turned its back on a certain ideology, which supposedly wanted the best for society but proceeded to try to achieve that goal by secret measures against people, despite the fact that people should be the very focus of all economic and social development. Thus, my delegation would like its vote not to be understood as support for a Government or regime guided by such an ideology.

Benin is fully committed to the democratic ideal and to fundamental human and people's rights. Hence my delegation cannot but endorse any measure that would ease the suffering of human beings. But what do we see? The international press—especially the American press—tells us what the situation is: The blockade against Cuba, which has been in force for several years, has had serious consequences for the lives of the Cuban people. When two elephants fight, their heads and trunks do not suffer; rather, it is the grass under their feet that is damaged. This is an old African proverb.

It is difficult for one to imagine the extent of the food restrictions to which the citizens of Cuba are subjected. According to press reports that we have all read, the situation worsened, after the major upheavals in East-West relations; that, in turn, has led to a fundamental change in the economic and commercial relations between Cuba and formerly Communist countries.

Benin is linked by sincere and deep friendship with all countries in the Western hemisphere. This friendship has been woven over centuries of history. The suffering of a people in this region is shared and felt by people on the other side of the Atlantic, where Benin is situated. Thus my delegation's vote will reflect the hope of people who are deprived of the necessities of life—medicines, fuel and basic commodities—in other words, the right to life and survival. So our vote will be a vote of hope. Our vote will be displayed in green.

My delegation will vote in favor of draft resolution A/47/L.20/Rev.1. It will do so without any bitterness, without any feeling of hostility against any country whatsoever. In so voting, we shall be issuing a friendly invitation to the parties—the United States of America and Cuba—finally to begin responsible negotiations to put an end to the enmity that has brought such suffering to their peoples. My delegation will vote for mankind, for humanism.

Mr. Richardson (United Kingdom): I am speaking on behalf of the European Community and its member States.

The opposition of the European Community and its member States to the extraterritorial application of national legislation is well known. The Community and its member States have consistently been on record in opposing the unilateral extension by the United States of the reach of trade measures implementing United States foreign or national security policies. Accordingly, they have opposed legislative initiatives, including the Cuban Democracy Act, intended to tighten further the United States trade embargo on Cuba by the extraterritorial application of United States jurisdiction.

They consider this to be a violation of the general principles of international law and the sovereignty of independent nations.

Although the European Community and its member States are fully supportive of the peaceful transition to democracy in Cuba, they cannot accept that the United States unilaterally determines and restricts European Community economic and commercial relations with any foreign nation which has not been collectively determined by the United Nations Security Council to be a threat to international peace and security.

The European Community and its member States believe, however, that the United States trade embargo against Cuba is primarily a bilateral matter for the Governments of the United States and Cuba.

The European Community and its member States will have these concerns in mind when voting on this draft resolution.

Mr. Van Dunem "Mbinda" (Angola): In recent years the world has been witness to profound changes in international relations with particular relevance to the end of the cold war, which opens an era of hope for the resolution of various international, regional and other conflicts that have appeared insoluble through dialogue. However, we note with concern that in some regions there still exist situations that will not benefit from this hope of the end of the cold war that we all share.

We should like to refer to the question that concerns us at this time: the economic and financial blockade imposed against Cuba by the United States of America.

As a matter of fact, Cuba has been suffering the effects of a severe blockade that has seriously affected its development, with serious consequences for the well being of its people. This situation has been aggravated with the adoption last October of the so-called Torricelli Law intended to strengthen the embargo and to extend its application beyond the borders of the United States of America.

This law affects not only Cuba but, as we can realize, also the sovereignty of other States, freedom of navigation and free international trade, as is acknowledged by various countries and international organizations, and especially the Economic Community, which has affirmed that "This law and other measures constitute a violation of the general principles of international law."

It would perhaps be an error in judgment if we concluded that this embargo and its strengthening through the Torricelli Law, seeks to strangle the economy and, accordingly, the social life of Cuba and to oblige that country to change its political system—this in flagrant violation of the principle of the self-determination of peoples, of their freely choosing their destinies without foreign interference, basic and fundamental principles set forth in the United Nations Charter, with which all Member States are obliged to comply.

In this context, we think that the right freely to determine their own destiny is a matter solely for the Cuban people to decide. It is also our conviction that the Cuban people should not be detached from the transformations that are taking place in the international arena.

For those reasons, and out of a profound respect for human rights, my delegation is in favour of the draft resolution calling for the lifting of the embargo, and it hopes that, through frank and open dialogue based on mutual respect and sovereign equality, the solution of this lengthy dispute will be possible. I am sure of that.

Mr. Butler (Australia): The Australian delegation regrets the way in which this draft resolution has come to the Assembly. One outcome of that passage of events has been some unfortunate imprecision in the language of the draft, and there is also of course the dissonance that exists between its title and its content.

In today's debate some speakers have stated their view that what is at issue in this draft resolution is the vital question of free and fair trade. On that subject, the commitment of Australia to free and fair trade under the rules of the General Agreement on Tariffs and Trade

(GATT) and to a successful conclusion of the Uruguay Round is a total commitment and widely known. We will continue to pursue that goal with every determination.

But because this draft resolution was born of a relatively narrow purpose, and is somewhat skewed, it is very unlikely to serve that wider purpose to which so many of us are committed, free and fair world trade. It is principally for that reason that my delegation will abstain in the voting on this draft resolution.

Mr. Kudryavtsev (Russian Federation) (interpretation from Russian): The Russian delegation will abstain in the voting on the draft resolution in document A/47/L.20/Rev.1 because we believe that, in order to resolve specific issues relating to trade and economic relations, it is more appropriate to consider them within the context of bilateral negotiations between States rather than in international forums.

At the same time we share the concern that has been expressed by a number of States in connection with the so-called Torricelli Law recently adopted in the United States. In our opinion that legislation is contrary to a whole series of provisions of contemporary international law.

Russia consistently advocates democratization and respect for human rights. However, we do not regard it as proper, from the legal viewpoint, to apply coercion and pressure in these matters, particularly measures that were part of the past cold war era.

As far as our economic relations with Cuba are concerned, they have been shifted onto a depoliticized, equal and mutually beneficial basis, onto a normal civilized level of inter-State relations.

Precisely such an approach is characteristic of the recent agreement concluded between the Russian Federation and Cuba relating to trade and economic cooperation, merchant shipping and other issues related to trade relations.

Mr. Malone (Canada): The draft resolution on which we shall now vote involves complex legal and political issues. Canada has experienced the effects of inappropriate attempts to assert extraterritorial jurisdiction, and we have developed our own means to deal with them. The draft resolution before us embodies certain legal principles that Canada believes must be respected. As a result, we shall vote for the resolution.

Our support for this draft resolution and the principles it embodies does not relate to the specific dispute between Cuba and the United States alluded to in the title of the draft resolution, nor does it in any way suggest complacency with respect to Cuba's human rights record.

Mr. O'Brien (New Zealand): New Zealand will vote for the draft resolution before us not because we are particularly attracted to the text as it stands, but because we do think that there is an important underlying principle at stake with direct implications for our own economic and trading interests. In particular, we think that countries such as our own must be able to go about their ordinary trade and commercial business free from the extraterritorial reach of legislation imposed unilaterally by third countries.

That said, New Zealand would have preferred a draft resolution on this subject to be concerned solely with the issue of principle at stake. We regret that certain extraneous material has been introduced by drawing selectively on the principles contained in the United Nations Charter. That does detract from the overall principle involved, but we do fully support that principle.

Mr. Piriz Ballon (Uruguay) (interpretation from Spanish): Independent of the specific, concrete case that led to the introduction of this draft resolution, and without prejudice to the reservations we might have about the legal appropriateness of the use of the word "embargo" in the heading of the draft resolution, Uruguay, which sees international law as the cornerstone of its foreign policy, cannot but support the text before us.

In fact, if every State in exercise of its sovereignty is totally free to decide with which other States it wishes to trade or to cease trading, it is then not possible to accept that a State might seek to extend to other countries the effects of its domestic legislation, thus imposing or threatening to impose damages against those third States for trading with the State that was the subject of such domestic legislation.

We are of the view that to apply such a policy is tantamount to seeking to extend the territorial jurisdiction of a State, which is a breach of the principle of sovereign equality of States; that it is in effect interference in the internal affairs of other States; and that it runs counter to the principles and norms of international law governing the freedom of trade and navigation.

The President (interpretation from French): I shall now put to the vote draft resolution A/47/L.20/Rev.1.

A recorded vote was taken.

* * *

[Member states were then offered an additional opportunity to explain their votes.—Eds.]

Mr. Yamamoto (Japan): Before proceeding with my statement in explanation of vote, I want to join you, Mr. President, and other delegations in conveying my sincere condolences to the delegation of the Lao People's Democratic Republic.

I wish to put on record the position of Japan, which abstained in the vote on draft resolution A/47/L.20/Rev.1.

First, Japan still has some doubts as to whether a discussion in the General Assembly can actually be conducive to resolving in a constructive way the question of the United States embargo against Cuba.

Secondly, various countries have expressed their concerns about the Cuban Democracy Act, as it contains some provisions that could affect the rights and interests of third nations. Japan fully understands such concerns.

Those points illustrate the very complex nature of this question. Japan wonders whether the draft resolution adopted this morning as resolution 47/19 can in fact properly address that complexity. If it cannot, the question will remain unresolved until a better way is found to achieve an appropriate solution.

Mr. Wide (Sweden): In the specific case of recent legislation applying to Cuba, which has possible extraterritorial effects, the Swedish Government has expressed its position of criticism based on certain principles of international law.

The preambular paragraph of the resolution adopted this morning is of a general character and seems to cover not only specific measures against Cuba but also a whole range of other measures with extraterritorial effects. Sweden thinks that the broader question of extraterritoriality is a complicated legal issue that can be thoroughly examined only in an appropriate context. Sweden therefore abstained in the vote on draft resolution A/47/L.20/Rev.1.

We note that 21 Ibero-American countries have requested the inclusion of a new agenda item concerning extraterritoriality, and that the General Assembly has decided to refer that item to the Sixth Committee.

Mr. Kabir (Bangladesh): My delegation abstained in the vote on draft resolution A/47/L.20/Rev.1. In explaining our abstention, I should like to point out that our abstention should not be construed as opposition to universally recognized principles of free trade and shipping or to relevant international law, including the internationally accepted norms of the non-extraterritoriality of domestic legislation.

Bangladesh firmly believes that, as was reiterated at the Tenth Summit Conference of non-aligned countries in Jakarta, peace, security and social and economic justice can only be based on the rule of law and the principles enshrined in the Charter. We also believe in the inadmissibility of the use of force and the assertion by States of claims to exercise extraterritorial rights. Inter-State and international relations are best governed by international law and respect for the sovereignty of nations.

We believe that the *rapprochement* between the United States and Cuba would contribute to the stability of the region. Bangladesh also believes that with the end of the cold war any differences can be resolved in a spirit of cooperation.

We abstained in the vote because this resolution, in our view, which rightly points out the supremacy of international law, may not contribute to the process of *rapprochement*. If the resolution had been subjected to wider consultations, perhaps a more unified approach could have emerged, thus facilitating adoption by consensus. This would have helped the process of reconciliation under the new political climate of *detente* and cooperation.

We hope sincerely that both the United States and Cuba will seize the opportunity offered by the momentum of peace and try to resolve their differences in order to lift the embargo by peaceful bilateral negotiations, thus further consolidating the post–cold war edifice of peace.

Mr. Chiaradia (Argentina) (interpretation from Spanish): In accordance with instructions I have received, I wish to set forth some of the reasons for the vote my Government cast on the draft resolution submitted under the item now before the Assembly.

First, my Government considers that the framework of the resolution is exceeded by an underlying political issue. The Republic of Argentina joins the rest of the international community in rejecting any limitation on State sovereignty in regard to free trade with third countries. This position has been clearly stated on a number of occasions, in particular in the joint statement by Presidents Salinas de Gortari and Menem last October in Mexico City.

Apart from that, and above and beyond the contents of the resolution, the Government of Argentina cannot but take into account the situation in which Cuba finds itself as a result of the persistence of a political system that does not make possible the full and effective exercise of individual and political rights. This situation is an anomaly in the Latin American region, where the democratic, representative system of government has been strengthened over the past few years.

Bearing in mind the principles involved and the political realities, the Government of Argentina decided to abstain in the vote on draft resolution A/47/L.20/Rev.1.

TALLY OF THE VOTE, NOVEMBER 24, 1992

[The recorded vote on Cuba's revised draft resolution, A/47/PV.70, November 24, 1992, is reprinted.—EDS.]

In favour:
Algeria, Angola, Barbados, Benin, Brazil, Burkina Faso, Burundi, Canada, Central African Republic, Chile, China, Colombia, Comoros, Congo, Cuba, Democratic People's Republic of Korea, Ecuador, Equatorial Guinea, France, Ghana, Guinea, Guinea-Bissau, Haiti, India, Indonesia, Iran (Islamic Republic of), Iraq, Jamaica, Kenya, Lao People's

Democratic Republic, Lebanon, Lesotho, Libyan Arab Jamahiriya, Madagascar, Malaysia, Mali, Malta, Mexico, Myanmar, Namibia, New Zealand, Niger, Nigeria, Pakistan, Papua New Guinea, Spain, Sudan, Swaziland, Syrian Arab Republic, Uganda, Ukraine, United Republic of Tanzania, Uruguay, Vanuatu, Venezuela, Viet Nam, Yemen, Zambia, Zimbabwe

Against:
Israel, Romania, United States of America

Abstaining:
Albania, Antigua and Barbuda, Argentina, Armenia, Australia, Austria, Azerbaijan, Bahamas, Bangladesh, Belarus, Belgium, Belize, Bolivia, Brunei Darussalam, Bulgaria, Cameroon, Chad, Costa Rica, Cote d'Ivoire, Czechoslovakia, Denmark, El Salvador, Ethiopia, Fiji, Finland, Gabon, Germany, Greece, Guatemala, Guyana, Honduras, Hungary, Iceland, Ireland, Italy, Japan, Jordan, Kuwait, Liechtenstein, Luxembourg, Maldives, Marshall Islands, Micronesia (Federated States of), Nepal, Netherlands, Nicaragua, Norway, Panama, Paraguay, Peru, Philippines, Poland, Portugal, Republic of Korea, Republic of Moldova, Russian Federation, Rwanda, Saint Lucia, Saint Vincent and the Grenadines, Samoa, San Marino, Singapore, Slovenia, Sri Lanka, Suriname, Sweden, Thailand, Trinidad and Tobago, Turkey, United Kingdom of Great Britain and Northern Ireland, Zaire.

Draft resolution A/47/L.20/Rev.1 was adopted by 59 votes to 3, with 71 abstentions (resolution 47/19).*

---

*Subsequently the delegation of Lebanon advised the Secretariat that it had intended to abstain.

PART II

SCOPE OF UNITED STATES ECONOMIC MEASURES

The comprehensive character of the United States measures is suggested by an interchange between the State and Treasury Departments in early 1961. The State Department was considering a "complete economic blockade of Cuba by the United States enforced if necessary by the naval and military forces." The Treasury Department responded that full exercise of the President's authority to prohibit commercial and financial dealings with Cuba pursuant to the Trading With the Enemy Act, 50 U.S.C. App. § 5(b), could "accomplish a significant proportion of all of the effects which might be desired to be obtained through the institution of an economic blockade."*

We first summarize the principal features of current United States prohibitions in both their bilateral and multilateral aspects. We also trace the statutory authority of the United States President to impose these measures under the Trading With the Enemy Act and other United States domestic law.

In the General Assembly proceedings, Cuba charged that the United States has gone beyond its regulatory measures in its effort to disrupt third-country trade and investment with Cuba. We provide a summary of reported incidents. We then provide a detailed chronology tracing the evolution of the United States administrative measures since they were first instituted in 1960. We conclude with an economic study examining Cuba's vulnerability to the current United States effort.

---

*Memorandum, Subject "Cuba–Total Blockade," May 16, 1961, Office of the Secretary to the Treasury, Department of the Treasury, as quoted in Morris H. Morley, *Imperial State and Revolution: The United States and Cuba, 1952–1986* 188 (1987).

The editors prepared the materials in Part II with the exception of the economic study, which Professor Andrew Zimbalist of Smith College contributed.

PRINCIPAL FEATURES OF THE UNITED STATES ECONOMIC MEASURES AGAINST CUBA

The United States prohibitions are set forth for the most part in the regulations of the United States Department of the Treasury, the Cuban Assets Control Regulations, 31 C.F.R. Part 515, and the United States Commerce Department, the Export Administration Regulations, 15 C.F.R. Parts 770 through 785. All transfers of property in violation of these regulations are null and void under the laws of the United States and cannot give rise to any title, interest or claim in the transferee. 31 C.F.R. § 515.203. Civil penalties may be imposed by the Treasury Department for any violation of these regulations, and knowing violations are punishable as criminal offenses, with prison terms up to ten years, substantial fines, or both. Additionally, property concerned in violations is subject to forfeiture. 50 U.S.C. App. § 16.

BILATERAL ASPECTS

1. *Imports.* The United States prohibits any imports from Cuba into the United States.

2. *Exports.* The United States prohibits any exports to Cuba from the United States.

3. *Transfers of money or property.* In addition to prohibiting imports and exports, the United States prohibits any United States person from transferring any money or property of any nature, wherever located, to Cuba or a Cuban national, wherever located, or engaging in any financial transaction involving Cuba or Cuban nationals.

4. *Travel.* The United States prohibits United States persons from paying Cuba or Cuban nationals for travel-related expenses such as payments for hotels and meals. This effectively precludes travel to Cuba for virtually all United States persons. There are limited exceptions: persons visiting close relatives in Cuba; journalists or documentary filmmakers; qualified persons pursuing full-time professional research about subjects which are specifically related to Cuba where the product of the research is very likely to be disseminated; and persons travelling on official business for the United States government, foreign governments, or international organizations. Even these persons are entitled to expend only $100 per day for their travel expenses in Cuba. United States charter companies are permitted to transport these persons, as well as persons fully hosted by the Cuban government, to and from Cuba.

5. *Credits and guarantees.* Prohibited transfers of property include the extension of any credits or guarantees.

6. *Technical data.* The prohibition against transfers of property also includes the transfer of technical data except for data which is publicly available. It also applies to the licensing of any rights to use or exploit technical data, whether public or not. Technical data is any information which can be used or adopted for use in connection with the production, manufacture, utilization or reconstruction of articles or materials.

7. *Services.* The United States prohibits United States persons from providing a "service" to Cuba or a Cuban national. The prohibition is so broad as to prohibit, for example, a United States scholar leading a seminar on academic subjects in Cuba.

8. *Relinquishing rights.* The United States prohibits United States persons from relinquishing a right in favor of Cuba or a Cuban national or forgiving a debt.

9. *Receiving property.* The United States prohibits any United States person from receiving property from Cuba or a Cuban national, receiving a service from Cuba or a Cuban national, or benefiting from a waiver of rights by Cuba or a Cuban national. This prohibition applies regardless of whether or not any consideration is given by the United States person.

10. *Aircraft.* The United States prohibits any aircraft departing from the jurisdiction of the United States for Cuba, or any aircraft wherever located from departing for Cuba if owned or controlled by United States persons.

11. *Vessels.* The United States prohibits any Cuban vessel from entering its ports and similarly closes its ports to any United States vessel carrying goods or passengers from or to Cuba or carrying goods in which Cuba has an interest.

12. *Brokering or transporting property.* The United States prohibits United States persons, whether located in the United States or abroad, from brokering the sale of Cuban property, transporting Cuban property or otherwise dealing in Cuban property, wherever located. The prohibition applies not only to transactions involving property in which Cuba currently has an interest—for example, property owned by Cuba or a Cuban national, but also property in which Cuba has had an interest at any time since July 8, 1963—for example, property of Cuban origin now owned by third persons.

13. *Third-country nationals in Cuba.* All the prohibitions applicable to transactions involving Cuban nationals are applicable to third-country nationals domiciled or permanently resident in Cuba and are applicable to partnerships, associations, corporations or other organizations

which have their principal place of business in Cuba wherever organized.

14. *Musical performances.* The United States prohibits any payment to Cuban musical artists for public performances in the United States. Ever since Congress permitted the sale of Cuban records in the United States in 1988, State Department policy has been to deny visas to Cuban musicians to perform in the United States even without fee. The State Department rationale is that performances in the United States would promote the sale of these artists' records.

15. *Contracts.* The United States prohibits any person from making a contract with Cuba or a Cuban national, even a contract conditioned upon the lifting of the United States prohibitions on dealings with Cuba.

16. *Freeze of property.* The United States has "frozen" all property within the territorial jurisdiction of the United States in which Cuba or a Cuban national has any interest of any nature whatsoever, direct or indirect. It similarly has frozen such property, wherever located, in the possession, custody or control of United States persons, wherever located. Frozen assets cannot be paid out, withdrawn, set off or transferred in any manner. The freeze is applicable to the private property of individual Cubans as well as any property of the Cuban government.

17. *Telephone service.* The United States by special license authorizes telephone service with Cuba, but the amounts due the Cuban telephone company for the provision of services are frozen.

18. *Permitted transactions.* There are a few transactions permitted by the current regulations:

a. *Family remittances.* United States persons may send up to $300 every three months to the household of a close relative in Cuba and up to $500 on a one-time basis to enable a close relative to emigrate from Cuba. United States persons may also provide $500 for travel between Cuba and the United States to a Cuban national who has already obtained an entry visa from the State Department to visit the United States.

b. *Informational materials.* By virtue of statutory exemptions enacted by Congress in 1988, 50 U.S.C. App. § 5(b)(4), it is possible to import into the United States Cuban books, films, audio or video tapes, periodicals, phonograph records, paintings, drawings, sculpture (up to a value of $25,000), photographs, posters and "other informational materials." United States persons similarly may obtain licenses from Cuban nationals to reproduce and distribute any such materials. Payment may be made to Cuba or Cuban nationals for these imports or licenses free of any blocking.

Excluded from the protection of this law, as interpreted by the Treasury Department, are live telecasts or radio transmissions, the transmission of data by telecommunications (for example, news wire feeds) or any transaction involving the substantive or artistic alteration or enhancement of the materials (for example, licensing the film rights to a Cuban novel). Also excluded is financing the creation of a new informational work—for example, a United States publisher giving an advance to a Cuban scholar to write a work of particular interest to the United States publisher.

Under this 1988 legislation, the flow of informational materials may proceed in the opposite direction as well. United States persons may export informational materials to Cuba or Cuban nationals and receive payments free of blocking.

c. *Gift parcels.* A United States person may send gift parcels to individual Cubans or Cuban educational, charitable or religious organizations. There is a one hundred dollar limit on the worth of gifts that may be sent per month to any one particular donee. The gifts can only be of articles such as clothing, food or medicine in dosage form.

d. *Humanitarian donations.* The Cuban Democracy Act of 1992, Title XVII, Pub. L. No. 102-484, §§ 1701 *et seq.;* 106 Stat. 2575 ("CDA"), authorizes the donation of medicines and medical supplies to nongovernmental organizations in Cuba. It also authorizes donations of medicines and medical supplies to the Cuban government, and sales of these items either to the government or to Cuban nationals, but only on condition that Cuba permits on-site inspections verifying that the exported medicines and medical supplies "are to be used for the purposes for which they were intended" and "for the use and benefit of the Cuban people." The Cuban Democracy Act also authorizes the donation of foods to nongovernmental organizations in Cuba but not to the Cuban government or Cuban nationals and makes no provision at all for the sale of foods. CDA § 1705.

19. *Specific licenses.* Both the Treasury and Commerce Departments may, in their discretion, license otherwise prohibited transactions upon individual application. However, the policy of the United States has been to deny such licenses in all but the rarest of situations.

PROHIBITIONS AFFECTING THIRD COUNTRIES

1. *Vessels.* The United States prohibits any third-country vessel from loading or unloading goods in any United States port for 180 days after its departure from a Cuban port it had entered to engage in the trade of goods or services. The United States also prohibits the entry into United States ports of any third-country vessel carrying goods or passengers to or from Cuba. It similarly closes United States ports to any

third-country vessel if it is carrying goods in which Cuba or Cuban nationals have an "interest" whatever the cargo's origin or destination. This prohibition applies to a third-country vessel carrying third-country goods which incorporate even trace amounts of Cuban-origin products or produce. CDA, § 1706(b).

2. *Exports incorporating United States-origin components.* The United States prohibits a corporation or other business entity organized under the laws of a third country and located and doing business in that country from exporting to Cuba products manufactured wholly in that third country, but which incorporate any United States component parts or materials. This is so irrespective of whether the component parts or materials have been completely transformed in the new product. Exceptions are possible only upon application by the third-country company demonstrating that the United States-origin component parts or materials constitute 20 percent or less of the value of the product. If the United States content value is 10 percent or less, then the product may be exported without the necessity of making an application. 15 C.F.R. § 774.1; 15 C.F.R. § 776.12; 15 C.F.R. § 785.1.

3. *Re-exports of United States-origin goods.* The United States prohibits nationals of third countries from re-exporting United States-origin goods to Cuba unless their re-exportation is specifically approved by the Commerce Department. It is the Commerce Department's policy to deny approval. It makes no difference whether or not the third-country national originally obtained the goods for resale or how long the third-country national has owned the goods. 15 C.F.R. § 774.1.

4. *Technical data.* The re-exportation restrictions apply equally to United States technical data, that is, information in any form, tangible or intangible, which can be used in the design, production or manufacture of products. Under the applicable restrictions, a third-country national may not re-export to Cuba technical data that originally was exported from the United States. Moreover, in many instances third-country nationals may not export products manufactured wholly in the third country and containing no United States components or materials simply because the products were produced by use of United States-origin technical data. 15 C.F.R. § 779.1; 15 C.F.R. § 779.8; 15 C.F.R. § 779.4.

5. *Third-country subsidiaries of United States corporations.* The Cuban Democracy Act of 1992, § 1706(a), prohibits third-country companies substantially owned or controlled by United States nationals from engaging in any transactions with Cuba or Cuban nationals to the same extent as United States corporations are prohibited from engaging in such transactions. A third-country company, moreover, may be found to be "controlled" by a United States entity and hence subject to the embargo even when the United States ownership interest in the

company is a minority share. The concept of "control" is applied flexibly and leaves the United States wide discretion in its enforcement.

Prior to the enactment of this legislation, the United States asserted jurisdiction over the foreign subsidiaries of United States corporations but granted them licenses on individual application to engage in certain transactions with Cuba or Cuban nationals. The United States normally issued licenses for import and export transactions but would not issue licenses for investments in Cuba, financing of Cuban commercial activities, or joint ventures with Cuban companies.

6. *Third-country branches of United States corporations.* The embargo prohibitions apply in full to the unincorporated branches of United States corporations in third-countries. The limited exception for separately incorporated subsidiaries, now repealed, never was applicable. 31 C.F.R. § 515.559; 31 C.F.R. § 515.329.

7. *Third-country corporations with minority Cuban participation.* The United States extends the embargo to third-country corporations and other business entities located and doing business in those countries if there is even a minority participation by Cuban nationals. Even as little as 25 percent ownership by Cuban nationals may be sufficient to subject the third-country company to the embargo. Such companies are considered "Cuban nationals" for all purposes and hence may not have any financial or commercial dealings with the United States or United States nationals. Any property the company may have in the United States will be frozen. 31 C.F.R. § 515.302.

8. *United States dollar-denominated transactions.* The United States prohibits third-country banks from maintaining United States dollar-denominated accounts for Cuba or Cuban nationals. It also prohibits any use of United States currency or United States dollar-denominated accounts in transactions between third-country nationals and Cuban nationals. United States State Department, *Background Briefing to Latin America Embassies* (July 12, 1963); Deputy Secretary of the Treasury Robert Carswell, in *Conference on the Internationalization of the Capital Markets* (March 1981); *Comptroller General's Report to the Congress of the United States* (November 14, 1980).

9. *Third-country imports incorporating Cuban-origin products.* The United States bars the importation of goods manufactured in a third country by a company organized under the laws of that country which are made of or derived even in part from any article which is a growth, produce or manufacture of Cuba. It makes no difference whether the Cuban article incorporated in the third-country product is only a raw material used in manufacturing the product, is found only in trace amounts or has been thoroughly transformed in the process of manufacture. 31 C.F.R. § 515.204.

10. *Designation of third-country companies as Cuban nationals.* The United States, through administrative designation, has declared that hundreds of corporations and other business entities organized under the laws of third countries and located and doing business in those countries are "specially designated" nationals of Cuba. Upon the issuance of such a declaration, all of the prohibitions of the embargo applicable to Cuban nationals automatically apply to the "specially designated" entity, and hence no United States national may have any commercial or financial dealings with the designated entity and all of its property located in the United States is frozen. The ground for designation is that the designated company has acted on behalf of the Government of Cuba or is owned or controlled directly or indirectly by the Government of Cuba. 31 C.F.R. § 515.306.

STATUTORY AUTHORITY FOR ADMINISTRATIVE MEASURES

The President of the United States has issued the measures described above principally pursuant to the authority conferred upon him by Congress in the Trading With the Enemy Act ("TWEA"), 50 U.S.C. App. § 5(b). Enacted as a war-time measure in 1917, TWEA was subsequently expanded to authorize the President to regulate property transactions involving a foreign country or a national thereof either during time of war or "during any other period of national emergency declared by the President."

In imposing economic measures against Cuba under the authority of TWEA in 1962, when there was no state of war between the two countries, President Kennedy relied upon the declaration of national emergency issued by President Truman in 1950 during the war in Korea. 64 Stat. A454C (December 16, 1950). The basis for that declaration, in turn, was the asserted danger to the security of the United States resulting from communist aggression and the worldwide communist movement. Neither then nor in the intervening years has the President of the United States declared any national emergency resulting from the conduct or activities of Cuba itself.

In the mid-1970s, Congress acted to nullify the 1950 Truman declaration of a national emergency and also limited the President's powers under TWEA to times of war. At the same time, it enacted a separate law to govern peacetime situations, the International Emergency Economic Powers Act ("IEEPA"), 50 U.S.C. §1701 *et seq.* Under IEEPA, the President may impose emergency economic measures, including prohibitions of transactions involving the property of foreign governments and their nationals, only in response to an "unusual and extraordinary threat, which has its source in whole or substantial part outside the United States, to the national security, foreign policy, or economy of the

United States, if the President declares a national emergency with respect to such threat." 50 U.S.C. § 1701(a).

The United States administration recognized that these legislative developments would place it in an awkward position with respect to its economic measures against Cuba as well as the other countries then under embargo (Vietnam, Cambodia and North Korea). It therefore requested that Congress exempt the Cuban and other existing embargoes from IEEPA's requirements and limitations and allow the President to continue to rely solely on the Trading With the Enemy Act with respect to those countries. Congress acquiesced because it wanted to avoid forcing the President to proclaim national emergencies under IEEPA in order to continue the embargoes against these countries when, in its view, no such emergencies existed. *See, e.g.,* H.R. Rep. No. 459, 95th Cong., 1st Sess. 11 (1977).

Accordingly, all that Congress required was that the President, to maintain the Cuban or other pre-existing embargoes, proclaim that continuation of those measures was in the "national interest" of the United States. Pub. L. No. 95-223, § 101(b), 91 Stat. 1626 *et seq.* No finding of a national emergency or finding of a threat to the national security, foreign policy, or economy of the United States was required. Nor has any such finding been made. Rather, the President has simply declared every year that continuation of the measures against Cuba is in the "national interest."

The Trading With the Enemy Act provides authority for all of the prohibitions described above and alone provides the President with the authority to prohibit financial transactions, freeze Cuban property, prohibit the provision of services, and regulate the conduct of persons outside the United States on the ground that they are nationals of the United States or otherwise persons subject to the jurisdiction of the United States. Thus, the prohibition against United States citizens traveling to Cuba and most of the extraterritorial reach of the United States measures rest upon the Trading With the Enemy Act alone and the President's simple declaration that such measures are in the "national interest" of the United States.

In 1961 Congress provided the President with concurrent authority to "establish and maintain a total embargo upon all trade between the United States and Cuba." Foreign Assistance Act of 1961, 22 U.S.C. § 2370(a)(1). Congress did not establish any standards for the President's exercise of his authority under this provision.

The President also has cited the Export Administration Act of 1979, 50 U.S.C. App. § 2401 *et seq.,* as providing concurrent authority to control exports and re-exports of goods or technology. The EAA's export authorities are to be exercised by the President only "to the extent necessary to further significantly the foreign policy of the United States or to fulfill its declared international obligations," 50 U.S.C. App. § 2405, or to restrict exports which "would make a significant contribution to the military potential of any other country or combination of countries which would prove detrimental to the national security of the United States," 50 U.S.C. App. § 2404, or for certain defined economic reasons.

The President is not required by these enactments to impose the cited economic measures against Cuba. In his sole discretion, the President may lift or modify those measures at any time.

LEGISLATIVE MEASURES AFFECTING TRADE WITH CUBA

The Cuban Assets Control Regulations and the Export Administration Regulations are the primary administrative measures through which the United States imposes its sanctions against Cuba. In addition, however, there are a number of statutes enacted by the United States Congress which regulate the President's authority in significant areas such as trade policy and the facilitation of loans by international financial institutions. Some of these provisions are specifically applicable to Cuba. In other cases, they apply generally to countries which, like Cuba, have nationalized property owned by United States nationals without payment of full compensation in accordance with the United States' view of the requirements of international law. Moreover, there are a large number of complex laws which regulate commerce between the United States and "communist" countries in general. Many of these have not been amended or repealed despite the dramatic changes in the former Soviet Union and Eastern Europe. Set out below is a survey of some of the most significant of these laws.

1. *Measures affecting third countries.* The United States has enacted several provisions designed to pressure third countries into adopting United States trade policies regarding Cuba and to ensure third country compliance with existing United States measures. Thus, for instance, § 305 of the Dire Emergency Supplemental Appropriations Act of 1990, Pub. L. No. 101-302, 104 Stat. 213, 244 (1990), which includes appropriations for foreign operations, multilateral and bilateral economic assistance and export assistance, prohibits any funds made available under the Act from being provided to any country that is providing military or economic assistance to Cuba.

Likewise, § 902(c) of Pub. L. No. 99-198, 99 Stat. 1354, 1444 (1985), as amended by § 903 of Pub. L. No. 101-624, 104 Stat. 3359, 3488 (1990), 7 U.S.C. § 1446 note, prohibits the President from allocating any portion of the United States sugar import quota to any country that is a net importer of sugar unless that country certifies that it does not import for re-export to the United States any sugar produced in Cuba. The President is also required to report to Congress yearly about actions taken by the President with regard to countries which have re-exported Cuban sugar to the United States.

The Cuban Democracy Act of 1992, § 1704 (b), authorizes, but does not require, the President to apply certain "sanctions" against any country that provides "assistance" to Cuba by declaring the country ineligible for assistance under the Foreign Assistance Act of 1961; ineligible for assistance or sales under the Arms Export Control Act; and ineligible under any program for the forgiveness or reduction of debt owed to the United States government. Third countries would be liable to these sanctions if, in the President's judgment, they provide assistance to or for the benefit of the Cuban government by grant; by concessional sale, guaranty or insurance; or "by any other means on terms more favorable than that generally available in the applicable market," including without limitation subsidies for exports to Cuba and favorable tariff treatment for Cuban-origin goods.

2. *Loans from international institutions.* There are a number of provisions which require the United States representative at international financial institutions to vote to block loans or other financial support to countries in certain circumstances. 22 U.S.C. § 287r instructs the United States Executive Director to the Inter-American Bank "to vote against any loan or other utilization of the funds of the Bank for the benefit of any country" which has expropriated property owned by United States nationals, unless prompt, adequate and effective compensation has been made, good faith negotiations are in progress, or the matter is in international arbitration. Unlike most of the statutes discussed above, moreover, there is no waiver provision explicitly providing the President with discretion in this matter. 22 U.S.C. § 284j provides identical instructions to the United States Executive Directors of the International Bank for Reconstruction and Development and the International Development Association.

22 U.S.C. § 286e-11 requires the Secretary of the Treasury to instruct the Executive Director of the United States to the International Monetary Fund "to actively oppose any facility involving use of Fund credit by any Communist dictatorship" unless the Secretary certifies that the extension of credit would meet a number of strict economic requirements, including that it would advance "market-oriented forces in that country."

3. *Tariffs.* As part of the Trade Act of 1974, Congress promulgated a tariffs scheme known as the Generalized System of Preferences, 19 U.S.C. §§ 2461-2465. This Generalized System provides for preferential duty-free treatment for a wide range of imports from "beneficiary developing countries." *See* § 2461. Under § 2462(b), however, a country

is ineligible to be a beneficiary developing country if it "has national-ized, expropriated or otherwise seized ownership or control of prop-erty" owned by United States nationals, unless the President determines that "prompt, adequate and effective compensation" has been made, good faith negotiations are in progress, or the matter has been submit-ted to international arbitration; or if it is a communist country, unless the President has extended most favored nation status to the country, the country is a party to the General Agreement on Tariffs and Trade and a member of the International Monetary Fund, and the country "is not dominated or controlled by international communism." The Presi-dent may still designate any country falling within the above exclu-sions, however, if he finds that doing so is in the "national economic interest of the United States." *See* 19 U.S.C. § 2702(b) (excluding Cuba from the duty free treatment afforded other countries of the Caribbean under the Caribbean Basin Economic Recovery plan and also disquali-fying any country which has nationalized United States-owned prop-erty without paying compensation or is a communist country unless the President finds the contrary will be in the "national economic or security interest" of the United States).

4. *Foreign assistance and other benefits.* There are a number of pro-visions which restrict the furnishing of foreign assistance and other benefits to Cuba. Foreign assistance includes the entire range of eco-nomic development and military assistance which the United States affords foreign countries each year.

Some of these restrictions are applicable specifically to Cuba. 22 U.S.C. § 2370(a)(1) provides flatly that no foreign assistance under the Foreign Assistance Act of 1961, 22 U.S.C. §§ 2159-2429, which is the general statutory scheme authorizing foreign economic and military assistance, shall be furnished to the "present government of Cuba." Significantly, there are no provisions which allow the President to waive this restriction. Likewise, § 2370(a)(2) provides that no assistance shall be furnished to *any* government of Cuba unless (a) the President deems it necessary "in the interest of the United States" *or* (b) the President determines that Cuba "has taken appropriate steps" to return to United States citizens the property which it expropriated after January 1, 1959 or to provide them with "equitable compensation" for the prop-erty taken. Even more significant, perhaps, is that § 2370(a)(2) goes so far as to prohibit Cuba from receiving any "benefit under *any* law of the United States" until the President makes such a determination (emphasis added). This presumably includes preferential tariffs and credits.

22 U.S.C. § 2370(f) specifically defines Cuba as a "Communist coun-try" and prohibits the furnishing of any foreign assistance to a "Com-munist country" unless the President finds: (a) that such assistance is

vital to the security of the United States, the recipient country is not controlled by the "international Communist conspiracy," and the assistance will "further promote the independence of the recipient country from international communism"; or (b) that furnishing assistance is "important to the national interest of the United States." *See* Foreign Operations, Export Financing, and Related Programs Appropriations Act of 1990, Pub. L. No. 101-167, §§ 512, 548, 103 Stat. 1194, 1219, 1235 (1989) (prohibiting the use of any funds made available under the Act from being used to finance directly or indirectly any assistance to Cuba, with waiver provision where "in the national interest"); Export-Import Bank Act, 12 U.S.C. § 635(b)(2) (similar restrictions on Bank credits with waiver provision where credits are "in the national interest").

RECENT UNITED STATES EFFORTS TO INTERFERE
WITH THIRD COUNTRY TRADE AND INVESTMENTS

In the General Assembly proceedings, Cuba charged that the United States has supplemented its extraterritorial administrative measures with an extralegal campaign of disrupting third-country trade and investment. We have prepared a summary of recent incidents cited by Cuba at the United Nations and of similar incidents reported elsewhere by Cuban authorities or by the international press.

THIRD-COUNTRY TRADE WITH NO UNITED STATES NEXUS

1. *Tabacalera, S.A.'s tourism investment.* Over the last several years, the Cuban government has invited Western capital to help develop tourism as a principal element of the country's economic strategy. To that end, Cuba has permitted foreign capital to form joint ventures with Cuban enterprises in the tourism as well as other sectors. These developments are described generally in the economic study provided *post* in this Part II.

In 1989, Cuba secured the commitment of the Spanish company Tabacalera, S.A., to form a joint venture with a Cuban enterprise for the development of Cayo Coco, an island off the north coast of Cuba, as a tourism center. Tabacalera is one of Spain's larger corporations, with international and domestic activities in tobacco as well as tourism. A majority of its shares are owned by the Spanish government. Tabacalera's involvement in the joint venture was to be through one of its several subsidiaries.

A few weeks after Tabacalera announced its plans, the Treasury Department's Office of Foreign Assets Control named it a "specially designated national of Cuba." 54 Fed. Reg. 49258 (November 29, 1989). By virtue of this designation, all the restrictions against United States persons dealing with Cuba applied to Tabacalera, so that it could not export its products to the United States, import products from the United States, or engage in any other financial or commercial transactions with United States nationals.

Several weeks of discussion reportedly took place between the Spanish and United States governments. On January 9, 1992 the Treasury Department withdrew the designation because Tabacalera "no longer comes within the scope of the definition of a specially designated national as defined in [31 C.F.R.] § 515.306 of the Regulations." 55 Fed. Reg. 2644-01 (January 26, 1990). On the following day Tabacalera announced it had withdrawn from the Cayo Coco joint venture for "economic reasons." A Spanish diplomat later told United States journalist Saul Landau that "it was a classic case of threat and intimidation. The United States officials said that if Tabacalera went ahead with the project there would be many obstacles to restoring trade between it and United States companies."

2. *VASP's transportation investment.* In April 1991 the private Brazilian airline company VASP sought an interest in the Cuban airline, Compañia Cubana de Aviación. VASP reportedly was willing to invest $800 million for a 60 percent interest, with the investment to be made through one of the several VASP companies. Cubana reportedly was seeking cash and new aircraft in order to support Cuba's current effort to expand tourism. The *Miami Herald* observed that this "could be the biggest deal since Cuba began accelerating its drive for foreign investment." *Miami Herald,* p. 11 (April 11, 1991).

VASP suddenly broke off negotiations in August 1991. "The problem was the American government," a senior VASP official was quoted as explaining. "We want to fly to the United States, and the American government just doesn't do business with people who deal with Cuba," he continued. A United States official confirmed that VASP "would have problems in other things" if it continued to negotiate with Cubana. An article in a Brazilian magazine—supposedly written with the collaboration of VASP's president—reported that "the United States government threatened to embargo VASP's purchase of airliners from the American companies Boeing and Douglas" if VASP entered into contracts with Cuba. "Brazilian Ends Talks With Cuba," *Miami Herald,* p. 1C (August 31, 1991). United States journalist Saul Landau has reported that a United States national security official, when asked of the incident, said, "We didn't threaten them or tell them not to go through with the deal. We just advised them about what might happen if they did." The United States apparently indicated that VASP would be unable to obtain United States-origin aircraft and parts to be used by VASP for its own operations unrelated to Cubana.

The *New York Times* has noted that reports of United States pressures on VASP are "widely believed." "Cuba, Long Forbidden, Wins Major Attention Abroad," *New York Times,* sec. 3, p. 5, col. 1 (April 19, 1992). The *Times* cited this incident in commenting that, "while allowing American subsidiaries to trade with Cuba, the United States quietly, but actively, discourages even foreign-owned companies from providing strategic goods to Cuba or resuscitating vital industries." The *Economist* has reported that, partially as a consequence of the VASP incident, many "big Latin American companies are still scared of reprisals from Washington" if they take advantage of attractive investment opportunities in Cuba. "Letting Cuba Down Gently," *Economist,* p. 90 (October 12, 1991).

3. *India's rice sale.* In December 1991 and again in February 1992, Cuban and Indian trade officials met to discuss the sale of large quantities of Indian rice. On February 27, 1992 United States Department of Agriculture Secretary Edward Madigan announced that he had told President Bush he opposed the sale of United States wheat to India under the United States' "export enhancement program" because of India's policy of selling rice to Cuba. "Wheat Trade Stunned re Madigan EEP/India Statement," *FWN Cable* (February 27, 1992). The announcement surprised Indian leaders because they already had held off making a rice sale to Cuba at the urging of the United States Ambassador. "India Officials Upset Over Madigan's Statement," *FWN Cable* (February 28, 1992). The Madigan announcement led to parliamentary inquiries and editorial denunciations, *Hindustan Times* (March 10, 1992); Editorial, *Times of India* (March 11, 1992), and the Indian government assured Parliament that it would not be influenced by "extraneous considerations" in its decision on the Cuban rice deal. "Gov't Conveys Concern to US," *Times of India* (March 10, 1992). India finally went ahead with the rice sale.

4. *Japan's brokering of sugar sales.* A senior official of a Japanese trading house was quoted as saying his firm was hesitant to set up a Cuba-South Korea sugar deal because of the "risk of angering the U.S. government. This could affect other business the trading house is doing in the United States." "Cuba OKs Sugar Sale to South Korea Despite Ties to North," *Miami Herald,* p. 4A (April 29, 1992).

5. *Threats to foreign employees.* It has been reported that, on at least half a dozen occasions since 1991, the families of third-country nationals planning to work in Cuba for their European or Latin American companies have received telephone threats of reprisals if the family members went forward with their plans.

6. *North American Free Trade Agreement.* On April 8, 1992 the Bush administration advised Congress that it would seek assurances under

the proposed North American Free Trade Agreement that Mexico will not buy sugar from Cuba and then export its own sugar production to the United States. Cable, *Reuters Monitor* (April 8, 1992). Under existing restrictions, Mexico, like any other third country, cannot export Cuban-origin sugar to the United States, but there is no restriction on its buying Cuban sugar for its own consumption provided it certifies that it is not re-exporting the sugar to the United States.

7. *Petroleum exploration.* The United States reportedly discouraged petroleum exploration and development by a third country in the Caribbean region. It warned that any such activity would provoke a strong reaction by Congress and would affect North American investments. *El Gobierno de EE.UU. contra Cuba: Revelaciones de la Agresión,* 31 (Ediciones Entorno, La Habana, 1992).

8. *Constricting airline service.* Reportedly, the United States has pressured Caribbean and other regional governments over the last two years not to allow Cubana to expand service within their jurisdictions, even to the point of urging that landing rights be denied. The stated ground was that enhanced air service would increase Cuban tourism. *El Gobierno de EE.UU.* 30.

THIRD-COUNTRY SUBSIDIARIES OF UNITED STATES CORPORATIONS

In October 1992 President Bush signed into law the Cuban Democracy Act of 1992, Title XVII, Pub. L. No. 102-484, §§ 1701 *et seq.*; 106 Stat. 2575, 2578-79, which, in § 1706, prohibits foreign subsidiary trade with Cuba. This ended the policy pursued since 1975 of licensing export/ import transactions with Cuba upon individual application. The United States had explained the partial relaxation of its prohibitions as an effort to remove an irritant in its relations with third-countries and to conform to the 1975 Organization of American States resolution permitting each country to determine its trade relations with Cuba. See Part IV.

Despite its publicly stated policy of accommodating the objections of third countries, scholarly studies based on government archives suggest that in the 1970s the United States frequently placed informal pressure on third country companies or their parents not to pursue trade with Cuba. *See* A.L.C. de Mestral and T. Gruchalla-Wesierski, *The Extraterritorial Application of U.S. Export Control Legislation: Canada and the U.S.A.* 161-69 (1990); Morris H. Morley, *Imperial State and Revolution, the United States and Cuba: A Study in Political Pressure on American Allies (1952-1986)* 178-239 (1987).

In the two years leading to passage of the Cuban Democracy Act there had been a rash of reported incidents in which third-country subsidiaries have discontinued trade with Cuba or showed no inclination to pursue trade even though it was commercially attractive.

Sometimes the companies explained that, inasmuch as they were owned by United States corporations they were prohibited from pursuing trade relations with Cuba—an incorrect statement of the law. Sometimes, the companies did not pursue even preliminary discussions, indicating a decision not to deal with Cuba for non-commercial reasons. It may be that in some instances the companies thought trade would be unlawful under United States export laws because their products contain more than 20 percent United States-origin parts, but this was rarely cited by the third-country companies. A sampling of these incidents follows.

9. *Lennox Canada—Canada.* In October 1991 this Canadian exporter of refrigeration equipment explained that, as a subsidiary of a U.S. corporation, it was not permitted to sell to Cuba.

10. *Square D—Canada.* In August 1991 this Canadian company, the subsidiary of a United States corporation, would not quote prices on electric switches even though it had engaged in trade with Cuba for years.

11. *Lobster sales—Canada.* For many years, a Canadian company, the subsidiary of a United States corporation, had imported Cuban lobsters for sale to restaurants. In May 1991 it suddenly discontinued all purchases.

12. *Robert Canada, Inc.—Canada.* In May 1991 this Canadian company, a subsidiary of a United States corporation, reneged on the sale of equipment for the preparation of food on board passenger aircraft.

13. *Hercules Canada—Canada.* In May 1991 this Canadian firm advised that it could not continue selling cellophane paper to Cuba because the firm had United States capital participation.

14. *Pepsi Cola Montreal—Canada.* In May 1991 Pepsi Cola Montreal advised a Canadian exporter that it would not fulfill a purchase order since the ultimate destination of the export would be Cuba. Pepsi Cola Montreal advised further that this decision was made after discussions with the United States head office of Pepsi Cola. The Canadian Ministry of External Affairs and International Trade wrote Pepsi Cola Montreal in June that the apparent interference of the head office of Pepsi Cola was inconsistent with the Canadian position on the extraterritorial application of United States law and with Canada's own policy favoring trade with Cuba. The incident, the Ministry wrote, was "of considerable concern" to the government.

15. *Dow Chemical Vickford Industries—Canada.* When asked for a quote on tape used in the production of telephone cables, this Canadian company advised it would be necessary for the Cuban party to direct its request to its parent company in the United States.

16. *Industria Fotográfica Interamericana—México.* This Mexican company asserted in May 1991 that, as a subsidiary of a United States corporation, it was not permitted to sell photographic products to Cuba.

17. *Coca-Cola de México—México.* The Mexican subsidiary of Coca-Cola was advised in May 1992 that it was prohibited from selling its product to Cuba for an international sporting event.

18. *Dorr-Oliver—Brazil.* In May 1991 this Brazilian company refused to sell parts used to filter cane juice, on the ground that it was a subsidiary of a United States corporation.

19. *Gates Export Corporation of Brazil—Brazil.* In January 1990 this Brazilian company advised it could not export its products to Cuba because it was a subsidiary of a United States corporation. It had previously fulfilled an export contract with Cuba.

20. *Woodward—Brazil.* In October 1990 this Brazilian company declined to give a quote on its ships products, on the ground that, as a subsidiary of a United States corporation, it could not engage in trade with Cuba.

21. *Editorial Interamericana, S.A.—Spain.* This Spanish publisher had enjoyed commercial relations with Cuba for many years. In 1990 it was purchased by McGraw-Hill, a United States publisher. McGraw-Hill advised the Spanish company that since it now was the subsidiary of a United States corporation, its personnel could not attend the Cuban book fair in Havana and the subsidiary could not make any future sales to Cuba. These instructions were not required by United States law: employees of third-country subsidiaries are permitted to travel to Cuba under Treasury Department regulations, 31 C.F.R. § 515.561, and Congress exempted the sale of books from the United States prohibitions against trade with Cuba, 50 U.S.C. App. § 5(b)(4).

22. *Dow Chemical Co. Ltd.—Italy.* This firm declined to sell resin for water treatment on instructions from its parent company in the United States.

23. *Lithographic equipment—European company.* A Cuban enterprise had commercial relations for many years with a European exporter of lithographic equipment. A subsidiary of a United States corporation, the European company had always sought and obtained United States Treasury Department licenses for the exports. In the spring of 1992, the European company advised by telex that it had neglected to renew its license and it therefore could not even give information concerning possible exports until the license was renewed. No date was given as to when that might occur.

UNITED STATES-ORIGIN PARTS

The United States prohibits third-country companies from exporting products manufactured in the third-country if they contain U.S.-origin parts or materials in excess of 20 percent of the value of the product. If the value is more than 10 percent but no more than 20 percent, the Commerce Department will entertain individual applications for permission; if no more than 10 percent, general authorization is provided in the Commerce Department regulations. 15 C.F.R. §§ 776.12(b)(3), 785.1(c). Several incidents suggest that the United States has become more restrictive in its construction of these regulations and more active in its enforcement efforts.

24. *Latin American chickens.* A Latin American company informed Cuba that it could no longer sell its poultry products because the United States had threatened to cut off the company's supply of United States-origin feed for its chickens. The apparent theory of the United States was that the United States-origin feed was incorporated into the chickens and their export thus would violate the United States prohibition against exporting a product with more than 20 percent United States-origin parts.

25. *Spare parts for Swedish filtration system.* Cuba had purchased a filtration system manufactured by a Swedish company. Even though the system contained filtration cartridges manufactured in the United States, the export of the system conformed to United States law since the cartridges amounted to less than 10 percent of the total value of the system.

In May 1991 the Swedish company refused to sell replacement cartridges for the system. It explained that, even though the cartridges would amount to less than 10 percent of the value of the system, United States law treated the replacement parts as distinct products which were 100 percent United States-origin and thus could not be exported to Cuba. This construction of the United States export laws could undermine the practical effect of the 20 percent rule in many instances.

26. *Siemens' sale of medical equipment. Business Week* has reported that "Washington is also toughening its curb on United States technology exports to Cuba." "Mr. Castro Goes to Market," *Business Week,* p. A17 (April 20, 1992). It gave the example of Washington barring the German company Siemens from selling a medical diagnostic machine on the ground that it is run by a United States-made microcomputer.

27. *Airbus sales.* In 1991 Cuba sought to purchase from a Western company two used Airbus planes for its tourism trade. The seller cancelled the contracts of sale when the United States objected. The United States asserted that the sale would violate United States export control laws in that, although the crafts were manufactured in Europe, the engines were made in the United States.

The Airbus, manufactured in Europe, is the major competitor with United States-made aircraft, but for the most part uses United States-origin engines. The United States' position therefore has broad implications for Cubana's ability to obtain modern aircraft in its effort to meet Cuba's growing tourism needs, particularly as production of aircraft in the former Eastern bloc nations has grown unreliable.

Also in 1991 the United States government blocked the sale of five Brasilia 30-passenger transport planes manufactured by the Brazilian Aeronautic Company to Cuba on the grounds that they contain several United States-made components. Press release, Cuban Ministry of Foreign Relations (May 7, 1991).

28. *Cunval Quebec, Nedco, Furnes Electric, Diamond Canapower, Simonds Industries, Servispect Prolux, Federal Pacific Electric of Canada.* In 1990 and 1991 these and other Canadian firms refused exports to Cuba on the ground that their products were of United States-origin.

CUBAN NICKEL

The United States prohibits the importation of third-country products if they contain any Cuban-origin nickel, even in trace amounts. After the principal clients for Cuban nickel had been disclosed in the press, officials from the United States embassies in Germany and Sweden reportedly visited all nickel consumer enterprises there, one by one, to question them about any possible purchases of Cuban nickel and to pressure them into discontinuing any such imports. Earlier, United States actions reportedly had compelled Acerinox, the major nickel consumer in Spain, to suspend its purchases of Cuban nickel.

NATIONALIZATION CLAIMS

Concomitant with intensified Cuban efforts to attract foreign investment beyond the tourist sector, the United States in 1991 began advising third-country governments and companies that investments in Cuba may conflict with claims of United States nationals arising from the Cuban nationalization of United States-owned property in 1960. In a series of diplomatic notes, the United States has "strongly" urged that foreign governments "encourage [their] nationals and business firms to avoid entering into contracts with the Government of Cuba, or investing in the Cuban economy, where such actions would involve assets located in Cuba that may be legally encumbered by unresolved claims to such assets by American citizens." One such diplomatic note reads in full as follows:

> The Embassy of the United States of America presents its compliments to the Ministry of Foreign Affairs of _____ and has the honor to request the cooperation of the Government of _____ in the following matter.
>
> The United States Government understands that the Government of Cuba may be offering foreign investors the opportunity to purchase land, manufacturing facilities, tourist resorts, and other assets in Cuba that belong to, or are the subject of outstanding claims by, American or

other foreign nationals. The Cubans may also be offering joint venture partnerships.

The United States originally imposed an economic embargo in 1962, after Cuba nationalized some 1.8 billion 1962 dollars worth of United States-owned property without paying prompt, adequate and effective compensation as required under international law. That embargo remains in effect.

There are 5,911 separate American claims pending against the Government of Cuba. These claims are today valued at over 5 billion dollars, including 6 percent interest per annum. United States claims against Cuba remain unsettled, and the United States expects that many of the claims will be actively pursued when United States-Cuban relations are normalized.

As a result of Cuba's support for insurgency abroad, policies of internal repression and lack of democratic institutions, the United States does not have full diplomatic or commercial relations with Cuba. The United States opposes investment in the Cuban economy as long as the Cuban government continues to pursue these policies.

The United States understands that the Government of _____ may have its own views on this. Nevertheless, the United States Government strongly urges the Government of _____ to take the necessary steps to encourage [its] nationals and business firms to avoid entering into contracts with the Government of Cuba, or investing in the Cuban economy, where such actions would involve assets located in Cuba that may be legally encumbered by unresolved claims to such assets by American citizens.

This will require careful verification on the part of such business people and firms to ensure that the Cuban Government has the unencumbered right to sell or otherwise dispose of the asset in question. To this end, business firms are encouraged to contact the Foreign Claims Settlement Commission of the United States to verify that the assets and properties of interest to them are not the subject of an outstanding claim. The Commission is located at 601 D Street NW, Washington DC 20579, U.S.A., telephone (202) 208-7730.

The Embassy of the United States of America avails itself of this opportunity to renew to the Ministry of Foreign Affairs of _____ the assurances of its highest consideration. Embassy of the United States of America,_____, 1991.

In April 1992 the State Department informed Congress that it "continually" urges foreign governments to heed this advice as part of its effort to isolate Cuba "by taking new measures tailored to the possibilities of a new era." Statement of Robert J. Gelbard, Principal Deputy Assistant Secretary of State for Inter-American Affairs, before the Committee on Foreign Affairs, House of Representatives, April 8, 1992.

When a French company, Total, S.A., entered into an offshore oil exploration agreement with Cuba, the United States approached the company for information on its Cuban activities. It also advised the

French government of possible complications arising from the fact that the Cuban government in 1960 had cancelled the oil concessions held by United States companies for the same acreage being explored by Total. The French company has proceeded with the exploration nonetheless. *Wall Street Journal,* p. A17 (April 15, 1992).

Historically, the United States has resolved nationalization claims through the negotiation of "lump sum" settlements with the nationalizing country. In exchange for a single sum provided by the foreign country, the United States waives all claims of its nationals arising from the nationalizations. The United States then distributes the lump sum to the claimants as it pleases. The inherent authority of the President to waive the nationalization claims of United States nationals was upheld in *Dames and Moore v. Regan,* 458 U.S. 654 (1981). Typically, the lump sum has been a fraction of the principal amount found by the United States Foreign Claims Settlement Commission, the administrative body which has certified the validity and amount of nationalization claims for the Secretary of State's possible espousal.

"Restoration of ownership to the original owner is virtually unknown in expropriation cases." American Law Institute, *Restatement of the Law, Third, Foreign Relations Law of the United States,* § 713, Comment k. *See also* Richard Lillich and Burns Weston, *International Claims: Their Settlement By Lump Sum Agreement, Vol. 1* (1974). Any demand for the return of properties, as distinct from a claim for compensation, presumably would conflict with the protection third countries would demand for the property of their nationals in Cuba.

On a number of occasions, Cuba has publicly expressed a willingness to discuss the nationalization claims along with claims against the United States arising from its economic measures against Cuba. Cuba has reached settlements with the other Western countries whose nationals suffered property losses. *Id., Vol. II* 339, 343.

PAST PRACTICES

The Cuban suggestion that the United States is engaged in extralegal and covert efforts to disrupt third-country trade with Cuba should be evaluated in light of historical experience. Morris H. Morley, *Imperial State and Revolution, the United States and Cuba: A Study In Political Pressure on American Allies 1952-1986* (1987), investigates the United States' construction of a "global economic blockade" between 1961 and 1968. Because of the passage of time, Professor Morley was able to obtain access to United States government archives for that period pursuant to the Freedom of Information Act and other programs for the release of declassified documents. Also instructive is A.L.C. de Mestral and T. Gruchalla-Wesierski, *The Extraterritorial Application of U.S. Export Control Legislation: Canada and the U.S.A.* (1990), which is based in large part on files of Canada's Department of External Affairs covering the 1960s and 1970s. Naturally, it is impossible to obtain similar access to current government files.

These scholarly studies describe how in the past, when the United States pursued with particular vigor its policy of isolating Cuba from the world economy, it went beyond its published embargo regulations to pressure third-country governments and, if that appeared unavailing or impolitic, to proceed directly against third-country companies. This covert economic campaign was systematic and intense, and yielded substantial results.

CHRONOLOGY OF UNITED STATES LEGAL MEASURES

We have prepared a chronology tracing the evolution of the United States administrative measures designed to limit Cuba's commercial, financial, and tourist relations with the United States and other countries. Beginning in 1959 the chronology runs through December 1, 1992 and provides important contextual information for understanding and evaluating current United States sanctions.

1. On May 17, 1959 Cuba adopted an agrarian reform law under which individual ownership of land was limited to a maximum of 995 acres; corporate ownership was likewise strictly limited. Compensation for expropriated holdings was offered in the form of redeemable twenty year government bonds with a maximum interest rate of 4 percent. The basis for valuation of the taken properties was the assessed value for purposes of taxation. Agrarian Reform Law of May 17, 1959, reprinted in *VII Leyes Del Gobierno Provisional de la Revolucion* (November 1960).* Significant United States-owned properties were potentially affected by the land reform measure.

2. On June 11, 1959 the United States asserted in a note to the Cuban government its view that expropriation of foreign owned property was permissible under international law only if accompanied by payment of "prompt, adequate and effective compensation" to the prior owner. The note further implied that if such compensation was not forthcoming the United States would consider implementing several policy options, including a reduction in the sugar quota, a prohibition on private investment in Cuba by United States nationals, and a termination of economic aid of any kind. Subsequently, United States-owned properties were expropriated under the agrarian reform law, leading to increased conflict between the countries.

---

*The Cuban laws cited in this chronology can be found in the official Spanish language Cuban government series *Leyes del Gobierno Provisional de la Revolucion* and *Leyes del Gobierno Revolucionario de Cuba.*

3. During most of 1959 and with increasing intensity during late 1959 and early 1960, Cuban exiles, under the supervision of the United States Central Intelligence Agency, conducted air raids against Cuba.

4. During 1959 the United States government undertook extensive efforts to prevent Western countries from selling military supplies to Cuba or providing it with military assistance. Notably, in 1959, the United States successfully persuaded the British government to cancel its plans to sell Hunter fighter jets to Cuba.

5. On February 13, 1960 Cuba and the Soviet Union entered into a trade agreement under which the Soviet Union agreed to purchase sugar and other products from Cuba and to supply Cuba with crude oil and other petroleum products.

6. In March, 1960 President Eisenhower approved a plan of covert action and economic sabotage against Cuba. The plan proposed the development of a unified opposition movement among Cuban exiles, the creation of a propaganda apparatus directed against the Cuban government, the creation of a covert intelligence and action organization within Cuba, and the creation of a paramilitary force made up of Cuban exiles for use in military operations against Cuba. These early preparations formed the basis for the later Bay of Pigs invasion of Cuba.

7. During the first three months of 1960, the United States government began an intense diplomatic campaign to prevent loans and credits from being extended to Cuba by Western European countries and Canada. In March, a consortium of Western European banks, under pressure from the United States government, cancelled plans to negotiate a $100 million loan to Cuba.

8. On May 17, 1960 the President of the National Bank of Cuba informed foreign-owned oil companies which operated refineries in Cuba—including Standard Oil, Texaco and Royal Dutch Shell—that oil from the Soviet Union would be arriving in Cuba and that the companies were expected to refine the oil at prices to be agreed upon. On June 6, 1960, acting at the urging of the United States government, the oil companies responded that they would not agree to refine the Soviet supplied petroleum and shortly thereafter refused delivery of Soviet crude oil. On July 1, 1960 the Cuban government took control of their operations, explaining that the oil companies' refusal was in violation of existing Cuban law requiring them to refine Cuban state oil. The oil companies were subsequently nationalized on August 6, 1960.

9. After the intervention of July 1, the oil companies instituted an international oil boycott of Cuba designed to restrict Cuba's access to oil and render the Cuban refineries unusable. The United States government played a central role in promoting the boycott, pressuring

governments such as Mexico not to sell oil to Cuba and shipowners not to ship oil to Cuba through threats of instituting shipping blacklists.

10. On July 6, 1960 the United States Congress amended the Sugar Act of 1948 under which the United States had set aside a yearly quota of sugar to be imported from Cuba. Sugar was Cuba's largest export product, and under the Sugar Act Cuba had been by far the largest foreign source of sugar for the United States. The purpose of the amendment was to afford the President of the United States discretionary authority to set aside the Cuban sugar quota. As amended, the Act afforded the President the authority to set Cuba's quota for the balance of 1960 and the first quarter of 1961, the effective period of the Act, in such amounts as the President found "to be in the national interest." Pub. L. No. 86-592, § 408(b)(1), 74 Stat. 330 (1960).

Thereafter, on the same date, Cuba enacted Law Number 851, which afforded the President of Cuba the authority to nationalize the property of United States companies operating in Cuba. The preamble to the law specifically cited the amendment of the Sugar Act as a measure of economic aggression requiring a counter-measure to protect Cuba's national interests:

> Whereas, the attitude assumed by the government and the Legislative Power of the United States of North America, which constitutes an aggression, for political purposes, against the basic interests of the Cuban economy, as recently evidenced by the Amendment to the Sugar Act just enacted by the United States Congress at the request of the Chief Executive of that country, whereby exceptional powers are conferred upon the President of the United States to reduce the participation of Cuban sugars in the American sugar market as a threat of political action against Cuba, forces the Revolutionary government to adopt, without hesitation, all and whatever measures it may deem appropriate or desirable for the due defense of the national sovereignty and protection of our economic development process.

On July 7, 1960 President Eisenhower exercised his authority under Pub. L. No. 86-592 and issued a proclamation declaring that Cuba's sugar quota for 1960 would be reduced by 700,000 tons to 2.42 million tons, almost all of which had already been imported. Pres. Proc. 3355, 25 Fed. Reg 6414 (July 6, 1960). In effect, therefore, the President cancelled the then unfulfilled balance of the Cuban sugar quota for 1960.

On August 6, 1960 the President of Cuba issued Resolution Number 1 under Law Number 851. That resolution ordered the nationalization of a number of the largest United States or United States-owned companies operating in Cuba. Thereafter, the President of Cuba issued additional resolutions under Law Number 851 which nationalized virtually all United States-owned property.

11. On October 19, 1960 the Commerce Department put in place the embargo of exports of United States goods and technical data to Cuba. At that time, the Commerce regulations divided the nations of the world into Country Groups O and R. Country Group O included all of the countries in North and South America, and Country Group R included all other nations. Within Country Group R, there was a Subgroup A which included the Communist nations. Exports to Subgroup A were severely restricted. Historically, Cuba was placed in Country Group O. *See, e.g.,* 15 C.F.R. § 371.3 (1960).

The regulations as amended on October 19, 1960 did not delete Cuba from Country Group O or place it in Subgroup A. Instead, they were revised to specifically exclude Cuba as a permitted destination from most of the general export licenses set forth in parts 371 and 385, thereby requiring special licenses for almost all exports to Cuba. *See* 15 C.F.R. §§ 371.8, 371.10, 371.16, 371.18, 371.25, 371.26, 385.2(b). Since the Commerce Department's policy was to deny virtually all license requests, the regulations imposed an almost total export embargo.

The embargo, moreover, was extraterritorial in scope. In addition to placing severe restrictions on exports of commodities and technical information from the United States, the regulations also prohibited the re-exportation from third countries of any commodities or technical data of United States origin to Cuba. *See* §§ 371.4 (commodities), 385.6 (technical data). Elaborate enforcement mechanisms were created to ensure third country compliance.

The Commerce Department did continue to permit a small number of exports to Cuba under extremely limited and restrictive general licenses. *See, e.g.,* §§ 371.9 (in-transit shipments), 371.11 (personal and household effects as baggage for personal use and tools of trade for personal use), 371.12 (dunnage necessary to store cargo), 371.13 (ship and plane stores), 371.20 (specified types of non-technical publications and motion pictures), 371.21 (gifts), 385.2(a) (technical data generally available in published form). The Commerce Department also promulgated a general license, GCU, specifically applicable to exports to Cuba. *See* §§ 371.27, 371.51, Supplement 4. This general license permitted the export of specified foodstuffs, animal oils, grains, medicines, and medical and hospital supplies. Under this scheme, Cuba was treated only slightly more favorably than the Subgroup A countries.

12. On December 19, 1960 President Eisenhower cancelled the Cuban sugar quota for the first quarter of 1961 pursuant to his authority under the amended Sugar Act. Pres. Proc. 3383, *Dep't St. Bull.,* p.18

(January 2, 1961). Thereafter, in a series of presidential proclamations, the Cuban sugar quota was cancelled for subsequent periods.

13. On January 3, 1961 the United States broke diplomatic relations with Cuba. On January 16, 1961 the State Department issued Public Notice 179, which proclaimed that travel by United States citizens to Cuba "would be contrary to the foreign policy of the United States and would be otherwise inimical to the national interest." Accordingly, Public Notice 179 declared all United States passports "invalid for travel to or in Cuba" unless specifically endorsed by the State Department as valid for such travel. An accompanying State Department press release explained that "U.S. citizens desiring to go to Cuba must until further notice obtain passports specifically endorsed" for such travel. This was said to be consistent with the normal practice of "limiting travel" to countries with which the United States had no diplomatic relations.

The State Department also made clear in its press release that it would endorse passports only in extremely limited instances, such as for newsmen and businessmen with established interests in Cuba. This was the practice it in fact pursued, and it expressly refused to endorse passports for tourism, even for "tourists" who wished to examine the political events in Cuba for themselves. This led to a test case in which the Supreme Court ultimately upheld the State Department's so-called "area restriction" on the use of passports in *Zemel v. Rusk,* 381 U.S. 1 (1965).

As reflected by the language of its January 16, 1961 Public Notice and press release, the government asserted it to be illegal for a United States citizen to travel to Cuba without a passport specially endorsed by the State Department for such travel. It soon put this position to the test when, on September 22, 1964, it filed criminal indictments against Levi Laub for organizing travel to Cuba of fifty-eight American citizens whose passports, although otherwise valid, were not specifically endorsed for travel to Cuba. The district court dismissed the indictment on May 5, 1966, holding that travel without a specifically endorsed passport was not a crime under a proper construction of the relevant statute. The government appealed directly to the Supreme Court, which upheld the district court in a decision issued January 10, 1967. *United States v. Laub,* 385 U.S. 475 (1967). Thus, from January 16, 1961 to January 10, 1967, the position of the United States government was that travel to Cuba without a specially endorsed passport was subject to criminal prosecution.

The position of the United States government on travel to Cuba was unprecedented. As the Supreme Court observed, never before had the government taken the view that "area restrictions" on the use of passports were criminal in nature, or that they had the effect of prohibiting travel to the designated country.

14. On April 17, 1961 the Bay of Pigs invasion of Cuba by forces organized and financed by the United States was launched.

15. On September 4, 1961 Congress enacted the Foreign Assistance Act of 1961, Pub. L. No. 87-195, 75 Stat. 424. Section 620(a), 22 U.S.C. §2370(a), provided that no assistance under the Act could be extended to the present government of Cuba. In addition, Congress authorized the President to establish and maintain "a total embargo upon all trade between the United States and Cuba." The President already had similar authority under the Trading With the Enemy Act, 50 U.S.C. App. § 5(b).

16. At the urging of the United States, on January 31, 1962, the Organization of American States voted to exclude Cuba from participation in the OAS system due to its having established a social and governmental system based upon Marxist-Leninist ideology and its acceptance of military assistance from the Soviet Union and China. Final Act, Eighth Meeting of Consultation of Ministers of Foreign Affairs Serving As Organ of Consultation in Application of the Inter-American Treaty of Reciprocal Assistance, Punta del Este, Uruguay, January 22-31, 1962, OEA/Ser. C/II.8 (1962). The vote was fourteen in favor, one opposed (Mexico) and five abstentions (Argentina, Brazil, Chile, Bolivia and Ecuador). In addition, the OAS passed a resolution adopting a collective embargo on trade with Cuba in arms and implements of war. *Id.*

17. On February 7, 1962 President Kennedy issued Proclamation 3447, 27 Fed. Reg 1085, which declared an embargo on all trade with Cuba. It specifically directed the Secretary of Commerce to continue the prohibitions on exports to Cuba and prohibited, *inter alia,* "the importation into the United States of all goods of Cuban origin and all goods imported from or through Cuba." On the same day the Treasury Department issued the Cuban Import Regulations, 31 C.F.R. § 515.201-801, which specifically implemented the Proclamation's import prohibition. Under these regulations, as amended shortly thereafter, the prohibition on imports extended to all merchandise "made or derived in whole or in part of any article which is the growth, produce, or manufacture of Cuba." § 515.201(c).

18. On August 1, 1962 Congress amended § 620(a) of the Foreign Assistance Act of 1961, 22 U.S.C. § 2730(a), to prohibit United States assistance "to any country which furnishes assistance to the present government of Cuba." Pub. L. No. 87-565, § 301(d)(1), 76 Stat. 255 (1962).

19. In early 1963 the United States acted to intensify pressure on third countries to isolate Cuba economically. National Security Action

Memorandum 220 of February 5, 1963 prohibited shipments of cargoes paid for by the United States government on foreign flag vessels which on or after January 1, 1963 had called at a Cuban port. This constituted a blacklist of all foreign vessels which engaged in trade with Cuba, and it was vigorously enforced through periodic publication in the Federal Register of the names of all ships which had called at a Cuban port. In addition, in December 16, 1963, Congress amended § 620(a) of the Foreign Assistance Act of 1961 to prohibit any United States assistance to countries which failed to take steps to prevent ships or aircraft under their registry from engaging in trade with Cuba. *See* Pub. L. No. 88-205, § 301(a), 77 Stat. 386.

20. On July 8, 1963 the Treasury Department replaced the Cuban Import Regulations with the Cuban Assets Control Regulations. 31 C.F.R. §§ 515.101-515.808. These regulations implemented the essential features of the economic embargo against Cuba, including a freeze of all Cuban owned assets in the United States, a prohibition on all unlicensed financial and commercial transactions between Cuba and the United States and between Cuban and United States nationals, and an embargo of Cuban imports. As construed, the regulations also prohibited any person or entity of any nationality and wherever located from engaging in unlicensed transactions with Cuba in United States dollars or dollar accounts. *See* § 515.201. This was confirmed in a State Department "Background Briefing" dated July 12, 1983, which was circulated to United States Embassies in Latin America and provided the State Department's interpretation of the regulations. According to the briefing, all banking transactions in United States dollars were prohibited by the regulations because "under banking practices, U.S. dollar transactions engaged in by Foreign banks must pass through American banks, and are thus affected by the Regulations." In addition, under the broad prohibitions of § 515.201, all exports of property subject to the jurisdiction of the United States were prohibited. This, in effect, incorporated the Commerce Department's export regulations into the Treasury regulations. *See* § 515.533.

Throughout the following years, the Treasury Department's policy was to deny licenses in almost all instances. Its enforcement against the import of Cuban origin products, such as nickel, or third country products containing Cuban origin materials, was particularly strict. Nickel products from a number of third countries, including Italy and France, were detained, and agreements were negotiated to ensure strict policing to prevent Cuban nickel from entering the United States.

The extraterritorial application of the regulations to United States controlled firms in third countries was accomplished in a more subtle manner. Section 515.541 permitted non-banking foreign firms owned or controlled by United States nationals to engage in transactions with

Cuba. However, by administrative interpretation, made explicit in a published regulation on July 10, 1974, § 515.412, Treasury required United States citizens who were directors, officers or managerial employees of such foreign firms to oppose any transactions with Cuba and prohibited them from participating in any such transactions. As a result, only those United States-owned or controlled firms whose local management was not controlled by United States citizen personnel were permitted to engage in any transactions with Cuba. Moreover, the Treasury Department vigorously pursued an informal policy of applying pressure to United States parent companies to ensure that their foreign affiliates "voluntarily" refrained from engaging in any transactions with Cuba. In published comments, Stanley Sommerfield, the head of the Treasury Department's Office of Foreign Assets Control, stated that this informal policy had been highly effective. Stanley Sommerfield, *Treasury Regulations Affecting Trade with the Sino-Soviet Bloc and Cuba,* 19 The Business Lawyer 861, 868 (1964). As a result, he indicated, Treasury had decided it was unnecessary to aggravate relations with United States allies by prohibiting foreign subsidiary trade altogether, but, he added, "[i]f it develops that a substantial amount of trade is being conducted by subsidiaries with Cuba (and constant checks are being made on this point) then the exemption will be reconsidered." *Id.*

In addition, Treasury imposed a number of other restrictions upon trade by foreign firms owned or controlled by United States nationals, including a prohibition on the use of United States dollar accounts or any other property subject to the jurisdiction of the United States in connection with such transactions, a prohibition on the transfer of United States-origin merchandise in connection with any such transactions, and a prohibition on the transportation aboard any vessel owned by such foreign firms of any merchandise either from any country to Cuba or from Cuba to any other country.

21. On May 14, 1964 the Commerce Department revoked general license GCU, thus requiring specific approval even for the export of foods and medicines to Cuba. The Commerce Department's policy, moreover, was to deny license requests for commercial transactions of this nature, permitting only limited humanitarian donations. The Atomic Energy Commission took parallel action with regard to exports of medicines having radioactive ingredients.

22. On July 26, 1964 the OAS voted to require its members to break diplomatic relations with Cuba; to impose a collective embargo on trade with Cuba except in foodstuffs, medicines and medical equipment for humanitarian purposes; and to suspend all sea transportation between their countries and Cuba. Final Act, Ninth Meeting of Consultation of Ministers of Foreign Affairs Serving as Organ of Consultation in

Application of the Inter-American Treaty of Reciprocal Assistance, OEA/ Ser.C/II.9, Doc.48, Rev.2 (1964). The vote was fifteen to four (Chile, Bolivia, Uruguay and Mexico) with one abstention. The reason cited for the resolution was Cuba's support for revolutionary movements in Venezuela.

23. In late July 1964 the Treasury Department froze the United States assets of a Mexican bank, Banco del Atlántico, on the ground that it had engaged in transactions with Cuban nationals in United States dollars. As noted the Treasury Department took the view that the regulations prohibited any transactions with Cubans in United States dollars even by foreign banks. Although the Mexican government objected to this extension of United States law, the bank ultimately agreed to cease conducting banking transactions with Cuba, and Treasury unblocked the frozen assets.

24. On October 6, 1964 the Commerce Department further strengthened its attempts to prevent foreign vessels from trading with Cuba. It amended the regulations to prohibit foreign ships calling in United States ports from obtaining bunker fuel if they intended thereafter to call at a Cuban port or if they had called at a Cuban port at any time after January 1, 1963. See 15 C.F.R. § 371.12(b)(2).

25. In 1965 the Commerce Department's Country Group designation system was amended. The countries were divided into six groups, Country Groups, T, V, W, X, Y and Z. Cuba was placed in Country Group Z, which is the most restrictive category. In most respects, the export restrictions remained substantially the same, although the few permitting exports at all were made even more restrictive. The extraterritorial application of the regulations was strengthened. Section 385.6, which prohibited the re-export by third countries of United States-origin technical data, was amended to prohibit, in addition, the re-export by third countries of the products of United States origin technical data.

26. After the Supreme Court's decision in *Laub,* discussed *ante,* on March 14, 1967, the State Department revoked Public Notice 179 and immediately replaced it with a new Public Notice imposing almost identical restrictions. It proclaimed "travel to, in or through Cuba is restricted" and recited that such travel "would seriously impair the conduct of U.S. foreign affairs." Similar notices were then issued periodically through 1976. These again provided that United States passports were not valid for travel to Cuba unless specifically endorsed by the State Department. In *Lynd v. Rusk,* 389 F.2d 940 (D.C. Cir. 1967), the court held that, although the government could prohibit use of a passport for travel to Cuba, there was no violation so long as the citizen did not present his passport to Cuban authorities—as evidenced by a Cuban visa being stamped in it.

The *Laub* decision of the Supreme Court made it possible for United States citizens to travel to Cuba, provided they did not violate the Treasury Department's regulations by making payment to Cuba or Cuban nationals for travel and living expenses (discussed *post*). Nonetheless, as the Supreme Court itself recognized in *Zemel* v. *Rusk,* the refusal to validate a passport for travel to Cuba had a deterrent effect on travel there. It proclaimed such travel to be against the national interest, and it implied at least a diminished ability or willingness to provide diplomatic protection to the traveler.

Even aside from its regulation of passports, the United States made travel to Cuba unlawful and impractical for most people through the Treasury regulations. As previously noted, those regulations essentially prohibited any United States citizen from engaging in any financial transaction, direct or indirect, with Cuba or Cuban nationals, except where specifically licensed by the Treasury Department. Inasmuch as Treasury pursued an extremely restricted licensing policy, this effectively prohibited United States citizens from making payment for travel expenses within Cuba or to pay for Cuban air services. Violation was subject to stiff criminal penalties. Although not explicitly recognized by the regulations, "hosted" travel was arguably not prohibited, that is, travel when Cuba paid all in-country expenses and the traveler either used non-Cuban air services or Cuba paid for the air services as well. Aside from the fact that the regulations ended any demand for such services, they also prohibited the financial transactions necessary to maintain regular air links with Cuba.

27. In 1969 the Commerce Department amended its export regulations to state expressly that its policy was to deny all applications to export commodities and technical data to Cuba except for "certain humanitarian transactions." The same policy was further elaborated upon in 1970.

28. On July 10, 1974 the Treasury Department added a number of provisions liberalizing the regulations in certain respects.

First, the import prohibition was eased to permit by specific license:

a. the importation of gifts of small value directly from Cuba (31 C.F.R. § 515.544);

b. the importation of Cuban books, publications, films, phonograph records, tapes, photographs, microfilm, microfiche and posters by universities, libraries, and research and scientific institutions as well as by scholars returning from Cuba to the extent necessary for their research (§ 515.545);

c. the importation of the materials listed in "b" above for commercial purposes so long as the payment for such materials was placed into a blocked account and not sent to Cuba (§ 515.545); and

d. the importation of newspapers, magazines, photographs, films, tapes, and other news materials by news-gathering agencies in the United States and by journalists and news correspondents returning from Cuba to the extent necessary for their journalistic assignments (§ 515.546).

Second, the travel restrictions were slightly relaxed. The Treasury Department promulgated 31 C.F.R. §§ 515.545 and 515.546. These regulations provided that specific licenses would be granted to scholars, journalists, and news correspondents for payment of expenses for travel to and from, and maintenance within, Cuba for the purpose of study and research in the case of scholars and gathering and transmitting news to the United States in the case of journalists and news correspondents. These specific licenses, however, would be granted only where the applicant had first obtained a passport validated for travel to Cuba from the State Department.

Third, a number of new provisions benefited Cuban emigrés by providing for the issuance of specific licenses unblocking certain of their assets which were otherwise frozen under the regulations. *See* §§ 515.549-515.558. The unblocked assets included proportionate amounts of joint bank accounts held by an emigré and a blocked Cuban national (§§ 515.550-515.551); proportionate shares of the proceeds of insurance policies where an emigré was a beneficiary, even though the insured and other beneficiaries were blocked Cuban nationals (§ 515.552); and proportionate shares of the assets of Cuban partnerships and sole proprietorships where an emigré was an owner, despite the fact that other owners were blocked Cuban nationals (§§ 515.557, 515.558).

29. On July 29, 1975 the OAS voted to rescind its mandatory sanctions against Cuba, leaving to each member state the right to determine its diplomatic and trade relations with Cuba. Final Act, Sixteenth Meeting of Consultation of Ministers of Foreign Affairs Serving as Organ of Consultation in Application of the Inter-American Treaty of Reciprocal Assistance, July 29, 1975, OEA/Ser.F/II. Doc. 9/75, Rev.2 (1975).

30. In response to the OAS resolution and to international pressure to relax the extraterritorial aspects of its economic measures, the United States eased the measures in a number of respects.

On October 8, 1975 the Treasury Department revoked 31 C.F.R. § 515.541 and replaced it with § 515.559. This change was a direct response to pressure by third countries objecting to the extension of the United States trade policy toward Cuba to foreign firms owned or controlled by United States nationals. Section 515.559 provided for the issuance of specific licenses for the export of goods to, or the import of goods from, Cuba by United States-owned or controlled firms in third countries where local law requires, or policy in the third country favors, trade with Cuba. This removed the requirement that United States national managerial personnel of the foreign firms oppose any transactions with Cuba. Foreign subsidiaries sharing a substantial number of officers or directors with the parent firm did not qualify for a license under § 515.559, an indirect but effective restraint on foreign subsidiary trade in many cases.

The prohibition on use of United States dollar accounts in licensed transactions was retained. In addition, these firms were still prohibited from engaging in a range of normal commercial transactions with Cuban nationals, including making investments in Cuban entities or extending credits. This special licensing scheme, moreover, applied only to firms organized under the laws of foreign countries and had no application to branches of United States companies operating in third countries.

The Commerce Department likewise relaxed the extraterritorial reach of the export regulations in a number of respects.

First, it eased the application of the regulations to exports by third countries of foreign-made products which contain "an insubstantial proportion of United States-origin materials, parts, or components." § 385.1. Under the previous regulations, if a foreign product contained any United States-origin parts, third country exports to Cuba were prohibited. Under the amended regulations, third country exports are permitted by special license "where local law requires, or policy in the third country favors, trade with Cuba," *id.*, and where the proportion of United States parts amounts to 20 percent or less of the value of the product. Where United States parts amount to more than 20 percent, approval is "less likely." *Id.*

Second, the Commerce Department revoked the regulation which denied bunker fuel to ships which intended after leaving the United States to call at a Cuban port or had, at any time after January 1, 1963, called at a Cuban port.

Third, the State Department issued a special notice invoking its power to nullify the prohibition in § 620(a) of the Foreign Assistance Act of 1961 on assistance to third countries which permit their vessels to trade with Cuba. Thereafter, in 1977, Congress repealed that portion of § 620(a), and the National Security Council rescinded National Security Action Memorandum No. 220 which had instituted the blacklist.

31. United States policy on travel to Cuba shifted dramatically in 1977 when the State Department under the Carter Administration permitted the passport restrictions on travel to Cuba to lapse on March 19 and the Treasury Department on March 21 promulgated a general license permitting all economic transactions incident to travel to Cuba. 31 C.F.R. § 515.560. This amounted to approval of United States tourist travel to Cuba. Section 515.560, as amended on May 18, 1977,

specifically approved transactions ordinarily incident to travel to and in Cuba, including for transportation and living expenses. It also permitted travel agencies in the United States to make arrangements for United States travelers, and banks and credit card companies to honor checks, traveler's checks and, under some restrictions, credit card transactions.

32. On January 9, 1978 the Treasury regulations were amended to permit United States residents to provide support payments to close relatives in Cuba. § 515.563. The payments, however, could not exceed $500 in any consecutive three month period. Payment of an additional $500 was also permitted for the purpose of enabling the payee to emigrate from Cuba.

33. On May 9, 1978 the Treasury regulations were amended to permit travel related transactions by Cuban travelers in the United States on a visa issued by the State Department. § 515.564.

34. In 1981 the Commerce Department amended its regulations to delete any reference to a policy permitting exports to Cuba even for humanitarian reasons. § 385.1.

35. The liberalization of the travel policy was short-lived. On April 20, 1982 the Reagan Administration's Treasury Department amended § 515.560 to severely restrict travel to Cuba. Expenditures incidental to travel to Cuba were prohibited without a special license except for three areas: (a) United States or foreign government officials on official business; (b) persons travelling to gather news, make documentary films, or engage in professional research or other similar activities; and (c) persons travelling to visit close relatives in Cuba. Transactions incidental to tourist and business travel were specifically prohibited and special approval was required for travel for "humanitarian reasons" or for purposes of "public performances" or other cultural or sports activities. In addition, previously permitted credit card and similar transactions were prohibited even for those permitted to travel to Cuba.

Shortly thereafter, on July 23, 1982 the Treasury Department amended § 515.560 again to further tighten the restrictions. Several lengthy subsections were added which defined narrowly the professional research exception to the travel ban. For example, the professional research exception was limited to full-time researchers who are specifically researching topics relating to Cuba and who are substantially likely to disseminate the product of their work. Moreover, while in Cuba, they may engage in recreational activities only to the extent "consistent with a full schedule of research activities." The new amendments expressly recognized what at least arguably had been implicit in the regulations from the beginning, that travel which is fully hosted—that is, paid for—by Cuba or a Cuban national, is not prohibited. Thus, so long as the United States citizens or residents do not spend any money or render any services in consideration of their expenses being paid, they may travel to Cuba.

In *Regan v. Wald,* 468 U.S. 222 (1984), the United States Supreme Court upheld these restrictions on the premise that they were not an effort to curtail the freedom of travel of United States citizens for political reasons but a foreign policy measure designed to deny Cuba hard currency.

36. On February 17, 1985 the Treasury Department added an appendix to 31 C.F.R. § 515.536 providing that any individual or organization in the United States may import single copies of any Cuban publication, including books, newspapers, magazines, films, phonograph records, tapes, photographs, microfilm, microfiche, posters and similar materials.

37. On August 21, 1985 the Treasury Department added § 515.567 which unblocks the *pro rata* shares of individuals resident in the United States or the authorized trade territory in the nationalized assets of Cuban corporations. These individuals are entitled to their net *pro rata* share of the United States-based assets after deducting the amount owed creditors for debts accrued prior to July 8, 1963, the effective date of the regulations. This regulation amounts to a partial liquidation in favor of the previous shareholders of all United States located assets of nationalized Cuban corporations.

38. On August 23, 1988, as part of a new trade bill, Congress enacted the "Berman Amendment" to the Trading With the Enemy Act denying the President authority to regulate or prohibit the importation from or exportation to Cuba, including for commercial purposes, of publications, films, posters, phonograph records, photographs, microfilms, microfiche, tapes or other informational materials. Omnibus Trade and Competitiveness Act of 1988, Pub. L. No. 100-418, § 2502, 102 Stat. 1371, 50 U.S.C. App. § 5(b)(4).

39. In August 1988 in another provision of the same trade bill, Congress instructed the administration to submit recommendations for enhancing enforcement of the embargo against Cuban-origin imports. Omnibus Trade and Competitiveness Act of 1988, § 1911. This congressional invitation to enhanced enforcement efforts seemingly marks the beginning of a still continuing period of efforts to tighten the blockade.

40. In October 1988 the Treasury Department's Office of Foreign Assets Control (OFAC) launched a "major initiative" to "identify Cuban merchant shipping front companies throughout the world and to block vessels operated by them from access to U.S. port facilities." *Report to Congress On Measures to Enhance Restrictions Against U.S. Imports from Cuba, as Required by Section 1911 of the Omnibus Trade and Competitiveness Act of 1988,* p.6. As a result of this initiative, thirty-two Cuban shipping companies operating out of Panama, Cyprus, Malta

and Liberia were designated as nationals of Cuba by the time the administration submitted its report to Congress pursuant to section 1911. The companies so designated, even though incorporated in third countries, are treated the same as Cuban corporations, with the effect that no United States person can have any dealings with them, and any of their property coming within the jurisdiction of the United States is frozen.

41. In late 1988 and through 1989 OFAC significantly expanded its enforcement capacities through the development of joint procedures with other federal agencies "for the early and continuous coordination of intelligence and investigative information, program development, technical assistance, case monitoring, effective prosecution and penalties for violations of controls." *Report,* p.12-13.

42. Also in late 1988 OFAC embarked upon a program of "expanded targeting of Cuba's global trading network." *Report,* p.12. "Working with international business information as well as with other government agencies," OFAC gave "increasing attention to Cuba's international trade ties." It pursued a program of "coordinated employment of all the Federal government's information gathering capabilities, special designations, blocking of assets, prosecutions," so that "Cuba's international trading network is effectively identified and monitored." This program "necessitates even further interagency planning and program development to bring the diverse authorities of the Federal agencies to bear most effectively on the key vulnerabilities of the Cuban economy and its embargo circumvention attempts." OFAC proceeded to "the next stage of planning and developing joint and integrated programs [with other federal agencies] to continue enforcing the Cuban embargo in the most effective manner possible." *Report,* p.12-13.

43. Also beginning in late 1988 OFAC developed a program of "public awareness" to alert the public and business communities about the embargo's restrictions. *Report,* p.6.

44. On November 23, 1988 OFAC established for the first time a licensing system for travel agents, air charterers and others who provide services to those wishing to travel to Cuba. 31 C.F.R. § 515.560(i), 53 Fed. Reg. 47527 (November 23, 1988). OFAC's stated purpose was to help ensure strict compliance with the limitations on travel to Cuba by United States nationals. It likewise established for the first time a licensing system for businesses which assist Cuban-Americans in forwarding remittances to close relatives in Cuba. 31 C.F.R. § 515.563, 53 Fed. Reg. 47529 (November 23, 1988). The stated purpose was likewise to ensure compliance with the limitations on family remittances.

45. Also on November 23, 1988 OFAC removed its prior requirement that, to be eligible for a license to do business with Cuba, a foreign

subsidiary of a United States corporation could have no more than a minority of United States nationals on its board of directors. 31 C.F.R. § 515.559, 53 Fed. Reg. 47527 (November 23, 1988).

46. Beginning in 1989 Senator Connie Mack (D-Fla.) made repeated efforts to secure the passage of legislation which would prohibit the foreign subsidiaries of United States corporations from engaging in trade with Cuba. Introduced as an amendment to other legislation, the so-called "Mack Amendment" was adopted by both houses of Congress several times. However, one bill to which the amendment was attached was vetoed by the President and several other bills also containing the amendment failed passage. The administration opposed passage of the Mack Amendment on the ground that it would unduly complicate United States relations with its allies but never stated the President would veto legislation simply because it contained the Mack Amendment. Ultimately, in April 1992, the administration advised Congress that it could accept the Mack Amendment as part of a comprehensive "Cuban Democracy Act of 1992" then under consideration by the Foreign Affairs Committee of the House of Representatives.

47. Also beginning in 1989 Congress considered other legislation, introduced principally by Florida's congressional delegation, including provisions conditioning assistance to the Soviet Union on its ceasing direct or indirect "assistance" to Cuba; instructing the administration to vote against International Monetary Fund membership for the U.S.S.R. or expanded Soviet access to IMF or European Bank for Reconstruction and Development facilities until the U.S.S.R. terminated "economic subsidies" to Cuba; conditioning most-favored-nation status to China upon its significantly cutting its aid to Cuba; reducing economic assistance to countries by an amount equal to their purchase of Cuban sugar; banning third-country vessels that trade with Cuba from United States ports; and instructing the administration to urge countries not to purchase Cuban sugar. These initiatives received substantial support in Congress but, largely for extraneous reasons, never became law.

48. On February 2, 1989 OFAC issued amendments purporting to bring its regulations into conformity with the Berman Amendment's exemption for the import or export of informational materials. For the most part OFAC took a narrow reading of the exemption, limiting its scope to the export or import of tangible items already in existence at the time of the import or export contract. Among other restrictions OFAC continued to prohibit a United States party financing the creation of a new informational work, such as a publisher paying an advance to a Cuban author to write a book. OFAC excluded altogether from the scope of the Berman Amendment live telecasts, news wire feeds, and other transmissions by electronic means. It also prohibited Cuba from appointing sales agents in the United States and prohibited

any travel by United States persons to Cuba to negotiate transactions in informational materials. Also excluded altogether from the protection of the Berman Amendment were paintings, drawings or sculpture. 31 C.F.R. §§ 515.206, 515.332, 515.545; 54 Fed. Reg. 5229 *et seq.* (February 2, 1989).

49. On February 2, 1989 OFAC lifted its freeze of the estates of decedent Cuban nationals to the extent the heirs are resident in the United States or elsewhere outside of Cuba. 31 C.F.R. § 515.524.

50. In February 1989 OFAC took the position that a United States filmmaker could not teach a one-week seminar at the International Film and Television School in Cuba on the ground that this would be providing a "service" to Cuba in violation of the embargo's prohibition against the transfer of "property" to Cuba or a Cuban national. OFAC thereafter prohibited similar educational exchanges on the same theory. Ultimately, on September 27, 1991, OFAC amended its regulations to specify the provision of "services" as a prohibited transaction. § 515.311.

51. In March, 1989 the State Department denied visas to the Cuban musical group Orquesta Aragón to perform without fee in a Caribbean arts festival in Chicago. This marked the beginning of the State Department policy of denying visas to Cuban musicians on the ground that their public performances will promote the sale of their records in the United States, now lawful under the Berman Amendment, and also enhance their reputation and thus the fees they can command in Europe and elsewhere. Prior to passage of the Berman Amendment, visas were granted to Cuban musicians to perform in the United States provided they did not receive any performance fees.

52. By August 2, 1989 OFAC's list of third-country companies or nationals specially designated as Cuban nationals for purposes of the embargo, on the ground that they were substantially owned or controlled by Cuba or act as agents for Cuba, had grown to 258 names. Statement of R. Richard Newcomb, Director, Office of Foreign Assets Control, before the Subcommittee on Human Rights and International Organizations, Subcommittee on Western Hemisphere Affairs, Subcommittee on International Economic Policy, of the House Committee on Foreign Affairs (August 2, 1989).

53. On August 25, 1989 OFAC imposed for the first time a limitation on the amount an authorized United States traveler can carry to Cuba to cover expenses: $100 per day. 31 C.F.R. § 515.569, 54 Fed. Reg. 35326 (August 25, 1989).

54. On September 20, 1989 OFAC listed as specially designated nationals of Cuba an additional fourteen companies and individuals, all of which were alleged to operate from Panama. 54 Fed. Reg. 8810 (September 20, 1989).

55. On November 3, 1989 Congress acted to substantially expand OFAC's staff and budget. It instructed the Secretary of the Treasury to

make available from Treasury's appropriations an amount for OFAC well above previous levels and also to staff OFAC well above previous levels. Treasury, Postal Service and General Government Appropriations Act, 1990, Pub. L. No. 101-136, 103 Stat. 783 (November 3, 1989). Congress cited effective enforcement of the sanctions program against Cuba in particular as requiring these measures. Making Appropriations for the Treasury Department, etc., Conference Report, H. R. Rep. No. 101-276, 101st Cong., 1st Sess. (October 11, 1989). Congress also instructed the Secretary of the Treasury to submit quarterly reports "on the successful enforcement of United States economic and trade policies from this enhancement" and stated Congress' expectation that future appropriations requests from Treasury will contain a detailed proposed budget for OFAC. Conference Report, p.8. These same instructions were repeated in the appropriations for the following fiscal years.

56. On October 24, 1989 OFAC announced its intention to impose a new requirement that the charter flights operating between Miami and Havana must arrive or depart from Miami during the general business hours of the United States Customs Service. The stated purpose was to ensure that there would be enough Customs service personnel in attendance to obtain compliance with the embargo's restrictions. 31 C.F.R. § 515.520, 54 Fed. Reg. 43304 (October 24, 1989). The restriction was made effective October 9, 1990.

57. On October 31, 1989 OFAC added thirty-four companies and individuals to its list of specially designated nationals of Cuba operating in Panama. 54 Fed. Reg. 45731 (October 31, 1989).

58. On November 17, 1989 OFAC announced that Japan had agreed to certify that nickel-bearing imports produced by the Shunan Works of Japan's Nisshin Steel Corporation do not contain any Cuban-origin nickel. As a consequence OFAC permitted nickel-bearing imports from that factory. 54 Fed. Reg. 47858 (November 17, 1989).

59. On November 29, 1989 OFAC listed sixty one additional companies and individuals as specially designated nationals of Cuba. Most were located in Mexico or Spain. 54 Fed. Reg. 49258 (November 29, 1989).

60. On December 1, 1989 OFAC denied the application of ABC Sports to pay Cuba a rights fee for the live telecast of the Pan American Games to be held in Havana.

61. On June 29, 1990 the United States announced agreement by the U.S.S.R. to certify that nickel and nickel-bearing products intended for export to the United States do not contain any Cuban-origin nickel. As a result OFAC lifted its ban on all nickel and nickel-bearing imports from the U.S.S.R. In agreeing to the certification program, the U.S.S.R.

joined France, the Federal Republic of Germany, Italy, Japan and the Netherlands.

62. On March 27, 1991 OFAC agreed to lift its embargo of Cuban paintings, drawings and sculpture in order to settle a lawsuit claiming the importation of these art works is protected by the Berman Amendment. 31 C.F.R. § 515.570, 56 Fed. Reg. 13284 (April 1, 1991).

63. On September 27, 1991 OFAC adopted a series of restrictions on payments to Cuba made by United States persons with family in Cuba. First, it reduced from $500 to $300 the remittances a United States person can send to the household of a close relative in Cuba every three months. Second, for the first time it imposed a limitation—$500— on the money United States persons can remit to Cuba or a Cuban national for the purpose of having a Cuban (usually a relative) visit the United States on a temporary visit. Third, OFAC for the first time imposed a limit—$500 annually—on the payment of Cuban government fees for visas and, in the case of Cuban-born United States persons, for the issuance or renewal of Cuban passports required for their travel to Cuba. 31 C.F.R. §§ 515.560, 515.564, 515.569; 56 Fed. Reg. 49246 (October 2, 1991).

64. On April 24, 1992 OFAC announced it would license the direct shipment of humanitarian gift parcels from the United States to Cuba, provided the parcels do not have a value of more than $100; no more than one such gift parcel is sent by a United States donor to the same Cuban donee per month; the parcel consists of goods, medicine or clothing; and no more than $5 per pound is paid to Cuba for duty, entry, delivery or other services. 57 Fed. Reg. 15216 (April 24, 1992).

65. On April 24, 1992 OFAC, acting pursuant to a Presidential directive, closed United States ports to any third-country vessel "carrying goods or passengers to or from Cuba or carrying goods in which Cuba or a Cuban national has an interest." 57 Fed. Reg. 15216 (April 24, 1992). No comparable restriction had been in effect since 1975, when the United States repealed its restrictions against third-country vessels trading with Cuba in order to conform to the Organization of American States resolution permitting each country to determine its own trade relations with Cuba.

66. On October 23, 1992 President Bush signed into law the Cuban Democracy Act of 1992, Title XVII, Pub. L. No. 102-484, §§ 1701 *et seq.;* 106 Stat. 2575 ("CDA"), which significantly expanded United States economic measures against Cuba in a number of respects:

a. It prohibits third-country companies substantially owned or controlled by United States nationals from engaging in any transactions with Cuba or Cuban nationals;

b. It prohibits third-country vessels from loading or unloading any freight at any place in the United States for 180 days after departing a Cuban port it entered to engage in the trade of goods or services;

c. It codifies the April 24, 1992 administrative regulation closing United States ports to third-country vessels carrying goods or passengers to or from Cuba or carrying goods in which Cuba or a Cuban national has an interest;

d. It instructs the President to maintain strict limits on remittances to Cuba by United States persons for the purpose of financing the travel of Cubans to the United States on temporary or permanent visits, "in order to ensure that such remittances reflect only the reasonable costs associated with such travel, and are not used by the Government of Cuba as a means of gaining access to United States currency";

e. It provides the Treasury Department for the first time with the authority to impose civil fines (up to $50,000) and to order the forfeiture of property for violation of the United States embargo regulations. The Treasury Department had long contended that this authority would substantially enhance its ability to enforce the embargo. Administrative fines, unlike criminal prosecutions, would not require Treasury to prove that the defendant knew of the embargo regulations and intentionally violated them, an element of proof the Treasury Department had found difficult to meet. Nor would Treasury have to convince a jury of the defendant's guilt or prove its case beyond a reasonable doubt. The CDA exempts from OFAC's new enforcement authority transactions incidental to news-gathering, research, or the export or import or transmission of information or informational materials, or transactions incidental to clearly defined educational or religious activities or activities of recognized human rights organizations that are reasonably limited in frequency, duration, and number of participants;

f. It authorizes the President to declare third countries providing "assistance" to Cuba ineligible for aid under the Foreign Assistance Act of 1961, assistance or sales under the Arms Export Control Act, or relief under any program for the forgiveness or reduction of debt owed to the United States government. The CDA broadly defines the "assistance" permitting imposition of these sanctions to include any trade on terms more favorable than generally available in the applicable market and also specifically includes subsidies for exports to Cuba and favorable tariff treatment of articles that are the growth, product, or manufacture of Cuba.

67. Also in October, 1992 Congress increased the criminal penalties for knowing violations of the Trading With the Enemy Act and hence the Cuban Assets Control Regulations to a maximum of $1 million in fines for corporations and $100,000 for individuals, ten years imprisonment, and the forfeiture of any property concerned in the violation.

Pub. L. No. 102-393, § 628, 106 Stat. 1729. Criminal violations of the Cuban Democracy Act are subject to the same maximum penalties. CDA, § 1710(d).

68. On November 16, 1992 OFAC narrowed somewhat the general license for transactions incidental to travel to Cuba for "professional research" by stipulating that the "professional research" must be "generally of a noncommercial, academic nature." At the same time, OFAC ended the practice of permitting third-country nationals entering the United States to bring with them as accompanying baggage Cuban-origin tobacco or alcohol products in noncommercial amounts for their personal consumption. It explained that this limited exception to the ban on imports of Cuban-origin products had permitted a brisk business for Cuban rum and cigars at airports in Canada and elsewhere. 57 Fed. Reg. 53997 (November 16, 1992).

ECONOMIC CONTEXT FOR THE CURRENT UNITED STATES MEASURES

[Professor Andrew Zimbalist has contributed an original paper to this volume analyzing the vulnerability of the Cuban economy to the measures being pursued by the United States. Professor Zimbalist is Robert A. Woods Professor of Economics at Smith College and a member of the Five College Graduate Faculty. He is the editor of a book series on "The Political Economy of Development in Latin America" for Westview Press and has published ten books and several dozen articles in the areas of comparative economic systems and economic development. His *The Cuban Economy: Measurement and Analysis of Socialist Performance* (with Swedish economist Claes Brundenius) was published by Johns Hopkins University Press in November 1989. Written in the spring of 1992, Professor Zimbalist's contribution anticipated passage of the Cuban Democracy Act then under consideration in Congress.]

ANDREW ZIMBALIST, THE COST OF THE UNITED
STATES EMBARGO AND ITS EXTRATERRITORIAL
APPLICATION TO THE CUBAN ECONOMY

The Cuban economy is amidst its worst crisis since 1959. After strong economic growth between 1970 and 1985, the Cuban economy stagnated between 1985 and 1989, declined by approximately 5 percent in 1990, fell by another 20 to 25 percent in 1991 and faces the prospect of a continuing output reduction of 10 percent or more in 1992. The proximate cause of Cuba's present predicament is not hard to identify— Cuba has a small and heavily trade-dependent economy. In the presence of the U.S. embargo, Cuba came to depend on the former Soviet trade bloc (CMEA) for over four-fifths of its imports. Without access to the U.S. market, with access to other markets restricted, and with imports from the former CMEA countries reduced by over two-thirds, Cuba's economy and its people are struggling to survive.

The Cuban government's response to the crisis has been deliberate but inadequate. A number of reforms initiated prior to 1989 are being continued,[1] others are being accelerated, and some new programs are being put in place. The current emphasis on foreign investment and tourism, structural reforms in the operation of foreign trade, and the impossibility of central planning in the presence of ubiquitous supply uncertainties have combined to transform the nature of Cuba's economic mechanism. Despite the promise of some extension of private enterprise and the market in the service sector, however, the needed and more concerted introduction of a broader market mechanism has not been forthcoming.

Cuba's Trade Dependency

Similar to other small economies, Cuba has always been very trade dependent. Indeed, during the triennium 1987 to 1989 Cuba's imports as a share of its *Ingreso Nacional Creado* (roughly Net Domestic Product minus "non-productive" services) averaged 61.5 percent and as a share of its estimated Gross Domestic Product (GDP) averaged 38.0 percent.[2] The more typical ratio of imports to GDP for small, medium-income countries in Latin America is around 25 percent.

Cuba's overall import dependency was aggravated by an excessive vulnerability to CMEA trade. During 1987 to 1989 an average 84.2 percent of Cuban imports came from Eastern Europe and the Soviet Union. Cuban imports from Eastern Europe, which accounted for approximately 15 percent of Cuban imports, fell by roughly one-half in 1990 and practically disappeared in 1991. Imports from the Soviet Union, which accounted for over 70 percent of Cuba's imports, fell by over 30 percent in 1990 (measured in current prices), and then dropped precipitously in 1991.[3]

1. For a full discussion of these reforms, see Andrew Zimbalist, *Industrial Reform and the Cuban Economy,* in Ian Jeffries, ed., *Industrial Reform in Socialist Countries: From Restructuring to Revolution* (1992), and Andrew Zimbalist and Wayne Smith, *Reform in Cuba,* in Ilpyong J. Kim and Jane S. Zacek, eds., *Transformation in Communist Systems: Comparing Perspectives* (1991).

2. The estimate is by this author. It is *Ingreso Nacional Creado* plus depreciation plus estimated non-productive services. The latter is estimated to be equal to 28 percent of Gross Domestic Product. *See* Andrew Zimbalist and Claes Brundenius, *The Cuban Economy: Measurement and Analysis of Socialist Performance,* ch. 4 (1989).

3. The 1990 figure for Soviet trade is from *Cuba Business,* October 1991, p. 2, and for trade with Eastern Europe it is estimated based on proportions in import reduction reported in Elena C. Alvarez, *Algunos efectos en la economía cubana de los cambios en la coyuntura internacional* 7 (Instituto de Investigaciones Económicas, Habana, Cuba, Junio de 1991). The 1991 estimate is from the opening speech of Fidel Castro at the Fourth Party Congress, October 10, 1991, reprinted in FBIS, *Daily Report Supplement: Latin America,* October 14, 1991. For a further elaboration, see Andrew Zimbalist, *Teetering on the Brink: Cuba's Post-CMEA Political and Economic Crisis,* Journal of Latin American Studies (1992).

A sense of the magnitude and importance of the reduction in Soviet exports to Cuba is conveyed by the following figures. In 1989 Cuba imported $5.52 billion worth of goods from the Soviet Union, including 13.11 million tons of petroleum (8.5 million tons of which was crude oil).[4] The revised trade agreement for 1991 called for Soviet exports of $3.363 billion to Cuba, including 10 million tons of petroleum. As of October 1, 1991, however, the Soviets had only exported $1.305 billion worth of goods, or 38.8 percent of the planned yearly total. By year's end Soviet exports reached around $1.7 billion, or just over 30 percent of the value of Soviet imports two years earlier.[5]

The collapse of the CMEA and the economies of Eastern Europe and the Soviet Union together led to a reduction of Cuba's overall imports of almost 60 percent. Since imports represent 38 percent of estimated GDP, this implies an import decrease equal to 22.5 percent of GDP. Further, since most of the would-be imports are raw materials and intermediate goods, their absence can have a multiplicatively downward effect on production.[6]

The Embargo

With the decimation of trade with the former Soviet bloc, apart from a modest increase in trade with China, Cuba's only remaining option is to increase trade with the West. The problems here are manifold: Cuba's industrial park is built overwhelmingly with CMEA technology and equipment; Cuba's export products in their selection, specification, and quality are geared for the CMEA; Cuba lacks the market contacts, information, and skills to readily penetrate Western markets; Cuba is prohibited from trading with its natural commercial partner in the West, the United States; and, the United States extraterritorially applies pressure and formal restraints on foreign countries and foreign companies to limit trade with Cuba.

4. These figures and others, unless otherwise noted, are from the *Anuario Estadístico de Cuba, 1989,* published by the Comité Estatal de Estadísticas and the *Resumen Estadístico del Comercio Exterior, 1986-88,* published by the Ministerio de Comercio Exterior.

5. These numbers are in current prices and it is likely that in constant prices the fall off would be a bit less sharp. This is because the price Cuba paid for Soviet oil fell approximately $7 a barrel between 1989 and 1991.

6. For some imports, however, the reduction in domestic output is minimal. For instance, some of the reduced oil imports resulted in more careful use of electricity in the household. Here all that is lost is the value added from domestic electricity generation—considerably less than the value of lost imports. Overall, we can estimate that an import fall of between 50 and 60 percent would result in a GDP drop on the order of 25 to 35 percent between 1989 and 1991. A further reduction in imports of 15 to 20 percent is possible for 1992, leading to an additional GDP drop of 10 percent or more. At such a level, however, the Cuban economy would appear to have hit bottom unless there are new external disruptions.

The transition from protected trade within the CMEA to competitive trade in world markets is a problematic and protracted process even without political and commercial restraints. Cuba's export role within the CMEA, however, left a product mix more amenable to penetrating Western markets than that in most other Soviet bloc countries. Cuba largely exported primary products that are basically homogeneous, such as sugar, nickel, tobacco, citrus, and fish products. With a few possible exceptions, their quality was sufficient to be sold in competitive markets. Not so with the manufactured consumer and capital goods exported by most other CMEA countries. Further, despite the absence of major political change, Cuba already has adapted substantially its foreign trade institutions and management training to facilitate the economy's reorientation to world markets. Thus, as difficult and painful as it would have been, Cuba's transition to the new international economy could have been accomplished with considerably more grace and celerity than what is being experienced in Eastern Europe and the Commonwealth of Independent States. It could have been accomplished, that is, were it not for the U.S. embargo and its extraterritorial application.

The evolution of the U.S. embargo policy is covered elsewhere in this volume. Suffice it to note here that since 1962 the embargo has been virtually comprehensive.

The Institute for Economic Research of Juceplan (the central planning board) presently is involved in a project evaluating the economic impact of the U.S. embargo. The study analyzes the impact sector by sector, considering only direct costs from lowered production, higher costs for obtaining goods, and lower prices for some of their foreign sales. Their estimates are obviously preliminary, but they do give some sense of the magnitude of the loss.[7] For the period 1960 to 1990, the total estimated cost of the embargo approached $38 billion. To put this figure in perspective, it is roughly 25 to 35 percent above the level of Cuba's GDP in 1989 or more than double the level of Cuban debt to the U.S.S.R. in that year.

Having lost the lion's share of its trade with the Soviet bloc and all of its aid, the impact of the embargo in 1991 and 1992 is more acute. One way to reckon this impact is to evaluate the possible level of trade that would prevail between Cuba and the United States absent the

7. The dynamic effect of the blockade is not explored in the study. For instance, if the inability of the Cubans to receive spare parts for the U.S. industrial park in the 1960s stimulated the development of Cuba's mechanical and metallurgy industry, then this possible positive influence is not considered. On the other hand, the methodology does not incorporate certain indirect costs. For example, the study considers the additional cost paid for purchasing and transporting medicine from the Soviet bloc, but it does not consider the cost of prolonged illness or death from not having access or timely access to certain medicines. Military defense costs are also excluded.

embargo. A recent study at the Johns Hopkins' School of Advanced International Studies suggested that the trade turnover between Cuba and the United States could reach $6.5 billion a year after the first few years of trade. Not all of this $6.5 billion would be an economic loss to Cuba; roughly half of it would be lower exports for U.S. corporations, and restricted access to Cuban goods and tourism for U.S. consumers.

Costs of the Extraterritorial Embargo (Blockade)

Cuba's efforts to enter the "free trade" of world capitalism has been blocked not only by its inability to conduct commerce with the United States but also by U.S. efforts to prevent Cuba from trading with companies from other countries. U.S. attempts to extend its embargo into a blockade take several forms. First, the U.S. government prohibits the importation of goods into the United States that contain even trace amounts of a Cuban input, whether or not that input has been thoroughly transformed in the course of manufacture. Thus, the French conglomerate *Le Creusot Loire* was told that it could not sell steel containing Cuban nickel to the United States. Understandably, the company then cancelled its contract with Cuba to build factories transforming bagasse into hardboard in exchange for Cuban nickel. Foreign confectionery companies are also affected by this policy. In theory at least they are not allowed to export chocolate bars to the United States that are made with Cuban sugar.

Second, companies operating outside the United States are not allowed to sell to Cuba goods that contain more than 20 percent U.S. inputs or that are based on a U.S. technological design. Foreign companies wishing to sell goods to Cuba that contain less than 20 percent U.S. inputs must apply for a license from the U.S. Treasury Department.[8] An example of this restriction occurred in May 1991 when the Swedish company Alfa-Laval was prohibited from exporting filtration equipment for the Cuban sugar industry because a component filter membrane was of U.S. origin. Third, the U.S. government has proscribed foreign banks which are fully owned by foreign nationals and operate solely on foreign soil from maintaining dollar denominated accounts for Cuba or from conducting dollar denominated commercial transactions involving Cuba. Fourth, U.S. nationals who are directors of companies operating outside of the United States are precluded from dealing with Cuba. Fifth, ships using Cuban ports are not allowed to use U.S. ports on the same voyage.

Sixth, threats and pressure have been employed to deter any economic relations with Cuba. Sometimes these threats are embodied in

8. Presently, goods with between 0 and 10 percent U.S. components have an automatic license and no application is necessary.

legislative initiatives, such as the current Torricelli bill, that call for sanctions to be taken against countries which engage in certain types of transactions with Cuba. Sometimes the pressures are simply in the form of letters or oral communications to companies or countries that the United States would look favorably on excluding Cuba from certain commercial activities or very unfavorably on including Cuba. Thus, for instance, Tabacalera, S.A. of Spain was induced to withdraw from a major and multifaceted investment in the development of tourist facilities on Cayo Coco, off Cuba's north coast.

Seventh, since 1975 subsidiaries of U.S. companies operating in foreign lands have been allowed, subject to certain restrictions, to engage in commerce with Cuba. To do so, however, they are required to apply for and obtain a special license from the U.S. Treasury Department. The total number of license applications grew from 164 in 1980 to 321 in 1990, and the value of this subsidiary trade turnover increased from $292 million in 1980 to $705 million.[9] Of this $705 million, $533 million or 76 percent was Cuban imports, and 71 percent of this was in foodstuffs. Although the balance of trade with U.S. subsidiaries was negative in 1990, it had been positive in 1989 and several previous years. In order of importance, the most active countries involved in this U.S. subsidiary trade in 1990 were Switzerland, Argentina, France, Canada, and Great Britain.

Presently there are two competing tendencies regarding U.S. subsidiary trade. On the one hand, with the collapse of the Eastern European and Soviet markets Cuba is more dependent on developing Western trade. Grain previously imported from the Soviet Union (often shipped in trilateral trade from Canada), for instance, will now have to be purchased directly from the West. Sugar sales to the former CMEA in excess of 5 million tons a year will now have to be sold on world markets. One large player in both the grain and sugar markets is the U.S.-based company, Cargill. In 1990 Cargill's subsidiaries in Switzerland and Canada obtained five different U.S. Treasury licenses to sell grain products to and import sugar from Cuba. Left unencumbered, this and other subsidiary trade would expand very rapidly. Sugar sales alone, at present world prices, would come to over $1 billion.

On the other hand, U.S. policy has become more aggressive. Despite the recognition of all U.S. administrations since 1975 that the curtailment of subsidiary trade impeded sovereign trade policy of foreign

9. This and other data on subsidiary trade comes from Donna Rich Kaplowitz and Michael Kaplowitz, *New Opportunities for U.S.-Cuban Trade* (1992), and from Office of Foreign Assets Control, *An Analysis of Licensed Trade with Cuba by Foreign Subsidiaries of U.S. Companies* (1991). The Treasury offers no figures on the number of license denials and the Cuba desk at the State Department claims that they are few. Officials at Treasury acknowledge, however, that companies call before applying for a license and are given a clear indication at that time whether they need bother applying or not.

nations and, hence, violated international law, the Bush administration now says that it will not veto either the Mack amendment to the Export Administration Act or the Torricelli/Graham bill. These bills, which appear to be on their way to passage, purport to proscribe all trade between U.S. subsidiaries and Cuba.

The key issue then becomes how and to what extent the prohibition is implemented. If it is strictly enforced along with the other extraterritorial restrictions, then Cuba could have severe difficulty placing its raw materials on international markets. In this case, not only U.S. subsidiaries dealing on these markets, such as Cargill and Continental Grain, but also many foreign companies will hesitate to buy Cuban products. The latter will balk because their clients may encounter increased restrictions or regulations about selling to the United States if their company purchases Cuban sugar, citrus, tobacco, coffee, fish products, nickel or cobalt. Or they will balk because the U.S. government will make their trade with other U.S. companies more difficult.

The Torricelli bill also contains a provision that would end all aid and special commercial arrangements for countries that offer Cuba preferential trade. Thus, Mexico and Venezuela may be shut out of preferential access to the U.S. market via CBI or GSP statutes if they sell oil to Cuba at below world market prices, as they do for other Caribbean countries under the San José Agreement. Even without the Torricelli bill, the U.S. government has applied strong pressure which thus far has succeeded in preventing such a deal for Cuba.

Overall, Cuba is exceptionally vulnerable. The value of Cuban imports fell from $8.12 billion in 1989 to $4.06 billion in 1991.[10] U.S. subsidiary imports in 1990 were $533 million. Figures for last year are not yet out, but if they grew by only 10 percent in 1991, they would have accounted for around 15 percent of Cuban imports. Further, as suggested above, the United States seems to have the capacity to affect a broader range of Cuba's commercial relations, for example, up to $1 billion in sugar sales. In November 1991 Ricardo Alarcón, Cuban Ambassador to the United Nations, gave a speech to the General Assembly in which he cited twenty seven different recent cases of trade contracts interrupted by U.S. pressure. Because Cuba's dependence on Western trade was minimal until 1990-91, the U.S. extraterritorial restrictions amounted to little more than a nuisance. Circumstances in 1992 and after are much different. Not only is Cuba more dependent, but U.S. policy is more aggressive.

Today, extraterritorial restrictions constitute a substantial economic threat to Cuba. There are questions, however, about how far or how successfully such policies can be extended. Despite presidential

10. José Luis Rodríguez, *La economía de Cuba ante la cambiante coyuntura internacional, Boletín de Información Sobre La Economía Cubana*, p. 9 (Febrero 1992).

candidate Bill Clinton's recent submission to the financial overtures of Mas Canosa's Cuban American National Foundation (CANF) in endorsing the Torricelli bill at a CANF fundraiser in Miami, there are several factors that mitigate against a strong application of new extraterritorial sanctions. First, neither Bush, nor Clinton, nor Perot can readily afford to alienate U.S. trading partners in the European Community or the Western hemisphere. Just as in 1975, pressure from foreign countries, particularly in the context of ongoing efforts to forge trade liberalization, will make it difficult to implement the Mack or Torricelli bills. Second, U.S businesses are increasingly anxious about losing Cuban trade and investment opportunities to competitors in other countries. They are already beginning to express their interests politically. The implicit promise of Bush administration policy over the last three years has been "just wait a few months, Castro will fall and then you'll have clear access." Each passing month brings new hollowness to this approach and greater agitation in the business community. Third, elementary common sense suggests that the blockade policy is counterproductive to its stated goals of improving human rights, stimulating political opening and promoting economic liberalization in Cuba. There is still some basis for hope that when the financial pressures of the 1992 elections pass, the U.S. approach may move away from the ideologically blinkered policy of blockade toward a more rational, humane, and productive policy of normalization.

PART III

UNITED STATES PROGRAM AND PURPOSES: 1989-1992

For three decades the United States justified its economic measures against Cuba by reference to some combination of Cuba's alliance with a hostile Soviet Union, its support for insurgencies in third countries, and its stationing troops abroad to influence regional conflicts. During the period of the Bush administration, these concerns disappeared from the official explanation of United States policy. There nonetheless was a pronounced intensification of the United States effort to isolate Cuba and undermine its economic viability. The Bush administration articulated the promotion of representative democracy and a market economy as the purpose of these enhanced measures. Congress picked up the same theme with its passage of the Cuban Democracy Act of 1992, intensifying still further the United States economic measures.

Cuba points to this intensification of sanctions notwithstanding abandonment of their traditional rationales as laying bare the fixed intention of the United States to restore its pre-revolution control over the island. Taken at face value, the United States shift in justification substantially reframes the legal and policy issues: Are economic measures of this scope and intensity permissible under international law for the purpose of promoting changes in the internal political character of a sovereign state, and in any event, do such measures advance either their stated goal or United States national interests?

We first set forth at length the Bush administration's explanation of its policies toward Cuba and the text of the Cuban Democracy Act. We provide, by way of contrast, our own review of the prior explanations offered by the United States for its program of economic sanctions. We then trace the intensification of United States efforts during the Bush administration. We also offer a sampling of views advanced in the domestic policy debate as alternative approaches to United States-Cuba relations. The legal issues are addressed in Parts IV and V.

Since the current rationale for the sanctions measures and much of the policy debate make certain assumptions about the Cuban political system, we conclude Part III with excerpts from recent remarks by President Castro on the democratic character of Cuban political institutions. As the documents submitted by Cuba during the General Assembly proceedings reflect, however, the Cuban position is that the nature of its political system is not relevant to an assessment of the United States economic measures. This is so, in Cuba's view, because the true aim of United States policy is unrelated to democratic concerns and, in any event, international law proscribes the United States effort to coerce changes in the political system of another sovereign state.

THE NEW RATIONALE: PROMOTION OF REPRESENTATIVE DEMOCRACY AND A MARKET ECONOMY

[Perhaps the fullest explanation of the Bush administration's purposes in not only continuing but intensifying economic measures against Cuba was provided by Robert S. Gelbard, Principal Deputy Assistant Secretary of State for Inter-American Affairs, in his April 8, 1992 statement to the House Foreign Affairs Committee. Neither there nor in President Bush's statements throughout 1992 is there any reference to the national security or foreign policy concerns which the United States cited in the past. Rather, Mr. Gelbard explained United States policy in these terms:

> The United States has followed a policy of isolating Cuba diplomatically and economically for three decades. We continue that policy today, in an effort to encourage a change to a democratic government in Cuba. To do otherwise would only bolster the regime's repression at home and delay democratic reform.

The Cuban Democracy Act of 1992, Title XVII, Pub. L. No. 102-484, §§ 1701 *et seq.,* 106 Stat. 2575 ("CDA"), contains an elaborate statement of the policy of the United States toward Cuba and specifies the conditions for lifting the United States economic measures. The Bush administration endorsed with enthusiasm the Cuban Democracy Act's goals and principles as identical to its own and, although initially expressing reservations about some of its substantive provisions, in the end embraced all of the statute's initiatives to expand the embargo. President George Bush's letter to Congress, September 22, 1992. The CDA, § 1708(a), provides that, before the President may waive the bill's prohibition on foreign subsidiary trade with Cuba or its restrictions on third-country vessels which trade with Cuba, he must first determine that the government of Cuba

(1) has held free and fair elections conducted under internationally recognized observers;

(2) has permitted opposition parties ample time to organize and campaign for such elections, and has permitted full access to the media to all candidates in the elections;

(3) is showing respect for the basic civil liberties and human rights of the citizens of Cuba;

(4) is moving toward establishing a free market economic system; and

(5) has committed itself to constitutional change that would ensure regular free and fair elections that meet the requirements of paragraph (2).

The CDA, § 1708(b), also links an end to the other aspects of the United States trade embargo to these changes in Cuba's internal political and economic order.

Mr. Gelbard's statement before the House Foreign Affairs Committee follows, as does the Cuban Democracy Act of 1992.]

STATEMENT OF ROBERT S. GELBARD, PRINCIPAL DEPUTY
ASSISTANT SECRETARY OF STATE FOR INTER-AMERICAN
AFFAIRS, BEFORE THE COMMITTEE ON FOREIGN AFFAIRS
OF THE HOUSE OF REPRESENTATIVES, APRIL 8, 1992

Mr. Chairman, thank you for this opportunity to discuss the situation in Cuba, U.S. policy toward that country, and the legislation pending before you, H.R. 4168 [subsequently enacted as the Cuban Democracy Act of 1992].

Cuba's government is isolated today as never before because of three factors: first, the collapse of the Soviet bloc; second, Cuba's own policies which resist democratic and economic reform, violate human rights and drive away new sources of support; and third, a consistent, 30-year U.S. policy of diplomatic and economic isolation.

While Cuba's government is isolated, the Cuban people are not. They know that democratic change has swept through Latin America and the former Soviet bloc. Although their own media contain many distortions, they are aware of world events through international broadcasts. They know relations with Cuba's former allies have changed dramatically. They have witnessed the departure from Cuba of technicians from once friendly nations and the return to Cuba of workers and students who were residents in the former East Germany, Czechoslovakia and the former Soviet Union.

One day the Cuban people—and they alone—will bring change to Cuba. No outsider can predict or determine when or how this will happen, but the depth of Cuba's crisis and the Cuban people's pent-up desire to improve their lives make it certain that change will come.

Many Cubans who work inside the system have done so because it is the only way to obtain education and advancement, not because they believe passionately in communism. But others have rejected the easy way out. More and more Cubans are standing up to the regime. Teachers, trade unionists, and human rights activists are bravely calling for democratic reform.

We are deeply concerned about the question of when and how the change comes. Our hope for a free Cuba is not just an aspiration for a better future for Cuba based on our humanitarian values. U.S. policy has consistently sought this end through a tough program of diplomatic and economic isolation of the Castro regime. Failure to continue this policy of isolation would only prolong the regime and delay the day when Cubans can decide their own future.

We take no pleasure in the suffering of the Cuban people, and we hope change comes soon. We hope it brings a genuine opening to democracy. And above all we hope for peaceful democratic change. Violence would do more than take innocent human lives—it could set off a cycle of revenge and recrimination, thereby preventing Cuba from turning promptly to the massive tasks of building new political institutions, freeing the economy and fostering national reconciliation.

Let me turn now to a discussion of the conditions in Cuba and the policy issues we face.

The Economic Situation in Cuba

1991 was the year when Cuba's economic benefits from the former Soviet bloc dropped precipitously. One top Cuban official, party ideology chief Carlos Aldana, referred to the end of Soviet and East European support as "the second blockade," which has caused an economic crisis that "has not bottomed out."

In 1991, economic aid from the former Soviet Union to Cuba totaled about $1 billion, compared to $4 billion the year before. With the collapse of the Soviet Union, President Yeltsin announced an end to all economic assistance to Cuba. In 1992, little, if any, aid remains. Many Russian civilian advisers have departed. Those that remain will have to be paid in hard currency by the Cuban government. While there may be some residual aid remaining—for example, in the form of technicians—it is clear that Russian aid to Cuba is coming to an end.

Reduced fuel supplies are causing dislocations throughout the Cuban economy, most importantly in the key export crop, sugar, but also in transportation, and in reduced activity throughout the economy. This year's sugar harvest is expected to drop to about 5.8 million tons, 24 percent less than last year. That in turn will further reduce Cuba's capacity to import oil. Public transportation has been cut by more than a third in Havana, and drastically between Cuban cities. Many factories have reduced their work forces due to lack of inputs, spare parts and fuel. Unemployment and under-employment is rapidly growing.

The economic crisis affects all aspects of daily life. Rationing continues on bread, meat, sugar, eggs, milk, basic staples, tobacco and fuel. Even in areas such as the health sector, where the government has long allocated substantial resources, hospitals have experienced shortages of medicine. On January 3, additional transportation cutbacks were announced in Havana, where 48 of 162 bus lines were eliminated. More fuel conservation measures were announced February 3. These include a nationwide program of job-swapping, where workers trade their current jobs for ones closer to their homes. Windmills, beasts of burden and bicycles are being used in increasing numbers to cut fuel consumption. Office workers are going to the countryside in large numbers to work two to four week stints on farms. Cuban officials and media reports are indicating that the government is encouraging some permanent resettlement of urban residents in rural areas to increase farm production. Military exercises are fewer, and military units are raising poultry, pigs, dairy herds and crops for their own consumption. Both Cuban and foreign press reports are describing a rising wave of so-called "economic crimes" such as illegal sales of goods at illegal prices, which are the result of Cubans trying to create sources of income, employment and supply where the state-planned economy is not functioning.

Absent a political decision to reduce the state's role in the economy and allow private initiative, the outlook for the Cuban economy is grim. In 1992, Russia and Kazakhstan have contracted to sell 1 million metric tons and 200,000 metric tons of oil, respectively, to Cuba, compared to 13 million metric tons that went to Cuba from the Soviet Union in 1989. Now that Cuba must pay world prices for oil, it will be able to buy only half of the amount it imported in 1989. Moreover, Cuba's total two-way trade, which in 1989 was $13.5 billion, is expected to be $4.8 billion in 1992.

Cuba is desperately seeking foreign investment and new trading partners. On the whole, it has been unsuccessful. Cuba has found few new trading partners, and has been completely unable to find sources for the products once supplied by the Soviet Union. Cuba is not receiving concessional assistance or favorable aid terms for its oil imports, despite Castro's personal request to Latin leaders. Cuba's total imports have fallen more than 50 percent. On the assistance side, no government has been willing to replace the former Soviet Union. Most governments have ended aid programs which were maintained during the 1980s.

The Political Situation

If 1991 answered a basic question about Cuba's prospects for continued subsidies from abroad, it also answered a key political question. Last year the regime relied increasingly upon repression and ideological discipline, not reform, to deal with its internal critics.

In the months preceding last October's Fourth Party Congress, the Cuban public hoped that the Congress would bring some important reforms. In the political sphere, direct elections to the National Assembly were mentioned; in the economic, the reopening of free farmers markets. These reforms, while far from revolutionary, would have represented an admission that a measure of economic and political freedom is needed to alleviate Cuba's crisis.

When the Congress did take place, few reforms were adopted. Finally, in March, the leadership announced that direct elections to the National Assembly would be carried out next October, but made it clear that the single party system would remain unaltered.

The idea of reestablishing farmers markets was derided at the Congress as an ideological error, even though, until their abolition in 1986, they contributed substantially to food supplies and to the six percent annual growth that the Cuban economy experienced in the early 1980s. Since the farmers markets were abolished in 1985, there has been no growth in the Cuban economy.

The National Assembly's December debate, rather than following up on the minor reforms proposed by the Party Congress, focused on revolutionary discipline: the interior minister warned about the threat of crime; party ideology chief Carlos Aldana called human rights activists "traitors to the nation" who will be summarily punished; and Castro himself extolled the creation of "rapid action brigades"—mobs that suppress dissent. Two months earlier, Archbishop Jaime Ortega of Havana had opposed the participation of Catholics in these brigades as activity contrary to Christian values. "Our Christian conscience," Ortega said, "not only says 'no' to participation in those actions; it also feels concern and suffers whenever those actions occur."

Human Rights

Assistant Secretary for Inter-American Affairs Bernard Aronson testified before this committee last July about Cuba's human rights record. Since then, the repression has worsened, and the international community has seen and condemned it. Cuba's human rights activists are people of extraordinary courage. They deserve even wider attention from the democratic community.

The protest last September of the Cuban Democratic Coalition in front of the Villa Marista, the state security headquarters in Havana, brought world attention to the Cuban regime's failure to allow peaceful transition. Coalition leaders Daniel and Tomas Aspillaga received sentences of up to two years for disorderly conduct and incitement to crime.

On October 7, the eleven groups making up the Cuban Democratic Convergence held a press conference three days before the Fourth Party Congress. They called on the Congress to make bold democratic reforms including formation of a provisional government, an elected constituent assembly and amnesty for political prisoners. Eighteen Democratic Convergence members were arrested; three got three-year prison terms for "clandestine publishing" and "incitement to crime." One Convergence leader, Luis Pita Santos, was arrested and sent to a mental hospital after he called for peaceful demonstrations against the regime. He was held without charge until late last month when he was suddenly put on trial for "illicit association," "clandestine printing," and "contempt."

Recently the Cuban government has used supposedly spontaneous demonstrations, called "acts of repudiation," to intimidate human rights activists. One of these occurred last November 19, when a mob of two hundred ransacked Alternative Criterion leader Maria Elena Cruz Varela's house, dragged her down four flights of stairs and forced papers she had written into her mouth. Filmmaker Marco Antonio Abad was arrested as he tried to videotape this attack. No one was punished for the attack; instead, a Cuban court sentenced the victim, Cruz Varela, to two years for "felonious association and slander." Six other Alternative Criterion members who faced mob violence were similarly treated in the courts. They are now serving one- to two-year sentences.

The Cuban government also took advantage of the capture of three Cuban exiles in December to impugn the motives of peaceful human rights activists. A regime-sponsored television program about the exiles alleged that they had a list of names, including those of human rights leaders who had called for peaceful change. Shortly thereafter, Gustavo and Sebastian Arcos of the Cuban Committee for Human Rights were assaulted by a mob and arrested; Sebastian Arcos and Harmony Movement leader Yndamiro Restano, who has been detained since December, now face trial for "rebellion."

The United States supports the brave people who are peacefully demanding greater respect for human rights and democracy in Cuba. Our Interests Section maintains contacts with these individuals, as do other diplomatic missions. We do not provide assistance to any group, as to do so would compromise their position as independent voices calling for reform. In our diplomatic contacts with other nations, we constantly return to the subject of the Cuban regime's deplorable treatment of those who dissent from its rule. And these discussions are bearing fruit.

In recent years, the United Nations Human Rights Commission (UNHRC) has been much more willing than in the past to call Cuba to account for its violations of fundamental human rights. It voted in 1991 to create for the first time a Special Representative for Cuba. The Special Representative, though prohibited by Castro from visiting the island, compiled a report containing nearly 150 instances of human rights violations. That report concludes that repression against those seeking "non-violent changes in circumstances which they find intolerable" has increased, and that "the rights of free expression, political participation and free association have been seriously curtailed."

On March 3 at the annual meeting of the UNHRC in Geneva, the international community responded to Cuba's most recent wave of attacks by deploring that country's human rights record and its failure to abide by the UNHRC's resolution and by upgrading the Special Representative to a Special Rapporteur. Incidentally, both Russia and Ukraine voted with the U.S. in favor of this upgrade. Despite its membership on the Commission, Cuba, which had defied the earlier resolution and refused to allow the Special Representative to visit Cuba, denounced what it called the UN's "interference" and announced its intention to likewise refuse to admit the UN Special Rapporteur.

In this hemisphere as well, more attention is being given to Cuba's human rights record. The Inter-American Commission on Human Rights (IACHR) recently expressed its "deep concern over the mounting restrictions" on dissidents in Cuba. The Commission noted that the regime had "hardened its attitude" toward dissent after it "failed to respond to repeated requests" from other nations in the hemisphere to relax its restrictions and open its political system.

Cuba in the International Community

The UN Human Rights Commission is but one measure of Cuba's growing international isolation. Last November, at the UN General Assembly, Cuba offered a resolution condemning the U.S. trade embargo. As the day of debate approached, only North Korea, Laos and Vietnam had shown interest. Ultimately, the resolution was withdrawn for lack of support. In 1989, Cuba succeeded in passing a general anti-embargo resolution through the General Assembly. We succeeded in defeating the 1991 effort because we convincingly argued that the embargo was justified because each country should be able to determine its own commercial relations. Had the embargo applied to U.S. companies in third countries, Cuba would likely have won the UN debate.

At the July summit at Guadalajara, Cuba was the sole dictatorship represented. President Lacalle of Uruguay described Castro's presentation as "a speech from the trenches about a state of siege, the closing of doors, and about staying entrenched in his old positions.... We know the consequences of the preachings of a man like him who made an entire generation believe that their country could be fixed with bullets and bombs."

At Guadalajara, President Perez of Venezuela called on Cuba to make democratic reforms. At a later summit in October on the Mexican island Cozumel, he and Presidents Salinas of Mexico and Gaviria of Colombia renewed a call for democratic reform. Furthermore, none of these Latin oil producers has stepped in to provide oil at concessional prices to replace the old Soviet subsidy. Just last month, the Rio Group called on Cuba to begin a "definitive democratization process."

U.S. Policy Toward Cuba

The United States has followed a policy of isolating Cuba diplomatically and economically for three decades. We continue that policy today in an effort to encourage a change to a democratic government in Cuba. To do otherwise would only bolster the regime's repression at home and delay democratic reform.

Thoughtful, respected analysts in the exile community and the academic world argue that the goal of peaceful change in Cuba would be better served by easing or ending the embargo. We respect their views, but we disagree. If the U.S. ended the embargo leaving the Castro dictatorship in place, we would have no leverage for reform in Cuba. We would leave the Cuban people without hope of a better future. Most seriously, U.S. trade and investment could strengthen communism in Cuba rather than helping to bring it to an end.

Those who argue to drop the embargo have the burden of demonstrating how new travel and investment would support independent Cubans rather than strengthen the state, and how it would create greater pressure for change than that which now exists due to the economic crisis. In our view, the Cuban government tightly controls foreign investment and the areas in which these investments may occur. This does not help the average Cuban, nor does it foster change. Most new foreign investment in Cuba is in tourism. But this effort more and more reminds the Cuban people of the type of society they were seeking to end when they rejected the Batista dictatorship. The regime's system of "tourist apartheid" is designed to keep Cubans away from foreigners who might bring ideas of freedom and free choice.

Our Cuba policy has responded to the collapse in the communist world not by changing basic principles, but by taking new measures tailored to the possibilities of a new era. Cuba has isolated itself through its own behavior, but U.S. policy has also played a significant part in increasing Cuba's isolation.

From the beginning of this Administration, we put Cuba at the center of the U.S.-Soviet agenda. In the March 1989 Bipartisan Accord, the Administration and Congress called on the Soviet Union and Cuba to stop their aid for subversion in Central America. In announcing that accord, President Bush pressed Cuba and the Soviets to live up to their pledge to support the Esquipulas treaty. We have also consistently urged the Soviets, and now the independent states, not to aid the Cuban government. We have pointed out that Soviet subsidies were inconsistent with the Gorbachev "new thinking," and even less so with the Yeltsin reform program. As Secretary Baker has noted, "we raise this issue every time we sit down with the Soviets." The fact that subsidies are disappearing reflects more than the movement to reform—it is a result of persistent U.S. diplomacy.

We also argue in regular, worldwide diplomatic contacts that the best way for democracies to promote change in Cuba is to press for democratic change and to back that up with reduced economic ties. Expanded trade or economic benefits only strengthen the Cuban government and delay inevitable reform. More and more, we find that Cuba's economic policies and the extreme climate of uncertainty are persuading people not to put money into Cuba.

We regularly review the effectiveness of the embargo, and make changes when needed. Last year, in response to the Cuban government's charging exorbitant processing fees—in dollars—for its citizens to be approved for tourist travel to the U.S., we changed our procedure. We sharply limited the amount that may be transferred to Cuba for travel to the U.S. In the past, Cuban fees averaged $700 to $1000 per person above the cost of airfare.

In addition, we continually encourage our allies not to aid the Cuban regime until it initiates democratic reform. Increasingly, they are following this advice. We urge them to review investment and trade with Cuba in light of the Cuban government's inability and unwillingness to pay its debt and its arbitrary treatment of foreign investment. We are particularly concerned about the property of U.S. citizens which was expropriated by the Cuban government without compensation. To this end, we have urged foreign governments to ensure that potential investors in Cuba are not becoming entwined in deals involving properties which do not have clear title.

Contingency Plans

We have analyzed a number of possible courses of events in Cuba and formulated some possible U.S. responses. I cannot discuss these in detail, but I can offer some general comments.

In the interest of encouraging peaceful change, we have worked to dispel the Cuban government's argument that the United States is poised to attack Cuba. In the past year, the President, the Secretary of State, and Assistant Secretary Aronson have publicly reiterated that we pose no threat and have no aggressive intentions toward Cuba. We hope for democratic change, but claim no right to order the affairs of Cuba.

The future of Cuba depends on the Cuban people. If there is violence in Cuba, we will seek the mediation of the Organization of American States and the United Nations. We will work with these organizations to end violence, to promote stability, and to secure a democratic transition.

We will not permit a mass migration to the U.S. The laws of the U.S. will be enforced. We expect all U.S. citizens and residents to obey the laws of this land. We seek to continue the current migration accord between the U.S. and Cuba in order to ensure orderly and normal migration. Under this accord over 23,000 Cubans have come to live in this country. Make no mistake, we do not intend to permit another Mariel boatlift.

No one knows how change will come to Cuba. However, people in Cuba and in the democratic community should know that we are serious in our desire to see peaceful democratic change come to Cuba—a change that is free of bloodshed and revenge, that opens the way to a genuine democratic system. When that change becomes possible, we will be prepared to help bring it about, and we will urge international support. That could include support for a democratic transition and elections. The possibilities will depend on decisions and actions taken by people in Cuba, and on whether those decisions represent a genuine effort to build democracy. The important point is that we are prepared to help. Like the rest of the democratic community, we are eager to build good relations with a democratic Cuba.

The Road Ahead

Mr. Chairman, we will continue to press for peaceful democratic change in Cuba, we will continue the embargo, we will continue to reiterate that we have no hostile intentions toward Cuba, and we will continue to inform the Cuban people—through Radio and TV Marti and other means—of world events in the hope that Cuba will also share in the return to democracy.

I would like to state here one basic principle that should guide our discussions. Today Cuba stands isolated because the world community—the UN, the European Community, Latin America, human rights monitors, even Russia—clearly recognizes that the Cuban government is denying freedom to its people. Cuba's government is violating the basic, minimal standards of this hemisphere's democratic community. That is where the focus should remain; on the conflict between Cuba's repressive government and the Cuban people's aspirations for freedom.

We commend the Cuban Democracy Act for its goal of bringing about peaceful democratic change in Cuba. We are impressed by its vision of future close and friendly relations between the U.S. and a democratic Cuba. We share this vision with the sponsors of the Cuban Democracy Act. Where we differ is not in the goal, but in aspects of the strategy. Where the Cuban Democracy Act would demand adherence by our allies to a policy similar to ours, we would respect their sovereignty and ask their cooperation. Where the proposed legislation would remove the focus on Cuba and shift the burden of action to the U.S., we would return the focus to Cuba and the failure of the Castro regime to implement change.

One provision in the Cuban Democracy Act, for example, instructs the U.S. to negotiate with governments which trade with Cuba agreements to restrict their trade in a manner consistent with U.S. policy. In short, we would be told to open talks to secure their agreement to an embargo on Cuba. In our view this provision would infringe severely on the President's constitutional authority to conduct foreign policy. Second, our attempts would be rejected. While many governments agree that Cuba should not receive aid, few want to impose an embargo against it.

Third, such a provision diminishes support for our Cuba policy. We believe we have had excellent results in persuading countries around the world to refrain from closer economic ties with Cuba. We have been successful because we are trying to convince, not demand cooperation from sovereign nations, and because Cuba's economy offers so little objective incentive to investment. It would do the democratic cause little good to give the Cuban government a new excuse to claim it is a victim of U.S. policy. It would shift the spotlight away from the Cuban government's refusal to permit democracy, and it would separate us from democracies whose cooperation we need to have to promote a peaceful transition in Cuba.

Another provision of the proposed legislation would deny U.S. aid and other benefits to any country which aids Cuba or provides favorable terms of trade. Although the independent states of the former Soviet Union have cut aid dramatically and significantly reduced trade to Cuba, this Act's definition of assistance is so broad that even a residual amount of trade or aid could disqualify these states from receiving badly-needed assistance from the U.S.—assistance that President Bush has pledged to give these new republics at a time of great opportunity and uncertainty. These results are clearly not the intended outcome of the sponsors, but it would be an unfortunate consequence. It would be doubly unfortunate at a time when world events are combining with U.S. policy to isolate Cuba and to place Havana under more pressure than it has ever faced before to abandon communism and give the Cuban people their freedom.

We share Congress' goal of a speedy transition to a peaceful and democratic Cuba. We agree that this goal may be best achieved through the economic and political isolation of Cuba. We have been successful in gaining the cooperation of our friends because they are equally concerned about the bitter future Cubans face, if there is no change in government. But measures that command their cooperation or demand their imposition of a policy similar to our own will only diminish their commitment to withhold aid from Cuba, and will result in their governments taking actions harmful to U.S. trade and investment.

The record shows that we will be successful if we work with the world community. There is very little aid going to Cuba. Since 1989, trade has fallen by over fifty percent. Cuba faces its most severe crisis in 33 years. The Cuban government's refusal to adopt economic and political reforms only deepens the crisis and hastens the day of change. If we stay the course, and work together, we can with the help of our friends—particularly those in Latin America, the OAS, and the UN—bring about a stable, prosperous, democratic Cuba.

We hope we can work with the Congress to resolve differences in approach. My colleagues and I are prepared to answer your questions about specific parts of the bill.

CUBAN DEMOCRACY ACT OF 1992

(Title XVII, Pub. L. No. 102-484, §§ 1701 *et seq.;* 106 Stat. 2575)

Sec. 1701. Short Title.

This title may be cited as the "Cuban Democracy Act of 1992."

Sec. 1701. Findings.

The Congress makes the following findings:

(1) The government of Fidel Castro has demonstrated consistent disregard for internationally accepted standards of human rights and for democratic values. It restricts the Cuban people's exercise of freedom of speech, press, assembly, and other rights recognized by the Universal Declaration of Human Rights adopted by the General Assembly of the United Nations on December 10, 1948. It has refused to admit into Cuba the representative of the United Nations Human Rights Commission appointed to investigate human rights violations on the island.

(2) The Cuban people have demonstrated their yearning for freedom and their increasing opposition to the Castro government by risking their lives in organizing independent, democratic activities on the island and by undertaking hazardous flights for freedom to the United States and other countries.

(3) The Castro government maintains a military-dominated economy that has decreased the well-being of the Cuban people in order to

enable the government to engage in military interventions and subversive activities throughout the world and, especially, in the Western Hemisphere. These have included involvement in narcotics trafficking and support for the FMLN guerrillas in El Salvador.

(4) There is no sign that the Castro regime is prepared to make any significant concessions to democracy or to undertake any form of democratic opening. Efforts to suppress dissent through intimidation, imprisonment, and exile have accelerated since the political changes that have occurred in the former Soviet Union and Eastern Europe.

(5) Events in the former Soviet Union and Eastern Europe have dramatically reduced Cuba's external support and threaten Cuba's food and oil supplies.

(6) The fall of communism in the former Soviet Union and Eastern Europe, the now universal recognition in Latin America and the Caribbean that Cuba provides a failed model of government and development, and the evident inability of Cuba's economy to survive current trends, provide the United States and the international democratic community with an unprecedented opportunity to promote a peaceful transition to democracy in Cuba.

(7) However, Castro's intransigence increases the likelihood that there could be a collapse of the Cuban economy, social upheaval, or widespread suffering. The recently concluded Cuban Communist Party Congress has underscored Castro's unwillingness to respond positively to increasing pressures for reform either from within the party or without.

(8) The United States cooperated with its European and other allies to assist the difficult transitions from Communist regimes in Eastern Europe. Therefore, it is appropriate for those allies to cooperate with United States policy to promote a peaceful transition in Cuba.

Sec. 1703. Statement of Policy.

It should be the policy of the United States—

(1) to seek a peaceful transition to democracy and a resumption of economic growth in Cuba through the careful application of sanctions directed at the Castro government and support for the Cuban people;

(2) to seek the cooperation of other democratic countries in this policy;

(3) to make clear to other countries that, in determining its relations with them, the United States will take into account their willingness to cooperate in such a policy;

(4) to seek the speedy termination of any remaining military or technical assistance, subsidies, or other forms of assistance to the Government of Cuba from any of the independent states of the former Soviet Union;

(5) to continue vigorously to oppose the human rights violations of the Castro regime;

(6) to maintain sanctions on the Castro regime so long as it continues to refuse to move toward democratization and greater respect for human rights;

(7) to be prepared to reduce the sanctions in carefully calibrated ways in response to positive developments in Cuba;

(8) to encourage free and fair elections to determine Cuba's political future;

(9) to request the speedy termination of any military or technical assistance, subsidies, or other forms of assistance to the Government of Cuba from the government of any other country; and

(10) to initiate immediately the development of a comprehensive United States policy toward Cuba in a post-Castro era.

Sec. 1704. International Cooperation

(a) Cuban Trading Partners—The President should encourage the governments of countries that conduct trade with Cuba to restrict their trade and credit relations with Cuba in a manner consistent with the purposes of this title.

(b) Sanctions Against Countries Assisting Cuba

(1) Sanctions.—The President may apply the following sanctions to any country that provides assistance to Cuba:

(A) The government of such country shall not be eligible for assistance under the Foreign Assistance Act of 1961 or assistance or sales under the Arms Export Control Act.

(B) Such country shall not be eligible, under any program, for forgiveness or reduction of debt owed to the United States Government.

(2) Definition of Assistance.—For purposes of paragraph (1), the term "assistance to Cuba"—

(A) means assistance to or for the benefit of the Government of Cuba that is provided by grant, concessional sale, guaranty, or insurance, or by any other means on terms more favorable than that generally available in the applicable market, whether in the form of a loan, lease, credit, or otherwise, and such terms include subsidies for exports to Cuba and favorable tariff treatment of articles that are the growth, product, or manufacture of Cuba; and

(B) does not include—

(i) donations of food to nongovernmental organizations or individuals in Cuba, or

(ii) exports of medicines or medical supplies, instruments, or equipment that would be permitted under section 1705(c) of this Act.

(3) Applicability of Section.—This section, and any sanctions imposed pursuant to this section, shall cease to apply at such time as the President makes and reports to the Congress a determination under section 1708(a).

Sec. 1705. Support for the Cuban People.

(a) Provisions of Law Affected.—The provisions of this section apply notwithstanding any other provision of law, including section 620(a) of the Foreign Assistance Act of 1961, and notwithstanding the exercise of authorities, before the enactment of this Act, under section 5(b) of the Trading With the Enemy Act, the International Emergency Economic Powers Act, or the Export Administration Act of 1979.

(b) Donations of Food.—Nothing in this or any other Act shall prohibit donations of food to nongovernmental organizations or individuals in Cuba.

(c) Exports of Medicines and Medical Supplies.—Exports of medicines or medical supplies, instruments, or equipment to Cuba shall not be restricted—

(1) except to the extent such restrictions would be permitted under section 5(m) of the Export Administration Act of 1979 or section 203(b)(2) of the International Emergency Economic Powers Act;

(2) except in a case in which there is a reasonable likelihood that the item to be exported will be used for purposes of torture or other human rights abuses;

(3) except in a case in which there is a reasonable likelihood that the item to be exported will be reexported; and

(4) except in a case in which the item to be exported could be used in the production of any biotechnological product.

(d) Requirements for Certain Exports.—

(1) On Site Verifications.—

(A) Subject to subparagraph (B), an export may be made under subsection (c) only if the President determines that the United States Government is able to verify, by on site inspections and other appropriate means, that the exported item is to be used for the purposes for which it was intended and only for the use and benefit of the Cuban people.

(B) Subparagraph (A) does not apply to donations to nongovernmental organizations in Cuba of medicines for humanitarian purposes.

(2) Licenses.—Exports permitted under subsection (c) shall be made pursuant to specific licenses issued by the United States Government.

(e) Telecommunications Services and Facilities.—

(1) Telecommunications services.—Telecommunications services between the United States and Cuba shall be permitted.

(2) Telecommunications facilities.—Telecommunications facilities are authorized in such quantity and of such quality as may be necessary to provide efficient and adequate telecommunications services between the United States and Cuba.

(3) Licensing of payments to Cuba.—

(A) The President may provide for the issuance of licenses for the full or partial payment to Cuba of amounts due Cuba as a result of the provision of telecommunications services authorized by this subsection, in a manner that is consistent with the public interest and the purposes of this title, except that this paragraph shall not require any withdrawal from any account blocked pursuant to regulations issued under section 5(b) of the Trading With the Enemy Act.

(B) If only partial payments are made to Cuba under subparagraph (A), the amounts withheld from Cuba shall be deposited in an account in a banking institution in the United States. Such account shall be blocked in the same manner as any other account containing funds in which Cuba has any interest, pursuant to regulations issued under section 5(b) of the Trading With the Enemy Act.

(4) Authority of Federal Communications Commission.—Nothing in this subsection shall be construed to supersede the authority of the Federal Communications Commission.

(f) Direct Mail Delivery to Cuba—The United States Postal Service shall take such actions as are necessary to provide direct mail service to and from Cuba, including, in the absence of common carrier service between the two countries, the use of charter service providers.

(g) Assistance to Support Democracy in Cuba—The United States Government may provide assistance, through appropriate nongovernmental organizations, for the support of individuals and organizations to promote nonviolent democratic change in Cuba.

Sec. 1706. Sanctions

(a) Prohibition of Certain Transactions Between Certain United States Firms and Cuba.—

(1) Prohibition.—Notwithstanding any other provision of law, no license may be issued for any transaction described in section 515.559 of title 31, Code of Federal Regulations, as in effect on July 1, 1989.

(2) Applicability to Existing Contracts.—Paragraph (1) shall not affect any contract entered into before the date of the enactment of this Act.

(b) Prohibitions on Vessels.—

(1) Vessels engaging in trade.—Beginning on the 61st day after the date of the enactment of this Act, a vessel which enters a port or place in Cuba to engage in the trade of goods or services may not, within 180 days after departure from such port or place in Cuba, load or unload any freight at any place in the United States, except pursuant to a license issued by the Secretary of the Treasury.

(2) Vessels carrying goods or passengers to or from Cuba.—Except as specifically authorized by the Secretary of the Treasury, a vessel carrying goods or passengers to or from Cuba or carrying goods in which Cuba or a Cuban national has any interest may not enter a United States port.

(3) Inapplicability of ship stores general license.—No commodities which may be exported under a general license described in section 771.9 of title 15, Code of Federal Regulations, as in effect on May 1, 1992, may be exported under a general license to any vessel carrying goods or passengers to or from Cuba or carrying goods in which Cuba or a Cuban national has an interest.

(4) Definitions.—As used in this subsection—

(A) the term "vessel" includes every description of water craft or other contrivance used, or capable of being used, as a means of transportation in water, but does not include aircraft; and

(B) the term "United States" includes the territories and possessions of the United States and the customs waters of the United States (as defined in section 401 of the Tariff Act of 1930 (19 U.S.C. 1401));and

(C) the term "Cuban national" means a national of Cuba, as the term "national" is defined in section 515.302 of title 31, Code of Federal Regulations, as of August 1, 1992.

(c) Restrictions on Remittances to Cuba.—The President shall establish strict limits on remittances to Cuba by United States persons for the purpose of financing the travel of Cubans to the United States, in order to ensure that such remittances reflect only the reasonable costs associated with such travel, and are not used by the Government of Cuba as a means of gaining access to United States currency.

(d) Clarification of Applicability of Sanctions.—The prohibitions contained in subsections (a), (b), and (c) shall not apply with respect to any activity otherwise permitted by section 1705 or section 1707 of this Act or any activity which may not be regulated or prohibited under section 5(b)(4) of the Trading With the Enemy Act (50 U.S.C. App. 5 (b)(4)).

Sec. 1707. Policy Toward a Transitional Cuban Government.

Food, medicine, and medical supplies for humanitarian purposes should be made available for Cuba under the Foreign Assistance Act of 1961 and the Agricultural Trade Development and Assistance Act of 1954 if the President determines and certifies to the Committee on Foreign Affairs of the House of Representatives and the Committee on Foreign Relations of the Senate that the government in power in Cuba—

(1) has made a public commitment to hold free and fair elections for a new government within 6 months and is proceeding to implement that decision;

(2) has made a public commitment to respect, and is respecting, internationally recognized human rights and basic democratic freedoms; and

(3) is not providing weapons or funds to any group, in any other country, that seeks the violent overthrow of the government of that country.

Sec. 1708. Policy Toward a Democratic Cuban Government.

(a) Waiver of Restrictions.—The President may waive the requirements of section 1706 if the President determines and reports to the Congress that the Government of Cuba—

(1) has held free and fair elections conducted under internationally recognized observers;

(2) has permitted opposition parties ample time to organize and campaign for such elections, and has permitted full access to the media to all candidates in the elections;

(3) is showing respect for the basic civil liberties and human rights of the citizens of Cuba;

(4) is moving toward establishing a free market economic system; and

(5) has committed itself to constitutional change that would ensure regular free and fair elections that meet the requirements of paragraph (2).

(b) Policies.—If the President makes a determination under subsection (a), the President shall take the following actions with respect to a Cuban Government elected pursuant to elections described in subsection (a):

(1) To encourage the admission or reentry of such government to international organizations and international financial institutions.

(2) To provide emergency relief during Cuba's transition to a viable economic system.

(3) To take steps to end the United States trade embargo of Cuba.

Sec. 1709. Existing Claims Not Affected.

Except as provided in section 1705(a), nothing in this title affects the provisions of section 620(a)(2) of the Foreign Assistance Act of 1961.

Sec. 1710. Enforcement.

(a) Enforcement Authority.—The authority to enforce this title shall be carried out by the Secretary of the Treasury. The Secretary of the Treasury shall exercise the authorities of the Trading With the Enemy Act in enforcing this title. In carrying out this subsection, the Secretary of the Treasury shall take the necessary steps to ensure that activities permitted under section 1705 are carried out for the purposes set forth in this title and not for purposes of the accumulation by the Cuban Government of excessive amounts of United States currency or the accumulation of excessive profits by any person or entity.

(b) Authorization of Appropriations.—There are authorized to be appropriated to the Secretary of the Treasury such sums as may be necessary to carry out this title.

(c) Penalties Under the Trading With the Enemy Act.—Section 16 of the Trading With the Enemy Act (50 U.S.C. App. 16) is amended—

(1) by striking "that whoever" and inserting "(a) Whoever"; and

(2) by adding at the end the following:

"(b)(1) The Secretary of the Treasury may impose a civil penalty of not more than $50,000 on any person who violates any license, order, rule, or regulation issued under this Act.

"(2) Any property, funds, securities, papers, or other articles or documents, or any vessel, together with its tackle, apparel, furniture, and equipment that is the subject of a violation under paragraph (1) shall, at the discretion of the Secretary of the Treasury, be forfeited to the United States Government.

"(3) The penalties provided under this subsection may not be imposed for—

"(A) news gathering, research, or the export or import of, or transmission of, information or informational materials; or

"(B) clearly defined educational or religious activities, or activities of recognized human rights organizations, that are reasonably limited in frequency, duration, and number of participants.

"(4) The penalties provided under this subsection may be imposed only on the record after opportunity for an agency hearing in accordance with sections 554 through 557 of title 5, United States Code, with the right to prehearing discovery.

"(5) Judicial review of any penalty imposed under this subsection may be had to the extent provided in section 702 of title 5, United States Code."

(d) Applicability of Penalties.—The penalties set forth in section 16 of the Trading With the Enemy Act shall apply to violations of this title to the same extent as such penalties apply to violations under that Act.

(e) Office of Foreign Assets Control.—The Department of the Treasury shall establish and maintain a branch of the Office of Foreign Assets Control in Miami, Florida, in order to strengthen the enforcement of this title.

Sec. 1711. Definition.

As used in this title, the term "United States person" means any United States citizen or alien admitted for permanent residence in the United States, and any corporation, partnership, or other organization organized under the laws of the United States.

Sec. 1712. Effective Date.

This title shall take effect on the date of the enactment of this Act.

NOTE ON THE PASSAGE OF THE CUBAN DEMOCRACY ACT

The Cuban Democracy Act passed the Senate on September 18, 1992 by a vote of sixty-one to twenty-four and passed the House on September 22, 1992 by a vote of 276 to 135. In signing the measure in a special ceremony in Miami, President Bush recognized the leaders of the Cuban-American community assembled there as "key forces behind this Cuban Democracy Act." Remarks on Signing the Cuban Democracy Act of 1992, 28 Weekly Comp. Pres. Doc. 2071 (October 23, 1992). The press has generally considered Jorge Mas Canosa of the Cuban American National Foundation to be the bill's chief architect. *See, e.g., Miami Herald,* p.1C (April 26, 1992); *Miami Herald,* p.1A (October 23, 1992). In April 1992 the Democratic candidate for President, Bill Clinton, had announced his support for the bill at a campaign stop in Miami organized by Mas Canosa. *Miami Herald,* p.1A (April 24, 1992). President Bush supported the measure with increasing vigor through the spring and summer of 1992 and, on the eve of its vote wrote the House to let each member "know that I strongly support" passage of this "important bill." Letter of September 22, 1992.

It is difficult to assess whether passage of the Cuban Democracy Act represented a true consensus on United States policy toward Cuba notwithstanding the lopsided votes in Congress and the bill's bipartisan support. At the time of the Democratic candidate's endorsement of the bill, polls showed a close presidential race and Florida appeared to be a key swing state, with the Cuban-American vote of possibly decisive weight. *Miami Herald,* p.1C (April 26, 1992). Whatever their view of its merits, both the Clinton campaign and the Democratic leadership in the Congress saw no electoral advantage in opposing the measure and some risk to their party's presidential ambitions in failing to support it. *See, e.g., Wall Street Journal,* p.A6 (September 25, 1992); *Newsweek,* p.48 (September 14, 1992). Polls show the country as a whole largely indifferent to Cuba-United States relations and so the new administration and Congress may have more political latitude than during the election. *See* Commission on U.S.-Latin American Relations, United States-Cuban Relations: An Issues Brief (March 1992).

It is noteworthy as well that, while the CDA's sponsor, Rep. Robert Torricelli (D-N.J.), and the delegation from Florida, strongly supported the measure, the Democratic chairs of the Senate Foreign Relations Committee and of its Subcommittee on Western Hemispheric Affairs opposed its passage, 138 Cong. Rec. S14058 *et seq.* (September 18, 1992), and that such key House figures as Rep. Lee Hamilton (D-Ind.), scheduled to replace Rep. Dante Fascell of Florida as chair of the House Foreign Affairs Committee, expressed substantial skepticism even though voting in the bill's favor. Transcript of Mark-Up Session, House Foreign Affairs Committee, May 21, 1992. It is also perhaps of some significance that at the same time as the House was approving the Cuban Democracy Act, the Democratic chairs of eleven House committees or subcommittees as well as Rep. Hamilton joined in co-sponsoring a bill which would eliminate the restrictions on United States citizens paying travel-related expenses to Cuba as well as other embargoed countries. H.R. 5406, 102d Cong., 2d Sess. (June 16, 1992). It may be recalled that in a short-lived relaxation of the United States measures, the last Democratic president, Jimmy Carter, had lifted the restrictions on travel to Cuba in 1977 as a step toward the normalization of relations.

NOTE COMPARING UNITED STATES POLICY TOWARD CHINA

In seeking to identify the underlying purposes of United States policy, consideration may be given not only to the recent shift in rationales but to the disparate treatment of Cuba and other countries which the United States considers equally undemocratic and repressive. Assistant Secretary of State Aronson offered an explanation for this disparate treatment in his July 11, 1991 testimony before the Subcommittee on Western Hemisphere Affairs, House Foreign Affairs Committee, *Cuba and A Changing World: The U.S.-Soviet-Cuban Triangle, Hearings before the Subcomm. on Western Hemisphere Affairs of House Comm. on Foreign Affairs*, 102d Cong., 1st Sess. 88 (1991). The colloquy follows.

Rep. Solarz: The president, as you know, has been urging the Congress to renew MFN status for China on the grounds that by maintaining our trading relationship with the People's Republic, we'll be in a better position to encourage progress in the area of democratization and human rights.

Can you perhaps enlighten those of us who have not been able to immediately grasp the logic behind our position as to why we think that MFN and a trading relationship is beneficial even in terms of democratization and human rights in China, but appears not to be beneficial in terms of Cuba, where I gather the president isn't considering asking us to lift the embargo, let alone provide MFN status to them? I'm not suggesting we do that—

Aronson: No, I understand. It's a fair question.

Rep. Solarz: —but I think it's important for you to give us the rationale.

Aronson: It's a fair question, though in terms of making the best case for why MFN should be granted to China, I would leave that to my colleague Dick Solomon; but there are differences. First of all, China had—the People's Republic of China had initiated market economic reforms before MFN was granted. That is not the case with Cuba. In fact, the opposite is the case. The Cuban government did initiate some modest market economic reforms in agriculture in the early '80s, which in fact were having some benefits and increasing production. The Communist Party then reversed course in 1986 and denounced these reforms and instituted a policy of rectification and eliminated them, including bonuses and overtime for workers. So that is one difference.

Secondly, we don't have a trade relationship with Cuba. We do have a trading relationship with China, so it's [MFN status] a relevant issue with China; it is not a relevant issue with Cuba.

And third, it is our policy to deny hard currency to the Cuban regime. That is a policy goal of the United States. And one reason we do this is the 32-year record of Cuban intervention in governments around the world, military and revolutionary intervention, which continues to this date. Now, there are analogues in China—we have missile proliferation concerns, but I would say that there is a fundamental difference.

Rep. Solarz: And finally, I gather it is the hope of the administration that somehow or other democracy will be established in Cuba. Could you tell us what, if anything, the administration is doing or is contemplating doing to facilitate the achievement of that objective beyond what we've been doing in Democratic and Republican administrations in the last 30 years, which is to maintain the embargo on Cuba and to try to mobilize diplomatic and political pressures against them? Is there anything new—any initiatives, any new thinking, any new ideas, any new approaches which are being considered, or is it kind of just stay the course and hope, you know, over time that the system falls of its own weight?

Aronson: I don't want to exaggerate what is new, but there are some modest initiatives. As you know, some of the groups under the National Endowment for Democracy have begun to build a relationship with some Cuban democratic groups and held a conference recently, I believe in Caracas, where a fairly strong statement was issued, and begun to support groups that are working for democratic change. TV Marti is another effort to offer sources of free information to the Cuban people. And frankly, I think President Bush's restatement of U.S. policy in more positive terms and the emphasis on elections offers a new element to some extent, though that was always implicit in U.S. policy.

The two points of distinction offered by Assistant Secretary Aronson were Cuba's unwillingness to initiate "market economic reforms" and its intervention in the internal affairs of third countries. Only the former remains; with the achievement of a political settlement in El Salvador, Cuban support for groups "violently assaulting democratic constitutional governments" disappeared entirely from the administration's explanation of its policies. The Cuban Democracy Act of 1992 makes reference to such support only in the past tense.

Assistant Secretary of State Aronson identified as "a new element," although "always implicit" in United States policy, President Bush's emphasis on elections in his radio message on May 20, 1991, the day "Cuban Americans commemorate the 89th anniversary of Cuban Independence." President Bush had stated, 27 Weekly Comp. Pres. Docs. 629 (May 20, 1991):

On Cuban Independence Day, our goals for the Cuban nation, shared by Cubans everywhere, are plain and clear; freedom and democracy, Mr. Castro, not sometime, not someday, but now. If Cuba holds fully free and fair elections under international supervision, respects human rights, and stops subverting its neighbors, we can expect relations between our two countries to improve significantly.

NOTE ON PREVIOUS EXPLANATIONS OF UNITED STATES POLICY

In 1983, at the beginning of the Reagan Administration, the United States had justified its restraint on any financial or commercial dealings with Cuba wholly by reference to Cuban support for the subversion of other governments of the Western hemisphere; Cuba's positioning 40,000 troops in Africa and the Middle East; and Cuba's efforts to further the Soviet Union's foreign policy and strategic goals in the Western hemisphere, Africa, and elsewhere. Moreover, the Reagan Administration asserted that the continuity in U.S. policy since 1960 lay precisely in its opposition to these elements of Cuba's international behavior. In an affidavit submitted in *Regan* v. *Wald,* 468 U.S. 222 (1984), the then Assistant Secretary of State for Inter-American Affairs, Thomas O. Enders, explained the Reagan Administration's position, and that of prior administrations, in the following terms:

5. It is the long-standing policy of the United States and that of President Reagan to promote the development of democratic government in Latin America and to contribute to the economic and social well-being of the region through the encouragement of free institutions. It has been and remains a principal objective of the Government of Cuba to stimulate and support the overthrow of non-Communist governments in the Western Hemisphere and to replace them with Marxist-Leninist regimes acceptable to Cuba. Cuban success would be contrary to the national interests of the United States. In view of the intensity of the conflict which these Cuban efforts have helped to generate in Central America and elsewhere in the region, this Administration has maintained and strengthened measures to suspend trade with Cuba which are continued pursuant to the Resolution adopted by the Sixteenth Meeting of Consultation of Ministers of Foreign Affairs, acting under the Inter-American Treaty of Reciprocal Assistance (ITAR), the "Rio Treaty," on July 29, 1975.

6. Since 1960 it has been a major objective of United States foreign policy with respect to Cuba to deny the Cuban Government the financial means for conducting a foreign policy of violence against friendly third countries, dedicated to undermining the security interests of the United States. For that reason the United States Government adopted extensive restrictions on trade with Cuba, including transactions related to travel, which was consistent with Resolution VIII of the Eighth Meeting of Consultation of Ministers of Foreign Affairs acting under the ITAR, on January 31, 1962, and with Resolution I of the Ninth Meeting of Consultation of Ministers of Foreign Affairs, July 22, 1964, basing its measures on the authority of the Trading with the Enemy Act. The criteria for licensing transactions related to travel to Cuba then adopted were subsequently relaxed in 1977 as part of efforts by the Carter Administration to improve bilateral relations with Cuba. Travel, however, remained within the scope of general and specific licensing authorities exercised under the Trading with the Enemy Act. The criteria for issuing licenses for transactions related to travel were tightened again in 1982 because the conduct of Cuba had resulted in a deterioration, rather than an improvement, in bilateral relations, and because Cuba had vigorously renewed efforts to overthrow non-Communist governments of the region by the use of subversion and violence.

7. The objective of the tightening in May 1982 of licensing criteria on transactions related to tourist and general business travel to Cuba was not to prevent travel. Rather its purpose was to deny Cuba the convertible currency income which would [sic] otherwise could have been generated by development of tourism from the U.S. on a commercial scale,

income which would then have become available for the advancement
of Cuban policy contrary to the national interests of the United States.

In the same litigation, Myles R. R. Frechette, then director of the
Office of Cuban Affairs in the State Department, also submitted an
affidavit, which read in relevant part as follows:

> 4. The United States does not now, and has not for many years,
> enjoyed good relations with the Government of Cuba. Since 1978, Cuba,
> with Soviet political, economic and military support, has provided wide-
> spread support for armed violence and terrorism in this hemisphere.
> Cuba also provides and maintains close to 40,000 troops in various
> countries in Africa and the Middle East where these forces impede
> political solutions to regional problems and further Soviet foreign policy
> interests. It is important to U.S. national security to counter Cuban
> efforts to further Soviet strategic goals.
>
> 5. Since 1963, the United States Government has blocked Cuban
> assets in this country and has maintained a near total embargo on
> trade in both goods and services between the United States and Cuba
> as a vital element of our overall foreign policy towards that country.
> These controls provide our principal means of expressing our rejection
> of Cuba's conduct and of increasing the cost to Cuba of its adventurism
> in this hemisphere and elsewhere.

In thus identifying the concerns which provided continuity in United
States policy, the incoming Reagan Administration was faithful to the
public explanations advanced in the first years of the sanctions program. President Kennedy justified the imposition of a total trade embargo on February 3, 1962 by asserting that Cuba's "alignment with
the communist powers" posed a threat to hemispheric security and
that the "loss of income" from the embargo "will reduce the capacity of
the Castro regime, intimately linked with the Sino-Soviet block, to
engage in acts of aggression, subversion, or other activities endanger-
ing the security of the United States and other nations of the hemisphere." "President Proclaims Embargo on Trade With Cuba," *Dep't St.
Bull.*, p.283 (February 19, 1962); *see also* Pres. Proc. 3447, 27 Fed. Reg.
1085 (February 3, 1962). A year and a half later, in going beyond a
trade embargo to institute the full measure of prohibitions against
dealings with Cuba or Cuban nationals in effect today—including the
freezing of Cuban assets and the ban on tourism, foreign subsidiary
trade, and other off-shore activity—the Secretary of State announced
that their purpose was "to counter Castro-Communist subversion in
the hemisphere." "United States Blocks Cuban Assets to Counter Communist Subversion," *Dep't St. Bull.*, p.160 (July 29, 1963).

The United States expressly grounded its comprehensive ban on trade
and other commercial or financial dealings on the actions of the

Organization of American States pursuant to Article 6 of the Inter-American Treaty of Reciprocal Assistance ("Rio Treaty"), 62 Stat. 1681, TIAS 1838, 21 UNTS 77 (September 2, 1947), which provided for the adoption of collective measures "if the inviolability or the integrity of the territory or the sovereignty or political independence of any American State should be affected by an aggression which is not an armed attack or by an extra-continental or intra-continental conflict, or by any other fact or situation that might endanger the peace of America." Meeting pursuant to this provision of the Rio Treaty from January 22 to 31, 1962, the OAS had adopted a resolution urging member states to undertake measures of "individual or collective self-defense" against the Cuban threat. Final Act of the Eighth Meeting of Consultation of Ministers in Application of the Inter-American Treaty of Reciprocal Assistance, OEA/Ser. C/LL.8 (1962). President Kennedy instituted the trade embargo two weeks later expressly "in accordance with the decisions of [this] recent meeting of foreign ministers of the Inter-American system." "President Proclaims Embargo on Trade With Cuba," *Dep't St. Bull.*, p.283 (February 19, 1962). The Secretary of State requested promulgation of the comprehensive prohibitions of July 8, 1963 "in accordance with a subsequent resolution adopted on July 3, 1963 by the Council of the Organization of American States urging member states to implement a series of recommendations to counter Castro-Communist subversion in the hemisphere." "United States Blocks Cuban Assets to Counter Communist Subversion," *Dep't St. Bull.*, p.160 (July 29, 1963).

Before the Organization of American States acted in January 1962, the United States had adopted significant measures but had chosen to predicate them publicly on a different ground—the need to protect United States trade interests. On July 6, 1960 President Eisenhower announced that he was reassigning Cuba's share in the balance of that year's sugar quota to other nations. Cuba's "policy of hostility toward the United States" and in particular its barter agreement with the Soviet Union raised serious questions "as to whether the United States can, in the long run, continue to rely upon that country for such large quantities of sugar." Statement by President Eisenhower, White House Press Release, July 6, 1960, *Dep't St. Bull.*, p.140 (July 25, 1960).

On October 19, 1960 the United States imposed controls prohibiting most exports to Cuba and explained these measures as a response to Cuba's "deliberate political policy to divert its trade away from the United States," presumably toward the Soviet Union. This policy was implemented by a "series of arbitrary, illegal and discriminatory economic measures which have injured thousands of American citizens and have drastically altered the hitherto mutually beneficial pattern of trade between the United States and Cuba." The United States specified Cuban manipulation of import taxes, currency control measures, and other trade regulations to that end. At the end of the list, the United States somewhat obliquely cited the nationalization of United States property as contributing to this disruption of the "the traditional pattern of trade between Cuba and the United States." "United States Institutes Controls on Exports to Cuba," *Dep't St. Bull.*, p.715 (November 7, 1960).

The courts of the United States later concluded that the rationale of economic protection advanced to explain the July 6, 1960 elimination of the Cuban sugar quota was pretextual. *Banco Nacional de Cuba v. Sabbatino*, 193 F. Supp. 375, 384 (S.D.N.Y. 1961), *aff'd*. 307 F.2d 845 (2d Cir. 1962), *rev'd. on other grounds* 376 U.S. 398 (1964). Internal government documents released years later by the Department of State's Office of the Historian as the "official record of the foreign policy of the United States," Department of State, *Foreign Relations of the United States, 1958-1960, Volume VI, Cuba* (1991), disclose the strong reluctance of the Eisenhower Administration to articulate security concerns before the OAS was ready to identify Cuba as a threat to the hemisphere and to authorize measures of self-defense. They also disclose a reluctance until the OAS acted to go beyond elimination of the sugar quota and export controls to impose the comprehensive sanctions in place today. It was thought that, if justified as measures of economic self-protection, elimination of the sugar quota and the export controls were within the "domestic jurisdiction" of the United States, could be defended against charges of economic coercion in violation of the OAS Charter, and were not subject to the requirements of the Rio Treaty, "which sanctions only multilateral action" to counter threats to the security of the hemisphere. However, any additional restrictions could not be explained as measures of economic protection since, among other reasons, they would require invocation of the Trading With the Enemy Act, 50 U.S.C. App. § 5(b), on grounds of national security. Once the OAS acted under the Rio Treaty, the United States went forward with its comprehensive sanctions program, then basing its measures on a security rationale.

The United States filed strong diplomatic protests with Cuba over the agrarian reforms instituted on May 17, 1959 and the subsequent nationalization decrees aimed specifically at the major United States corporate interests in Cuba. Nonetheless, the United States made little reference to the nationalization of United States-owned property when announcing its economic measures against Cuba or when defending them in international forums. *Dep't St. Bull.*, p.958 (June 29, 1959); *Dep't St. Bull.*, p.171 (August 1, 1960). This is perhaps attributable in part to the long-standing and sharp disagreements between Latin

America and the United States on the question of nationalizations and the lack of any consensus in the international community generally on the subject. As the United States Supreme Court acknowledged in 1964 in ruling that the domestic courts of the United States should not pass judgment on the legality of the Cuban nationalizations, "there are few if any issues in international law today on which opinion seems to be so divided as the limitations on a state's power to expropriate the property of aliens." *Banco Nacional de Cuba v. Sabbatino*, 376 U.S. 398, 429 (1964). As the Supreme Court also observed, "the disagreement as to relevant international law standards reflects an even more basic divergence between the national interests of capital importing and capital exporting nations and between the social ideologies of those countries that favor state control of a considerable portion of the means of production and those that adhere to a free enterprise system." *Id.* at 430.

Intensification of United States Economic Measures

[At least so far as the public record reveals, the United States began a new period in its economic campaign against Cuba roughly in August 1988. At the initiative of the Florida delegation, Congress instructed the administration to "prepare appropriate recommendations for improving the enforcement of restrictions on the importation of articles from Cuba." Omnibus Trade and Competitiveness Act of 1988, Pub. L. No. 100-418, § 1911, 102 Stat. 1320 (August 23, 1988).

Before the end of the year the administration responded with a report to Congress identifying the efforts it recently had made to tighten not only import restrictions but all its restrictions on trade or financial dealings with Cuba and outlining plans for still greater vigor in its enforcement efforts. We reproduce pertinent excerpts.]

REPORT TO CONGRESS ON MEASURES TO ENFORCE
RESTRICTIONS AGAINST UNITED STATES IMPORTS
FROM CUBA, AS REQUIRED BY SECTION 1911 OF THE
OMNIBUS TRADE AND COMPETITIVENESS ACT OF 1988

*   *   *

The comprehensiveness of the trade restrictions and the geographical proximity of Cuba, just 90 miles from Key West, have aided the effectiveness of the U.S. embargo in denying Cuba hard currency earnings. The inability of Cuba to trade with the country that, by reasons of geography and history, otherwise would be its major trading partner compounds the difficulties the country already experiences as a result of its inefficient state-owned economic system.

The current embargo inflicts obvious hard currency shortages and other costs on the Cuban economy. In December 1986, Castro admitted that the embargo had placed "mountains of difficulties and obstacles" in his way.

The Office of the United States Trade Representative, along with the agencies responsible for implementing the embargo against Cuba (Departments of Treasury, Commerce and State), share Congress' concern that the restrictions on Cuban imports be effectively enforced. This report offers a welcome opportunity to review current efforts as well as to recommend measures which could enhance the U.S. Government's enforcement capabilities.

*   *   *

FAC [Office of Foreign Assets Control, U.S. Department of the Treasury] is charged with responsibility for investigating alleged violations of the various economic sanctions programs it administers. Over the past year, FAC has been developing and instituting joint procedures with other Federal agencies for the early and continuous coordination of intelligence and investigative information, program development, technical assistance, case monitoring, effective prosecution and penalties for violations of controls.

Focal points for these efforts include the U.S. Customs Service; the Office of Export Enforcement of the Department of Commerce; the Federal Bureau of Investigation; the Justice Department's Criminal Division; and the United States Attorneys' offices around the nation.

FAC has also been developing and instituting a program for the systematic training of inspectors, agents, and other Customs personnel in the scope and nature of the economic embargo and sanctions programs which the office enforces. Additionally, FAC personnel function as resource people for the other cooperating agencies.

The office also has developed and instituted a program of "public awareness" for both public and private sectors. This effort has enabled FAC to identify areas where violations are most likely to occur and to publicize FAC requirements more widely to selected groups.

In an effort to expand enforcement of sanctions against Cuba, a major initiative was launched in October 1988 to identify Cuban merchant shipping front companies throughout the world and to block vessels operated by them from access to U.S. port facilities. As a result of this initiative, 32 Cuban shipping front companies operating out of Panama, Cyprus, Malta and Liberia have so far been identified as specially designated nationals.

*   *   *

FAC has enhanced its licensing compliance function in the past year and is closely monitoring all licensed Cuban activity. The office has imposed stringent reporting requirements as a condition of many licenses. It has also initiated compliance programs involving specific industries, such as Cuban art, overflights, and financial transactions.

*   *   *

Enforcement results

The following actions are representative of the results of recent enforcement initiatives undertaken by FAC:

Individuals pled guilty to conspiracy to violate the Trading With the Enemy Act in connection with the exportation of merchandise to Cuban front companies located in Panama.

Enforcement actions were undertaken which resulted in the cancellation of planned recreational tours to Cuba.

Administrative monetary sanctions were imposed via a consent decree against a U.S. banking institution for violations of the Trading With the Enemy Act for engaging in an unauthorized business relationship with Cuba.

A Cuban-owned merchant vessel was blocked for entering U.S. territorial waters and subsequently released under a $250,000 consent agreement.

A shipment of Cuban-origin cigars, with an estimated value of $22,800, was seized in Miami for illegally transiting the United States.

Prize money won by a Cuban national in a chess tournament was ordered to be paid into a blocked bank account in the United States.

An aircraft belonging to a specially designated national of Cuba was seized and subsequently sold at auction and the proceeds were placed in a blocked bank account in the United States.

Auction houses have agreed to follow specific Treasury guidelines in determining whether artwork taken on consignment for sale comply with Treasury regulations prohibiting any dealings in or importing of property in which Cuba has an interest.

A third country-flag oil tanker was seized in Puerto Rico for carrying Cuban-origin cargo into the United States in violation of the Trading With the Enemy Act.

Since 1985, more than 180 front companies and individuals identified as acting on behalf of the Cuban government worldwide have been barred from engaging in any form of financial or trade transaction with the United States under the specially designated nationals provision of the Treasury Department's Cuban Assets Control Regulations. The special initiative against Cuban merchant shipping front companies worldwide was launched as a part of this program.

*   *   *

Enhanced Enforcement of the Embargo.

FAC has been working to enhance enforcement of the Cuban embargo both by increasing awareness by Federal enforcement personnel of the purpose and nature of the embargo, the Cuban Assets Control regulations and TWEA, and of the types of activities that constitute violations of the embargo. FAC will expand these efforts through training sessions and through direct assistance and advice to U.S. Attorneys' offices and other investigative agencies. Violations of the embargo will be vigorously pursued.

Expanded Targeting of Cuba's Global Trading Network.

Cuba's trading ties throughout the world bring the country significant foreign exchange earnings and provide the Cuban government with a key means for attempting to circumvent the United States embargo. Working with international business information as well as with other government agencies, FAC is increasing its attention to Cuba's international trade ties.

Coordinated employment of all the Federal government's information gathering capabilities, special designations, blocking of assets, prosecutions and—if authority is granted, civil penalties—should be pursued so that Cuba's international trading network is effectively identified and monitored.

Expanded Interagency Program Planning and Development.

Enforcement efforts by FAC, such as the targeting of Cuba's global trading network discussed above, will necessitate even further interagency planning and program development to bring the diverse authorities of Federal agencies to bear most effectively on the key vulnerabilities of the Cuban economy and its embargo circumvention attempts. Interagency cooperation and coordination should move into the next stage of planning and developing joint and integrated programs to continue enforcing the Cuban embargo in the most effective manner possible.

NOTE ON RECENT EFFORTS TO ISOLATE CUBA

Following its submission of this report to Congress, the United States initiated a still continuing series of administrative measures to restrict dealings with Cuba even further. They are set out in detail in Part II in the chronology presented there. During the same period the United States reportedly pursued, with considerable success, additional means to deter third-country companies from pursuing trade and investment relations with Cuba. In Part II we summarize thirty or so reported incidents of United States pressure on third-country companies.

The United States' contemporaneous government-to-government efforts were even more intense and, according to the Bush administration, had a decisive effect upon the Cuban economy. President Bush, in a June 4, 1992 letter to Congress, wrote that "my administration will continue to stress to other nations that continued direct economic or military assistance to the Cuban dictatorship is not acceptable and will seriously affect their relationship with the United States, including the provision of assistance." By August 1992 Robert S. Gelbard, Principal Deputy Assistant Secretary of State for Inter-American Affairs, reported to Congress that "Russian leaders claim that all economic aid and subsidized trade, which peaked at an estimated $5 billion a year, have ended. Total two-way trade between Russia and Cuba in 1992 may amount to an estimated $500 million compared to $8.7 billion in 1989." Statement to the Senate Foreign Relations Committee, Subcommittee For Western Hemisphere and Peace Corps Affairs, August 5, 1992.

The Bush administration claimed full credit for these cataclysmic changes in Cuba's economic relations with the former Soviet Union. Mr. Gelbard asserted that the "Russians have taken these steps not only for domestic economic reasons, but also in order to cooperate with us to promote democratic reform in Cuba." He continued:

It happened because of a strong and active Bush Administration policy to discourage Soviet—and later Russian—support for Cuba. President Bush and Secretary Baker wasted no words in letting President Gorbachev and, subsequently, President Yeltsin, know that we expected Soviet military and economic support to Cuba to end.

Mr. Gelbard also spoke of the Bush administration's vigilance in "enforcing the embargo" as contributing to Cuba's economic isolation in other respects.

By these combined efforts, Mr. Gelbard made clear, the Bush administration sought and, in his view, had achieved nothing short of "Cuba's economic collapse." Mr. Gelbard explained:

Cuba's economic collapse—for in truth that is what we are witnessing— is not taking place because of a passive American policy. It is happening for four reasons:
* The termination of Cuba's economic relationship with the former Soviet empire.
* The refusal of Fidel Castro to adapt to the wave of democracy that has swept the world. The Cuban economy—like its political system—cannot survive in isolation. The communist era is over.

* Our long-standing American policy of economic and political isolation of Cuba.

* Our firm and clear policy on the administration and enforcement of the embargo of Cuba.

Statement of Robert S. Gelbard, before the Senate Foreign Relations Committee, Subcommittee For Western Hemisphere and Peace Corps Affairs, August 5, 1992.

Congress decided to place additional pressure on Cuba by adopting the Cuban Democracy Act of 1992. Enacted in October 1992, the CDA significantly escalated the United States measures in two respects. First, the CDA prohibits third-country companies substantially owned or controlled by United States nationals from engaging in any transactions with Cuba or Cuban nationals. This reverses the policy the United States had pursued since 1975 of licensing foreign subsidiaries to pursue export/import transactions with Cuba.

With Cuba's attempt to reorient its economy away from the Soviet Union, this trade had grown dramatically since 1988. In 1988 its dollar value was reportedly $246 million; by 1990 its dollar value was $705 million and available information indicates that this rate of growth was continuing. Moreover, the character of the trade had abruptly shifted. In 1988 Cuban exports had accounted for 60 percent of the trade; by 1990 Cuba's purchase of goods from foreign subsidiaries accounted for 76 percent of the trade. Foodstuffs accounted for almost three-quarters of these imports. Donna Rich Kaplowitz and Michael Kaplowitz of the Cuban Studies Program, The Paul H. Nitze School of Advanced International Studies, Johns Hopkins University, *New Opportunities for U.S.-Cuban Trade* (1992).

Second, the CDA revived the practice of "blacklisting" third-country vessels which the United States had also abandoned in 1975 under pressure from third countries. It prohibits third-country vessels from loading or unloading any freight at any place in the United States for 180 days after departing a Cuban port it entered to engage in the trade of goods or services. The CDA also codified the Bush administration's April 24, 1992 administrative regulation closing United States ports to third-country vessels carrying goods or passengers to or from Cuba. The direct effect is to add to the already high freight costs caused by the United States economic measures, which make it necessary for Cuba to ship long distances what it otherwise could buy or sell ninety miles away.

The Cuban Democracy Act also enhanced the President's ability to pressure third-country governments to join in the economic pressure against Cuba. It authorizes the President to declare third countries providing "assistance" to Cuba ineligible for aid under the United States's principal foreign aid program (the Foreign Assistance Act of

1961), for assistance or sales under the Arms Export Control Act, or for relief under any program for the forgiveness or reduction of debt owed to the United States government. The CDA broadly defines the "assistance" permitting the imposition of these sanctions to include any trade on terms more favorable than generally available in the applicable market and specifies subsidies for exports to Cuba and favorable tariff treatment of articles that are the growth, product, or manufacture of Cuba.

ALTERNATIVE APPROACHES TO UNITED STATES-CUBA RELATIONS

[We set out here some of the views advanced in the United States domestic policy debate as alternatives to the policy pursued by the Bush administration and exemplified in the Cuban Democracy Act of 1992.]

ROBERT S. MCNAMARA, JANUARY 21, 1992

[Robert S. McNamara was United States Secretary of Defense from 1961 to 1968. On January 21, 1992 he delivered the following remarks at a press briefing in Washington, D.C. held after the Havana session of the "Tripartite Conference on the October Crisis of 1962," organized by Brown University's Center for Foreign Policy Development and Thomas J. Watson Jr. Institute for International Studies.]

[At the prior sessions of the conference in Moscow and Antigua, the Cubans were not willing to discuss] their military relations with the Soviets or their support of subversive attempts to overthrow established governments in the hemisphere, actions which led us to see them as a threat to our security. They did so in Havana. And in particular, they addressed our concerns as to how they would behave in the future.

The Cubans were quite forthright, saying that yes, they did indeed support revolutionary movements; they did carry out subversions of established governments in the hemisphere and they referred particularly to action in the Dominican Republic, Nicaragua, Salvador, Chile and Venezuela. They were equally candid in saying what they were going to do in the future. Fidel Castro was very, very specific. He said, and I'm quoting, "Did we support revolutionary movements in the past? Do we admit it? Yes, we admit it." Then he went on to say, "If you ask me if that's still Cuba's policy today, I would tell you no. There's a new situation in Latin America. Have we changed? Yes, we've changed. Therefore that kind of activity by Cuba no longer exists."

A few hours later, in a session in the afternoon, he expanded on that thought, and he said, there's been substantial movement toward political stability in Latin America, but in his opinion, that apparent stability covers up very severe social and economic problems which may erupt and lead to instability in many countries in the hemisphere, and then he made a very important statement, and he said, and I quote again, "Would Cuba take advantage of that instability"—that is to say, by support of revolutionary movements? And he answered very clearly, "No."

So as I suggested, at the meetings in Moscow, Antigua and Havana, we've each learned much about why the others acted as they did, and based on that, we're in a far better position to ensure that the next 30 years of relationships among our countries, particularly between Cuba and the U.S., do not reflect the fear, the hostility, that has shaped our relations in the past. There is no threat to the U.S. today from Cuba. And I say that quite categorically. I say it as one who spent seven years of my life worrying about such threats and believing, rightly or wrongly, that we were indeed endangered by the actions of the Cubans and the Soviets. That danger no longer exists. I am very positive about that. But I am equally positive that today there's no threat to the security of Cuba from the United States. I hope the Cubans are beginning to believe that. I know why they didn't believe it in the past. I hope our actions in the present, particularly in the future, will lead them to a new evaluation of the potential for improving relations between our countries.

I don't want to suggest we don't face divisive issues today; I don't want to suggest we won't continue to face them. We in the U.S., for example, are concerned about what we consider to be restrictions on political freedoms and constraints on civil rights. In speaking of civil rights, let me digress for a moment. We in the United States tend to equate human rights with civil rights, but the most basic human right is the right to lead and to live a productive life, and I want to say in that respect, I admire immensely what Cuba has done to advance the welfare of its people in two sectors — health and education. I don't know any third world nation that has advanced as far, and as a U.S. citizen, I'm embarrassed to admit to you that infant mortality in Cuba is lower than it is in the capital of the richest country in the world, the District of Columbia.

But I return to my point. There are major issues between the U.S. and Cuba. They're not going to go away soon. However, they're not issues of security, and therefore there's no basis for continuing to base our relationship on fear and hostility. Cuba's not the only nation with which the U.S. has disagreements on issues of political freedom and human rights, civil rights. And the U.S. is not the only nation which criticizes Cuba in those regards. These are issues which can and should be handled through normal diplomatic dialogue. So much, then, for the major purpose of the meeting. It was accomplished beyond anything that I could have hoped for.

REPRESENTATIVE DAVID NAGLE (D-IOWA), STATEMENT
BEFORE THE COMMITTEE ON FOREIGN AFFAIRS OF THE
HOUSE OF REPRESENTATIVES, APRIL 2, 1992

Chairman Fascell, Representative Torricelli and other members of the full committee, thank you very much for the opportunity to share with you my thoughts concerning United States policy toward Cuba and specifically H.R. 4168, the "Cuba Democracy Act of 1992."

While we strongly support the purpose of the legislation as set forth in the statement of policy section: "to seek a peaceful transition to democracy and a resumption of economic growth in Cuba," the question of the best means to accomplish this objective is the reason for these hearings and the subject of serious and thoughtful debate. I strongly support a U.S. policy that fosters change in Cuba, but embargoes are not policies in and of themselves, they are instruments of foreign policy. Since we agree on the objectives of our policy, our debate should consider the effectiveness of the instrument, as well as other foreign and domestic implications of the particular instrument.

As Cuba has become less of a national security threat, the issue of our policy towards the neighboring country has increasingly been influenced by domestic concerns. Yet, I believe that it still merits foreign policy consideration; and in addressing domestic concerns, implications for all geographical areas of the country should be considered.

We did not embargo Eastern Europe or the Soviet Union, even when those countries were clear threats to our national security. In fact, many of us believe that U.S. contact with these countries served as a catalyst for the future democratic movements that developed. In the past, those who supported a different policy towards Cuba than towards Eastern Europe argued that due to the geographic proximity to the United States, Cuba represented a greater threat and should therefore be embargoed and isolated, rather than engaged.

With Cuba heavily dependent on the Soviet Union both militarily and economically, there was no incentive to change our policy. But, as we all recognize, the world has changed drastically in the past three years. Like many of my colleagues here, I have had the privilege recently to receive briefings on Cuba from our intelligence agencies, including the Defense Intelligence Agency. Without revealing specifics, our intelligence agencies have concluded that Cuba poses no military threat to the United States or its surrounding neighbors.

Given this fact, one would expect a serious review of our policy to take place. These hearings are providing the opportunity to initiate this process. I would argue, however, that instead of pursuing a policy of increasing the economic hardships of the Cuban people, as proposed by H.R. 4168,—which, in turn, increases tensions as well as lack of confidence in the United States, we should opt for a policy of rapprochement and engagement.

I would like to read a portion of a recent U.S. Army War College report and ask unanimous consent to insert the report in its entirety into the record. The thirty-five participants, including experts from the defense, foreign policy, intelligence, and academic communities, reached the following consensus:

U.S. policy is counterproductive and is one of the factors enabling Castro to remain in power. Castro plays the "confrontation game" extremely well. Over the years, he has been highly successful in manipulating the specter of the "Yankee threat" to mobilize the Cuban people behind his leadership and policies. In effect, successive U.S. administrations, both Republican and Democratic, have repeatedly played into his hands by enabling him to wrap himself in the cloak of besieged nationalism. In contrast, Castro plays the "peace game" much less skillfully. The sooner the United States can change the nature of the relationship in a way that opens up the island to U.S. influence, the better. Such a change would undermine the rationale for the garrison state (continuing sacrifice and vigilance) and make the regime's task of political and social control much more difficult. Among the suggested measures that might be taken were the total or partial removal of the U.S. embargo, the encouragement of more travel to Cuba by U.S. citizens, the provision of humanitarian aid, the closing of TV Marti, and the end of U.S. military maneuvers in the vicinity of Cuba.

I concur in this assessment. I recognize H.R. 4168 takes several small steps in this direction, but I believe we should go further. Not only should we permit the donation of medicines, we should exempt all foods and medicines from the embargo, lift the restrictions on travel and take a closer look at the political impact that economic reform may have on Cuba's political system.

From a humanitarian standpoint the U.S. has a long tradition of excluding medicines and foods from embargoes, even in time of armed conflict. During the most severe freezes of the Cold War, many of my constituents in Iowa were allowed to sell their grain to the Soviet Union. More recently, one need only compare the U.N. sanctions on Iraq with those applied to Cuba to realize a vastly different standard is being applied. As a matter of principle and national policy, I think our policy is wrong—the U.S. should not be in the business of preventing people access, regardless of their country's government, to foods and medicines.

H.R. 4168 would limit the availability of medicines and foods for the Cuban population by restricting U.S. subsidiary trade with Cuba (the Mack Amendment). Mr. Chairman, I would like to introduce for the record a July 1991 Special Report published by the Office of Foreign Assets and Control of the Treasury Department, "An Analysis of Licensed Trade with Cuba by Foreign Subsidiaries of U.S. Companies."

The report demonstrates an increase of over 300 million dollars of exports to Cuba by U.S. subsidiary companies in 1990—more than 90 percent of these exports were in grains, wheats and other consumables. On the other hand, Cuban sales to U.S. subsidiaries have not increased; therefore, the greatest impact of this provision of the bill will be on the availability of these products in Cuba while not having a great impact on Cuban exports.

Furthermore, this aspect of the bill along with other provisions could have a serious impact on our foreign relations with those countries affected by the legislation. Canada and England have already passed legislation to block the effects of the Mack amendment. H.R. 4168 would impact on an even greater number of countries. The sanctions on governments that provided "assistance" to Cuba, according to the definition of "assistance" provided in the bill, would apparently affect a number of Latin American countries. Several normal trade practices are included in this definition: guarantees, insurance and tariff agreements, for example. Some of these practices do not only benefit Cuba, but rather are bilaterally beneficial. In practice, how could we enforce this legislation? Do we plan to set up a U.S. government review process of trade agreements between our allies and Cuba?

In addition, the proposed sanctions against these countries stipulate that they would be ineligible for partnerships under the Enterprise for the Americas; free trade agreements; and debt reduction. Are these not programs that benefit the United States also, not only the other country?

I would argue that from a practical standpoint, not only will our allies not abide by the provisions of this bill, but that American companies will be left behind—locking out American producers of foods and medicines while their European, Canadian and Latin American competitors establish a foothold.

As important as the market opportunities are for U.S. companies the potential impact that the presence of American business people could have in creating a more open and democratic Cuban society cannot be overemphasized. Contact and commerce promotes democratic change, as it did in the case of Cuba's former allies. It does not take much imagination to contemplate the effect normal trade and commerce would have on Cuba—an island of ten and a-half million people; with a language spoken by a large and increasing segment of our population; ninety miles from the U.S.; with a long, albeit tumultuous, history with the United States.

In my opinion, America should allow its most valuable asset, its citizens, to travel freely to Cuba and to any other country, assuming their safety is not in jeopardy. These "roving ambassadors" will convey through their words and actions the values we as Americans hold dear.

A change in our policy is clearly supported by the majority of our citizens as indicated by the recent poll conducted by the Terrance Group and Greenberg-Lake. I would also like to submit these results for the record.

Although pursuing a policy of sticks may be in the interest of some constituency groups, there are many others that do not agree with the policy changes proposed in H.R. 4168 as we have seen in the process of these hearings. The bill has also been controversial among Cuban Americans, who had formally been considered monolithically in favor of greater restriction.

In conclusion, if enacted, this bill could lead to serious complications—increased tensions in Cuba could result in violence 90 miles from our coast and a flood of new immigrants attempting to enter the United States. We must ask if this is the entire nation's best interest?

In my opinion, a further tightening of the embargo is not in our national interest. Rather it continues to allow Castro to divert attention from his regime's economic failures, and has the unquestionable effect of punishing the Cuban people. We should opt for a policy of rapprochement in those areas that increase contact between both of our nations; provide for humanitarian needs to be met through the sale of medicines and food; benefit our farmers and industries; and assure U.S. citizens their rights to freely travel. This alternative policy would not only increase the internal political space for the democratic forces inside of Cuba, but would initiate a process of confidence-building measures with Cuba as well as with our allies who have for so long been at odds with us over this issue.

Mr. Chairman, thank you very much for the opportunity to appear before this distinguished committee this morning. I encourage this committee, and the other committees that have jurisdiction over this legislation, to continue the effort to reach out to a wide spectrum of interests. I strongly believe the contributions and insights of these groups will provide invaluable assistance to Congress and the Administration as together we begin to reformulate our policy toward Cuba in the post-Cold War era. These hearings are an important first step and I commend you.

In closing, I would like to request that I be permitted to insert in the record some statistical information on trade between Cuba and its trading partners in Western Europe and the Americas and an assessment of the economic and political effectiveness of our embargo against Cuba.

Thank you Mr. Chairman and members of the committee. If you have any questions, I will be glad to try to answer them.

JORGE I. DOMINGUEZ, STATEMENT BEFORE
THE COMMITTEE ON FOREIGN AFFAIRS OF THE
HOUSE OF REPRESENTATIVES, APRIL 2, 1992

[Jorge I. Dominguez is Professor of Government at Harvard University. A past President of the Latin American Studies Association and a member of the Inter-American Dialogue, he is the author of two books and many articles on Cuba, among other topics. He is President of the Institute for Cuban Studies and co-editor of the journal *Cuban Studies*.]

The first crucial question to consider in assessing U.S. policy toward Cuba in the immediate future is: How important is Cuba for the foreign policy of the United States and how much cost should the United States be willing to incur to advance worthwhile goals with regard to Cuba?

The chairman and many members of this committee have for many years pondered the question of Cuba. Thus you know that Cuba today matters much, much less to U.S. foreign policy than it did five, ten, or twenty years ago.

If these Hearings had been held ten years ago, we would be discussing the tens of thousands of Cuban troops in Angola. Those troops are gone.

Ten years ago we would have been discussing the thousands of Cuban troops and military advisers in Ethiopia and in several other African countries, in Grenada, and in Nicaragua. Those forces are gone as well.

Into the very recent past, we would have been discussing Cuban assistance to revolutionary movements in Latin America and other parts of the world. For the most part, these activities have ended.

For thirty years we were concerned about the Soviet-Cuban military alliance and about Soviet military, political, and economic support for Cuba. The Soviet Union exists no more, and the successor republics no longer subsidize the Cuban government.

For many years Cuba, though a small country, had behaved as if it were a major power on the world stage. No more. Many throughout the world who had opposed such Cuban activity, including members of this Committee, should feel encouraged.

In short, Cuba today is much less significant for the United States than at any time since Fidel Castro came to power.

This takes us to a second question: How should U.S. policy toward Cuba be situated within the central strategic considerations of U.S. foreign policy today? The key question for U.S. foreign policy today is how to construct a world order safe for the interests and values of the United States.

In order to help construct such a world, the United States should consolidate its relations with Russia and other former Soviet republics to prevent the re-installation of authoritarian rule and to reduce the threat of nuclear weapons proliferation and of nuclear war. Compared to these concerns, the Cuban question is trivial. It makes no sense to burden U.S. relations with Russia and other successor states with the Cuban question, especially given that none of these republics wishes to subsidize Cuba.

The Cuban question is also trivial in the context of the U.S. objective to build a stronger and more open world economy or in relation to building a free trade area with Mexico and Canada and ultimately with the rest of the hemisphere. To achieve these worthwhile goals, the United States needs the cooperation of those that have been its allies and economic partners at a critical juncture for the future of the U.S. economy and world trade and investment.

It is, therefore, inappropriate to burden the future of a new world economic order with attempts to impose U.S. extraterritorial jurisdiction on the subsidiaries of U.S. firms operating in third countries. The U.S. government should not contribute to world economic disorder at a moment when constructive cooperation is especially important. Moreover, for those of us who believe that the future competitiveness of the U.S. economy will be greatly advanced through a North American free trade area that would encompass Mexico, the United States, and Canada, the injection of the Cuban question as an obstacle to the realization of such a strategic vision seems ill advised.

To help construct a world safe for its values and its interests, the United States has a special stake in strengthening its relations with other countries of the Americas even beyond the formation of a North American free trade area. We ought to seek the cooperation of other countries in Latin America and the Caribbean because they have and will continue to have a major impact on the United States. As several Latin American economies have begun to recover in the recent past, we see that U.S. exports to them have increased by substantial and rapid rates. Much of the potential future export growth of the United States lies in Latin America. Moreover, our societies are and are likely to become even more closely inter-connected as the result of migration, the need for cooperation to protect the environment, or the need to address drug-trafficking, among other topics.

This takes us to a third question: What should be U.S. policy toward Cuba and how best to implement it?

With the Soviet-Cuban alliance gone, the United States should fashion a policy toward Cuba that is part of U.S. policy toward Latin America. Latin American countries seek to foster a mutually respectful relationship of cooperation with the United States. Bullying tactics are not the way to build such a relationship, even if the bullying is aimed at a government such as Cuba's that now has little support among the other governments of the Americas. Latin American governments oppose unilateral U.S. actions, especially those intended to coerce them toward policies that they consider ill-advised and imprudent. Today, more than ever, Latin American governments engage the government of Cuba in order to seek to bring about fundamental but peaceful changes within Cuba. In their own way, these Latin American governments are advancing goals with regard to Cuba that we in the United States share. Thus the United States should encourage its Latin American neighbors to continue to engage the Cuban government.

What, then, might the United States itself do to facilitate changes in Cuba? From long experience we know that the Cuban government is especially adept at adjusting to economic hardship, in part by repression but in part by using U.S. hostility to gain the support of many Cubans. Actions that seek to impose greater economic hardship on Cuba are thus not likely to be effective in bringing about regime change, particularly if they allow the Cuban government to portray itself as a victim of U.S. aggression. They may even be counter-productive.

In contrast, the Cuban government has never handled openness well. The single most politically destabilizing event experienced by Fidel Castro's government was the visits in 1979 of 100,000 Cuban-Americans to see their relatives. Through their conversations, their ideas, and their example, they helped countless Cubans to see that their future could be different.

A positive feature of the bill before this committee, H.R. 4168, is that it recognizes that freer communications can facilitate domestic change in Cuba. From the perspective of exposing Cubans to more diverse ideas, frankly it does not matter if the Cuban government earns some money right away from improved telephone communications. The Cuban government has rejected AT&T's first offer to improve such communications because that proposal deferred full payment to Cuba for several years. Instead of haggling about small sums of money, the United States should act to improve communications now, quickly, broadly, even if it means paying the Cuban government its full share of the telephone business every year. The policy of facilitating openness should be extended to the sale of FAX equipment and to the lifting of all barriers that prevent U.S. citizens from visiting Cuba as tourists. So, too, the U.S. government should support artistic, journalistic, and scholarly exchanges as a way for U.S. citizens to manifest in Cuba the full meaning of expressive freedoms, and for Cubans to experience the benefits of the First Amendment first-hand in the United States. The communications part of the U.S. embargo policy has never made any sense and should be dismantled.

The members of this committee know that freedom has consequences. Trust those instincts as you think about U.S. policy toward Cuba. The principal way to foster freedom is with freedom itself, not with embargoes, blockades, or punishments. The policy of the United States toward Cuba should seek the cooperation of its allies in the Western hemisphere to involve Cuba and Cubans in the free exchange of ideas and experiences as the principal means to create the circumstances within Cuba that will make authoritarian rule less and less possible.

The Cuban government claims that it would welcome the U.S. government's adoption of many of these policies in the confidence that such contact would not undermine its rule. In contrast, you and I have faith that the contagion of freedom that has swept over the world could reach Cubans as well. Dare the Cuban government to open up its borders to people and ideas in response to the recommended changes in U.S. policy, and let Cubans respond. In a short time we will be able to assess whose vision of the Cuban people is right.

If you think that the Cuban government is wrong in its self-assessment that it can withstand the end of the communications and travel embargoes, if you think that the free roaming of U.S. citizens, including Cuban-Americans, and their ideas in Cuba is likely to induce openings in Cuba, if you believe that freedom builds upon itself, then foster a different U.S. policy.

The U.S. government should stop being Fidel Castro's secret accomplice. Do not help him censor ideas and the free travel of peoples. Do not help him invoke the specter of U.S. aggression. Do not help him justify the failings of his economy with reference to U.S. economic aggression.

Guarantee, instead, that the United States will let Cubans choose their own future. Encourage other countries to retain their cultural, artistic, and academic relations with Cuba, especially the former communist countries of Europe that have much to communicate by their example. Take whatever steps you can to work with other governments of this hemisphere to open up Cuban politics, consistent with a strategic vision of the future that has faith in freedom's intrinsic value and in its enormous capacity to foster change.

DR. RICHARD LESHER, PRESIDENT, UNITED STATES
CHAMBER OF COMMERCE, MAY 9, 1992

[On the May 9, 1992 edition of "It's Your Business," a weekly television program of the United States Chamber of Commerce, Dr. Richard Lesher, the Chamber's president, discussed "Trade with Cuba" with Representative David Nagle (D-Iowa), Senator Connie Mack (R-Fla.), Representative Robert G. Torricelli (D-N.J.) and Meryl Comer, the program's moderator. Excerpts follow that include the totality of Dr. Lesher's comments that day.]

Ms. Comer: The 29-year-old trade embargo bars U.S. companies from doing business in Cuba. However, as reported in the *Sunday New York Times,* foreign subsidiaries of U.S. companies take advantage of a 1975 amendment to the American embargo that allows them to trade nonstrategic goods with Cuba. Now, that's a loophole that Senator Mack is trying to close.

Congressman Nagle, how do you react to that? Is that a short focus in terms of policy?

Mr. Nagle: It is a short focus, and the reality is that we can't despite our best attempts, isolate—quote—Cuba. We can't prohibit the Canadians from trading with them, the Mexicans from trading with them, or anyone else that seeks to have an economic relationship with them. The only thing we're doing when we cut off trade with Cuba for United States companies and their subsidiaries is we just simply give the market to someone else. It's an ineffective tool.

Dr. Lesher: That's why embargoes don't work, because you never have that control. And I don't think our relationship with the rest of the Western hemisphere is worth risking...

Ms. Comer: Let me just ask Senator Mack, Western European investors—France, Spain, even Canada—have moved into Cuba. They're looking at oil; they're looking at luxury resorts. How do you say to American businesses we're going to continue to keep you out of this market?

Mr. Mack: I say that we're going to continue to keep you out and we're going to do our best to try to keep others out as well. We have been able to do that in areas like Cambodia and Vietnam. We certainly ought to be able to make it in Cuba.

Ms. Comer: Is that realistic today in today's trading environment?

Dr. Lesher: Wait, wait. You're keeping investors and traders out of Vietnam? Who is?

Mr. Mack: The embargo that we have in Vietnam and Cambodia is to stop all investment, and we have been doing that.

Dr. Lesher: You haven't stopped anybody. You think the Japanese are not there investing? Come on.

*   *   *

Dr. Lesher: They [Latin American leaders] do support you [Rep. Torricelli] philosophically, but they don't want you coming down there and writing their laws for them. That'll be big bad America again if we do that, and that's what—you're going too far trying to tell them exactly what to do.

*   *   *

Dr. Lesher: Bob [Rep. Torricelli] you've said several times the world has changed. Let me tell you why the world has changed. What happened in Eastern Europe and the Soviet Union? Because we had trade, because we had tourism, because we had a comparison of our system to their system for the last 18 years, that's why the wall came down.

STATEMENT OF PASTORS FOR PEACE, MAY 1992

[Founded in August 1988, Pastors for Peace is an ecumenical organization devoted to providing humanitarian and development aid to Central America and the Caribbean as well as undertaking educational work in the United States on related issues. It is located in Minneapolis, Minnesota.]

Cuba is in an economic crisis and the people of Cuba are suffering. The crisis is due, in large part, to the U.S. trade embargo against this small island nation. Recently, the Bush administration has extended the embargo to other nations, in violation of international law, effectively making it a blockade.

We find this embargo to have no moral basis and to be a gross violation of the human rights of the Cuban people. Cuba is not our enemy. We are not now and have never been threatened by Cuba. The embargo deprives our brothers and sisters of badly needed medicines, food, petroleum and other items required in daily life.

The embargo is also a violation of the rights of U.S. citizens. It restricts our right to travel freely to Cuba, to exchange information and culture, and to engage in business. These limitations have helped to perpetuate a grossly misguided U.S. policy toward Cuba for the past 32 years. Without a free exchange of information, it is impossible for U.S. citizens to understand the real situation in Cuba and to make intelligent choices concerning policy decisions.

Unfortunately, the U.S. has a long history of interference in the internal affairs of Cuba. Since 1900, U.S. military forces have occupied Cuban territory on three different occasions. The U.S Navy still maintains a naval base on Cuban territory, in direct contradiction to the wishes of the Cuban people.

Since 1959, Cubans have been in charge of their own affairs. The past three decades have been the most productive and promising in terms of quality of life and democratic process in the history of Cuba. The U.S. must respect the sovereignty of Cuba.

STATEMENTS OF PRESIDENT CASTRO ON DEMOCRACY IN CUBA

[In the Cuban view, one state may not use coercive economic measures to dictate change in another state's political system whatever its nature and so the democratic character of the Cuban political system *vel non* is of no moment to the present issues of international law. Nonetheless, since much of the United States policy debate makes certain assumptions about the nature of the Cuban political system, we set out remarks by President Fidel Castro on democracy in Cuba.]

SPEECH GIVEN BY PRESIDENT FIDEL CASTRO RUZ AT
THE OPENING SESSION OF THE FIRST IBERO-AMERICAN
SUMMIT, GUADALAJARA, MEXICO, JULY 18, 1991

*   *   *

The goal of unity and integration which encourages us today allows us to analyze—in the framework of respect for sovereignty and the self-determination of our countries and within the diversity which characterizes us—better forms of participation and equality of opportunities in the heart of our societies as the only possible way to expand and deepen democracy on the continent and the full exercise of individual, social and political rights. We will only be able to achieve the lofty ideal of democracy to which we aspire if we resolve the serious problems of abject poverty in which half the continent's population lives.

It is not possible to speak of democracy and participation to those who live with the utter lack of basic rights and to those for whom equality is an empty and abstract concept. We will be capable of achieving these aspirations and objectives to the extent that we resolve the economic crisis and make the structural changes necessary to allow us to overcome inequality, ensure a just and equitable distribution of wealth and create conditions so that the entire population has access to social benefits and political rights. Only in this way can we completely democratize our societies and only in this way will each people, in the full exercise of its sovereignty and independence, be able to choose the ways and means to organize its society and the most direct and effective forms for all of its citizens to participate in this society.

The political system, the forms of government, the election mechanisms which ensure the genuine and effective participation of all the people in political life are the sovereign decision of each country. These are determined by the history, traditions, experiences and aspirations of each people. In the case of Cuba, our democracy is the result of a concrete historical experience, a conquest based on national unity, social property and the people's participation. The people's participation in the decisions which govern their destinies is the essence of our democracy, which proves its worth through concrete measures linked to the satisfaction of our society's development needs.

Our Constitution was approved eleven years ago through direct and secret ballot, by more than 97 percent of our population. More than 95 percent of the eligible voters regularly participate in our elections, which, just because people in other countries don't know about them, shouldn't be undervalued or distorted as to their profoundly democratic content. The premises of our electoral system are multiple and direct nomination of candidates by the majority of freely acting voters; the voters' constant feedback about what their representatives do, including the possibility of recalling an elected representative; the mass participation of citizens with the right to vote in elections, through direct and secret ballot. Our socialist state, our political and social system, our economic organization, along with our territory, are defended by the people themselves, who have the weapons in their hands.

In ongoing and daily practice our democracy has within it—not just because it is elective, but also and above all because of its participatory and grass-roots nature—the potential for its own improvement, because we are convinced that the search for better forms of organization should never stop. Nor should the improvement of a political system like ours, which emerged from an authentic, American people's revolution and, together with the recovery of our sovereignty and the nation's wealth which had been in the hands of foreigners, created conditions of equality and of unprecedented rights for our people.

For this reason today, even under conditions of harassment, hostility and threats from outside, in consultation with the people we have undertaken studies on how to improve our system, deepening even more the peoples' participation and improving the structures of government.

*   *   *

PRESS CONFERENCE GIVEN BY PRESIDENT FIDEL
CASTRO RUZ ON THE OCCASION OF HIS PARTICIPATION
AT THE SUMMIT CONFERENCE OF THE GROUP OF THREE,
COZUMEL, MEXICO, OCTOBER 23, 1991

(*Granma International,* p.8 (November 3, 1991))

*   *   *

Epigmenio Ibarra (Imevision).—Mr. President, a compound question. In the first place, during the Congress, the direct election of deputies to the National Assembly was approved. What is the electoral body that will sanction these elections? Furthermore, do you see the possibility of the Communist Party losing its majority in the Assembly during these elections? If this were to happen, what would be your position?

*   *   *

Fidel Castro.—I think there is a lot of ignorance concerning our present electoral system: It is not well known, yet it was approved in 1976, through a plebiscite in which more than 97 percent of the population participated.

At that time we made considerable efforts to find new ways of selecting candidates and running elections that did not resemble those of any other socialist country; neither were they similar to those of capitalist, semi-capitalist or countries aspiring to capitalism.

We established the principle of direct nomination by the people; we divided the country into electoral districts in which the residents, meeting within their electoral districts—which I believe were much more democratic than the famous Greek ones, where neither slaves nor citizens outside the law, the immense majority, could vote—there could be eight, ten, twelve meetings depending on the size of the district, and each district proposed its candidates. There could be no more than eight and no less than two candidates in a district, and these nominated neighbors went up for election. If none of the candidates obtained more than 50 percent of the vote, there was a second round. In my electoral district, for example, we almost always had to vote two Sundays in a row, because none of the candidates had obtained more then 50 percent. That was our system; that is to say, the Party did not propose the delegates, the people did directly.

Those delegates constituted the municipal assembly. Depending on the size of the municipality, there could be 80, 200, 300 delegates and they elected the executive board, which had to be made up of delegates from the district; at the same time they elected the delegates to the Provincial Assembly.

Our country is not a federal state. It has never been, it does not have those traditions; but, despite this, the delegates from the electoral district elected the provincial delegates and also the deputies to the National Assembly, the highest state authority in our country. While the delegates from the electoral district were nominated and elected directly, this was not the case with those in the provincial assemblies of the National Assembly.

What we have recently established, starting from these ideas dating back to 1976—which, it seems to me, were very correct—is that now the provincial delegates and the deputies to the National Assembly also have to be elected directly.

Now the key problem is who will nominate. You know that throughout the world as far as we know, parties and party members nominate candidates, not the people. We have established a procedure in which residents nominate their neighbors, the people nominate and not the Party.

Now that we will move on to electing the provincial delegates and the deputies to the National Assembly, it will be the very same district delegates who will nominate the delegates to the provincial assemblies and the same district delegates who will nominate the deputies to the National Assembly. This does not exist anywhere else and I believe it is an extraordinary step forward.

The Party does not nominate even in our present system; the Party will have to guarantee that the principles and norms are followed, but it does not nominate. It will therefore be the people directly and the delegates of the people who will nominate. Before they nominated and elected, now they will nominate but not elect; they will nominate, but the voters will elect directly both the provincial delegates and the national deputies—that is, the members of the National Assembly, which number approximately 500—this number grows with the population, from which the rest of the powers of the state emanate.

Electoral commissions are organized to prepare this whole process. Elections are not simple, as you know well, and as it is known everywhere: all the ballots, all the candidates, all the vote counts, everything, and we have the agencies that will take care of that.

The Congress does not establish this, the Congress can establish its by laws but it cannot dictate the law to the National Assembly; the Congress recommends a policy, proposes a thesis, lays down certain principles, and it is the National Assembly that has to put those principles into practice.

*　　　*　　　*

Question number three is what if we lose. Simply, if the Revolution lacks the support of the majority of the people, it loses—not just now, it has always been the case, if the Revolution had only received a minority of the votes.

This advance, which in our minds is considerable, was not undertaken as a concession to anyone, but is part of our aim of increasingly improving and democratizing our society. Victory will require the majority of the people as before, but this majority will be improved. If the majority is not with the Revolution, the Revolution will lose power. This does not mean that if the Revolution loses power it will surrender, that everyone will hang himself, that there will be mass suicide. We have made no plans in that event, but I can tell you that we are revolutionaries and we are people with principles, we have always acted this way and always will. We would be faced with the situation of a minority revolution and then we all have to see how to go about defending the Revolution from a minority position, respecting the laws, respecting the principles and respecting the results, of this no one should harbor any doubts whatsoever.

PART IV

MEASURES AFFECTING THIRD COUNTRIES: THE INTERNATIONAL LAW ISSUES

Cuba asserted before the General Assembly that the United States has gone well beyond suspending trade and financial relations between its own nationals and Cuba. Through a series of extraterritorial measures, Cuba charged, the "United States has exceeded the confines of its national jurisdiction under international law and has violated the sovereignty of other States as well as that of Cuba." Cuba's specification of those extraterritorial measures and its memoranda arguing their illegality under international law appear in Part I. The United States responded that its measures against Cuba are bilateral in nature and within the parameters of a sovereign's discretion to determine its own trade relations.

The reach of the United States measures has long generated controversy, not only between the United States and Cuba, but between the United States and third-countries, including traditional United States allies. That controversy grew sharper when Congress, in October 1992, passed the Cuban Democracy Act of 1992, Title XVII, Pub. L. No. 102-484, §§ 1701 *et seq.*, 106 Stat. 2575, prohibiting trade between third-country subsidiaries of United States corporations and Cuba; prohibiting third-country vessels from loading or unloading freight in the United States for 180 days after departing from any Cuban port they had entered to engage in the trade of goods or services; and closing United States ports to third-country vessels carrying goods or passengers to or from Cuba or carrying goods in which Cuba had an interest whatever their origin or destination. In addition, the Cuban Democracy Act authorized the President to exclude third countries from United States foreign assistance, arms procurement, and debt forgiveness programs if they provide "assistance" to Cuba. The statute also provided that the "President should encourage the governments of countries that conduct trade with Cuba to restrict their trade and credit relations" with Cuba in a manner consistent with United States objectives. See Part III, where the full text of the Cuban Democracy Act is set out. In 1991 the Bush administration had assured the international community that it opposed the legislative effort to extend the United States economic measures' extraterritorial reach but in the end President Bush supported passage of the legislation.

A month after passage of the Cuban Democracy Act, in November 1992 at the General Assembly's forty-seventh session, the international community rejected decisively the United States' assertion of extraterritorial jurisdiction as violative of international law. In debating the Cuban draft resolution, twenty-nine member states addressed the General Assembly in addition to Cuba and the United States. Indonesia spoke on behalf of the nonaligned countries; the United Kingdom on behalf of the European Community. Whether voting in favor of the draft resolution or abstaining, almost all to speak criticized the United States' assertion of extraterritorial jurisdiction as violative of international law and many made reference to the Cuban Democracy Act in that context. None defended the extraterritorial reach of the United States measures. See Part I for the full record of the General Assembly debate.

The General Assembly adopted the Cuban draft resolution condemning the extraterritorial reach of the United States measures by a vote of fifty-nine in favor to three against (Israel, Romania, United States), with seventy-one abstentions. Two members of the European Community, Spain and France, voted for the resolution. Although the ten other members of the European Community abstained, they expressed through the remarks of the U.K. representative criticism of the extraterritorial aspects of the embargo as a "violation of the general principles of international law and the sovereignty of independent nations." Canada, like Spain and France, an important Western trading partner with Cuba as well as a close ally of the United States, voted in favor of the resolution. Cuba's principal Latin American trading partners—Mexico, Brazil, Venezuela, and Colombia—voted in favor of the resolution, as did several other Latin American countries (Chile, Ecuador, and Uruguay). Argentina, although it abstained, joined in the general criticism of the United States on the extraterritoriality issue.

In condemning the extraterritorial reach of the United States measures, the European Community and Canada expressed their long-held positions on the issue. Over the course of several years, the European Community and Canada had submitted to Congress and the President their strong objections to pending legislative proposals to prohibit foreign subsidiary trade. They also had objected to President Bush's April 18, 1992 administrative measure closing United States ports to third-country vessels carrying goods or passengers to or from Cuba and to the legislative initiative to "blacklist" third-country vessels for 180 days after trading in Cuban ports. We begin Part IV with several of these *démarches* and other communications.

After Congress passed the Cuban Democracy Act of 1992, Canada and the United Kingdom issued executive orders blocking any application of the United States legislation in their territories. We reprint those orders as well.

The fullest statement of the European Community's legal position on the extraterritorial reach of the United States embargo laws may be found in the memorandum that the EC issued in 1982 objecting to the United States sanctions against the Soviet Union. In short-lived regulations, the United States prohibited European companies owned or controlled by United States corporations from exporting goods, technology or services to the Soviet Union for the construction of a natural gas pipeline between the U.S.S.R. and Western Europe. At the same time, the United States prohibited European companies without any United States ownership or control from re-exporting any United States-origin machinery or technical data for use in construction of the gas pipeline project; exporting products incorporating United States-origin parts; or exporting any products manufactured through the use of United States-origin technical data. The European Community argued that these measures exceeded the United States' jurisdiction under international law and rejected them. Since the United States has made comparable assertions of jurisdiction in its Cuban sanctions program, we reprint the European Community memorandum.

The EC cited in support of its position rulings of the International Court of Justice and of several national courts on prior assertions of extraterritorial jurisdiction. In the only judicial decision to pass upon the United States' 1982 measures, the Netherlands' District Court at the Hague found the United States to have exceeded its jurisdiction under international law. Its decision in *Compagnie Europeenne des Petroles S.A.* v. *Sensor Nederland B.V.* is reprinted in 22 I.L.M. 66 (1983).

In 1975 the Organization of American States lifted the collective sanctions it had imposed in 1964 and permitted each country to determine its own trade relations with Cuba. For the express purpose of conforming to the OAS resolution, the United States liberalized measures affecting third country trade with Cuba which the Cuban Democracy Act of 1992 restored. We therefore reprint the 1975 OAS resolution and materials reflecting the United States' original understanding of its import.

For the concluding section of this Part IV, we have prepared a synopsis of the United States legal position on the scope of its jurisdiction under international law. We reprint as well the State Department's exposition of its legal position on two occasions.

EUROPEAN COMMUNITY AND CANADIAN OBJECTIONS

DÉMARCHES AND OTHER COMMUNICATIONS, 1990–1992

[In a 1990 *démarche,* the European Community made clear its objections to the then current restrictions on foreign subsidiary trade with Cuba as well as to the proposals for the outright prohibition of such trade. As reported in A.L.C. de Mestral and T. Gruchalla-Wesierski, *Extraterritorial Application of Export Control Legislation: Canada and the U.S.A.* 168 (1990), Canada objected to these restrictions as early as September 28, 1978 in a note to the State Department. The 1990 EC *démarche* follows.]

The Delegation of the Commission of the European Communities and the Embassy of France present their compliments to the Department of State and wish to refer to Amendment No. 333 to the Senate version of the Foreign Relations Authorisation Bill which was passed by the Senate on 20 July.

This Amendment would have the effect of repealing Section 515.559 of the Treasury Department's Cuban Assets Control Regulations which provides for the issue of licences to allow U.S.-owned or controlled firms in third countries to do business with Cuba. These Regulations otherwise prohibit virtually all transactions by persons purportedly subject to the jurisdiction of the United States with Cuba or with Cuban nationals.

The European Community and its Member States have on many occasions made clear their objections to the application of U.S. requirements to the activities outside the U.S. of companies incorporated within the EC. Such extraterritorial extension of U.S. jurisdiction is unacceptable to the European Community and its Member States as a matter of law and policy.

The European Community and its Member States accordingly reject the application of the Cuban Assets Control Regulations to the activities outside the U.S. of companies incorporated within the EC. There is, in their view, no basis in international law for the United States to claim the right to license non-U.S. transactions with Cuba by such companies, whatever their ownership or control.

The Amendment, if enacted and implemented, would inevitably lead to even greater conflict and argument over the extraterritorial application of the Regulations. It would also have a significant impact on the trade interests of the Community. In these circumstances, the EC and its Member States would be bound to react to protect all their legitimate GATT rights.

The European Community and its Member States therefore urge the Department of State to work with the other agencies concerned to amend the Regulations so as to avoid the imposition of requirements on companies incorporated in the EC, and in any case to do all that it can to prevent enactment of the Amendment now under consideration.

The Delegation of the Commission of the European Community and the Embassy of France avail themselves of the opportunity to renew to the Department of State the assurance of their highest consideration.

APRIL 18, 1990 EUROPEAN COMMUNITY DÉMARCHE

The Delegation of the Commission of the European Communities and the Embassy of Ireland present their compliments to the Department of State and wish to refer to the Smith amendment incorporated in Bill HR 4445, entitled "The Emerging Democracies Act of 1990," as well as to similar language included in Bill S 2444 introduced in the Senate by Senator Mack and others.

The amendment and the Bill contain three objectionable elements.

*   *   *

As regards the proposed seizure, forfeiture and sale by the United States of vessels which entered Cuban ports and subsequently U.S. ports, the European Community considers that this measure, which even in war time would be an infringement of the international law on neutral shipping, is completely unacceptable in peace time.

In addition, the amendment contains measures to withhold assistance from countries importing sugar from Cuba. The European Community considers this a measure with potentially damaging and disturbing effects on international relations for a number of third countries, including from the European Community and some of the states to which both the United States and the European Community and its Member States give aid within the framework of the C-24 process.

The European Community and its Member States therefore urge the Department of State to do all that it can to prevent the enactment of Bill HR 4445 in its current version and of Bill S 2444.

FEBRUARY 14, 1991 EUROPEAN COMMUNITY
LETTER TO CONGRESS

Dear Senator,

We are writing to you in relation to the Bill to reauthorise the Export Administration Act of 1979 (S320) which will shortly be considered by the full Senate.

The European Community and its Member States have followed the Congressional debate on this legislation very closely because contained within the Bill are two sections which have the potential to have a negative impact on the Community's interests and indeed on EC-U.S. relations as a whole.

*   *   *

Much the same considerations underlie our concerns about Section 128 of the Bill one of whose effects would be to prohibit U.S.-owned subsidiary companies located outside the U.S. from trading with Cuba. Notwithstanding our objections to the extraterritorial extension of U.S. law to which this provision gives rise we would point out also that it is in sharp contradiction with the view frequently expressed by the U.S. government that U.S. enterprises domiciled in foreign countries should benefit from national treatment (i.e. be treated no less favourably than enterprises from the home country). By considering U.S. subsidiaries in the EC trading with Cuba as falling within U.S. jurisdiction, these companies are in effect being denied the very treatment that is espoused for them in other contexts.

We would ask you to take these views into account as the Senate debates the reauthorisation of the Export Administration Act in the next few days.

OCTOBER 21, 1991 EUROPEAN COMMUNITY DÉMARCHE

The Delegation of the Commission of the European Communities and the Embassy of the Netherlands present their compliments to the Department of State and wish to refer to HR 2508, the International Cooperation Act of 1991, which authorises U.S. foreign assistance programmes for fiscal years 1992 and 1993. This Bill contains a provision introduced by Senator Mack which would have the effect of prohibiting U.S. owned subsidiary companies domiciled outside the U.S. from trading with Cuba.

The European Community and its Member States have repeatedly stated that such an extraterritorial extension of U.S. jurisdiction is unacceptable and clearly expressed the rationale of their concern in their letter to Congress on the 6th of September, 1991.

The Department of State is no doubt aware that certain countries, including EC Member States, have already decided to invoke their blocking statutes if this legislation comes into effect. The European Community and its Member States consider the Mack amendment to be a measure with the potential to cause grave and damaging effects to bilateral EC/U.S. trade relations. Furthermore, passage of such a measure would be totally inappropriate and inconsistent with the new climate of reinforced Transatlantic Cooperation.

It is the view of the European Community and its Member States therefore that the Administration should take all steps available to it to prevent the Mack amendment from passing into law.

The Delegation of the Commission of the European Communities avails itself of this opportunity to review to the Department of State the assurances of its highest consideration.

FEBRUARY 7, 1992 EUROPEAN COMMUNITY
LETTER TO CONGRESS

Dear Senator,

We are writing to you in connection with S. 320 and HR 3489, Bills to reauthorise the Export Administration Act (EAA) of 1979.

The European Community and its Member States continue to be very concerned about a provision contained in both House and Senate versions of the Bill (the "Mack amendment") which would have the effect of prohibiting U.S.-owned subsidiary companies domiciled outside the United States from trading with Cuba.

As was made clear in letters sent by the Embassy of the Netherlands and the Delegation of the Commission of the European Communities to Congress on 6 September 1991, such an extraterritorial extension of U.S. jurisdiction is unacceptable as a matter of law and policy to the European Community and its Member States. Indeed, we consider the Mack amendment to be a measure with the potential to cause damaging effects to transatlantic relations in general and to bilateral EC/U.S. trade relations in particular. This would be all the more regrettable in the light of the new climate of reinforced Transatlantic Cooperation.

Our concerns about the Mack amendment are such that some Member States of the Community have decided to invoke their blocking statutes if this legislation comes into effect. This would have the result that U.S. companies would be subjected to conflicting requirements, a state of uncertainty which can only be damaging for trade. Measures such as the Mack amendment are also prompting debate within the Community about whether it would be desirable to have a blocking statute at Community level in order to defend the interests of companies lawfully established in Europe.

In the light of the above considerations, we would urge you to oppose this provision when it comes before the conference on renewing the Export Administration Act.

APRIL 7, 1992 EUROPEAN COMMUNITY DÉMARCHE
(JOINED BY SWEDEN AND CANADA)

The Delegation of the Commission of the European Communities and the Embassy of Portugal present their compliments to the Department of State and wish to refer to HR 4168, the Cuban Democracy Act of 1992, which was recently introduced in the House, by Representative Torricelli (D-N.J.) and others.

The European Community and its Member States are seriously concerned about Section 6 of the bill which would have the effect of prohibiting U.S.-owned or controlled subsidiary companies domiciled outside the U.S. from trading with Cuba.

As has been made clear to the Department of State on a number of occasions, most recently in a *démarche* of October 21 1991 (attached), the European Community and its Member States cannot accept the extraterritorial extension of U.S. jurisdiction as a matter of law and policy.

In addition, the European Community and its Member States note with concern that the bill would introduce discriminatory tax penalties against U.S. companies with subsidiaries overseas which trade with Cuba, thereby providing a draconian economic disincentive against transactions which would be permitted in other jurisdictions.

The bill, if adopted, would also prohibit any vessel from engaging in trade with the United States if the vessel has entered a port in Cuba during the preceding 180 days. Such a measure would be in conflict with long-standing rules on comity and international law, would injure international shipping and would adversely affect the European Community's trade with the United States.

The European Community and its Member States consider that these collective provisions have the potential to cause grave and damaging effects to bilateral EC/U.S. trade relations. Furthermore, passage of these provisions would be totally inappropriate and inconsistent with the new climate of reinforced Transatlantic Cooperation.

The European Community and its Member States request therefore that the Administration takes measures to prevent the bill from passing into law.

The Embassies of Sweden and Canada fully associate themselves with this *démarche*.

The Delegation of the Commission of the European Communities and the Embassy of Portugal avail themselves of this opportunity to renew to the Department of State the assurance of their highest consideration.

JUNE 1992 EUROPEAN COMMUNITY "TALKING POINTS"

We are writing to you to express our concerns about certain provisions included in HR 5323, *The Cuban Democracy Act of 1992,* which was recently passed by the House Foreign Affairs Committee. The provisions in question are the "Mack" amendment (which would prevent U.S. subsidiaries located outside the U.S. from trading with Cuba) and new shipping restrictions (which would prohibit any vessel from visiting U.S. ports for 180 days after having engaged in trade with Cuba).

The European Community and its Member States have repeatedly stated that measures which extend U.S. jurisdiction extraterritorially are unacceptable as a matter of law and policy. A summary of our concerns on HR 5323 in the form of "Talking Points" is attached. We hope that full account will be taken of these views as the Bill is marked up in other Committees of the House.

Talking Points

We have commented on a number of occasions about the extraterritorial use of U.S. law with respect to Cuba. *Démarches* to the Department of State were made on 7 April 1992, 21 October 1991, and letters sent to Congress on 6 September and 14 February 1991.

The U.S. Administration has signaled to Congress its support for the passage of a *Cuban Democracy Act,* most recently in a letter from the President to Congressman Broomfield, the Ranking Minority Member of the Committee on Foreign Affairs of the House of Representatives. The draft legislation which has passed the House Foreign Affairs Committee contains two provisions to which we object. These are:

–The Mack amendment, which would deny licenses under the *Cuban Assets Control Regime* to U.S. subsidiaries located outside the U.S. which are owned or controlled by U.S. parent companies;

–A provision which would effectively prohibit any vessel, which had entered Cuba to engage in trade, from visiting U.S. ports for 180 days after departure from Cuba, irrespective of the cargo on board.

This latter measure would reinforce new regulations promulgated by the Treasury Department in April 1992 which will have the affect of prohibiting the entry of any vessel into a U.S. port if the vessel is carrying goods or passengers to or from Cuba or carrying goods in which Cuba or a Cuban national has an interest. These regulations are in conflict with long-standing rules on comity and international shipping and will adversely affect the European Community's trade with the United States. Since the prohibition on the entry of vessels will not seemingly apply to specifically licensed foreign subsidiary trade, the regulations could also have a discriminatory effect in favor of U.S.-owned or controlled firms located abroad which, regarding their licensed trade with Cuba, would not be subject to shipping restrictions.

We are concerned at the apparent willingness of the U.S. Government to endorse passage of a Cuban Democracy Act containing extra-territorial elements which will disrupt the normal business activities of companies and shipping lines based in Member States of the European Community. These measures would constitute the second batch of actions (following the Treasury Regulations referred to above) which would be aimed at forcing foreign persons outside the proper jurisdiction of the U.S. to submit to U.S. law and foreign policy.

As we have reiterated on countless occasions, such extraterritorial extension of U.S. jurisdiction is unacceptable as a matter of law and policy. It is also in outright contradiction with the view frequently expressed by the U.S. government, most notably in the framework of the EC-1992 programme, that U.S. enterprises domiciled in foreign countries should benefit from national treatment. Forcing such enterprises to submit to U.S. law denies them the national treatment that the U.S. espouses for them in other contexts.

We hope that the U.S. Administration and Congress will reflect further on the expediency of supporting legislation which has the capacity to cause damage to trade relations at a time when the bilateral and multilateral agenda is already overcharged. Recognition by allied countries of different economic and foreign policy approaches to countries should be a normal result of international discourse between them. Attempts to force one country's agenda on the other can only lead to conflict and to a denial of the principles that the EC-U.S. Transatlantic Declaration is designed to underpin.

OCTOBER 8, 1992 EUROPEAN COMMUNITY PRESS RELEASE

The European Community and its member states are urging the US President to veto the Cuban Democracy Act which is included in the Defense Authorization Bill (HR 5006), submitted by Congress to the President for signature on October 6, 1992. An official *démarche* was made yesterday pointing out that the extension of the US trade embargo against Cuba has the potential to cause grave damage to the transatlantic relationship.

The Cuban Democracy Act seeks to speed up the transition to democracy in Cuba through the imposition of a reinforced trade embargo under which US and Cuban trading partners would have to comply with US prohibitions for economic and trade operations outside the jurisdiction of the United States. Until now the trade boycott with Cuba allowed some flexibility.

The European Community and its member states are seriously concerned about the reinforcement by the US Congress of the trade embargo against Cuba. Furthermore, the Act's proposed sanctions for vessels that enter a port in Cuba would be in conflict with long standing rules on comity and international law, and adversely affect international shipping as well as the European Community's trade with the United States.

Until now, through a licensing regime, EC-based subsidiaries of US companies were allowed to carry on commercial operations with Cuba. The Cuban Democracy Act implies that EC-based companies would be facing US civil and criminal penalties if they trade with Cuba.

The EC has persistently voiced its opposition to the unilateral extension by the US of the reach of trade measures implementing US foreign or national security policies.

During the last two years, the European Community has been on record with other nations such as Canada in opposing legislative initiatives to tighten further the US trade embargo upon Cuba. Such actions would have to be applied extraterritorially of the US jurisdiction, in violation of the general principles of international law and the sovereignty of independent nations.

Although the EC is fully supportive of a peaceful transition to democracy in Cuba, it cannot accept that the US unilaterally determines and restricts EC economic and commercial relations with any foreign nation which has not been collectively determined by the United Nations Security Council as a threat to peace or order in the world of nations.

UNITED KINGDOM AND CANADIAN BLOCKING ORDERS, 1992

[Immediately upon Congress' adoption of the Cuban Democracy Act, the United Kingdom and Canada issued orders to counter its effects within their jurisdictions. Numerous other states reportedly are taking similar measures, formal or informal.

The United Kingdom's Protection of Trading Interests (U.S. Cuban Assets Control Regulations) Order, 1992 No. 2449, Statutory Instruments (Oct. 14, 1992) on its face appears to go beyond the CDA's prohibition of foreign subsidiary trade and preclude compliance with any of the extraterritorial features of the United States embargo. It provides that "no person or persons in the United Kingdom shall comply, or cause or permit compliance, whether by themselves, their officers or agents with any requirement or prohibition imposed on them pursuant to [the Cuban Assets Control Regulations] in so far as such requirement or prohibition affects trading activities carried on in the United Kingdom or the import of goods to or the export of goods from the United Kingdom." "Trading activities" is defined to include "any activity carried on in the course of a business of any description." The Canadian measure, Foreign Extraterritorial Measures (United States) Order (1992), *Canada Gazette*, p.4048 (October 21, 1992), is set out below.]

Whereas the United States is proposing to adopt a measure, set out in section 1706(a)(1) of the National Defense Authorization Act for Fiscal Year 1993, as passed by the United States Congress on October 5, 1992, which affects section 515.559 of the Cuban Assets Control Regulations, 31 C.F.R., Part 515, and constitutes a measure affecting trade or commerce between Canada and Cuba;

And whereas, in the opinion of the Attorney General of Canada, those measures is likely to adversely affect significant Canadian interests in relation to international trade or commerce between Canada and Cuba involving business carried on in whole or in part in Canada or is otherwise likely to infringe Canadian sovereignty;

Therefore, the Attorney General of Canada, with the concurrence of the Secretary of State for External Affairs, pursuant to section 5 of the *Foreign Extraterritorial Measures Act,* hereby revokes the Foreign Extraterritorial Measure (United States) Order (1990), made on October 31, 1990, and makes the annexed Order requiring persons in Canada to give notice of communications relating to, and prohibiting such persons from complying with, an extraterritorial measure of the United States that adversely affects trade or commerce between Canada and Cuba in substitution thereof.

Ottawa, October 9, 1992
Kim Campbell,
Attorney General of Canada

Concurred;
Barbara McDougall
Secretary of State for
External Affairs.

Annex

Short Title
1. This Order may be cited as the *Foreign Extraterritorial Measures (United States) Order (1992).*

Interpretation
2. In this Order, "corporation" means an undertaking that is registered or incorporated under the laws of Canada or a province and that carries on business in whole or in part in Canada; *(personnel morale);*

"extraterritorial measure of the United States" means the measure set out in section 1706(a)(1) of the National Defense Authorization Act for Fiscal Year *1993,* as passed by the United States Congress on October 5, 1992.

Notice

3. Every corporation and every officer thereof that receives, in respect of any trade or commerce between Canada and Cuba, directives, instructions, intimations of policy or other communications relating to an extraterritorial measure of the United States from a person who is in a position to direct or influence the policies of that corporation in Canada shall give notice thereof to the Attorney General of Canada.

Prohibition

4. No corporation shall comply with any extraterritorial measure of the United States in respect of trade or commerce between Canada or Cuba, or with any directives, instructions, intimations of policy or other communications relating thereto that are received from a person who is in a position to direct or influence the policies of the corporation in Canada.

Regulatory Impact Analysis Statement
(This statement is not part of the Order.)

Description

The *Foreign Extraterritorial Measures Act,* s. 5, permits the Attorney General of Canada to issue an order blocking the application in Canada of foreign legislation or other legal measures which will have an extraterritorial effect in Canada. This may be done if, in the opinion of the Attorney General, the foreign measure has or will likely have a significant adverse effect on Canadian interests in relation to international trade or commerce involving business carried on in whole or part in Canada, or if the foreign measure otherwise infringes Canadian sovereignty. This Order is issued with the concurrence of the Secretary of State for External Affairs.

The United States Congress has adopted legislation dealing in part with the *Cuban Assets Control Regulations* that would have the effect of potentially prohibiting, under United States law, all trade with Cuba originating in Canada by any company that is U.S. owned or controlled. This extraterritorial application of United States law would adversely affect approximately 30 million dollars of Canadian trade with Cuba annually, as well as restrict possible opportunities for trade growth. Such a displacement of Canadian law and policy by United States law and policy constitutes an infringement of Canadian sovereignty.

As a result of the above factors and considerations, the Attorney General of Canada, with the concurrence of the Secretary of State for External Affairs, has issued the *Foreign Extraterritorial Measures (United States) Order (1992)*. The order accomplishes two things. First, it prohibits compliance with the United States regulation concerning the *Cuban Assets Control Regulations,* thereby counteracting the violation of Canadian sovereignty. This will assist in protecting present trade with Cuba, and in preserving opportunities for increased trade. Second, the Order requires that all directions given by persons in a position to influence compliance with the United States law by the company carrying on business in Canada be reported to the Attorney General. This will increase the effectiveness and success of the order.

*   *   *

Alternatives Considered

Two types of alternatives were considered. The first was to issue no order until the Act. This would have left the infringement of Canadian sovereignty unanswered, and the adverse affect on Canadian international trade unchecked. This option was, therefore, unacceptable.

The second option was to have a different content to the order. The present content, however, was seen as best achieving the result of protecting all companies carrying on trade between Canada and Cuba from the application of the relevant United States provision. Although the interpretation provided for the term "corporation" is broad, this Order, when read as a whole, effectively applies only to those businesses that are incorporated or registered in Canada and are American owned or controlled, and therefore intended to be caught by the amended United States measure. The present order is, therefore, considered to be effective and reasonable.

*   *   *

Anticipated Impact

This Order may be expected to directly impact on American owned or controlled businesses operating in Canada that presently conduct, or that may conduct, international trade with Cuba. The order bars compliance with the application in Canada of the United States measure prohibiting trade with Cuba, and requires these businesses to report to the Attorney General of Canada, and not comply with any directions given by persons in a position to influence their decisions in this regard.

It may be expected that the order will place some companies in a situation where they cannot comply with the United States law. This will, however, be due to the extraterritorial imposition of United States law to Canada in violation of Canadian sovereignty, and in violation of generally accepted principles of international law. One might note here that should any corporation be prosecuted in the United States for a violation of the amended regulation, the existence of this Order can be considered by the American courts. Its precise impact, though, will be for those courts to determine.

The order may also be expected to attract considerable political attention both in the United States and in Canada. The highest level of consideration of these potential impacts lies behind the concurrence given by the Secretary of State for External Affairs to the issuance of the order. It is seen as a necessary measure to protect and safeguard Canadian sovereignty.

*   *   *

Consultation

Consultations have taken place on the diplomatic level, through the Department of External Affairs.

*   *   *

Compliance Mechanism

The *Foreign Extraterritorial Measures Act*, section 7, provides for the prosecution of violations of this Order, including the reporting requirement, by indictment or summary conviction. Maximum penalties are $10,000 and $5,000 respectively, each with the additional or alternative penalty of up to five years in prison. Proceedings under the Act must be instituted with the consent of the Attorney General of Canada.

NOTE ON THE GENERAL AGREEMENT
ON TARIFFS AND TRADE

Some consideration may be given to the provisions of the General Agreement on Tariffs and Trade, 61 Stat. Parts (5), (6), TIAS 1700, 55-61 UNTS, in connection with the European Community's objections to President Bush's April 18, 1992 order on third-country vessels and its objections to the even more restrictive provision of the Cuban Democracy Act of 1992. GATT is a legally binding instrument to which the United States, Cuba, and more than 100 other states are parties.

Article V of GATT recognizes "the freedom of transit through the territory of each contracting party, via the routes most convenient for international transit" of goods, vessels and other means of transport "to or from the territory of other contracting parties." This right of free transit applies irrespective of the "place of origin, departure, entry, exit or destination, or on any circumstances relating to the ownership of [the] goods." The United States refusal to permit third-country vessels to enter United States ports because they are carrying cargo in transit to or from Cuba must be evaluated in light of its obligations to third countries under Article V.

Article XI of GATT forbids any "prohibitions or restrictions other than duties, taxes or other charges" upon the importation of a product of another contracting state. President Bush's April 18, 1992 order appears to impose a restriction not authorized by Article XI, namely, that the imported goods not be shipped to the United States aboard vessels which also are carrying cargo in transit to or from Cuba. The Cuban Democracy Act of 1992 would appear to conflict with Article XI for the same reasons, since it would restrict importations to ships that had not traded in Cuba for 180 days.

Article XXI of GATT relieves a contracting party from these and other obligations to the extent necessary for the "protection of its essential security interests...in time of war or other emergency in international relations." As noted in Part III, the United States no longer asserts that Cuba threatens its security interests. See Part V for a further discussion of GATT.

THE EUROPEAN COMMUNITY'S 1982 DIPLOMATIC NOTE AND LEGAL COMMENTS ON THE EXTRATERRITORIAL ISSUES PRESENTED BY UNITED STATES ECONOMIC MEASURES AGAINST THE U.S.S.R., PRESENTED TO THE UNITED STATES DEPARTMENT OF STATE ON AUGUST 12, 1982

Diplomatic Note

*   *   *

1. With reference to the interim Rules promulgated on 22 June 1982 by the Department of Commerce under the Export Administration Act of 1979, and to the Community's note presented on 14 July 1982, the European Community wishes to present further Comments on the new Export Administration Rules, with the request that this note and these comments be transmitted to the Department of Commerce in accordance with that Department's invitation for public comments to be made by 21 August 1982.

2. The European Community wishes to draw attention to the importance that it attaches to the legal, political and economic aspects of the United States measures, including their impact on the commercial policy of the Community. As to the legal aspects, the European Community considers the United States measures contrary to international law,

and apparently at variance with rules and principles laid down in United States law.

3. As to the political and economic aspects, it is clear that the United States measures are liable to affect a wide variety of business activities, while their primary purpose is to delay the construction of the pipeline to bring Soviet gas to Western Europe. The European Community holds that it is unlikely that the United States measures will in fact delay materially the construction of the pipeline or the delivery of the gas.

The pipeline from Siberia to Western Europe can be completed using Soviet technology and production capacity diverted from other parts of their current programme. Furthermore the recent United States measures provide the Soviets with a strong inducement to enlarge their own manufacturing capacity and to accelerate their own turbine and compressor developments, thus becoming independent of Western sources. Gas could still flow to the Community starting as scheduled in 1984 owing to the existence of substantial spare capacity in the existing pipeline system, sufficient to cover the requirements of the early phases of the programme of deliveries.

4. One of the main elements of the Community's policy of reducing the vulnerability of its energy supply is based on diversification of sources. Gas from the Soviet Union will help to conserve the Community's own stock of gas, oil and other fuels, and will reduce the Community's reliance on other foreign sources. Use of Siberian gas will not create a dangerous dependence on that source. Even when gas is flowing at the maximum rate, in 1990, it will represent less than 4 percent of the Community's total energy consumption.

5. Whatever the effects on the Soviet Union, the effects on European Community interests of the United States measures, applied retroactively and without sufficient consultation, are unquestionably and seriously damaging. Many companies interested as sub-contractors, or suppliers of components, have made investments and committed productive capacities to the pipeline project, well before the American measures were taken. Though they may use no American technology, they will suffer complete loss of business if the European contribution to the project is blocked. Some of these companies may not survive. Major European companies that can survive the immediate loss of business, will nevertheless suffer from lower levels of capacity utilization and loss of production and profits, while workers will be laid off temporarily or permanently.

6. In the longer term, European Community companies may be damaged by the disruption of their contracts concluded in good faith, because they may cease to be reliable suppliers in the eyes not only of the Soviet Union, but also of their actual and potential business partners

in other countries. One inevitable consequence would be to call in question the usefulness of technological links between European and American firms, if contracts could be nullified at any time by decision of the United States Administration. Another consequence to be feared is that the claim of United States jurisdiction accompanying United States investment will create a resistance abroad to the flow of United States investment. Thus, these export control measures run counter to the policy aims of the United States of easing the transfer of technology and of encouraging free trade in general. There will be other far-reaching effects upon business confidence. These measures thus add to the climate of uncertainty that is already pervading the world economy as a whole.

7. The European Community therefore calls upon the United States Authorities to withdraw these measures.

Comments

I. *Introduction*

1. On June 22, 1982, the Department of Commerce at the direction of President Reagan and pursuant to Section 6 of the Export Administration Act amended Sections 376.12, 379.8 and 385.2 of the Export Administration Regulations. These amendments amounted to an expansion of the existing U.S. controls on the export and re-export of goods and technical data relating to oil and gas exploration, exploitation, transmission and refinement.

The European Community believes that the U.S. regulations as amended contain sweeping extensions of U.S. jurisdiction which are unlawful under international law. Moreover, the new Regulations and the way in which they affect contracts in course of performance seems to run counter to criteria of the Export Administration Act and also to certain principles of U.S. public law.

2. The main thrust of the Regulations may be summarized as follows:

First of all, persons within a third country may not re-export machinery for the exploration, production, transmission or refinement of oil and natural gas, or components thereof, if it is of U.S. origin, without permission of the U.S. Government.

Moreover, any person subject to the jurisdiction of the United States[1] is required to get prior written authorization by the Office of Export Administration for export or re-export to the U.S.S.R. of non-U.S. goods

---

1. Now defined as (i) Any person wherever located who is a citizen or resident of the United States; (ii) any person actually within the United States; (iii) any corporation organized under the laws of the United States; or (iv) any partnership, association, corporation or other organization, wherever organized or doing business, that is owned or controlled by persons specified in paragraphs (i), (ii) or (iii).

and technical data related to oil and gas exploration, production, transmission and refinement.

Finally, no person in the U.S. *or in a foreign country* may export or re-export to the USSR foreign products directly derived from U.S. technical data[2] relating to machinery etc. utilized for the exploration, production or transmission or refinement of petroleum or natural gas or commodities produced in plants based on such U.S. technical data.

This prohibition applies in three alternative situations, namely:

–if a written assurance was required under the U.S. export regulations when the data were exported;

–if any person subject to the jurisdiction of the USA (as defined in note (1)) receives royalties or other compensation for, or has licensed, the use of the technical data concerned, regardless of when the data were exported from the U.S.;

–if the recipient of the U.S. technical data has agreed (in the licensing agreement or other contracts) to abide by U.S. export control regulations.

3. The following comments will discuss *firstly* the international legal aspects of the U.S. measures, including (a) the generally recognized bases on which jurisdiction can be founded in international law and (b) other bases of jurisdiction which might be invoked by the U.S. Government; *secondly* the rules and principles as laid down in U.S. law, in particular the Export Administration Act, and as applied by U.S. Courts, which would seem to be at variance with the Amendments of June 22, 1982.

II. *The Amendments under International Law*

A. *Generally accepted bases of jurisdiction in international law*

4. The U.S. measures as they apply in the present case are unacceptable under international law because of their extra-territorial aspects. They seek to regulate companies not of U.S. nationality in respect of their conduct outside the United States and particularly the handling of property and technical data of these companies not within the United States.

They seek to impose on non-U.S. companies the restriction of U.S. law by threatening them with discriminatory sanctions in the field of trade which are inconsistent with the normal commercial practice established between the U.S. and the EC.

In this way the Amendments of June 22, 1982, run counter to the two generally accepted bases of jurisdiction in international law; the territoriality and the nationality principles.[3]

2. This expression is very broadly defined in 15 CFR para. 379.1.

3. *See Restatement, Second, Foreign Relations Law of the United States (1972)*, paras. 17 and 30 respectively.

5. The *territoriality principle* (i.e. the notion that a state should restrict its rule-making in principle to persons and goods within its territory and that an organization like the European Community should restrict the applicability of its rules to the territory to which the Treaty setting it up applies) is a fundamental notion of international law, in particular insofar as it concerns the regulation of the social and economic activity in a state. The principle that each state—and *mutatis mutandis* the community insofar as powers have been transferred to it—has the right freely to organize and develop its social and economic system has been confirmed many times in international fora. The American measures clearly infringe the principle of territoriality, since they purport to regulate the activities of companies in the EC, not under the territorial competence of the U.S.

6. The *nationality principle* (i.e. the prescription of rules for nationals, wherever they are) cannot serve as a basis for the extension of U.S. jurisdiction resulting from the Amendments, i.e. (i) over companies incorporated in EC Member States on the basis of some corporate link (parent-subsidiary) or personal link (e.g. shareholding) to the U.S.; (ii) over companies incorporated in EC Member States, either because they have a tie to a U.S.-incorporated company, subsidiary or other "U.S. Controlled" company through a licensing agreement, royalty payments, or payment of other compensation, or because they have bought certain goods originating in the U.S.

7. *ad (i)* the Amendments in two places purport to subject to U.S. jurisdiction companies, wherever organized or doing business, which are subsidiaries of U.S. companies or under the control of U.S. citizens, U.S. residents or even persons actually within the U.S. This implies that the United States is seeking to impose its corporate nationality on companies of which the great majority are incorporated and have their registered office elsewhere, notably in EC Member States.

Such action is not in conformity with recognized principles of international law. In the *Barcelona Traction Case*, the International Court of Justice declared that two traditional criteria for determining the nationality of companies; i.e., the place of incorporation and the place of the registered office of the company concerned, had been "confirmed by long practice and by numerous international instruments." The Court also scrutinized other tests of corporate nationality, but concluded that these had not found general acceptance. The Court consequently placed primary emphasis on the traditional place of incorporation and the registered office in deciding the case in point.[4] This decision was taken within the framework of the doctrine of diplomatic protection, but reflects a general principle of international law.

4. CJ Reports 1970, 3, at 43.

8. *ad (ii)* The notion inherent in the subjection to U.S. jurisdiction of companies with no tie to the U.S. whatsoever, except for a technological link to a U.S. company, or through possession of U.S. origin goods, can only be that this technology or such goods should somehow be considered as unalterably "American" (even though many of the patents involved are registered in the Member States of the European Community). This seems the only possible explanation for the U.S. Regulations given the fact that national security is not at stake here (see below under B).

Goods and technology do not have any nationality and there are no known rules under international law for using goods or technology situated abroad as a basis of establishing jurisdiction over the persons controlling them. Several Court cases confirm that U.S. jurisdiction does not follow U.S. origin goods once they have been discharged in the territory of another country.[5]

9. The Amendments of 22 June 1982, therefore, cannot be justified under the nationality principle, because they ignore the two traditional criteria for determining the nationality of companies reconfirmed by the International Court of Justice and because they purport to give some notion of "nationality" to goods and technologies so as to establish jurisdiction over persons handling them.

The purported direct extension of U.S. jurisdiction to non-U.S. incorporated companies not using U.S. origin technology or components is *a fortiori* objectionable to the EC, because neither of these (in themselves invalid) justifications could apply.

10. The last mentioned case exemplifies to what extent the wholesale infringement of the nationality principle exacerbates the infringement of the territoriality principle.[6] Thus even EC incorporated companies in the example mentioned above according to the Amendments would have to ask special written permission not of the EC, but of the U.S. authorities in order to obtain permission to export goods produced in the EC and based on EC technology from the territory to which the EC Treaties apply in the USSR. The practical impact of the Amendments to the Export Administration Regulations is that EC companies are pressed into service to carry out U.S. trade policy towards the USSR, even though these companies are incorporated and have their registered office within the Community which has its own trade policy towards the USSR.

5. *American President Lines* v. *China Mutual Trading Co.,* 1953 A.M.C. 1510, 1526 (Hong Kong Sup. Ct.) and *Moens* v. *Ahlers North German Lloyd,* 30 R.W. 360 (Tribunal of Commerce Antwerp (1966).

6. The application of the nationality principle would imply *ipso facto* some overlapping with the application of the territoriality principle and this is acceptable under international law, in some instances, but we are not in such a situation in this case.

The public policy (*"order public"*) of the European Community and of its Member States is thus purportedly replaced by U.S. public policy which European companies are forced to carry out within the EC, if they are not to lose export privileges in the U.S. or to face other sanctions. This is an unacceptable interference in the affairs of the European Community.

11. Furthermore, it is reprehensible that present U.S. Regulations encourage non-U.S. companies to submit "voluntarily" to this kind of mobilization for U.S. purposes.

Even when submission to a foreign boycott is entirely voluntary, such submission *within* the U.S. has been considered to be undesirable and contrary to U.S. public policy.[7] By the same token it must have been evident to the U.S. Government that the statutory encouragement of voluntary submission to U.S. public policy in trade matters *within* the EC is strongly condemned by the European Community. Private agreements should not be used in this way as instruments of foreign policy. If a Government in law and in fact systematically encourages the inclusion of such submission clauses in private contracts the freedom of contract is misused in order to circumvent the limits imposed on national jurisdiction by international law.

It is self-evident, moreover, that the existence of such submission clauses in certain private contracts cannot serve as a basis for U.S. regulatory jurisdiction which can properly be exercised solely in conformity with international law. Nor can a company prevent a state from objecting to any infringement which might occur of the jurisdiction of the state to which it belongs.

B. *Other bases of jurisdiction*

12. There are two other bases of jurisdiction which might be invoked by the U.S. Government, but which have found less than general acceptance under international law. These are:

a) the protective principle (para. 33 of the 2nd Restatement), which would give a State jurisdiction to proscribe acts done outside its territory but threatening its security or the operation of its governmental functions, if such acts are generally recognized as crimes by States with reasonably developed legal systems;

b) the so-called "effects doctrine," under which conduct occurring outside the territory but causing direct, foreseeable and substantial effects—which are also constituent elements of a crime or tort—within the territory may be proscribed (para. 18 of the 2nd Restatement).

13. However, it is clear *ab initio* that the extension of U.S. jurisdiction implicit in the Amendments cannot be based on the principles mentioned under 12(a) or (b).

---

7. Cf. Section 8 of the *Export Administration Act* and below under II.A.

The "protective principle" has not been invoked by the U.S. Government, since the Amendments are based on Section 6 (Foreign Policy Controls) and not on Section 5 (National Security Controls) of the Export Administration Act. The U.S. Government itself, therefore, has not sought to base the Amendments on considerations of national security.

The "effects doctrine" is not applicable. It cannot conceivably be argued that exports from the European Community to the USSR for the Siberian gas pipeline have within the USA direct, foreseeable and substantial effects which are not merely undesirable, but which constitute an element of a crime or tort proscribed by U.S. law. It is more than likely that they have no direct effects on U.S. trade.

14. For the reasons expounded above, it is clear that the U.S. measures of June 22, 1982 do not find a valid basis in any of the generally recognized—or even the more controversial—principles of international law governing state jurisdiction to prescribe rules. As a matter of fact the measures by their extraterritorial character simultaneously infringe the territoriality and nationality principles of jurisdiction and are therefore unlawful under international law.

III. *The Amendments Under U.S. Law*

A. *U.S. Reactions to measures similar to the June 22 Amendments*

15. If a foreign country were to take measures like the June 22 Amendments, it is doubtful whether they would be in conformity with U.S. law and they would therefore probably not be recognized and enforced by U.S. courts.

The kind of mobilization of EC companies for U.S. purposes to which the Community objects was subject to strong American reactions and legislative counter-measures, when U.S. companies were similarly mobilized for the foreign policy purposes of other states.

The anti-foreign-boycott provisions of Sections 8 of the *Export Administration Act* are testimony to that. In the same way as the U.S. could not accept that its companies were turned into instruments of the foreign policy of other nations, the EC cannot accept that its companies must follow another trade policy than its own within its own territorial jurisdiction.

It is noteworthy that the anti-boycott provisions of the Export Administration Act can be invoked in response to a boycott that takes a less direct form than the June 22 Amendments, namely a boycott which merely tries to dissuade persons from dealing with a third country by refusing to trade with such persons. An export restriction patterned on the June 22 Amendments, in contrast, would directly prohibit a person from dealing with a particular country under the threat of government-imposed penalties. Therefore, the latest Amendments would appear to be even more far-reaching than a boycott which might give rise to the application of the anti-boycott provisions.

16. Even if for some reason the foreign boycott provisions of the Export Administration Act were not considered applicable, a foreign country imposing such restrictions as those imposed by the June 22 Amendments would probably be viewed by U.S. Courts as attempting to extend its laws beyond its territory without sufficient nexus with the U.S. entity to justify such an extension. This certainly would be the case with respect to a mere licensee of a foreign concern.

If a foreign government complained that a U.S. licensee of a foreign company was not complying with that foreign government's export restrictions prohibiting such exports, a U.S. federal court would decline jurisdiction, because U.S. Courts will not enforce foreign penal statutes.[8]

If the observance of a foreign export control by a U.S. subsidiary or licensee were to become an issue in litigation between the latter and its foreign parent company or licensor, a federal or state court would probably not refuse jurisdiction, but would decline to enforce the export restrictions of the foreign country on the grounds that it would be contrary to the strong public policy of the forum and not in the interest of the United States to do so.[9]

This being the reaction of the U.S. legislature and judiciary to foreign measures comparable to its own measures of June 22, the U.S. Government should not have inflicted these measures on the EC companies concerned in the virtual knowledge that these measures would be regarded as unlawful and ineffective by public authorities in the EC.

B. *Conflicts of Jurisdiction and Accommodation of Interest*

17. In cases where the conflicting exercise of jurisdiction to prescribe leads to conflicts of enforcement jurisdiction between states, each state, according to para. 40 of the Restatement (2nd) Foreign Relations Law of the U.S., is required by international law to consider, in good faith, moderating the exercise of its enforcement jurisdiction. In this connection the following factors should be considered:

a) vital national interests of each of the states;

b) the extent and the nature of the hardship that inconsistent enforcement actions would impose upon the person;

c) the extent to which the required conduct is to take place in the territory of the other state;

d) the nationality of the other person....

8. *Wisconsin* v. *Pelican Insurance Company,* 127 US 265, 290 (1888); Restatement (2d) Conflict of Laws para. 89.

9. Restatement (2d) Conflict of Laws pp. 90.

18. Over the past year various U.S. Courts of Appeal have pronounced themselves in favour of this "balancing of interests" approach.

In the case of the *Timberlane Co.* v. *Bank of America*[10] Judge Choy suggested that comity demanded an evaluation and balancing of relevant factors, and continued: "The elements to be weighed include the degree of conflict with foreign law or policy, the nationality or allegiance of the parties, and the locations or principal places of businesses or corporations, the extent to which enforcement by either state can be expected to achieve compliance, the relative significance of effects on the United States as compared with those elsewhere, the extent to which there is explicit purpose to harm or affect American commerce, the foreseeability of such effect, and the relative importance to the violations charged of conduct within the United States as compared with conduct abroad.

A similar approach was followed in *Mannington Mills*[11] and is set out in paragraph 40 of the Second Restatement.

19. Although this "balancing of interest" approach applies in the first place to courts, there are good reasons why the U.S. Government should exercise such restraint already at the rule-making stage.

20. First, Section 6 of the Export Administration Act in several places enjoins the President to consider the position of other countries before taking or extending export controls.

Thus para. (b): "... the President shall consider: (3) the reaction of other countries to the imposition or expansion of... export controls by the United States."

In para. (d): "...the President shall determine that reasonable efforts have been made to achieve the purposes of the controls through negotiations or other alternative means."

Finally in para. (g): "...the President shall take all feasible steps to initiate and conclude negotiations for the purpose of securing the cooperation of such foreign governments in controlling the export to countries and consignees to which the U.S. export controls apply of any goods or technology comparable to goods or technology controlled under this section."

21. In the second place, these Amendments to the Export Administration Regulations may not be subject to substantive judicial review. This means that U.S. Courts may not be able to apply their balancing of interests approach in a class of enforcement jurisdictions. It is therefore appropriate for the executive to apply it at the rule-making stage.

22. Finally, the direction in which informed legal opinion in the U.S. is moving on this issue is demonstrated by the new draft Restatement (3rd) of the *Foreign Relations Law of the U.S.*

10. *Timberlane Lumber Co.* v. *Bank of America,* 1977-1 Trade Cases No. 61.233.
11. *Mannington Mills Inc.* v. *Congoleum Corp.* 1979-1 Trade Cases No.62.547.

It does away with the rather artificial distinction between the right to assert a jurisdiction to prescribe and restraint in exercising it. It simply considers that the exercise of a jurisdiction to prescribe may be unreasonable; to decide whether this is so or not draft para. 403[12] enjoins the evaluation of such factors as place of the activity to be regulated, links of persons falling under the regulation with other states, consistency with the traditions of the international system, interest of other states in regulating the activity concerned, and the existence of justified expectations to be affected by the regulation.

23. Whatever approach is adopted by the U.S. Government in balancing U.S. interests against the interests of the European Community, the following considerations have been neglected.

The interest of the European Community in regulating the foreign trade of the nationals of the Member States in the territory to which the Community Treaties apply is paramount over any foreign policy purposes that a third country may have.

The conduct required by the Amendments is to take place largely in territory to which the EC Treaties apply and not in U.S. territory.

The nationality and other ties of many persons whose conduct is purportedly regulated by the June 22 Amendments link them primarily to EC Member States and not to the U.S.

There are justified expectations on the part of EC companies which are seriously hurt by the U.S. measures.

C. *Criteria under Section 6 (b) of the Export Administration Act*

24. It can hardly be claimed that the U.S. measures satisfy the criteria laid down in the Export Administration Act, and therefore it is doubtful whether the restrictions are properly applied in terms of U.S. law. Criterion 1 refers to the probability that the controls will achieve the intended foreign policy purposes. Soviet Authorities have clearly stated their intention to deliver gas to Western Europe as scheduled, and there is little reason to doubt their ability to do so, even without American or European equipment since the existing Soviet pipeline system already has sufficient spare capacity, at least to cover the requirements of the early phases of the programme of deliveries. If the pipeline is built with Soviet technology and the gas flows on time, these U.S. export controls are at best ineffectual, and may well be self-defeating, as instruments of foreign policy.

25. Criterion 3 requires that the reaction of other countries to the imposition or expansion of such export controls be taken into account. In view of the extra-territorial application, and retroactive effect of the U.S. measures, the European Community cannot fail to denounce the

---

12. Cited in Harold G. Maier, *Extraterritorial Jurisdiction at a Crossroads: an Intersection between Public and Private International Law*, 76 *American Journal of International Law* 1982, 280, at 300-301.

measure as unlawful under international law; and in view of their damaging economic and political consequences, has already protested in the strongest terms.

26. Criterion 4 requires consideration of the effects of the proposed controls on the export performance of the United States. Here again, confirmation of the U.S. measures despite criterion 4 would involve complete disregard for damaging effects not only immediately, but also in the longer term, owing to the grave doubts that are bound to arise in future about the U.S. as a reliable supplier of equipment under contract, or as a reliable partner in technology-licensing arrangements. This danger had already been pointed out to the President of the United States by the U.S. Chamber of Commerce.

D. *Compensation for damage resulting from U.S. measures*

27. The U.S. measures inasmuch as they refer to exports from countries outside the U.S. are the more objectionable, as they affect contracts that were free from restrictions imposed by the U.S. Authorities at the time of their conclusion.

The main contractors of the Siberian pipeline, a number of major sub-contractors and suppliers as well as other exporters, will suffer substantial economic and financial losses for which no compensation is provided. For many sub-contractors who for the most part have nothing to do with American goods or technology for gas transport, the practical consequences of the Amendments will be particularly severe and may actually force them out of business. Lay-offs of a considerable number of workers will result in any case from the Amendments.

28. The idea that compensation is due in case private property or existing contracts are seriously affected by government action is also familiar in the U.S. legal system. If the U.S. Government takes private property by eminent domain it has to compensate the owner. The Supreme Court has indicated many times that if regulatory legislation virtually deprives a person of the complete use and enjoyment of his property the law of eminent domain applies.[13]

Justice Brandeis has written: "It is true that the police power embraces regulations designed to promote public convenience or the general welfare.... But when particular individuals are singled out to bear the cost of advancing the public convenience, that imposition must bear some reasonable relation to the evils to be eradicated or the advantages to be secured."[14] It is self-evident that for European contractors and sub-contractors within the EC cost imposed upon them by the Amendments does not bear a reasonable relation to the advantage of furthering American export policy.

13. Most recently in *Goldblatt* v. *Town of Hempstead,* 369 US 590, 594 (1962).
14. *Nashville C. and St. L. Ry* v. *Walters,* 294 US 405, 429 (1935).

29. This lack of provision for compensation or protection is all the more disconcerting, because the Amendments of June 22 purport to regulate not merely U.S. external trade,[15] but EC external trade as well. Moreover, these are considerations which obviously have played a role in the imposition of foreign trade embargoes in the past. Firstly, both the Cuban Assets Control Regulations (1981) and the Iranian Assets Control Regulations (1979) exempted to a large extent foreign incorporated firms with ties to U.S. firms from otherwise stringent or even absolute trade prohibitions.[16] Secondly, both the trade embargo connected with the Iranian hostage crisis and the embargo on grain shipments to the USSR permitted existing contracts to be honoured.

IV. *Conclusion*

30. The European Community considers that the Amendments to the Export Administration Regulations of June 22, 1982 are unlawful since they cannot be validly based on any of the generally accepted bases of jurisdiction in international law. Moreover, insofar as these Amendments tend to enlist companies whose main ties are to the EC Member States for purposes of American trade policy *vis-a-vis* the USSR, they constitute an unacceptable interference in the independent commercial policy of the EC. Comparable measures by third states have been rejected by the U.S. in the past.

31. Even from the standpoint of U.S. law, the European Community considers that the United States has not adopted a proper "balance of interests" approach. The European Community further considers that the Amendments are of doubtful validity under the criteria of the Export Administration Act of 1979.

32. For these reasons, the European Community calls upon the U.S. Authorities to withdraw these measures.

ORGANIZATION OF AMERICAN STATES

[On January 31, 1962 the Organization of American States adopted resolutions excluding Cuba from participating in the OAS system and imposing an embargo on trade with Cuba in arms and implements of war. Final Act, Eighth Meeting of Consultation of Ministers of Foreign Affairs Serving as Organ of Consultation in Application of the Inter-American Treaty of Reciprocal Assistance, Punta del Este, Uruguay, January 22-31, 1962, OEA/Ser.C/II.8 (1962). The resolution cited, in explanation for the action taken, Cuba's having established a social and governmental system based

---

15. *Buttfield* v. *Stranahan*, 192 US 470, 493 (1904) indicates that insofar as it concerns U.S. external trade it may be difficult to assert Fifth Amendment rights.

16. This is not to say that the EC agrees in principle to the way in which these Regulations handle the problem of extraterritoriality.

upon Marxist-Leninist ideology and its acceptance of military assistance from the Soviet Union and China. The vote on the resolution was fourteen to one (Mexico) with five abstentions (Argentina, Brazil, Chile, Bolivia and Ecuador).

Thereafter, on July 26, 1964 the OAS passed a further resolution requiring all member states to break diplomatic relations with Cuba; to impose a collective embargo on trade with Cuba except in foodstuffs, medicines and medical equipment for humanitarian purposes; and to suspend all sea transportation between member states and Cuba. Final Act, Ninth Meeting of Consultation of Ministers of Foreign Affairs Serving as Organ of Consultation in Application of the Inter-American Treaty of Reciprocal Assistance, OEA/Ser.C/II.9, Doc. 48, Rev.2 (1964). In explanation of these actions, the OAS cited Cuba's support for revolutionary movements in Venezuela. The vote in support of the resolution was fifteen to four (Chile, Bolivia, Uruguay and Mexico) with one abstention.

The 1964 sanctions resolution was never fully effective in preventing trade or diplomatic contacts between Latin American countries and Cuba; Mexico, for instance, never broke diplomatic ties with Cuba. Between 1973 and 1975 the effectiveness of the resolution broke down almost completely. By then it was clear that a majority of the member states of the OAS no longer supported mandatory sanctions against Cuba: Cuba had already reestablished diplomatic ties with a number of these countries and significant trade relations with many more. It had also begun to participate in many regional economic organizations.

On July 29, 1975 the OAS adopted a resolution rescinding its sanctions against Cuba and leaving to each member state the right to determine its diplomatic and trade relations with Cuba. The vote was sixteen to three (Chile, Paraguay and Uruguay) with two abstentions (Nicaragua and Brazil). The United States joined the majority. Final Act, Sixteenth Meeting of Consultation of Ministers of Foreign Affairs, Serving as Organ of Consultation in Application of the Inter-American Treaty of Reciprocal Assistance, July 29, 1975, OEA/Ser.F/II.Doc.9/75, Rev.2 (1975).

The 1975 resolution is set out below, as are three documents reflecting the United States' response. In the first, the State Department announced that it would take steps to comply with the resolution by modifying those economic measures which impact upon third countries. In the second, the Commerce Department, making express reference to the OAS resolution, liberalized restrictions on third-country exports to Cuba containing 20 percent or less United States components, parts, or materials.

The third document is an excerpt from the testimony of then Assistant Secretary of State for Inter-American Affairs William D. Rogers before Congress elaborating upon the significance of the OAS resolution. He concluded that the OAS resolution "made it inconsistent for us to continue to apply our own restrictions to third countries that trade with and ship to Cuba."

The Cuban Democracy Act of 1992 substantially restored the pre-1975 restrictions on third-country shipping and imposed a complete ban on foreign subsidiary trade, doing away with the policy of licensing such trade in effect since 1963 and liberalized in 1975 in response to the 1975 OAS resolution.]

1975 OAS RESOLUTION

(Final Act, Sixteenth Meeting of Consultation of Ministers of Foreign Affairs, Serving as Organ of Consultation in Application of the Inter-American Treaty of Reciprocal Assistance (TIAR), July 29, 1975, OEA/Ser. F/II. Doc. 9/75 Rev. 2.)

Considering:

That the States Parties to the TIAR have renewed their adherence to the principles of Inter-American solidarity and co-operation, nonintervention and reciprocal assistance enunciated in the TIAR and the Charter of the Organization, and

Desiring:

To promote Inter-American relations in the broadest possible way,

Resolves:

1. To reaffirm solemnly the principle of nonintervention and to urge States Parties to ensure that it is observed throughout the continent, in accordance with the Charter of the Organization, to which end they once more proclaim their solidarity and reiterate their will to co-operate constantly with a view to fulfilling the purposes of a policy of peace,

2. To grant the States Parties to the TIAR freedom to normalize or conduct their relations with the Republic of Cuba in accordance with their own national policy and interests, and at the level and in the manner which each State deems appropriate, and

3. To transmit the text of this resolution to the Security Council of the United Nations.

STATE DEPARTMENT RESPONSE TO THE OAS RESOLUTION

(Dep't St. Bull. p.404 (September 15, 1975))

The Organ of Consultation of the OAS, acting under the *Rio Treaty,* adopted a resolution on July 29 which allows each member state to determine for itself the nature of its economic and diplomatic relations with the Government of Cuba. That action grew out of an earlier decision by the members of the OAS, on July 25, to adopt a Protocol of Amendment to the *Rio Treaty* which, once ratified, will lift sanctions by a simple majority vote.

In keeping with this action by the OAS, the United States is modifying the aspects of our Cuban denial policy which affects other countries. Effective today, August 21, 1975, it will be U.S. policy to grant licenses permitting transactions between U.S. subsidiaries and Cuba for trade in foreign-made goods when those subsidiaries are operating in countries where local law or policy favors trade with Cuba. Specific licenses will continue to be required in each case and they will remain subject to regulations concerning U.S. origin parts, components, strategic goods and technology.

In order to conform further with the OAS action, we are taking appropriate steps so that effective immediately countries which allow their ships or aircraft to carry goods to and from Cuba are not penalized by loss of U.S. bilateral assistance. We are initiating steps to modify regulations which deny bunkering in the United States to third country ships engaged in the Cuba trade. We will also seek legislation to eliminate similar restrictions on Title I, Public Law 480 food sales to third countries.

AMENDMENT TO COMMERCE DEPARTMENT
REGULATIONS IN RESPONSE TO OAS RESOLUTION

(40 Fed. Reg. 55314, November 28, 1975)

(b) *Cuba.* On August 21, 1975, the U.S. Government announced modifications in those aspects of U.S. restrictions on trade with Cuba which affect third countries, in order to bring them into accord with the policy of the Organization of American States to allow each member state to determine for itself the nature of its economic and diplomatic relations with the Government of Cuba. In this context, the Department of Commerce generally will consider favorably on a case-by-case basis requests for authorization for the use of an insubstantial proportion of U.S.-origin materials, parts, or components in nonstrategic foreign-made products to be exported to Cuba, where local law requires, or policy in the third country favors, trade with Cuba. U.S.-origin content will generally be considered insubstantial when it amounts to 20 percent or less of the value of the product to be exported from the third country. Approval of requests for authorization for the use of U.S.-origin materials, parts, or components amounting to more than 20 percent by value of the foreign-made product to be exported from the third country to Cuba will be less likely.

STATEMENT OF WILLIAM D. ROGERS, ASSISTANT SECRETARY
FOR INTER-AMERICAN AFFAIRS, DEPARTMENT OF STATE

(United States Trade Embargo of Cuba, Hearings before Subcommittees
on International Trade and Commerce and International Organizations
of House Comm. on Int'l Rel., 94th Cong., 1st Sess. 360 (1975))

Mr. Rogers: Thank you, Mr. Chairman.

I appear before the Subcommittee on International Trade and Commerce, and the Subcommittee on International Organizations to testify on developments in the evolution of our Cuba policy since my last appearance before you on June 11 of this year. It is a pleasure to be here.

Let me lay down a few general principles:

We are ready. We are prepared to improve our relations with Cuba. Hostility is not a permanent and unalterable part of our policy.

We are willing to enter into a dialog with Cuba. But the dialog must be on a basis of reciprocity.

The process to this end must be direct discussion between parties. We will not bargain through the press or through intermediaries.

We are prepared to engage in such direct exchanges without preconditions or ultimatum.

Resolution of the problems between us will not be easy, and will not be furthered by calculated offense to the other party.

We cannot put aside the interests of a half-million Cuban refugees to whom we have given asylum. The human dimension of our relations with Cuba is at the top our agenda.

Nor can we ignore the substantial claims for compensation held by U.S. nationals.

In all events, our negotiations toward these ends must be sober and businesslike.

This afternoon I would like to begin by reviewing the events of significance in United States-Cuban relations since my last appearance here. These are: the termination of mandatory OAS sanctions against Cuba at San Jose (which you may want to pursue with your former colleague, Ambassador Bill Mailliard, who is here with me); our lifting of third country restrictions; and various developments in the world affecting the emergent United States-Cuban dialog, as well as United States and Cuban official statements and gestures.

The San Jose Action

I discussed at length the multilateral constraints on trade with Cuba during my last appearance before your subcommittees. At that time, I said we wanted to clear the multilateral decks of this issue in order to remove a divisive issue and restore the integrity of the Rio Treaty.

This was accomplished at the end of July in a manner reflecting a healthy consensus of opinion within the OAS.

A conference of plenipotentiaries was held July 16 through the 26 in San Jose, Costa Rica, to consider amendment of the Inter-American Treaty of Reciprocal Assistance—Rio Treaty. A protocol amendment was signed on July 26.

The key amendment was the provision that a vote to rescind sanctions against a state would be taken by a vote of an absolute majority rather than by a vote of two-thirds as is required by the existing Rio Treaty.

These amendments are, of course, subject to ratification and will be submitted soon to the Senate for its advice and consent.

As a result of a resolution of the OAS Permanent Council held in San Jose on July 26, the OAS representatives met at the Sixteenth Meeting of Consultation of Ministers of Foreign Affairs on July 29, serving as Organ of Consultation under the Rio Treaty.

The delegations of Argentina, Colombia, Costa Rica, Ecuador, Haiti, Honduras, Mexico, Panama, Peru, Trinidad and Tobago, and Venezuela cosponsored a draft resolution which solemnly reaffirmed the principle of nonintervention and left parties to the Rio Treaty freedom of action in deciding whether or not to continue to desist from trade and diplomatic relations with Cuba.

The action of San Jose removed an anomaly—the anomaly of mandatory sanctions which were no longer acceptable to a majority of the OAS members. The United States saw the San Jose result as a practical, diplomatic, as well as legally sound means of restoring the integrity of the Rio Treaty. Therefore, we gave our support to the resolution and voted in favor of it along with 15 other OAS members.

Those who voted against were Chile, Paraguay and Uruguay. Brazil and Nicaragua abstained. All the other nations, 16 in all, voted for the resolution. It is now in effect. The member states have freedom of action either to continue the suspension of or to reinstitute commercial and diplomatic ties with Cuba.

Lifting Our Third Country Constraints.

As a logical and practical corollary to the termination of mandatory OAS sanctions, the U.S. Government, on August 21, announced modifications of those aspects of our Cuban denial policy which affect other countries.

*   *   *

This action did not resolve, and was not put forward as the resolution of a bilateral issue with Cuba. As Secretary Kissinger has made clear, bilateral issues, including our own direct trade ban, will be subject to negotiations with the Cubans on a basis of reciprocity.

This was basically a measure to remove a recurrent source of friction between the United States and friendly countries both in this hemisphere and overseas which, for reasons of their own, have engaged in or never ceased to trade with Cuba.

The termination of the mandatory aspect of the OAS sanctions at San Jose made it inconsistent for us to continue to apply our own restrictions to third countries that trade with and ship to Cuba.

THE UNITED STATES LEGAL POSITION

NOTE ON THE STATE DEPARTMENT AND THE AMERICAN LAW INSTITUTE'S RESTATEMENT OF THE FOREIGN RELATIONS LAW OF THE UNITED STATES

Soon after the U.S.S.R.-Western Europe gas pipeline controversy, the Legal Adviser to the Department of State cited with approval the *Restatement, Second, Foreign Relations Law of the United States* (1965) on the question of national jurisdiction and criticized the successor *Restatement* then under consideration in draft form. David R. Robinson, *Conflicts of Jurisdiction and the Draft Restatement,* 15 Law and Policy in Int'l Business 1147 (1983). Consideration of the two *Restatements* is therefore useful to illuminate the United States position, particularly as, for the most part, "theories of jurisdiction regarding export controls have not been elaborated by the Executive Branch or Congress nor have they been appraised, in terms of international law, by the courts." W. Michael Reisman and William D. Araiza, *United States of America,* in Karl M. Meessen, ed., *International Law of Export Control: Jurisdictional Issues* 163, 172 (1992). Formulated by the American Law Institute, a private body composed of leading United States judges, lawyers, and law teachers, the *Restatements* are "an attempt to state and clarify existing" international law. *Restatement Second,* p. xi.

Issued in 1965 the *Restatement Second* identified links of territory and nationality as the traditional bases for a state prescribing a rule of law. It also recognized the prescriptive jurisdiction of a state with respect to external threats to its security or to the operation of its governmental functions, provided the external conduct is generally recognized as a crime under the law of states that have reasonably developed legal systems (for example, counterfeiting of a state's currency). The *Restatement Second* found states to have jurisdiction over at least three matters of universal concern as well: piracy, collision and salvage on the high seas, and fisheries conservation. *Restatement Second,* §§ 10, 33, 34-36.

The *Restatement Second,* § 17, stated the territorial principle as follows:

Jurisdiction to Prescribe with Respect to Conduct, Thing, Status, or Other Interest within Territory

A state has jurisdiction to prescribe a rule of law

(a) attaching legal consequences to conduct that occurs within its territory, whether or not such consequences are determined by the effects of the conduct outside the territory, and

(b) relating to a thing located, or a status or other interest localized, in its territory.

Within the scope of this territorial principle is certain conduct that occurs outside the territory but causes an effect within the territory. *Restatement Second*, § 18.

The United States has predicated its regulation of third-country companies re-exporting United States-origin products or technical data on this territorial principle, treating re-export control as a condition of the original authorization to export from the territory of the United States. 15 C.F.R. § 774; *Restatement, Third, Foreign Relations Law of the United States*, § 402, Comment c, p. 239 (1987); Homer E. Moyer, Jr. and Linda A. Mabry, *Export Controls as Instruments for Foreign Policy: The History, Legal Issues and Policy Lessons of Three Recent Cases*, 15 Law and Policy in Int'l Business 127 (1983). This assertion of jurisdiction is usually, although not always, bolstered by the United States requiring the foreign importers' agreement to abide by any changes in the United States laws on re-exports. At hearings before Congress on the gas pipeline controls, Lionel Olmer, Under Secretary for International Trade Administration of the Commerce Department, testified in 1982 as follows:

> We do state unequivocally our position that we have such authority [to regulate re-exports]. Without getting into a legal debate, I would say to you that the contracts undertaken by those people in Europe [the importers of U.S.-origin goods or technical data] included a clause that committed them to keep current regarding U.S. export regulations, and committed them to receiving authorization for the re-export of any products and U.S. technology which might go to the Soviet Union.
>
> So, that is to say, we maintain that our export control laws come into force and effect at the time of re-export. It is not a new phenomenon created in December or in June, but it is a part and parcel of the means by which we have applied our export control regulations over time, with the knowledge and obviously with the consent of our foreign trading partners.

Economic Relations with the Soviet Union, Hearings before the Subcommittee on International Economic Policy of the Senate Committee on Foreign Relations, 97th Cong., 2nd Sess. 20 (1982).

The *Restatement Second*, § 27, acknowledges that a corporation has the nationality of the state under whose laws it is organized and is thus subject to that state's regulation under the nationality principle. The *Restatement Second* also finds jurisdiction on the basis of the nationality principle in the state of those who own or control the third-country corporation. Comment d to § 27 provides:

> When the nationality of a corporation is different from the nationality of the persons (individual or corporate) who own or control it, the state of the nationality of such persons has jurisdiction to prescribe, and to enforce in its territory, rules of law governing their conduct. It is thus in a position to control the conduct of the corporation even though it does not have jurisdiction to prescribe rules directly applicable to the corporation.

Under this approach, there may be conflicting assertions of jurisdiction with respect to the foreign subsidiaries of United States corporations, just as there may be conflicts with respect to re-exports on the basis of the *Restatement Second*'s territorial principle once the goods are outside the United States. In these and other conflicts between two states prescribing different rules of conduct, the *Restatement Second* found that "international law is normally neutral, provided both states have bases of jurisdiction that international law recognizes." *Id.*, § 39, Reporter's Notes, p. 113. "There is no developed rule of international law that precludes exercise of jurisdiction solely because another state has jurisdiction," and further, "international law, in most situations, does not provide for choosing among competing bases of jurisdiction to prescribe rules of conduct." *Restatement Second,* § 39, Comment b.

It is upon this analysis that the United States maintains that it may apply its trade restrictions to a company organized under the laws of a third country but owned or controlled by United States nationals. Ownership or control provides a basis for jurisdiction, and it suffices no matter the basis or strength of the third-country's jurisdictional claims.

While it finds no qualification in international law to a state's jurisdiction once any jurisdictional basis is found, the *Restatement Second* does require a state "to consider" moderating enforcement of its rules when another state with jurisdiction has established conflicting rules. Section 40 provides as follows:

Limitations on Exercise of Enforcement Jurisdiction

Where two states have jurisdiction to prescribe and enforce rules of law and the rules they may prescribe require inconsistent conduct upon the part of a person, each state is required by international law to consider, in good faith, moderating the exercise of its enforcement jurisdiction, in the light of such factors as

(a) vital national interests of each of the states,

(b) the extent and the nature of the hardship that inconsistent enforcement actions would impose upon the person,

(c) the extent to which the required conduct is to take place in the territory of the other state,

(d) the nationality of the person, and

(e) the extent to which enforcement by action of either state can reasonably be expected to achieve compliance with the rule prescribed by that state.

The *Restatement, Third, Foreign Relations Law of the United States* (1987), issued more than two decades later, found in the intervening controversies over jurisdiction and their resolution the emergence of a principle of international law supplanting the *Restatement Second*'s position. Now, even when one of the bases for prescriptive jurisdiction is present, "a state may not exercise jurisdiction to prescribe law with respect to a person or activity having connections with another state when the exercise of such jurisdiction is unreasonable." *Restatement Third,* § 403. "In contrast to prior § 40 [of the *Restatement Second*], reasonableness is understood here not as a basis for requiring states to consider moderating their enforcement of laws, but is an essential element in determining whether, as a matter of international law, the state may exercise jurisdiction to prescribe." *Restatement Third,* § 403, Reporter's Note 10, p.254. The *Restatement Third* also modified the formulation of the traditional bases of jurisdiction so that they too embrace "broader criteria" of reasonableness. *Id.,* Subchapter A, Introductory Note, p.237.

Sections 402 and 403 of the *Restatement Third* read as follows:

§ 402. Bases of Jurisdiction to Prescribe

Subject to § 403, a state has jurisdiction to prescribe law with respect to

(1)(a) conduct that, wholly or in substantial part, takes place within its territory;

(b) the status of persons, or interests in things, present within its territory;

(c) conduct outside its territory that has or is intended to have substantial effect within its territory;

(2) the activities, interests, status, or relations of its nationals outside as well as within its territory; and

(3) certain conduct outside its territory by persons not its nationals that is directed against the security of the state or against a limited class of other state interests.

§ 403. Limitations on Jurisdiction to Prescribe

(1) Even when one of the bases for jurisdiction under § 402 is present, a state may not exercise jurisdiction to prescribe law with respect to a person or activity having connections with another state when the exercise of such jurisdiction is unreasonable.

(2) Whether exercise of jurisdiction over a person or activity is unreasonable is determined by evaluating all relevant factors, including, where appropriate:

(a) the link of the activity to the territory of the regulating state, i.e., the extent to which the activity takes place within the territory, or has substantial, direct, and foreseeable effect upon or in the territory;

(b) the connections, such as nationality, residence, or economic activity, between the regulating state and the person principally responsible for the activity to be regulated, or between that state and those whom the regulation is designed to protect;

(c) the character of the activity to be regulated, the importance of regulation to the regulating state, the extent to which other states regulate such activities, and the degree to which the desirability of such regulation is generally accepted;

(d) the existence of justified expectations that might be protected or hurt by the regulation;

(e) the importance of the regulation to the international political, legal, or economic system;

(f) the extent to which the regulation is consistent with the traditions of the international system;

(g) the extent to which another state may have an interest in regulating the activity; and

(h) the likelihood of conflict with regulation by another state.

(3) When it would not be unreasonable for each of two states to exercise jurisdiction over a person or activity, but the prescriptions by the two states are in conflict, each state has an obligation to evaluate its own as well as the other state's interest in exercising jurisdiction, in light of all the relevant factors, Subsection (2); a state should defer to the other state if that state's interest is clearly greater.

In the light of these newly emergent principles, the *Restatement Third* addressed the United States regulation of foreign subsidiaries differently than the *Restatement Second*. Its § 414 reads as follows:

§ 414. Jurisdiction with Respect to Activities of Foreign Branches and Subsidiaries

(1) Subject to §§ 403 and 441,* a state may exercise jurisdiction to prescribe for limited purposes with respect to activities of foreign branches of corporations organized under its laws.

(2) A state may not ordinarily regulate activities of corporations organized under the laws of a foreign state on the basis that they are owned

---

*Section 441 provides in relevant part as follows:

§ 441. Foreign State Compulsion

(1) In general, a state may not require a person

(a) to do an act in another state that is prohibited by the law of that state or by the law of the state of which he is a national; or

(b) to refrain from doing an act in another state that is required by the law of that state or by the law of the state of which he is a national.

or controlled by nationals of the regulating state. However, under § 403 and subject to § 441, it may not be unreasonable for a state to exercise jurisdiction for limited purposes with respect to activities of affiliated foreign entities

(a) by direction to the parent corporation in respect of such matters as uniform accounting, disclosure to investors, or preparation of consolidated tax returns of multinational enterprises; or

(b) by direction to either the parent or the subsidiary in exceptional cases, depending on all relevant factors, including the extent to which

(i) the regulation is essential to implementation of a program to further a major national interest of the state exercising jurisdiction;

(ii) the national program of which the regulation is a part can be carried out effectively only if it is applied also to foreign subsidiaries;

(iii) the regulation conflicts or is likely to conflict with the law or policy of the state where the subsidiary is established.

(c) In the exceptional cases referred to in paragraph (b) the burden of establishing reasonableness is heavier when the direction is issued to the foreign subsidiary than when it is issued to the parent corporation.

Under the *Restatement Third*'s exposition in particular, the shift in the United States' articulated purposes and goals in its Cuban sanctions program, see Part III, would require a fresh consideration of the United States regulation of foreign subsidiary trade with Cuba and its limitations on the re-export of United States-origin goods or technical data to Cuba. In determining whether these assertions of jurisdiction are "unreasonable" and hence violative of international law, attention must be paid to the "importance of regulation to the regulating state." *Restatement Third*, § 403 (2)(c). The importance to the United States of promoting democracy in Cuba may be evaluated differently than the importance of the national security and foreign policy interests previously asserted as justification for the Cuban sanctions program, namely, deterring Cuban support for subversion of third countries, Cuba's strategic alliance with the Soviet Union, and Cuba's efforts to influence regional conflicts by stationing substantial troops abroad. Under the *Restatement Second*'s approach, in contrast, the shift in rationale simply would require the United States to consider moderating its enforcement of the rule of law it has prescribed.

In his 1983 article State Department Legal Adviser Robinson wrote that the United States' view of international law, as well as its state practice, coincided with that suggested by the *Restatement Second* rather than the *Restatement Third*. The latter's § 403, stating a requirement of reasonableness, "does not accurately reflect the state of international law." *Conflicts of Jurisdiction and the Draft Restatement*, 15 Law and Policy in Int'l Business 1147, 1152 (1983). Moreover, the United States does not generally support the development of international law in the direction indicated by § 403. Once any basis for jurisdiction is present, then, in the United States' view, the matter for the most part is one best left to the realm of diplomacy and foreign policy rather than law:

> Any effort to limit questions of conflicts of jurisdiction to purely legal questions of the power, or even the propriety, of exercising jurisdiction is bound to impose an analytical rigidity inconsistent with the flexibility required by the widely-varying demands of diplomacy and foreign policy. The effort is also unlikely to be adequately responsive to the legitimate domestic concerns behind the laws in question.

*   *   *

In the opinion of the Office of the Legal Adviser this effort to "legalize" disputes over conflicts of jurisdiction is ill-advised. Section 403, as currently drafted, does not accurately reflect the state of international law. Nor would it constitute a desirable change in the law because it fails to take into account the diplomatic and policy aspects of conflicts of jurisdiction. While some have criticized the current balancing test for being too "political" and insufficiently "legal," changing the question from how to resolve conflicts of jurisdiction to how to determine which state has sole jurisdiction does not alter the underlying problem. The answers to conflicts of jurisdiction cannot be found by reducing all disputes to legal battles over the exclusive authority of states.

Id. at 1149, 1152. *See also* Secretary of State Shultz, "Trade, Interdependence, and Conflicts of Jurisdiction," *Dep't St. Bull.* p.33 (June 1984).

The United States position articulated by Legal Adviser Robinson in 1983 was evident in the remarks that same year by Deputy Secretary of State Kenneth Dam occasioned specifically by the gas pipeline controversy and was evident as well in the remarks of Legal Adviser John R. Stevenson in 1970 occasioned in part by United States efforts to regulate the Canadian subsidiaries of United States corporations wishing to pursue trade with Cuba. We reprint Secretary Dam and Legal Adviser Stevenson's remarks, which were published in *Dep't St. Bull.* p.48 (June 1983) and *Dep't St. Bull.* p.425 (October 12, 1970), respectively.

KENNETH W. DAM, DEPUTY SECRETARY OF STATE,
"EXTRATERRITORIALITY AND CONFLICTS OF JURISDICTION,"
ADDRESS BEFORE THE AMERICAN SOCIETY OF INTERNATIONAL
LAW, WASHINGTON, D.C., APRIL 15, 1983

*   *   *

The legal dispute was over what is sometimes called extraterritoriality. I prefer the term "conflicts of jurisdiction," which describes the issue more neutrally and analytically. In a wide variety of situations, the United States and other countries attempt to apply their laws or regulations to conduct or property beyond their national boundaries. The resulting international disputes can become particularly serious when the legal arguments embody major disagreements over foreign policy, as in the Polish sanctions case. Thus conflicts of jurisdiction are at the intersection of law and diplomacy, making the topic especially appropriate for a Deputy Secretary of State to discuss before this learned society.

One of the aims of the American Society of International Law has been "to promote the establishment and maintenance of international relations on the basis of law and justice." That is a good statement of one of our principal national objectives in both international law and foreign policy.

Let me give you a brief survey of the conflicts problem, and then I shall outline the program of concrete steps that the U.S. Government is taking to show its willingness to resolve, or ease, the kinds of difficulties that have arisen.

Roots of the Problem

The international problem of conflicts of jurisdiction has an ancient history. The concept of extraterritoriality antedated the nation-state as we now know it. Through Roman and medieval times, a citizen was subject to the jurisdiction of his sovereign wherever he traveled. More recently, for centuries, consuls of some powerful states were able to exercise criminal and civil jurisdiction over their nationals in foreign countries. As early as the 15th century, Venetians traveling in the Ottoman Empire gained exemption from Ottoman jurisdiction. Soon Sardinians, Tuscans, Austrians, Russians, and others carved out similar privileges in Ottoman domains. The other most famous case is China in the 19th century. Many European colonial powers gained the right to apply their own laws to their nationals in China through diplomatic or consular courts.

The United States engaged in the practice as well. We gained extraterritorial rights in regions of the Ottoman Empire by the 1830 Treaty of Commerce and Navigation with Turkey. These rights lasted until 1949. In China, the United States obtained extraterritorial jurisdiction through the 1844 Treaty of Peace, Amity and Commerce and did not terminate it until 1943.

When the treaty to relinquish extraterritorial rights in China was before the U.S. Senate in 1943, the Foreign Relations Committee somewhat nostalgically observed that the practice of extraterritoriality had had a benign purpose. It had been intended, the committee said "to diminish friction, minimize causes of conflict, and contribute to the maintenance of conditions of law and order." As we now know, the practice had the opposite effect. The Chinese today view it as a symbol of the humiliations imposed on them by the colonial powers during the period of their national weakness. The issue had quite literally revolutionary implications.

In this modern age of nationalism, every nation is extraordinarily sensitive to other countries' assertions of jurisdiction that seem to impinge on the sacred domain of national sovereignty. The irony is that the modern world also generates its own, almost unavoidable, conditions of jurisdictional conflict.

We live in a world of increasing economic interdependence. The rapidly growing scale of international trade and investment in the postwar period has brought with it a vast expansion of law regulation, and legal complexity. The result is that even among the closest allies, claims of jurisdiction are bound frequently to collide. Consider the enormous expansion of world trade: The decade of the 1970s was a period of oil shocks and recessions; nevertheless, between 1970 and 1980 world exports increased from $328 billion to over $2 trillion. American exports alone increased from $43 billion to over $220 billion. Foreign direct investment in the United States increased almost fivefold.

In this modern environment of commercial expansion and interaction, the United States and other nations often judge that their civil and criminal law must reach conduct abroad that has substantial and direct effects on their economies, their interests, and their citizens. Needless to say, one nation's assessment of its legal necessity often runs up against another nation's conception of its national sovereignty.

*   *   *

The United States has resorted to economic controls in several instances as an instrument of foreign or national security policy. In the case of our export controls over trade with communist countries, there have been many instances of disagreement with our trading partners. In a famous example in the mid-1960s, French President de Gaulle reopened trade relations with China at a time when U.S.-China relations were still locked in bitter hostility. This action quickly found its way into court in the *Freuhauf* case.

In 1965, the United States attempted to prevent the French subsidiary of Freuhauf, an American manufacturer of tractor trailers, from selling trailers to China. The subsidiary sought relief from a French court, which took over operation of the subsidiary and appointed a receiver who required delivery of the trailers to China. In the end, the territorial sovereign—in this case, France—was allowed to control the enterprise at issue. But the underlying policy conflict endured, at least until 1971, when one of the jurisdictions involved—that is, the United States—began to harmonize its China policy with that of the other.

The dispute over Polish sanctions was an even more vivid example of a legal dispute that was in its essence a dispute over policy. We and our allies condemned the Soviet-backed declaration of martial law in Poland and the suppression of human rights. To signify that "business as usual" could not continue with those who oppressed the Polish people, the President imposed economic sanctions against the Soviet and Polish Governments. These sanctions included, *inter alia,* controls over exports of oil and gas equipment and technology to the USSR.

The President imposed the sanctions under the Export Administration Act of 1979. That act authorizes controls over goods or technology "subject to the jurisdiction of the United States or exported by any person subject to the jurisdiction of the United States" where necessary to further our national security or foreign policy objectives. Where "national security" controls are involved, fewer disputes arise between the United States and its allies. Goods and technology which make a direct and significant contribution to Soviet military potential are prohibited by all allied countries. When the controls are imposed on "foreign policy" grounds, however—such as in the Polish case—different perspectives are more likely to exist.

The legal dispute with our allies over Polish sanctions focused on the American effort to reach conduct abroad and on the issue of sanctity of contracts. The sanctions announced on December 29, 1981, prohibited exports and reexports of oil and gas equipment and technology to the Soviet Union regardless of preexisting contractual obligations; the sanctions extended to goods of U.S. origin already in foreign hands. On June 18, 1982, the controls were extended to prohibit the export by foreign subsidiaries of wholly foreign-made goods, and the export by licensees of foreign products incorporating previously obtained U.S. technology. Our allies objected to the interruption of contracts already signed. They further objected to the so-called "extraterritorial" reach of the sanctions.

American parents of the foreign subsidiaries, such as Dresser Industries, and licensees of American technology brought numerous administrative proceedings and lawsuits against the U.S. Department of Commerce. In response, this government took the same position that administration after administration and Congress after Congress have taken—namely, that the relationship between a parent and a subsidiary, or the use of American technology by a licensee, justifies the assertion of American jurisdiction when substantial American interests are involved.

But the issue was not resolved in the courts. It was settled by diplomacy. The underlying dispute was on the broader question of economic relations with the Soviet Union.

*   *   *

There is an important lesson here, and, indeed, it is the main theme I want to put before you tonight. When these disputes over jurisdiction turn out to be grounded in disputes over policy, the most effective solution is a major effort to harmonize our policies. This may not make the legal disputes go away, but it will surely make them less divisive. The democratic nations have an even deeper interest in resolving these policy conflicts—not only to make lawyers' lives easier but to preserve the political unity of the Western alliance. And that alliance is, without exaggeration, the foundation of the legal, economic, and political system of the democratic West.

In the coming decades, the problem of maintaining allied cohesion over foreign policy will not necessarily become easier. In the early years of the postwar period, American power was so preponderant within the alliance that our prescriptions often received ready acceptance from allies weakened by the war and dependent on American economic aid and military protection. Today, our allies are strong, self-confident, and independent minded. Unanimity will hardly be automatic. The United States still has the responsibility to state its convictions, and act on them, on matters of vital importance to free world security. Harmonizing policies will require determined effort on the part of all.

Measures for the Future

The United States is prepared to do its part in finding cooperative solutions to the problems I have discussed. We are prepared to be responsive to the concerns of others. If our allies join with us in the same spirit, much can be done.

First of all, the United States will continue to seek to resolve the policy differences that underlie many of these conflicts of jurisdiction. Thus, for example, we will work with our allies toward the goal of a new consensus on the important strategic issue of East-West trade.

Second, the United States can seek to minimize conflicts by shaping and applying appropriate guidelines to govern assertions of authority over conduct abroad where those assertions conflict with foreign law. The American Law Institute is now considering a third draft *Restatement of Foreign Relations Law.* The draft now gives a prominent place to the balancing of competing state interests in determining the existence of jurisdiction over foreign conduct. We in the Department of State are not altogether satisfied with making a balancing test the prerequisite to the existence of jurisdiction. As a practical matter, however, a careful weighing of the interests of the states concerned is obviously a useful procedure and a deterrent to unwarranted conflicts. We welcome the Federal courts' use of a general balancing analysis in private cases like *Timberlane, Mannington Milts,* and *Mitsui.* Balancing can certainly help to ensure that decisions affecting significant foreign concerns are not taken lightly.

Third, the United States is making clear its intention to avoid further problems of retroactive application of economic controls. We know that the reliability of contracts is essential to the health and growth of commerce. Last week the President transmitted to Congress legislation to amend and extend the Export Administration Act of 1979. The Administration bill strengthens the national security export controls and their enforcement while at the same time easing some of the problems we have had in the past over foreign policy controls.

The bill declares explicitly that "it is the policy of the United States, when imposing new foreign policy controls, to minimize the impact on pre-existing contracts and on business activities in allied or other friendly countries to the extent consistent with the underlying purpose of the controls."

The bill also explicitly recognizes the sanctity of contracts as a limitation which will insulate many existing contracts from disruption by new foreign policy export controls. Specifically, the bill protects existing sales contracts that require delivery within 270 days from the imposition of controls, unless the President determines that a prohibition of such exports is required by the "overriding national interest" of the United States.

To strengthen enforcement of the national security export controls, the bill authorizes restrictions on future imports into the United States of goods or technology from persons abroad who violate these controls. Controls on imports into the United States by particular foreign violators are obviously territorial and, therefore, are clearly within our jurisdiction under international law.

*   *   *

The Need for Cooperation

These measures will not eliminate the problem of conflicts of jurisdiction. But the United States is eager to do what it can to minimize such problems in the future. We value our relations with our partners.

Any one of our countries may, on some occasion in the future, feel that its national interest or public policy cannot be served without an assertion of jurisdiction which leads to a disagreement with its partners. The complexity of the modern interdependent world, and the reality of greater equality among the major industrial nations, make these occurrences almost inevitable.

The problem is ripe for creative legal thinking. It also calls for statesmanship to ensure that the fundamental political and moral unity of the democracies is not torn by disputes over policy. All of the industrial democracies face the same larger responsibility: How do we reconcile our sovereign independence as nations with the imperative of our unity as allies? How do we balance our interest in expanding trade and jobs and prosperity with our interest in not contributing to the growth of Soviet power? Once again the great enterprise of the law touches upon some of the most profound questions of our national and international life.

JOHN R. STEVENSON, LEGAL ADVISER TO THE STATE
DEPARTMENT, "EXTRATERRITORIALITY IN CANADIAN-UNITED
STATES RELATIONS," COMMENTS TO THE CANADIAN
BAR ASSOCIATION, OCTOBER 12, 1970

A consequence of the close ties between the United States and Canada is a shared awareness of the special problems that arise out of the proximity of the two countries—a proximity that is more than merely geographic. What the United States does is watched and often felt in Canada, and there is an understandable sensitivity in this country to some of our actions that impinge on Canadian interests. The United States Government is aware of this sensitivity, having discussed with your Government candidly and usually fruitfully some of the problems I shall refer to this afternoon; we are concerned that every effort be made to explain United States interests, policies, and views and to understand those of Canada.

I think we might begin by putting in perspective the concept of extraterritoriality, which describes the effect in one state of the attempt by another to attach legal significance to conduct. In other words, it is an exercise of jurisdiction by a state as seen from the standpoint of a second state. Some writers have contended that no exercise of jurisdiction by a state may have effects outside that state's territory; for them, extraterritoriality is synonymous with invalidity. However, one need only look at some of the features of our shrunken world—multinational corporations, contracts involving performance in more than one country, and international aviation—to realize that it is not only practiced and permitted but also sometimes desirable or necessary that some exercises of jurisdiction have extraterritorial effects. I believe that this proposition is well enough established in state practice that it need not be belabored. But I want to emphasize that the concept of extraterritoriality does no more than help describe the effect of an exercise of jurisdiction. Whether that exercise is valid under international law depends on various considerations, only one of which is its effect in other states.

We should also bear in mind the fact that extraterritorial effects work in more than one direction. For example, when a foreign country's law tolerates, protects, encourages, or requires an anticompetitive arrangement among persons or companies subject to its jurisdiction that affects the U.S. economy, that country's law is having an extraterritorial effect in the United States. If the United States wants to do something about such a situation, it must often exercise jurisdiction in a manner that other states would characterize as extraterritorial. The problem is to reconcile the "extraterritorialities."

Principles of Jurisdiction

Though authorities and state practices differ over the question of jurisdiction to prescribe and enforce rules of law, there are certain traditional bases that have generally been applied by the courts of the United States and have formed part of the general background of assumptions for the framing of our legislation.

The *Restatement, 2d,* of the Foreign Relations Law of the United States, as adopted by the American Law Institute, reflects a recent formulation of this aspect of international law. It sets forth three principal bases of jurisdiction:

The first is jurisdiction within territory, the first part of which relates to conduct within the territory. The second part of the territorial basis, which produced considerable controversy within the American Law Institute while it was being considered, allows a state to prescribe a rule of law with respect to conduct that occurs outside its territory and causes an effect within its territory, if certain conditions are met. This part will generally apply only to aliens, since nationals' conduct abroad may be covered by the nationality principle. It has support in the *Case of the S.S. "Lotus"* (P.C.I.J. Ser. A, No. 10 (1927)), in which the Permanent Court of International Justice found that the effect on a Turkish ship of negligent conduct occurring on a French ship provided a valid basis for Turkish jurisdiction to attach consequences to that conduct. It was this basis of jurisdiction to prescribe that Judge Hand used to construe the reach of the Sherman Act in the famous Alcoa case (*U.S.* v. *Aluminum Co. of America et al,* 148 F. 2d 416 (2d Cir. 1945)).

The second basis of jurisdiction set forth in the *Restatement* is the nationality principle.

A third basis is the so-called protective principle relating to the security of a state or the operation of its governmental functions. This principle is little used in the United States.

In my opinion the *Restatement* expresses reasonable, if not universally accepted, principles of jurisdiction. I also believe that in the overwhelming majority of cases United States courts and the executive branch have acted consistently with them and that where problems have arisen they have not been the result of invalid exercises of jurisdiction but rather of two or more valid, but conflicting, exercises of jurisdiction. The question is rarely how to prevent a state from asserting an invalid jurisdiction, but how to reconcile conflicts resulting from two states prescribing different legal rules for the same conduct. Discussion of a few areas of concern might help illustrate this point.

*   *   *

Subsidiaries of U.S. Corporations in Canada

Another area in which problems have arisen concerns the application of certain U.S. laws to subsidiaries of U.S. corporations in Canada and to officers of Canadian corporations who are U.S. citizens. The basis for this jurisdiction is the nationality principle. In this area as in antitrust, possibilities for conflicts are abundant.

The substantive area in which many of the problems occur, the regulations under the Trading With the Enemy Act (50 U.S.C. App. §1-44), is an area in which the United States has long considered its vital interests to be engaged. Of course, we are fully aware of the sensitive conflicts that result from the legitimate Canadian concern about control of Canadian corporations from foreign territory. It is important to recognize here, as in the antitrust field, that these conflicts are due to two separate but valid exercises of jurisdiction and that they can and should be narrowed by mutual efforts at understanding and accommodation.

The United States has been increasingly educated to this problem, and the practice has been instituted in some cases of issuing licenses for certain transactions by U.S. subsidiaries in Canada that would otherwise be prohibited by U.S. regulation of the parent. There are other signs of change in this field, as with the recent relaxation of controls on transactions with Communist China.

PART V

ECONOMIC COERCION AND FREE TRADE IN INTERNATIONAL LAW

In the General Assembly proceedings and elsewhere, Cuba has charged that the United States measures violate international law because they are meant to coerce Cuba into abandoning its political and economic system. Cuba has also claimed that the United States sanctions program violates international norms promoting free trade, economic development, and a new international economic order.

In response the United States has advanced the broad view that its economic measures against Cuba, irrespective of their purpose, are strictly an internal matter of no concern to the international community. As it explained during the General Assembly proceedings, "[e]very government has a right and a responsibility to choose the governments with which it wishes to have commercial and political relations." And again, "[b]ilateral trade is first and foremost a question of national sovereignty. Governments make decisions to initiate trade, to end trade, to adjust the terms of trade, to suspend trade and to restore trade based on national interest."

There is a new clarity to this debate, notwithstanding that it dates back to the very beginnings of the Cuban revolution in 1959. For the first time in three decades, the United States now states that it is pursuing economic measures principally to coerce change in Cuba's political and economic system. There is no longer any reference to Cuban support of subversion in third countries, Cuba's strategic alliance with a hostile Soviet Union, or Cuba's stationing of troops abroad to influence regional conflicts—international behavior cited for thirty years as reason and justification for the United States economic campaign to isolate and weaken Cuba. See Part III, where we trace the evolution of the United States explanations for its measures.

There is another new element to this debate. The United States has intensified its always formidable economic pressure at precisely the moment when Cuba is most vulnerable. It predicts Cuba cannot survive for much longer, and in the view of some observers, the question is a close one. See Part III for a recounting of the intensification of United States efforts and Part II for Professor Zimbalist's analysis of their impact.

In this Part we provide materials helpful to an evaluation of the international law issues presented by the opposing positions of Cuba and the United States. We first set forth in pertinent part the principal international instruments relied upon by Cuba for its assertion that international law prohibits the use of economic measures to advance the neocolonial ambitions it attributes to the United States or even to advance the democratic goals asserted by the United States. We then set forth recent General Assembly resolutions which place the issue of economic coercion in the context of relations between the developed and the developing states.

After setting forth the relevant international instruments, we provide materials expressing a range of views on their import and on related legal principles. These include a report summarizing the views expressed by a group of legal experts at a meeting convened by the United Nations. The International Court of Justice in its decision in the *Nicaragua* case found no violation of customary international law in the United States economic measures against that country, *Case Concerning Military and Paramilitary Activities in and Against Nicaragua (Nicaragua v. United States of America) (Merits)*, 1986 I.C.J. Rep. 14 (Judgment of June 27, 1986). We reprint the brief portions of the I.C.J. opinion on this point and discuss their significance.

We next set out a number of statements expressing the traditional United States position on economic coercion and then turn to what appears to be the emerging position of the United States that economic coercion—indeed, force—is permitted to promote democracy. We set forth a variety of materials reflecting the reception which the United States position has received in the international community and the extent to which recent events may have altered the nonintervention principle upon which Cuba rests.

Thereafter, we note the United States' prior reliance on the 1975 resolution of the OAS leaving each member state free to determine its diplomatic and trade relations with Cuba as an authorization for its economic measures and provide pertinent materials. Similarly, we include notes considering the significance of the Cuban nationalization of United States-owned property in 1959 and 1960 and the United States allegations of human rights violations by the Cuban government.

Finally, we include materials concerning the validity of economic sanctions under the General Agreement on Tariffs and Trade ("GATT") and other international instruments on free trade, development, and the new international economic order.

The bearing of the General Assembly's November 24, 1992 resolution on these questions is inconclusive. The focus of its concern, and condemnation, is the "extraterritorial" aspects of the United States measures, not the measures as a whole, although it reaffirms the fundamental principles upon which Cuba relies, "the sovereign equality of states, [and] nonintervention and non-interference in their internal affairs." Those member states that addressed Cuba's economic coercion claim in the debate on the resolution expressed differing opinions on the legal issue and even on the advisability of the General Assembly's consideration of the United States measures beyond those aspects affecting third countries. With some nuances, their views tended to divide along North-South lines. See Introduction to Part I for a fuller discussion of the remarks of member states on this point and the transcript of the November 24, 1992 debate.

Indonesia, for instance, speaking on behalf of the non-aligned states and reaffirming an earlier statement of the non-aligned conference condemning the United States measures, supported the Cuban position; in contrast, the members of the European Community, through the remarks of the U.K. representative, indicated their view that the United States measures, except insofar as they affect third countries, are primarily a bilateral matter between the governments of the United States and Cuba. Among the Latin American states to address the General Assembly, Brazil, Ecuador, and Mexico expressed views similar to that of the non-aligned states; Venezuela indicated agreement with the E.C. position; and Argentina appears to accept the view that economic coercion to promote democracy is an exception to the nonintervention principle.

Although the General Assembly's position has thus yet to be determined, it is likely to face the question again in the near future. The resolution directs that the item "Necessity of Ending the Economic, Commercial and Financial Embargo Imposed by the United States of America against Cuba" be placed on the provisional agenda for the General Assembly's next session.

INTERNATIONAL INSTRUMENTS

CHARTER OF THE ORGANIZATION OF AMERICAN STATES

[The Charter of the Organization of American States, 2 UST 2394, TIAS 2361, 119 UNTS 3, was signed on April 30, 1948 and contained what were then perhaps the broadest and most explicit statements of the principles prohibiting intervention in the internal affairs of states and the use of coercive economic measures. The Charter is a binding treaty obligation of both Cuba and the United States. We set forth its pertinent provisions.*]

* * *

Article 6

States are juridically equal, enjoy equal rights and equal capacity to exercise these rights, and have equal duties. The rights of each State depend not upon its power to ensure the exercise thereof, but upon the mere fact of its existence as a person under international law.

* * *

Article 15

No State or group of States has the right to intervene, directly or indirectly, for any reason whatever, in the internal or external affairs of any other State. The foregoing principle prohibits not only armed force but also any other form of interference or attempted threat against the personality of the State or against its political, economic and cultural elements.

Article 16

No State may use or encourage the use of coercive measures of an economic or political character in order to force the sovereign will of another State and obtain from it advantages of any kind.

CHARTER OF THE UNITED NATIONS

[The United Nations Charter, 59 Stat. 1031, TS 993, 3 Bevans 1153 (June 26, 1945), does not include any express statement of the principle of non-intervention. Nevertheless, it is generally agreed that various provisions when considered together affirm this principle implicitly. Pertinent provisions of the Charter are set out below.]

Article 1

The Purposes of the United Nations are:

* * *

---

*The Charter was amended on February 27, 1967, 21 UST 607, TIAS 6847, but the quoted provisions were unaffected, except that they were renumbered Articles 9, 18, and 19.

2. To develop friendly relations among nations based on respect for the principle of equal rights and self-determination of peoples, and to take other appropriate measures to strengthen universal peace;

3. To achieve international cooperation in solving international problems of an economic, social, cultural, or humanitarian character, and in promoting and encouraging respect for human rights and for fundamental freedoms for all without distinction as to race, sex, language, or religion....

Article 2

*   *   *

1. The Organization is based on the principle of the sovereign equality of all its Members.

*   *   *

4. All Members shall refrain in their international relations from the threat or use of force against the territorial integrity or political independence of any state, or in any other manner inconsistent with the purposes of the United Nations.

*   *   *

7. Nothing contained in the present Charter shall authorize the United Nations to intervene in matters which are essentially within the domestic jurisdiction of any state or shall require the Members to submit such matters to settlement under the present Charter; but this principle shall not prejudice the application of enforcement measures under Chapter VII [which deals with threats to international peace and security].

*   *   *

Article 51

Nothing in the present Charter shall impair the inherent right of individual or collective self-defense if an armed attack occurs against a Member of the United Nations, until the Security Council has taken measures necessary to maintain international peace and security....

UNITED NATION'S DECLARATION ON PRINCIPLES OF
INTERNATIONAL LAW CONCERNING FRIENDLY RELATIONS AND
CO-OPERATION AMONG STATES IN ACCORDANCE WITH
THE CHARTER OF THE UNITED NATIONS

[In 1970 the General Assembly adopted unanimously the Declaration on Principles of International Law concerning Friendly Relations and Cooperation among States in accordance with the Charter of the United Nations. G.A. Res. 2625 (XXV) (October 24, 1970). Its purpose was to provide an authoritative declaration of the pertinent legal principles established in the Charter and the pertinent principles of customary international law, and it is widely recognized as such. The Declaration largely adopts the formulations of the nonintervention and economic coercion principles originally set forth in the OAS Charter. We reprint the relevant provisions.

After the adoption of the Declaration on Friendly Relations in 1970, there followed a number of other General Assembly resolutions which contained provisions on nonintervention and economic coercion largely to the same effect. Some of these were controversial resolutions in many respects, but in those instances in which the United States opposed, abstained, or stated reservations, it did not indicate any disagreement with the reiteration of the nonintervention and economic coercion principles established in the Declaration on Friendly Relations. The resolutions included the Resolution on Permanent Sovereignty Over Natural Resources of Developing Countries, G.A. Res. 3016 (XXVII) (December 18, 1972), which was supported by 102 countries, opposed by none, with twenty-two abstentions (including the United States and other developed countries); the Resolution on Permanent Sovereignty Over Natural Resources, G.A. Res 3171 (XXVII) (December 17, 1973), which was supported by 108 countries, opposed by one (United Kingdom), with sixteen abstentions (including the United States and other developed countries); the Declaration on the Establishment of a New International Economic Order, G.A. Res. 3201 (S-VI) (April 9-May 2, 1974), which was adopted by consensus although with reservations on the part of the United States and others; and the Charter of Economic Rights and Duties of States, G.A. Res. 3281 (XXIX) (December 17, 1974), which was supported by 120 countries, opposed by six (including the United States and other Western European countries), with ten abstentions (also largely Western European countries).]

G.A. Res. 2625 (XXV) (October 24, 1970)

The General Assembly,

*   *   *

Deeply convinced that the adoption of the Declaration on Principles of International Law concerning Friendly Relations and Co-operation among States in accordance with the Charter of the United Nations during the celebration of the twenty-fifth anniversary of the United Nations would contribute to the strengthening of world peace and constitute a landmark in the development of international law and of relations among States, in promoting the rule of law among nations and particularly the universal application of the principles embodied in the Charter,

*   *   *

1. *Approves* the Declaration on Principles of International Law concerning Friendly Relations and Co-operation among States in accordance with the Charter of the United Nations, the text of which is annexed to the present resolution.

*   *   *

Annex

Declaration on Principles of International Law concerning Friendly Relations and Co-operation among States in accordance with the Charter of the United Nations

Preamble

The General Assembly,

*   *   *

Bearing in mind the importance of maintaining and strengthening international peace founded upon freedom, equality, justice and respect for fundamental human rights and of developing friendly relations among nations irrespective of their political, economic and social systems or the levels of their development,

*   *   *

Convinced that the strict observance by States of the obligation not to intervene in the affairs of any other State is an essential condition to ensure that nations live together in peace with one another since the practice of any form of intervention not only violates the spirit and letter of the Charter of the United Nations but also leads to the creation of situations which threaten international peace and security,

Recalling the duty of States to refrain in their international relations from military, political, economic or any other form of coercion aimed against the political independence or territorial integrity of any State,

*   *   *

Reaffirming, in accordance with the Charter, the basic importance of sovereign equality and stressing that the purposes of the United Nations can be implemented only if States enjoy sovereign equality and comply fully with the requirements of this principle in their international relations,

*   *   *

Convinced that the principle of equal rights and self-determination of peoples constitutes a significant contribution to contemporary international law, and that its effective application is of paramount importance for the promotion of friendly relations among States, based on respect for the principle of sovereign equality,

*   *   *

Considering that the progressive development and codification of the following principles:

*   *   *

(c) The duty not to intervene in matters within the domestic jurisdiction of any State, in accordance with the Charter,

*   *   *

(e) The principle of equal rights and self-determination of peoples,
(f) The principle of sovereign equality of States,

*   *   *

Having considered the principles of international law relating to friendly relations and co-operation among States,
1. Solemnly proclaims the following principles:

*   *   *

The principle concerning the duty not to intervene in matters within the domestic jurisdiction of any State, in accordance with the Charter

No State or group of States has the right to intervene, directly or indirectly, for any reason whatsoever, in the internal or external affairs of any other State. Consequently, armed intervention and all other forms of interference or attempted threats against the personality of the State or against its political, economic and cultural elements, are in violation of international law.

No State may use or encourage the use of economic, political or any other type of measures to coerce another State in order to obtain from it the subordination of the exercise of its sovereign rights and to secure from it advantages of any kind.

*   *   *

Every State has an inalienable right to choose its political, economic, social and cultural systems, without interference in any form by another State.

*   *   *

The principle of equal rights and self-determination of peoples

By virtue of the principle of equal rights and self-determination of peoples enshrined in the Charter, all peoples have the right freely to determine, without external interference, their political status and to pursue their economic, social and cultural development, and every State has the duty to respect this right in accordance with the provisions of the Charter.

*   *   *

Every State has the duty to promote through joint and separate action universal respect for and observance of human rights and fundamental freedoms in accordance with the Charter.

*   *   *

The principle of sovereign equality of States

All States enjoy sovereign equality. They have equal rights and duties and are equal members of the international community, notwithstanding differences of an economic, social, political or other nature.

In particular, sovereign equality includes the following elements:

(a) States are juridically equal;

(b) Each State enjoys the rights inherent in full sovereignty;

(c) Each State has the duty to respect the personality of other States;

(d) The territorial integrity and political independence of the State are inviolable;

(e) Each State has the right freely to choose and develop its political, social, economic and cultural systems;

(f) Each State has the duty to comply fully and in good faith with its international obligations and to live in peace with other States.

* * *

General part

2. *Declares* that:
In their interpretation and application the above principles are interrelated and each principle should be construed in the context of the other principles,

* * *

3. *Declares further* that:
The principles of the Charter which are embodied in this Declaration constitute basic principles of international law, and consequently appeals to all States to be guided by these principles in their international conduct and to develop their mutual relations on the basis of their strict observance.

UNITED NATIONS RESOLUTIONS ON THE USE OF
ECONOMIC COERCION BY DEVELOPED COUNTRIES
AGAINST DEVELOPING COUNTRIES

NOTE ON THE HISTORY OF THE GENERAL
ASSEMBLY RESOLUTIONS

On December 20, 1983 the General Assembly adopted a resolution titled "Economic Measures as a Means of Political and Economic Coercion Against Developing Countries" G.A. Res. 197 (XXXVIII). This was the first in a series of similar resolutions condemning what the General Assembly views as the increasing use by some developed countries of coercive and restrictive economic measures as a means of exerting political pressure on some developing countries. The General Assembly found these measures to violate the Charter of the United Nations, the Charter of Economic Rights and Duties of States, and the General Agreement on Tariffs and Trade and deplored "the adoption by certain developed countries, taking advantage of their predominant position in the international economy, of economic measures to exert coercion on the sovereign decisions of developing countries." It likewise reaffirmed "that developed countries should refrain from threatening or applying trade restrictions, blockades, embargoes and other economic sanctions incompatible with the provisions of the Charter of the United Nations, and in violation of undertakings contracted multilaterally or bilaterally, against developing countries as a form of political and economic coercion which affects their economic, political and social development."

The 1983 General Assembly resolution arose out of, *inter alia*, earlier resolutions of the Latin American Economic System ("SELA") (a regional organization consisting of twenty-six Latin American states) and the United Nations Conference on Trade and Development ("UNCTAD"), which had in similar terms condemned the use of coercive economic measures by developed states against developing states. For SELA, *see, e.g.,* Final Report on the Eighth Ordinary Meeting of the Latin American Council, Decision Number 112 (August 1982).

The UNCTAD resolution (Resolution Number 152 (VI)), titled Rejection of Coercive Economic Measures, was adopted on July 2, 1983 and became the basis for the General Assembly resolutions which followed. It was supported by 81 countries, opposed by 18, with 18 abstentions. Those opposed and abstaining included most of the developed nations of the world, the United States among them. The votes on the General Assembly resolutions followed the same pattern. G.A. Res. 197 (XXXVIII) (December 20, 1983) (119 in support, 19 opposed and 15 abstaining); G.A. Res. 210 (XXXIX) (December 18, 1984) (116 in support, 19 opposed and 6 abstaining); G.A. Res. 185 (XL) (December 17, 1985) (128 in support, 19 opposed and 7 abstaining); G.A. Res. 165 (XLI) (December 5, 1986) (115 in support, 23 opposed and 3 abstaining); G.A. Res. 173 (XLII) (December 11, 1987) (128 in support, 21 opposed and 5 abstaining); G.A. Res. 125 (XLIV) (December 22, 1989) (118 in support, 23 opposed and 2 abstaining); G.A. Res. 210 (XLVI) (December 20, 1991) (97 in support, 30 opposed and 9 abstaining) (change in vote due principally to change in votes of former East Bloc countries).

We reprint the 1983 UNCTAD resolution. An official summary of the statements made by various governments in support and in opposition to the resolution sets forth the reasons why developed countries, including the United States, opposed the resolution. Proceedings of the United Nations Conference on Trade and Development, Sixth Session, June 6–July 2, 1983, paragraphs 338–368. It is noteworthy that their opposition was not based upon disagreement with the underlying legal principles upon which the resolution was premised, but rather upon their view that the resolution was political in nature and failed to condemn evenhandedly the use of coercive economic measures by developing countries against both developed and developing countries. The United States representative made specific reference in this regard to the 1973 Arab oil boycott directed against it and other countries which had proved to be highly disruptive of international trade.

In addition, we reprint General Assembly Resolution 210 (XLVI), adopted in 1991, which is the most recent in the line of nearly annual General Assembly resolutions on this subject. The General Assembly's increasing sense of urgency about the failure of its earlier resolutions to curb the use of coercive measures is evident. The General Assembly resolutions have each called upon the Secretary-General to prepare reports on the use of coercive economic measures against developing countries, and, in response, the Secretary-General has now prepared six such reports. *See* Report of the Secretary-General, September 27, 1984, A/39/415; Report of the Secretary-General, October 16, 1985, A/40/596; Report of the Secretary-General, October 24, 1986, A/41/739; Report of the Secretary-General, October 19, 1987, A/42/660; Report of the Secretary-General, October 10, 1989, A/44/510; Note by the Secretary-General, October 15, 1991, A/46/567.

UNITED NATIONS CONFERENCE ON TRADE AND
DEVELOPMENT, RESOLUTION 152 (VI), JULY 2, 1983
REJECTION OF COERCIVE ECONOMIC MEASURES

The United Nations Conference on Trade and Development,

Considering the relevant articles of the Charter of the United Nations,

Considering Article 32 of the Charter of Economic Rights and Duties of States,

Bearing in mind the principles and rules of the General Agreement on Tariffs and Trade, and paragraph 7(iii) of the Ministerial Declaration adopted by the Contracting Parties to GATT at their thirty-eighth session,

Bearing in mind also the General Principles governing international trade relations and trade policies conducive to development adopted by the Conference at its first session,

Considering that some developed countries are resorting more and more frequently to the application of coercive and restrictive measures of increasing scope, as an instrument for exerting political pressure on some developing countries,

Recognizing that these measures are at variance with the Charter of the United Nations, the Charter of Economic Rights and Duties of States, and the General Agreement on Tariffs and Trade,

Considering that coercive measures have a negative effect on external trade, which plays a crucial part in the economies of developing countries, particularly during the present international economic crisis,

Considering further that such measures do not help to create the climate of peace needed for development,

Reiterates that all developed countries shall refrain from applying trade restrictions, blockades, embargoes and other economic sanctions incompatible with the provisions of the Charter of the United Nations, and in violation of undertakings contracted multilaterally, against developing countries as a form of political coercion which affects their economic, political and social development.

GENERAL ASSEMBLY RESOLUTION 210 (XLVI), DECEMBER 20, 1991
ECONOMIC MEASURES AS A MEANS OF POLITICAL AND
ECONOMIC COERCION AGAINST DEVELOPING COUNTRIES

The General Assembly,

Recalling the relevant principles set forth in the Charter of the United Nations,

Recalling also its resolutions 2625 (XXVI) of 24 October 1970, 3201 (S-VI) and 3202 (S-VI) of 1 May 1974 and 3281 (XXIX) of 12 December 1974, containing the Charter of Economic Rights and Duties of States,

Reaffirming article 32 of the Charter of Economic Rights and Duties of States, which declares that no State may use or encourage the use of economic, political or any other type of measures to coerce another State in order to obtain from it the subordination of the exercise of its sovereign rights,

Bearing in mind the general principles governing international trade and trade policies for development contained in the relevant resolutions and rules of the United Nations Conference on Trade and Development and the General Agreement on Tariffs and Trade,

Reaffirming its resolutions 38/197 of 20 December 1983, 39/210 of 18 December 1984, 40/185 of 17 December 1985, 41/165 of 5 December 1986, 42/173 of 11 December 1987 and 44/215 of 22 December 1989, and considering that further work needs to be undertaken in order to implement them,

Gravely concerned that the use of coercive economic measures adversely affects the economy and development efforts of developing countries and creates a general negative impact on international economic cooperation and on the world-wide effort to move towards a non-discriminatory, open, trading system,

Taking into account the note by the Secretary-General prepared in response to Assembly resolution 44/215, and his assessment of how to continue his task,

Concerned that the mandate provided in paragraph 6 of resolution 44/215 has not been fully implemented,

1. *Calls upon* the international community to adopt urgent and effective measures to eliminate the use by some developed countries of unilateral economic coercive measures against developing countries with

the purpose of exerting, directly or indirectly, coercion on the sovereign decisions of the countries subject to those measures;

2. *Deplores* the fact that some developed countries continue to apply economic measures and, in some cases, have increased their scope and magnitude, as evidenced by trade restrictions, blockades, embargoes, freezing of assets and other economic sanctions incompatible with the Charter of the United Nations;

3. *Calls upon* developed countries to refrain from making use of their predominant position in the international economy to exercise political or economic coercion through the application of economic instruments with the purpose of inducing changes in the economic, political, commercial and social policies of other countries;

4. *Requests* the Secretary-General to pursue fully his mandate as contained in paragraph 6 of Assembly resolution 44/215, through the Office of the Director-General for Development and International Economic Cooperation and in close cooperation with the United Nations Conference on Trade and Development;

5. *Also requests* the Secretary-General to report to the General Assembly at its forty-eighth session on the implementation of the present resolution.

THE 1989 UNITED NATIONS GROUP OF LEGAL EXPERTS
AND THE INTERNATIONAL COURT OF JUSTICE

NOTE ON THE EXPERTS' VIEWS AND THE NICARAGUA OPINION

In May 1989 the Secretary-General of UNCTAD convened a meeting of legal experts to consider effective approaches to the elimination of the use of coercive economic measures against developing countries. Although there were differing views on various subsidiary questions, there was general consensus that the intention of the state imposing the coercive measures was a key criterion and that at a minimum it was impermissible for the pressuring state to seek "to influence changes in the non-economic policies—domestic or foreign—of another State. This included intent of a non-economic nature, for example, to influence the target State in its choice of government, in its foreign policies towards third countries and in its allowing individuals and groups in the State to enjoy various political and civil rights." The Secretary-General of the United Nations included a report of the experts meeting, which we reprint, as an annex to his October 10, 1989 report to the General Assembly on coercive economic measures, A/44/510.

In 1986 the International Court of Justice issued its decision on the merits in *Case Concerning Military and Paramilitary Activities in and Against Nicaragua (Nicaragua v. United States of America) (Merits)*,

1986 I.C.J. Rep. 14 (Judgment of June 27, 1986). Nicaragua's principal claim, upon which it prevailed, was that United States support for the paramilitary operations of the *"contras"* and related activities, including its mining of a Nicaraguan port, violated the customary international law prohibition on the use of force in international relations. In addition, Nicaragua contended that United States support for the *contras* and its economic measures against Nicaragua violated both the customary international law prohibition on nonintervention in the internal affairs of other states and the Treaty of Friendship, Commerce and Navigation between the two countries. The United States economic measures included the elimination of bilateral assistance, the reduction of sugar imports, the blocking of loans from international financial organizations, and ultimately the prohibition of export/import trade between the two countries and the barring of Nicaraguan vessels from United States ports and Nicaraguan aircraft from air transportation to and from the United States. Although similar in these respects to the measures against Cuba, the Nicaraguan measures were not nearly as comprehensive.

In support of its intervention claim, Nicaragua argued that the United States' purpose in supporting the *contras* and imposing these economic measures was to overthrow the government of Nicaragua and to secure its replacement by a government acceptable to the United States. Although the United States did not participate in this phase of the case, it had previously contended that its purpose was to convince Nicaragua to cease supplying weapons to the armed opposition in El Salvador.

In resolving Nicaragua's intervention claim for support of the *contras,* the International Court of Justice found it unnecessary to decide which was the United States' true goal. Instead, it found that the *contras'* purpose was to overthrow the government and that under international law that purpose had to be attributed to the United States in light of its support for their activities. It then found the imputed purpose impermissible and, accordingly, United States support for the *contras* to constitute unlawful intervention in the internal affairs of Nicaragua.

In contrast, the Court rejected Nicaragua's claim regarding the United States economic measures. It provided little explanation of the underlying basis for its decision, stating only that "the Court has merely to say that it is unable to regard such action on the economic plane as is here complained of as a breach of the customary-law principle of nonintervention." *Id.,* paragraph 245. It is unclear from the opinion whether in so ruling the Court accepted the United States' contention that its sole purpose was to deter Nicaragua from continuing the flow of weapons to the armed opposition in El Salvador. In the context of the economic measures, there was no basis for attributing the purposes of the *contras* to the United States.

As a result of the conclusory manner in which the Court treated Nicaragua's claim on this point, it is difficult to predict how it would view a similar claim made by Cuba, given the differences in scope, intensity, justifications for and purposes of the United States measures against Cuba. The Court's brief comment that it did not consider the economic measures against Nicaragua "here complained of" to be a breach of the customary international law prohibition on intervention, however, suggests that the imposition of economic measures under some circumstances would violate the principle. This is likewise suggested by the Court's exposition of the nonintervention principles elsewhere in its decision, which affirms that "coercion" defines, "and indeed forms the essence of prohibited intervention" and that it is only most "obvious in the case of an intervention which uses force." *Id.,* paragraph 205 (set forth in full, *post*).

It may be noted, moreover, that due to the United States multilateral treaty reservation to its declaration accepting compulsory jurisdiction, the Court could not consider whether the United States economic measures violated the principles of the United Nations Charter or the express prohibition on economic coercion contained in the OAS Charter. Therefore, Nicaragua's intervention claim was premised solely on the customary international law prohibition on intervention. It is perhaps noteworthy as well that there is no indication in the Report of the Expert Group Meeting, included in the Secretary-General's 1989 report and reprinted here, that any of the experts viewed the Court's decision as reflecting upon the scope of the international law prohibition on economic coercion.

Having rejected Nicaragua's claim under customary international law, the Court nevertheless went on to hold that the trade embargo was so inconsistent with the spirit of the Friendship Treaty that it violated the international law principle that a party to a treaty may not take actions which defeat its object and purpose. It likewise found the prohibition on Nicaraguan vessels entering United States ports to violate the specific terms of the Treaty. There is no Friendship Treaty in force between the United States and Cuba.

REPORT OF THE SECRETARY-GENERAL
ECONOMIC MEASURES AS A MEANS OF POLITICAL AND
ECONOMIC COERCION AGAINST DEVELOPING COUNTRIES

(A/44/510, October 10, 1989)

*   *   *

Report Of The Expert Group Meeting

*   *   *

2. *Current state of international law*

4. Putting aside for the moment the difficulties in defining what coercive economic measures are, it was the general view of the experts that international law lacked a clear consensus as to when those measures were improper. The international legal system also lacked adequate mechanisms for monitoring and dealing with the use of those measures.

5. Those gaps in international law existed in spite of commendable efforts in the past—through treaties and through declarations and resolutions in international organizations—to develop norms limiting the use of coercive economic measures. The principal exception to the situation was provided by GATT (see sect. 4).

3. *Defining coercive economic measures*

6. In theory, a host of economic activities might qualify as coercive economic measures. States and entities controlled by them engaged in or affected international economic activity in many ways every day. These activities could be grouped roughly into five major categories, as limits on:

(a) Bilateral government programmes, such as foreign assistance, low-interest credit, fishing rights and aircraft landing rights;

(b) Exports from the country that is imposing the measures (the "sender" State);

(c) Imports from the country that is the object of the measures (the "target" State);

(d) Private financial transactions, such as on bank deposits, loans related to trade and loans for investment;

(e) The activities of the international financial institutions, such as the International Monetary Fund (IMF), the World Bank and the regional development banks.

7. The experts generally agreed that many of these activities could be proper. Seeking to limit some of these activities would be inappropriate and even counterproductive. The problem was to identify those activities which should be eliminated or limited.

8. Some of the experts also thought that "economic sanctions" constituted something different from coercive economic measures as that concept was discussed at the meeting, although the experts did not necessarily agree on the differences between the two. In any event, the experts generally preferred to avoid the use of the phrase "economic sanctions" when trying to define coercive economic measures.

9. There was general consensus that the intent of the sender country was an important criterion in determining what constituted a coercive economic activity, that is, one that should be eliminated or limited. Intent that seemed to be acceptable [i.e., should be eliminated or limited—EDS.] was where the sender State sought to influence changes in the non-economic policies—domestic or foreign—of another State. This included intent of a non-economic nature, for example, to influence the target State in its choice of government, in its foreign policies towards third countries and in its allowing individuals and groups in the State to enjoy various political and civil rights.

10. The intent criterion, however, did not include many economic activities, for example, and probably most importantly, those against a target State to get it to change its tariff or non-tariff trade barriers. The experts generally believed that it would be over-inclusive and counterproductive at that point to expand the fledgling concept of economic coercive measures to include the large and complex mix of sender States' economic activities for economic purposes. Some experts also noted that GATT already provided a developed international legal framework that covered many such economic activities undertaken for economic reasons.

11. Most of the experts also thought that for an economic measure to be defined as coercive there should be some impact on the target State. While international and domestic law often prohibited "attempts"—that is, attempted actions—in many situations, most of the experts thought that the developing concept of coercive economic measures should focus at least initially on cases where a country actually suffered some harm. These were presumably the most important cases. The experts also generally agreed that the impact should be at least "material," or clearly observable.

*   *   *

15. In measuring impact, most of the experts agreed that offsetting benefits that a target country might receive from a third country should not be counted in determining whether the minimum requisite effect existed or not. Those offsetting benefits might occur when a third State began purchasing the exports of the target country after the sender State had imposed a trade embargo. Several of the experts noted that

any effort to take offsetting benefits into account would often be difficult to measure. It would be hard to determine, for example, whether the actions of the third State were intended to be an offsetting measure and or were simply normal commercial activity. The calculation would also be further complicated by the fact that the target State might have had to pay some price (not always obvious) to enter into new arrangements with the third country.

16. On the other hand, some experts noted the general agreement of the experts, discussed above, that the sender State's actions should have some economic impact to be coercive. If a third country's activities more than made up for the sender State's action, then there was an issue of whether the threshold test of requisite impact was satisfied.

17. There was considerable discussion whether affirmative as well as negative economic activities should be included at that point in the concept of coercive economic measures. Affirmative economic activities were those where a country was offering a benefit or "carrot" to the other country to encourage economic or political developments. A prime example would be bilateral foreign aid. The country receiving such assistance might be paying a price for it in one subtle way or another in terms of reduced independence.

18. It was generally agreed that only negative economic activities, such as trade embargoes and asset freezes, could be considered coercive economic measures. It did not seem advisable at that point to include affirmative economic activities.

Although these activities could have a material impact on the target country, favourable economic relations between countries should be encouraged. To begin to delve into the subjective motivation for, say, a grant of bilateral foreign aid would probably be unworkable and might make it more difficult for recipient countries to obtain foreign assistance in the future.

4. *Allowable exceptions*

19. There was a general consensus that the exceptions to the criteria developed above should be limited in both number and scope. The experts were concerned that exceptions were subject to abuse, or would at least raise problems of interpretation. Moreover, there also seemed to be a sense that the initial criteria had been drawn relatively narrowly so that most acceptable economic activities were not caught in the concept of coercive economic measures as developed so far.

20. The experts generally agreed that there should be a security, or self-defence, exception. Thus, a State could take what would otherwise be a coercive economic activity if it were necessary for its security interests. Nevertheless, the experts also generally agreed that the exception should be defined narrowly.

21. Some experts suggested that other exceptions found in GATT, such as those in Article XX, might also be allowed. However, other experts noted that most of those exceptions were designed for evaluating economic activity for economic purposes and not for the non-economic purposes that were being considered here.

22. Some experts suggested that there should be a general exception allowing activity that was pursuant to international treaty obligations. This was not refined further, but it was taken for granted that there should definitely be a provision at least recognizing that States could take economic measures pursuant to a Security Council resolution under Article 41 of the Charter of the United Nations. The measures against South Africa were an example.

23. Some experts suggested a possible exception to allow activity to protect human rights. Other experts thought that would be providing a loophole to allow activity that should not be permissible.

24. One expert suggested allowing an exception for activity that was taken in response to the target State's breach of an international obligation that entailed a material injury and had not been compensated for fairly. The response would have to meet the equivalence standard (see the Vienna Convention on the Law of Treaties, 1969). Moreover, the responding State would still have an obligation under Article 33 of the Charter of the United Nations to seek to resolve any dispute by peaceful means. Other experts questioned the need for an explicit exception for such a situation.

*   *   *

Appendix

List of Participants

Mr. Barry E. Carter
Georgetown University Law Center
United States of America

Mr. Sada Shankar Saxena
Director-General
Indian Institute for Foreign Trade
India

Mr. Omar Yousif Elagab
Advocate, Senior Lecturer in Law
Ealing College of Higher Education
United Kingdom of Great Britain
and Northern Ireland

Mr. Jeffrey J. Schott
Institute for International
Economics
United States of America

Mr. Jeffrey L. Gertler
Legal Affairs Officer
General Agreement on
Tariffs and Trade
Switzerland

Mrs. Elizabeth Zoller
Professeur Agrégé des Facultés de
Droit à l'Université de Strasbourg
France

Mr. Drago Kisic W.
Director
Macroconsult S.A.
Peru

United Nations, New York
Mr. Albrecht Horn
Principal Officer
Office of the Director-General for
Development and International
Economic Co-operation

Mr. Roberto Mac Lean
Banco Central de Reserve del Peru
Peru

UNCTAD Secretariat, Geneva
Mr. K.K.S. Dadzie
Secretary-General
Mr. A. Belkora
Officer-in-Charge
Protectionism and Market
Access Programme
International Trade Programmes

Mr. N.A. Markov
Scientific Co-ordinative Centre
Ministry of Foreign Affairs
Union of Soviet Socialist Republics

CASE CONCERNING MILITARY AND PARAMILITARY
ACTIVITIES IN AND AGAINST NICARAGUA (NICARAGUA V.
UNITED STATES OF AMERICA) (MERITS)

(1986 I.C.J. Rep. 14 (Judgment of June 27, 1986))

* * *

123. Nicaragua has complained to the Court of certain measures of an economic nature taken against it by the Government of the United States, beginning with the cessation of economic aid in April 1981, which it regards as an indirect form of intervention in its internal affairs. According to information published by the United States Government, it provided more than $100 million in economic aid to Nicaragua between July 1979 and January 1981; however, concern in the United States Congress about certain activities attributed to the Nicaraguan Government led to a requirement that, before disbursing assistance to Nicaragua, the President certify that Nicaragua was not "aiding, abetting or supporting acts of violence or terrorism in other countries" (Special Central American Assistance Act, 1979, Sec. 536 *(g)*). Such a certification was given in September 1980 (45 Federal Register 62779), to the effect that

> "on the basis of an evaluation of the available evidence, that the Government of Nicaragua 'has not co-operated with or harbors any international terrorist organization or is aiding, abetting or supporting acts of violence or terrorism in other countries.'"

An official White House press release of the same date stated that

> "[t]he certification is based upon a careful consideration and evaluation of all the relevant evidence provided by the intelligence community and

by our Embassies in the field. . . . Our intelligence agencies as well as our Embassies in Nicaragua and neighboring countries were fully consulted, and the diverse information and opinions for all sources were carefully weighed."

On 1 April 1981 however a determination was made to the effect that the United States could no longer certify that Nicaragua was not engaged in support for "terrorism" abroad, and economic assistance, which had been suspended in January 1981, was thereby terminated. According to the Nicaraguan Minister of Finance, this also affected loans previously contracted, and its economic impact was more than $36 million per annum. Nicaragua also claims that, at the multilateral level, the United States has acted in the Bank of International Reconstruction and Development and the Inter-American Development Bank to oppose or block loans to Nicaragua.

124. On 23 September 1983, the President of the United States made a proclamation modifying the system of quotas for United States imports of sugar, the effect of which was to reduce the quota attributed to Nicaragua by 90 percent. The Nicaraguan Finance Minister assessed the economic impact of the measure at between $15 and $18 million, due to the preferential system of prices that sugar has in the market of the United States.

125. On 1 May 1985, the President of the United States made an Executive Order, which contained a finding that "the policies and actions of the Government of Nicaragua constitute an unusual and extraordinary threat to the national security and foreign policy of the United States" and declared a "national emergency." According to the President's message to Congress, this emergency situation had been created by the "the Nicaraguan Government's aggressive activities in Central America." The Executive Order declared a total trade embargo on Nicaragua, prohibiting all imports from and exports to that country, barring Nicaraguan vessels from United States ports and excluding Nicaraguan aircraft from air transportation to and from the United States.

*   *   *

239. The Court comes now to the application in this case of the principle of nonintervention in the internal affairs of States. It is argued by Nicaragua that the "military and paramilitary activities aimed at the government and people of Nicaragua" have two purposes:

"(a) The actual overthrow of the existing lawful government of Nicaragua and its replacement by a government acceptable to the United States; and *(b)* The substantial damaging of the economy, and the weakening of the political system, in order to coerce the government of Nicaragua into the acceptance of United States policies and political demands."

Nicaragua also contends that the various acts of an economic nature, summarized in paragraphs 123 to 125 above, constitute a form of "indirect" intervention in Nicaragua's internal affairs.

240. Nicaragua has laid much emphasis on the intentions it attributes to the Government of the United States in giving aid and support to the *contras*. It contends that the purpose of the policy of the United States and its actions against Nicaragua in pursuance of this policy was, from the beginning, to overthrow the Government of Nicaragua. In order to demonstraté this, it has drawn attention to numerous statements by high officials of the United States Government, in particular by President Reagan, expressing solidarity and support for the *contras,* described on occasion as "freedom fighters," and indicating that support for the *contras* would continue until the Nicaraguan Government took certain action, desired by the United States Government, amounting in effect to a surrender to the demands of the latter Government. The official Report of the President of the United States to Congress of 10 April 1985, quoted in paragraph 96 above, states that: "We have not sought to overthrow the Nicaraguan Government nor to force on Nicaragua a specific system of government." But it indicates also quite openly that "United States policy toward Nicaragua"—which includes the support for the military and paramilitary activities of the *contras* which it was the purpose of the Report to continue—"has consistently sought to achieve changes in Nicaraguan government policy and behavior."

241. The Court however does not consider it necessary to seek to establish whether the intention of the United States to secure a change of governmental policies in Nicaragua went so far as to be equated with an endeavour to overthrow the Nicaraguan Government. It appears to the Court to be clearly established first, that the United States intended, by its support of the *contras,* to coerce the Government of Nicaragua in respect of matters in which each State is permitted, by the principle of State sovereignty, to decide freely (see paragraph 205 above); and secondly that the intention of the *contras* themselves was to overthrow the present Government of Nicaragua. The 1983 Report of the Intelligence Committee refers to the *contras* "openly acknowledged goal of overthrowing the Sandinistas." Even if it be accepted, for the sake of argument, that the objective of the United States in assisting the *contras* was solely to interdict the supply of arms to the armed opposition in El Salvador, it strains belief to suppose that a body formed in armed opposition to the Government of Nicaragua, and calling itself

the "Nicaraguan Democratic Force," intended only to check Nicaraguan interference in El Salvador and did not intend to achieve violent change of government in Nicaragua. The Court considers that in international law, if one State, with a view to the coercion of another State, supports and assists armed bands in that State whose purpose is to overthrow the government of that State, that amounts to an intervention by the one State in the internal affairs of the other, whether or not the political objective of the State giving such support and assistance is equally far-reaching. It is for this reason that the Court has only examined the intentions of the United States Government so far as they bear on the question of self-defence.

242. The Court therefore finds that the support given by the United States, up to the end of September 1984, to the military and paramilitary activities of the *contras* in Nicaragua, by financial support, training, supply of weapons, intelligence and logistic support, constitutes a clear breach of the principle of nonintervention.

* * *

244. As already noted, Nicaragua has also asserted that the United States is responsible for an "indirect" form of intervention in its internal affairs inasmuch as it has taken, to Nicaragua's disadvantage, certain actions of an economic nature. The Court's attention has been drawn in particular to the cessation of economic aid in April 1981; the 90 percent reduction in the sugar quota for United States imports from Nicaragua in April 1981; and the trade embargo adopted on 1 May 1985. While admitting in principle that some of these actions were not unlawful in themselves, counsel for Nicaragua argued that these measures of economic constraint add up to a systematic violation of the principle of nonintervention.

245. The court does not here have to concern itself with possible breaches of such international economic instruments as the General Agreement on Tariffs and Trade, referred to in passing by counsel for Nicaragua; any such breaches would appear to fall outside the Court's jurisdiction, particularly in view of the effect of the multilateral treaty reservation, nor has Nicaragua seised the Court of any complaint of such breaches. The question of the compatibility of the actions complained of with the 1956 Treaty of Friendship, Commerce and Navigation will be examined below, in the context of the Court's examination of the provisions of that Treaty. At this point, the Court has merely to say that it is unable to regard such action on the economic plane as is here complained of as a breach of the customary-law principle of nonintervention.

TRADITIONAL UNITED STATES POSITION
ON ECONOMIC COERCION

The Declaration on Friendly Relations

NOTE ON THE UNITED STATES POSITION

In the General Assembly proceedings, the United States took the position that its economic measures against Cuba are not subject to international law constraints, since every state has the right to choose the governments with which it wishes to have commercial relations. It provided no elaboration on how it reconciled this position with the prohibitions on intervention and economic coercion set forth in the international instruments relied upon by Cuba and set forth above. We present a number of previous statements made by the United States on the subject of nonintervention and economic coercion, which elaborate more fully on its views. Some of these statements were made in the context of discussions in international forums and, when considered in that context, have the added value of indicating the views of other states as well.

The first document concerns the United States position in the deliberations leading to the adoption of the 1970 Declaration on Friendly Relations. The United States voted for the Declaration, and when the final draft resolution was before the drafting committee, the United States representative spoke in favor, indicating United States support for its provisions on nonintervention and economic coercion. *See* Report of the Special Committee on Principles of International Law Concerning Friendly Relations and Co-operation Among States, General Assembly Twenty-Fifth Session, Supp. No.18 (A./8018) (1970).

In the deliberations leading to adoption of the 1970 Declaration, the United States representative, in conjunction with other sponsors, had proposed a draft resolution, A/AC.125/L.13, which in Section 3A provided: "Nothing in the foregoing shall be construed as derogating from (A) the generally recognized freedom of States to seek to influence the policies and actions of other States, in accordance with international law and settled international practice and in a manner compatible with the principle of sovereign equality of States and the duty to co-operate in accordance with the Charter." This draft was ultimately rejected by the committee and the quoted language was criticized on a number of grounds by various delegations. The comments of the United States representative in support of the draft resolution indicate the United States view that the nonintervention principle should not be construed to prohibit states from seeking "to influence the policies and actions of other States in the normal course of relations." These comments, as well as those of other states in support and opposition to the draft resolution, are reprinted here.

THE 1966 SPECIAL COMMITTEE ON PRINCIPLES OF
INTERNATIONAL LAW CONCERNING FRIENDLY
RELATIONS AND CO-OPERATION AMONG STATES
(Summary Records of the Fourteenth, Fifteenth and Sixteenth
Meetings, March 17–18, 1966, A/AC.125/SR.14, 15, 16)

1. *Mr. Hargrove* (United States of America), speaking on behalf of his own delegation and the other sponsors, introduced the joint proposal (A/AC.125/L. 13) to the Special Committee. He wished to stress particularly the relationship between its provisions and those of the Declaration embodied in General Assembly resolution 2331 (XX). In company with many others, his delegation had stated that the Declaration represented a milestone in the development of the political attitudes of the General Assembly towards certain of the most pressing problems of the day. At the same time, the Declaration was not intended as a legal document and could therefore not be substituted for the formulation of the principle which the Special Committee had been instructed to draft. What the Declaration might have gained in eloquence, it had lost, by its very nature, in accuracy, precision and exhaustiveness, which were necessary for a legal text. What the sponsors of the proposal (A/AC.125/L.13) had done reflected, in fact, the idea expressed by the representative of Lebanon, who had suggested that the Special Committee should extract the legal content of the Declaration. The result of their work was a text which was perhaps less extensive than that on which it was based but which had lost nothing in potency.

*   *   *

5. He then drew the Committee's attention to *paragraph 3* of the proposal (A/AC.125/L.13). The sponsors were fully aware of the danger of trying to state what was in effect an exception to the principle, designed to take account of normal diplomatic practice. The Committee had already discussed the proposal put forward by the delegation of Sweden on the basis of the Vienna Conventions. However, in proposing paragraph 3A the sponsors had sought to avoid another danger: that of producing a purportedly accurate legal text which so cut across and into the very stuff of everyday State-to-State relations that no national Government would take it seriously.

*   *   *

7. *Mr. Sinclair* (United Kingdom) said that his delegation could add very little to the statement made by the United States representative on the structure of the proposal (A/AC.125/L.13), of which the United

Kingdom was a sponsor. Nevertheless, he felt it useful to comment on the text, in his turn, in order to make clear to the Committee the purpose which the sponsors had had in mind.

*   *   *

9. As the United Kingdom delegation had pointed out to the Committee, it was extremely important that the text of the principle should include positive provisions which balanced the negative aspect of the formulation of prohibitions. That concern was reflected in paragraph 3A of the proposal, which attempted to state what acts were lawful in day-to-day relations.

*   *   *

20. *Mr. Pechota* (Czechoslovakia) said that the proposal in document A/AC.125/L.13 seemed to ignore the efforts that the General Assembly had made to reach an agreement on the scope and content of the principle of nonintervention and that it tended to water down the rules so clearly stated in resolution 2131 (XX).

*   *   *

21. Furthermore, the peremptory nature of the principle of nonintervention was weakened by paragraph 3A of the proposal. It was not advisable to try to devise artificial limitations of the concept of nonintervention. What was essential was to define not the forms of influence that States exerted on each other, but rather the forms of manifestly unlawful pressure. In that regard the proposal was conspicuously silent.

*   *   *

3. *Mr. Vanderpuye* (Ghana) thanked the sponsors of document A/AC.125/L.13....

4. As for paragraph 3A, it seemed incompatible with the purposes of the United Nations, especially that of developing friendly relations and co-operation among nations. It was hard to see how freedom could be given to States to "seek to influence the policies and actions of other States" without violating the principle of sovereign equality and respect for the political independence of States.

*   *   *

12. *Mr. Mishra* (India) said that the introduction of the proposal in document A/AC.125/L.13 had changed the situation.

*   *   *

17. If the words "freedom of States to seek to influence the policies and actions of other States" in paragraph 3A could be construed to include intervention, then the paragraph would amount to an international institutionalization of intervention. There was no "generally recognized freedom" of States to intervene in the affairs of other States. On the other hand, if the words referred only to ordinary diplomatic and consular activities, there was no need for the provision. The principle of nonintervention had never been considered to prohibit such activities, which were now governed by the Vienna Conventions on Diplomatic Relations and Consular Relations.

*   *   *

19. *Mr. Chammas* (Lebanon)

*   *   *

23. In view of the statement in paragraph 1 as to the right of a State freely to choose the form and degree of its associations with other States, meaning that States had the right to enter freely into alliances and regional arrangements and hence to allow their foreign policies to be influenced by their partners in those alliances and arrangements, and bearing in mind the readiness to influence and be influenced because of obligations emanating from such arrangements, the intent of paragraph 3A was to call upon the Assembly to sanction through international law unlimited and undefined rights for States to influence the policies of other States. Areas of influence in international relations had not been defined, nor was there a settled international practice in that respect. This was why the delegation of Lebanon could not accept the concept proposed in paragraph 3A and opposed the inclusion of such a concept in the drafting of this principle.

24. *Mr. Gottlieb* (Canada) said that he would like to associate his delegation with the explanations of the proposal in document A/AC.125/L.13 given by some of the other sponsors, particularly the representative of Australia.

*   *   *

29. With regard to the Indian representative's comment on paragraph 3A, he would like to give assurances that it was in no way intended to suggest that intervention was permissible. In drafting that paragraph the sponsors had had in mind the fact that when general principles were formulated it was often necessary to put in a saving clause to indicate what it was that those general principles did not affect. The relationship of Article 51 of the Charter to Article 2(4) was a case in point. Also, it should be noted that the freedom referred to in paragraph 3A of the proposal was specifically to be exercised in accordance with international law. The idea underlying that paragraph was that in the modern world States were interdependent and were called upon by the Charter to co-operate in maintaining international peace and security. There might be many instances in which States should try to influence others to follow policies consistent with the maintenance of peace and security—or, to give another example, with the principle of respect for human rights. Thus the idea that States should have freedom to influence the policies of other States seemed to his delegation to be essential to the fulfillment of the obligations of States to the international community.

*   *   *

24. *Mr. Ignacio-Pinto* (Dahomey) said that he would try to sum up the discussion on the principle of nonintervention....

*   *   *

27. His delegation felt that the Special Committee should return to the text adopted by the Assembly and raise the level of the debate with a view to defining the principle of nonintervention and thus serving the cause of peace. If it was true, as he believed, that the members of the Special Committee were engaged in forging new international law, based, in accordance with the Charter, on friendship and co-operation among nations, it was distressing to note that the sponsors of proposal A/AC.125/L.13 referred them in paragraph 3A to "settled international practice." If what was meant was the practice which for decades had been a source of threats and was associated with a troubled past, then such practice was no longer acceptable today.

*   *   *

37. *Mr. Rohrmoser* (Guatemala) said that he could not accept the fact that the sponsors of document A/AC.125/L.13 had omitted intervention in the external affairs of States from paragraph I of their proposal, thus departing from resolution 2131 (XX), which recapitulated a

whole series of ideas set forth in Article 15 of the Charter of the Organization of American States. As regards the "generally recognized freedom of States to seek to influence the policies and actions of States," referred to in paragraph 3A, he was unaware of what sources of international law recognized the freedom mentioned and could therefore not accept that provision, which seemed to legitimize intervention.

*   *   *

39. *Mr. Arangio Ruiz* (Italy)

*   *   *

Finally, the representative of India had objected to paragraph 3 A on the grounds that it stated a principle already embodied in the Vienna Convention on Diplomatic Relations. Such a statement was not, however, superfluous. In formulating a principle on nonintervention, it was essential to say that the ban on intervention did not extend to admitted practices of international intercourse which were generally recognized as not being unlawful in international law and in which all countries habitually engaged.

*   *   *

50. *Mr. Sinclair* (United Kingdom) said that the sponsors of draft resolution A/AC.125/L.13 had endeavoured to draw up, with the greatest care, a text expressing the concepts set forth in resolution 2131 (XX) in the clearest possible legal terms.

*   *   *

53. Furthermore, the use in paragraph 3A of the draft of the words "in accordance with...settled international practice," which had also been criticized, was justified by the fact that the ways in which the freedom to seek to influence the policies and actions of other States could be exercised might not be governed by generally accepted rules of international law. For example, the Vienna Convention covered only certain aspects of that freedom, since it did not cover special missions. That omission was rectified by the words which had been criticized.

54. *Mr. Hargrove* (United States of America)

*   *   *

56. Paragraph 3A had also been criticized because it allegedly constituted a distinct exception to the legal prohibition of intervention.

The sponsors had, however, guarded against that possibility by referring not only to the principle of sovereign equality of States and the duty to co-operate in accordance with the Charter, but also to respect for international law and consequently to respect for the Charter. In any case, a provision recognizing the freedom to seek to influence the policies and actions of other States in the normal course of relations was necessary. Otherwise it could be said, for example, that the United States delegation to the special Committee and the other delegations were guilty of intervention every time they sought to influence—as they did constantly—the policies and actions of other delegations.

*　　*　　*

61. *Mr. Mishra* (India)

*　　*　　*

62. Nobody would claim that the act of seeking to influence the opinion of another State constituted intervention, a point on which his delegation agreed with that of the United States.

That being so, if paragraph 3A was not designed to limit the principle of nonintervention in the affairs of other States, it was out of place in a formulation of principles on the prohibition of intervention. If, on the other hand, it did seek to limit that principle, his delegation would be unable to accept it.

*Opinions of the Office of the Legal Adviser
to the State Department*

NOTE ON THE STATE DEPARTMENT'S VIEW OF
THE NONINTERVENTION PRINCIPLE

In 1974 George Aldrich, Acting Legal Adviser to the State Department, prepared a legal memorandum acknowledging that the various formulations of the nonintervention principle could be given a broad interpretation but also emphasizing their ambiguity, especially insofar as they prohibit interference by means other than force. If applied literally, he notes, "absurd consequences" would follow since many acts of a great power significantly impact upon other countries. "Thus, a decision by the United States to increase or decrease bilateral assistance to a specific country, to send a diplomatic note respecting a particular bilateral problem, to restrict or encourage the export of a U.S. product, or to support the position of one hemispheric government at the expense of another, might be attacked.... Such an interpretation is not, however, supported by the negotiating history."

Similarly, Aldrich acknowledged that the Declaration on Friendly Relations "clearly prohibits...actions designed to coerce a state to secure advantages from it in contravention of its rights." However, he pointed out that in accepting this provision the United States was "careful to interpret it as avoiding any condemnation of economic or other pressures designed to protect or enforce the rights of the state imposing the pressures." In addition, he noted that the United Nations Charter internationalized the protection of human rights and thereby rendered "at least certain actions to promote respect in another state for internationally protected human rights" immune from condemnation as "impermissible intervention, but where beyond that the line between the conflicting rights should be drawn cannot be decided in the abstract and must be determined on a case-by-case basis." The State Department synopsis of the Legal Adviser's memorandum is reprinted.

In 1976 David Small, an Assistant Legal Adviser, prepared a further memorandum on the subject. He indicated that international law traditionally considered a state to have an inherent right "to exercise full control over its trade relations, including the withholding of exports and prohibition of imports with respect to any other state or states, absent treaty commitments to the contrary." The Declaration on Friendly Relations' provision on economic coercion represented a change from the traditional position and was acceptable because of "its ambiguity." It prohibits two types of measures, "that which attempts to coerce a state not to exercise its legal rights and that which attempts to extort advantages." The right to use coercive economic measures as a countermeasure in response to another state's violation of international law would not be affected. We reprint this memorandum as well.

It is noteworthy that the current position of the United States—that its measures against Cuba are solely an internal matter—appears to be a return to the traditional position and, arguably, to be inconsistent with the views stated by Aldrich and Small, which acknowledge some limitations on the right to use economic coercion. The current rationale of the measures—to promote democracy in Cuba—likewise does not appear to fall within the category of permitted measures indicated by Aldrich, that is, economic coercion to protect or enforce the rights of the state imposing the measures. We consider the question of human rights *post.*

GEORGE H. ALDRICH, ACTING LEGAL ADVISER,
DEPARTMENT OF STATE, OCTOBER 25, 1974

(As summarized in *Digest of United States Practice
in International Law* 5–8 (1974))

In a memorandum of law dated October 25, 1975, George H. Aldrich, Acting Legal Adviser of the Department of State, set forth the current international law with respect to intervention in the internal affairs of states. The memorandum dealt first with the development of the general principle of international law prohibiting states from intervening in the internal affairs of another state. Cited as of primary significance in the development of the general principle were the United Nations Charter, the Inter-American system, the 1961 Vienna Convention on Diplomatic Relations, and the 1970 U.N. Declaration on Friendly Relations.

Concerning the UN Charter, Mr. Aldrich cited Article 2, paragraphs 3, 4, and 7, and said that while the language of paragraphs 3 and 4 "does not in terms proscribe 'intervention' in the internal affairs of other states...it is certainly capable of being interpreted as proscribing hostile acts not involving the threat or use of force." Further, the wording of paragraph 7 "may indicate that the drafters of the Charter deliberately avoided use of the term 'intervention' in dealing with the rights and duties of states, as opposed to those of the UN organization. Be that as it may, the language of the Charter was open to subsequent interpretation."

With respect to the Inter-American system, Mr. Aldrich cited Article 18 of the OAS Charter, whose roots are in the Monroe Doctrine and in U.S. activities in the hemisphere in the early 1900s. The memorandum summarizes the history of this period through the addition of the Roosevelt Corollary (1904), the "Good Neighbor" Policy (1933), and the "somewhat reluctant support" by the United States of the 1933 Montevideo Convention on the Rights and Duties of States (TS 881; 49 Stat. 3097; 3 Bevans 145; entered into force for the United States December 26, 1934, subject to a reservation). Article 8 of the Montevideo Convention provides that "no state has the right to intervene in the internal or external affairs of another." While this was the "first formal treaty commitment by the United States to a broad principle of nonintervention," a U.S. reservation to the Convention noted *inter alia* U.S. support of the "general principle of nonintervention" and its regret that during the conference which drafted the Convention there was not time "to prepare interpretations and definitions of these fundamental terms that are embraced in the report." The reservation tied U.S. actions to the policies of the Roosevelt Administration rather than to the specific terms of the Convention.

The next nonintervention treaty commitment entered into by the United States was the 1951 OAS Charter (TIAS 2361; 2 UST 2394; entered into force for the United States December 13, 1951, subject to a reservation). Article 18 of the Charter provides:

> No state or group of states has the right to intervene directly or indirectly, for any reason whatsoever, in the internal or external affairs of any other state. The foregoing principle prohibits not only armed force but also any other form of interference or attempted threat against the personality of the state or against its political, economic and cultural elements.

Mr. Aldrich stated that the history of the nonintervention principle as embodied in the OAS Charter suggests "(a) that the United States recognized that it had accepted a somewhat more broadly stated commitment to avoiding such activity than had heretofore been accepted, although the basic obligation remained the same, (b) that the new language was designed to deal with the serious types of intervention which were taking place in Eastern Europe at the time the drafters were meeting, and (c) that the impetus for the principle in the Charter and the Montevideo Convention was at least in part the overt military interventions of the United States during the first quarter of the 20th century. Thus, what is now Article 18 was designed to encompass both military intervention and less direct forms."

Mr. Aldrich then continued:

> ...the precise scope of Article 18—beyond its applicability to military interventions—is by no means clear. If applied literally, absurd consequences would follow. For example, any action or failure to act by the United States could be argued to come within the prohibition, as most such acts by a great power have an important impact on many countries in this hemisphere. Thus, a decision by the United States to increase or decrease bilateral assistance to a specific country, to send a diplomatic note respecting a particular bilateral problem, to restrict or encourage the export of a U.S. product, or to support the position of one hemispheric government at the expense of another, might be attacked as contrary to the language of Article 18. Such an interpretation is not, however, supported by the negotiating history.... Only the practice of states and the subsequent further development of the law can give it meaning.

The 1961 Vienna Convention on Diplomatic Relations (TIAS 7502;23 UST 3227; entered into force for the United States December 13,1972) provides in Article 41 that all persons enjoying diplomatic privileges and immunities "have a duty not to interfere in the internal affairs" of the host state. This is different from a prohibition against state intervention, and the remedy for Article 41 violations is the declaration of a diplomat as *persona non grata* and his consequent withdrawal from the host country.

The 1970 Declaration on Friendly Relations provides *inter alia* that:

> No state or group of states has the right to intervene, directly or indirectly, for any reason whatever, in the internal or external affairs of any other state. Consequently, armed intervention and all other forms of interference or attempted threats against the personality of the state or against its political, economic and cultural elements, are in violation of international law.

The Declaration also provides that "Every state has an inalienable right to choose its political, economic, social and cultural systems, without interference in any form by another state."

The Declaration sets forth some guidance on the meaning of the nonintervention principle. It proscribes "armed intervention and all other forms of interference or attempted threats against the personality of the state or against its political, economic and cultural elements." It prohibits "economic, political or any other type of measures to coerce another state in order to obtain from it the subordination the exercise of its sovereign rights and to secure from it advantages of any kind." It bars states from assisting "subversive, terrorist or armed activities directed toward the violent overthrow of the regime of another state." It forbids a state to "interfere in civil strife in another state." Mr. Aldrich continued:

> A close reading of the Friendly Relations text suggests that, aside from the use or threat of force, the Declaration clearly prohibits actions designed to assist groups endeavoring to overthrow violently a foreign government and actions designed to coerce a state to secure advantages from it in contravention of its rights. In accepting this language, we were careful to interpret it as avoiding any condemnation of economic or other pressures designed to protect or enforce the rights of the state imposing the pressures. The text also seems to avoid condemnation of assistance to dissident political groups not directed toward the violent overthrow of the government. However, it gives very little guidance as to what, short of the threat or use of force, might be prohibited interference with the right of a state to choose its political, economic, social and cultural systems. As with most international legal instruments, the Declaration was the product of compromise and leaves many ambiguities and uncertainties. Over time, some of these will gradually be resolved by the practice of states, but that process has only just begun.
>
> It may be asked, for example, whether financial assistance by one state to newspapers, political parties, or other groups within another state is illegal intervention under the principles set forth in the Friendly Relations Declaration. This cannot be decided by textual analysis or by reference to negotiating history, but can be determined only over time

by the practice of states. It may confidently be assumed that, if the issue of whether such activities are proscribed by the principle of nonintervention were to be put to a vote today in the United Nations General Assembly, the vast majority would hold that they are; but whether the practice of those states will come to support that conclusion remains to be seen.

Finally, it should be noted that in any situation there may well be conflicting rights and duties of states. Thus, the United Nations Charter, while laying the foundation on which the Friendly Relations Declaration was built concerning nonintervention, also internationalized the protection of human rights. Prior to the Charter, the relation between a state and its nationals was, in general, considered a domestic matter, not properly the subject of international concern. However, each Member of the United Nations has pledged, in Articles 55 and 56, to "take joint and separate action in cooperation with the organization for the achievement" of a number of purposes, including "universal respect for, and observance of, human rights and fundamental freedoms for all without distinction as to race, sex, language, or religion." Thus, at least certain actions to promote respect in another state for internationally protected human rights cannot legitimately be prohibited by the principle of nonintervention. Certainly raising questions about violations of such human rights is not impermissible intervention, but where beyond that the line between the conflicting rights should be drawn cannot be decided in the abstract and must be determined on a case-by-case basis.

In summary, recent developments in international law have provided a principle of nonintervention as part of the legal structure in which sovereign states co-exist. The application of that principle to different factual situations is difficult and uncertain and is likely to remain so at least until an extended period of state practice has been accumulated and can be examined. The threat or use of force, assistance to armed revolutionaries, and coercion designed to secure advantages from a state in contravention of its rights are the only state acts clearly and expressly prohibited by the legal principle, but it may well be extended further by the practice of states.

DAVID H. SMALL, ASSISTANT LEGAL ADVISER FOR
NEAR EASTERN AND SOUTH ASIAN AFFAIRS,
DEPARTMENT OF STATE, NOVEMBER 12, 1976

(Digest of United States Practice in International Law 576–78 (1976))

Export controls over individual commodities have been imposed under American law for economic and strategic reasons as far back as World War I. The Export Control Act of 1949 [63 Stat. 7;50 U.S.C. App. 2021-2032] bluntly declared it to be the policy of the United States to use export controls to "further the foreign policy of the United States." Similarly, its replacement legislation, the Export Administration Act of 1969 [83 Stat. 841; 50 U.S.C. App. 2041-2413], declared it to be United States policy "to use its economic resources and trade potential to further...its national security and foreign policy objectives." The Trading With the Enemy Act [40 Stat. 415; 50 U.S.C. App 1 *et seq.*] authorizes far-reaching blocking actions against persons who are "designated nationals" of an enemy. Such persons...need not be nationals of an enemy state. Indeed, U.S. citizens could be so designated.

...[T]hese acts gave rise to an extensive, complex system of regulations, which include the grouping of countries into different categories for different treatment with respect to U.S. exports. Similarly, the United States has established separate tariff schedules treating imports differently, depending on country of origin, and basing classification on political or ideological orientation. The Treasury Regulations under the Trading With the Enemy Act place political restrictions on the use of U.S. dollars or dollar accounts by anyone anywhere.... Similarly, dollar accounts belonging, for example, to the People's Republic of China, or persons resident there, were frozen by the U.S. Treasury wherever these accounts were located, and some were in European banks. Beyond such controls, the United States has, on occasion, initiated total boycotts against other countries, such as the trade embargoes imposed upon North Korea, North Vietnam, and Cuba.

Traditional international law adopted a *laissez-faire* approach toward the economic rights and duties of states, and it has long been considered an inherent right of an independent, sovereign state to exercise full control over its trade relations, including the withholding of exports and prohibition of imports with respect to any other state or states, absent treaty commitments to the contrary....

The Charter of the United Nations contains a number of very important and far-reaching restrictions on the use of armed force, but it says nothing at all about restrictions on the use of economic measures of coercion by individual states or groups of states. Conceivably, economic measures could give rise to a dispute, "the continuance of which is likely to endanger the maintenance of international peace and security" within the meaning of article 33 of the Charter, but even that is nowhere made clear. Economic pressure may be unfriendly and even unfair, but economic coercion, *per se,* cannot generally be said to be prohibited by the U.N. Charter.

In 1970, the twenty-fifth General Assembly attempted to elaborate the law of the U.N. Charter by adopting a resolution approving the "Declaration on Principles of International Law concerning Friendly Relations and Cooperation among States." ...[T]here are two provisions relevant to economic coercion. A preambular provision recalls "the duty of states to refrain in their international relations from military, political, economic or any other form of coercion aimed against the political independence or territorial integrity of any state." This seems to acknowledge the existence of a duty not to use economic coercion for the purpose of destroying or dismembering a state. This is scarcely a radical rule. While the passage could imply more, its possible further implications are not widely agreed. The second reference to economic coercion in the Declaration is more important. In elaborating on the duty not to intervene in matters within the domestic jurisdiction of a state, it says:

> No state may use or encourage the use of economic, political or any other type of measures to coerce another state in order to obtain from it the subordination of the exercise of its sovereign rights and to secure from it advantages of any kind.

This latter provision is far from clear, but it seems to mean that two types of economic coercion are prohibited: that which attempts to coerce a state not to exercise its legal rights and that which attempts to extort advantages. The origin of this provision is to be found in article 15 of the Charter of the Organization of American States (TIAS 2361; 2 UST 2394).... [I]t seems fair to say that the broad acceptability of this formulation results from its ambiguity. Under it...the United States can defend suspension of economic assistance pursuant to the...Hickenlooper amendment [22 U.S.C. 2370(e)(2)] on the grounds that the other state has no legal right to expropriate property without paying just compensation—and, on the contrary, that the other state has a duty to pay such compensation. In seeking to square the Arab boycott with the Declaration, the boycott's defenders label it a legitimate measure of self-defense, rather than an effort to secure advantages from Israel.

In view of the extensive use of economic coercion by one state against another throughout the twentieth century, and in view of these rather modest legal efforts to restrict it, existing international law can probably best be described as narrowing only slightly the permissive legal regime of the past. The direction of development of the law is toward greater restriction on the use of economic coercion, but it has been a slow movement with, thus far, limited effects.

United States Justification for its Economic Sanctions against Argentina

NOTE ON THE UNITED STATES VIEW OF ECONOMIC COERCION UNDER THE OAS CHARTER

In October 1982 the United States representative to the OAS addressed the issue of economic coercion in comments to the Inter-American Economic and Social Council, which we reprint. The United States, along with the European Economic Community, had imposed economic sanctions against Argentina during the conflict over the Malvinas/Falkland Islands. The United States measures included the suspension of export credits and a ban on military exports. On April 28, 1982 the OAS approved a resolution deploring "the adoption by members of the European Economic Community and other states of coercive measures of an economic and political nature, which are prejudicial to the Argentine nation" and urging them "to lift those measures, indicating that they constitute a serious precedent, inasmuch as they are not covered by Resolution 502 (1982) of the United Nations Security Council and are incompatible with the Charters of the United Nations and of the OAS and the General Agreement on Tariffs and Trade (GATT)." Resolution I of the Twentieth Meeting of Consultation of Ministers of Foreign Affairs, OEA/Ser.F/II.20 (April 28, 1982).

Thereafter, in October 1982, when the ensuing war had ended, the Inter-American Economic and Social Council took up the issue of economic coercion against Argentina and developing countries in general. It adopted a resolution declaring that the economic measures against Argentina were in violation of the United Nations and OAS Charters, the Declaration on Friendly Relations, and other related international instruments and constituted a "grave precedent for future relations between the developed countries and the developing countries of the American continent and throughout the world." More generally, it rejected "the imposition of embargoes and economic blockades, the freezing of funds, the suspension of credits and all other economic measures of a coercive nature directed against any developing country for the purpose of undermining or obstructing the full exercise of its sovereignty over its territory or natural and economic resources, or of placing obstacles in the way of economic and social policies that any one of them may have established on the basis of a sovereign decision by its people and government." CIES/RES.234 (XVII-O/82), included in XVII Annual Meeting of the Inter-American Economic and Social Council at the Ministerial Level, October 19-22, 1982, OEA/Ser.H/XII.40, pp.12-13 (1982).

In explaining the United States opposition to the resolution, which was adopted by a vote of twenty to one with four abstentions, the United States representative defended the United States measures, *inter alia,* by invoking the traditional view that international law does not constrain states in adopting the kind of measures which the United States had imposed on Argentina. Although the measures against Argentina were mild in comparison to those against Cuba, the United States position presaged its stance in the General Assembly in 1991 and 1992: "The United States measures focused on official programs in support of exports and regulations relating to traffic in arms, which all nations have the sovereign right to regulate. The United States had no legal duty to provide Argentina the benefits it withdrew."

Furthermore, the United States representative placed a gloss on the language of the OAS Charter, implicitly interpreting its prohibition on the use of coercive economic measures "to force the sovereign will of another State and obtain from it advantages of any kind" as inapplicable to measures designed solely to coerce a sovereign to comply with its legal obligations under the Charter. According to the United States representative, the United States measures did not violate the Charter because they were not "designed, in the words of Article 19 of the OAS Charter, to obtain from Argentina advantages of any kind. Rather, they were designed to demonstrate United States adherence, consistent with all relevant legal obligations, to the principle of peaceful dispute settlement that forms the bedrock of the OAS Charter." This reading of the OAS Charter would presumably apply as well to the nearly identical language of the Declaration on Friendly Relations and related General Assembly resolutions, the formulations of which were based on the OAS Charter.

It may be considered whether the United States may invoke this legal position in support of its measures against Cuba in addition to its traditional *laissez-faire* view of sovereign discretion. In this connection, whether the United States is seeking "advantages of any kind" would be critical. It bears mention that in order to continue the measures against Cuba under the Trading With the Enemy Act, the President is required to certify annually that the measures are in the "national interest," 50 U.S.C. App. § 5(b) note, which he has done since 1977, most recently on September 14, 1991. Presidential Determination No. 91-52, 56 Fed. Reg. 48415 (September 13, 1991). The Principal Legal Officer of the General Secretariat of the OAS, expressing his own views, considered a similar certification by the President to be dispositive of the United States claim that its measures against Argentina were not designed to secure advantages from it. Domingo E. Acevedo, *The U.S. Measures Against Argentina Resulting From the Malvinas Conflict,* 78 A.J.I.L. 323, 342 (1984).

In addition, it may also be noted that the United States in the case of Argentina made reference to the pacific settlement of disputes, which is a fundamental requirement of international law contained in the OAS Charter. In the case of Cuba, the United States stated purpose is the promotion of democracy. Unlike its requirement of pacific settlement of disputes, the OAS Charter simply provides with respect to democracy that: "The American States reaffirm the following principles:...d) The solidarity of the American States and the high aims which are sought through it require the political organization of those States on the basis of the effective exercise of representative democracy." OAS Charter, Article 3. It may be considered whether there is a difference between measures which attempt to coerce adherence to a legally binding obligation and those which attempt to coerce the achievement of this goal. *See Case Concerning Military and Paramilitary Activities in and Against Nicaragua (Nicaragua v. United States) (Merits)*

1986 I.C.J. Rep. 14 (Judgment of June 17, 1986), paragraphs 259, 261. It is also significant that notwithstanding the United States arguments, the member states voted twenty to one to condemn its economic measures against Argentina.

EXPLANATION OF THE UNITED STATES VOTE ON
RESOLUTION 234 (XVII-0/82) OF THE INTER-AMERICAN
ECONOMIC AND SOCIAL COUNCIL

(Final Report, XVII Annual Report Of The Inter-American
Economic And Social Council At The Ministerial Level,
October 19-22, 1982, OEA/Ser.H/XII.40 (1982))

The United States objects firmly to characterization of the measures adopted by the U.S. in April of this year as "coercive economic measures" in violation of international law and, in particular, Article 19 of the OAS Charter. The modest measures adopted by the United States, which it should be noted have now been withdrawn, demonstrated United States adherence to fundamental principles of international order to which we all must subscribe. They were fully consistent with our international obligations and, in particular, with the relevant resolution of the UN Security Council.

The United States measures focused on official programs in support of exports and regulations relating to traffic in arms, which all nations have the sovereign right to regulate. The United States had no legal duty to provide Argentina the benefits it withdrew; nor was there any violation of Argentina's rights under any existing agreement. The United States measures did not seek illegitimately to impair the political independence, territorial integrity, or sovereign rights of Argentina; nor were they designed, in the words of Article 19 of the OAS Charter, to obtain from Argentina advantages of any kind. Rather, they were designed to demonstrate United States adherence, consistent with all relevant legal obligations, to the principle of peaceful dispute settlement that forms the bedrock of the OAS Charter.

It is therefore with astonishment and sadness that my delegation finds, in this draft resolution, these important principles of international law turned on their heads. Fully legal measures plainly designed to manifest disapproval of an illegal use of force and encourage compliance with law cannot constitute 'unlawful economic coercion'; yet so the draft resolution would assert. My delegation does not believe that such unfortunate assertions should be allowed to divert this body from the truly important, productive topics on our full agenda.

For this reason the United States Mission disassociates itself from any implied approval or responsibility for this document.

THE EMERGING UNITED STATES POSITION AND ITS
INTERNATIONAL RECEPTION: ECONOMIC COERCION
TO PROMOTE DEMOCRATIC CHANGE

*International Court of Justice's Consideration
of Intervention to Promote Democracy*

NOTE ON THE REJECTION OF THE REAGAN AND BUSH
DOCTRINES BY THE INTERNATIONAL COURT OF JUSTICE

The United States' current stated purpose in imposing economic measures against Cuba is to promote democratic change. Although in the General Assembly proceedings the United States did not attempt to articulate any international law support for imposing measures for this purpose, relying instead on the argument that its measures were solely an internal matter, this legal position is at least implicit in its statements on the issue. Cuba, of course, challenges this claimed purpose as pretextual. It further contends that the use of coercive economic measures constitutes impermissible intervention precisely when it is imposed to promote change, democratic or otherwise, in the internal political and economic system of a sovereign state.

In this section we indicate the degree of acceptance which this emerging position of the United States has received in the international community. It would appear there is growing international concern with democratic rights but that in accordance with the nonintervention principle states have generally expressed their concerns through diplomatic persuasion and international censure. There is some indication of an acceptance of the use of multilateral economic sanctions to promote democracy in states where an existing democratic government has been overthrown and the state had previously agreed that collective measures could be adopted against it in the event of an interruption of its democratic governmental institutions. There does not, however, appear to be support for the imposition of sanctions to promote democracy on a unilateral basis or in the absence of the state's prior consent.

In recent years the United States has on a number of occasions used military force or coercive economic measures against states where one of its principal stated purposes was the desire to promote democracy in the target country. Perhaps the most dramatic example was the United States economic measures against Panama in 1988, which were followed by an invasion in 1989. The United States arrested the then leader of the country, General Manuel Noriega, and installed a new government composed of the electoral victors in a previous election who had never acceded to power due to the intervention of General Noriega. Among other purposes, the United States repeatedly cited in support of first its economic measures and then the invasion the desire to promote democracy in Panama. Other examples include the United States invasion of Grenada, its economic measures against Nicaragua and support for the *contras,* and its economic measures against Haiti (considered in more detail *post*).

When defending its actions in international forums, the United States has not advanced the legal position that the use of military force may be justified by a desire to promote democratic changes. Instead, it has rested upon more traditional legal justifications, while at the same time bolstering its position by reference to its purpose to promote democracy. Nevertheless, commentators have interpreted United States government policy as implicitly premised on this position, which some have dubbed the "Bush Doctrine." *See, e.g.*, David J. Scheffer, *Use of Force After the Cold War: Panama, Iraq, and the New World Order,* in Louis Henkin, Stanley Hoffmann, Jeane J. Kirkpatrick, Allan Gerson, William D. Rogers, and David J. Scheffer, EDS., *Right v. Might: International Law and the Use of Force* 109, 119 (2d ed. 1991).

In this respect the policy of the Bush administration has gone a step further than that articulated during the previous administration as the "Reagan Doctrine." The Reagan Doctrine asserted the legal and political legitimacy of providing support to "pro-democratic" insurgencies fighting "totalitarian" regimes supported by the Soviet Union. Such support was viewed as proper because it sought to promote democratic change and was necessitated by an initial Soviet "intervention," albeit in favor of an existing government. Jeane J. Kirkpatrick and Allan Gerson, *The Reagan Doctrine, Human Rights, and International Law,* in *Right v. Might,* 19, 34 (1991). The Bush administration's policy eliminates the need for any foreign involvement and justifies military intervention solely to promote democracy. The rationale for this policy, moreover, applies as well to the use of coercive economic measures to promote democracy. *A fortiori,* if military force may be used for this purpose, economic coercion may be as well. See Lori Fisler Damrosch, *Politics Across Borders: Nonintervention and Nonforcible Influences Over Domestic Affairs,* 83 A.J.I.L. 1 (1989), for a view that use of economic coercion is permissible to promote democratic change.

The first document we reprint is an excerpt from the International Court of Justice's decision in the *Nicaragua* case. In the context of Nicaragua's claim based upon United States support for the paramilitary activities of the *contras,* the Court considered whether the United States actions were in violation of both the prohibition on the use of force and the broader nonintervention principle. On the latter question, the Court held that the principle of nonintervention, which it found was a norm of customary international law, was fully applicable irrespective of whether the United States actions were an attempt to promote democratic changes in Nicaragua. *Id.,* paragraphs 202-09, 257-68. Its ruling is thus a repudiation of the underlying premise of the Bush and Reagan doctrines. Given the United States failure to appear before the Court, the Court was unwilling even to assume that the United States would assert this position as a legal justification for its conduct. "The United States authorities have on some occasions clearly stated their grounds for intervening in the affairs of a foreign State for reasons connected with, for example, the domestic policies of that country, its ideology, the level of its armaments, or the direction of its foreign policy. But these were statements of international policy, and not an assertion of rules of existing international law." *Id.,* paragraph 209.

The legal analysis applicable to the use of force raises a number of issues which are not applicable to a legal analysis of the use of coercive economic measures. The portion of the Court's opinion which we include, however, explicates the general nonintervention principle, and the Court's reasoning was expressly not limited to interventions involving the use of force. As the Court explained:

A prohibited intervention must accordingly be one bearing on matters in which each State is permitted, by the principle of State sovereignty, to decide freely. One of these is the choice of a political, economic, social and cultural system, and the formulation of foreign policy. Intervention is wrongful when it uses methods of coercion in regard to such choices, which must remain free ones. The element of coercion, which defines, and indeed forms the very essence of, prohibited intervention, is particularly obvious in the case of an intervention which uses force....

Id., paragraph 205. Thus, the portions of the opinion we set out are of interest in considering the application of the nonintervention principle in the context of coercive economic measures.

CASE CONCERNING MILITARY AND PARAMILITARY
ACTIVITIES IN AND AGAINST NICARAGUA (NICARAGUA
V. UNITED STATES OF AMERICA) (MERITS)

(1986 I.C.J. Rep. 14 (Judgment of June 27, 1986))

*   *   *

202. The principle of nonintervention involves the right of every sovereign State to conduct its affairs without outside interference; though examples of trespass against this principle are not infrequent, the Court considers that it is part and parcel of customary international law. As the Court has observed: "Between independent States, respect for territorial sovereignty is an essential foundation of international relations" (*I.C.J. Reports 1949,* p. 35), and international law requires political

integrity also to be respected. Expressions of an *opinio juris* regarding the existence of the principle of nonintervention in customary international law are numerous and not difficult to find. Of course, statements whereby States avow their recognition of the principles of international law set forth in the United Nations Charter cannot strictly be interpreted as applying to the principle of nonintervention by States in the internal and external affairs of other States, since this principle is not, as such, spelt out in the Charter. But it was never intended that the Charter should embody written confirmation of every essential principle of international law in force. The existence in the *opinio juris* of States of the principle of nonintervention is backed by established and substantial practice. It has moreover been presented as a corollary of the principle of the sovereign equality of States. A particular instance of this is General Assembly resolution 2625 (XXV), the Declaration on the Principles of International Law concerning Friendly Relations and Co-operation among States. In the *Corfu Channel* case, when a State claimed a right of intervention in order to secure evidence in the territory of another State for submission to an international tribunal (*I.C.J. Reports 1949*, p.34), the Court observed that:

> "the alleged right of intervention as the manifestation of a policy of force, such as has, in the past, given rise to most serious abuses and such as cannot, whatever be the present defects in international organization, find a place in international law. Intervention is perhaps still less admissible in the particular form it would take here; for, from the nature of things, it would be reserved for the most powerful States, and might easily lead to perverting the administration of international justice itself." (*I.C.J. Reports 1949*, p.35.)

203. The principle has since been reflected in numerous declarations adopted by international organizations and conferences in which the United States and Nicaragua have participated, e.g., General Assembly resolution 2131 (XX), the Declaration on the Inadmissibility of Intervention in the Domestic Affairs of States and the Protection of their Independence and Sovereignty. It is true that the United States, while it voted in favour of General Assembly resolution 2131 (XX), also declared at the time of its adoption in the First Committee that it considered the declaration in that resolution to be "only a statement of political intention and not a formulation of law" (*Official Records of the General Assembly, Twentieth Session, First Committee*, A/C.I/SR.1423, p.436). However, the essentials of resolution 2131 (XX) are repeated in the Declaration approved by resolution 2625 (XXV), which set out principles which the General Assembly declared to be "basic principles" of international law, and on the adoption of which no analogous statement was made by the United States representative.

204. As regards inter-American relations, attention may be drawn to, for example, the United States reservation to the Montevideo Convention on Rights and Duties of States (26 December 1933), declaring the opposition of the United States Government to "interference with the freedom, the sovereignty or other internal affairs, or processes of the Governments of other nations"; or the ratification by the United States of the Additional Protocol relative to Nonintervention (23 December 1936). Among more recent texts, mention may be made of resolutions AG/RES.78 and AG/RES.128 of the General Assembly of the Organization of American States. In a different context, the United States expressly accepted the principles set forth in the declaration, to which reference has already been made, appearing in the Final Act of the Conference on Security and Co-operation in Europe (Helsinki, 1 August 1975), including an elaborate statement of the principle of nonintervention; while these principles were presented as applying to the mutual relations among the participating States, it can be inferred that the text testifies to the existence, and the acceptance by the United States, of a customary principle which has universal application.

205. Notwithstanding the multiplicity of declarations by States accepting the principle of nonintervention, there remain two questions: first, what is the exact content of the principle so accepted, and secondly, is the practice sufficiently in conformity with it for this to be a rule of customary international law? As regards the first problem—that of the content of the principle of nonintervention—the Court will define only those aspects of the principle which appear to be relevant to the resolution of the dispute. In this respect it notes that, in view of the generally accepted formulations, the principle forbids all States or groups of States to intervene directly or indirectly in internal or external affairs of other States. A prohibited intervention must accordingly be one bearing on matters in which each State is permitted, by the principle of State sovereignty, to decide freely. One of these is the choice of a political, economic, social and cultural system, and the formulation of foreign policy. Intervention is wrongful when it uses methods of coercion in regard to such choices, which must remain free ones. The element of coercion, which defines, and indeed forms the very essence of, prohibited intervention, is particularly obvious in the case of an intervention which uses force, either in the direct form of military action, or in the indirect form of support for subversive or terrorist armed activities within another State. As noted above (paragraph 191), General Assembly resolution 2625 (XXV) equates assistance of this kind with the use of force by the assisting State when the acts committed in another State "involve a threat or use of force." These forms of action are therefore wrongful in the light of both the principle of non-use of force, and that of nonintervention. In view of the nature of Nicaragua's

complaints against the United States, and those expressed by the United States in regard to Nicaragua's conduct towards El Salvador, it is primarily acts of intervention of this kind with which the Court is concerned in the present case.

206. However, before reaching a conclusion on the nature of prohibited intervention, the Court must be satisfied that State practice justifies it. There have been in recent years a number of instances of foreign intervention for the benefit of forces opposed to the government of another State. The Court is not here concerned with the process of decolonization; this question is not in issue in the present case. It has to consider whether there might be indications of a practice illustrative of belief in a kind of general right for States to intervene, directly or indirectly, with or without armed force, in support of an internal opposition in another State, whose cause appeared particularly worthy by reason of the political and moral values with which it was identified. For such a general right to come into existence would involve a fundamental modification of the customary law principle of nonintervention.

207. In considering the instances of the conduct above described, the Court has to emphasize that, as was observed in the *North Sea Continental Shelf* cases, for a new customary rule to be formed, not only must the acts concerned "amount to a settled practice," but they must be accompanied by the *opinio juris sive necessitatis*. Either the States taking such action or other States in a position to react to it must have behaved so that their conduct is

> "evidence of a belief that this practice is rendered obligatory by the existence of a rule of law requiring it. The need for such a belief, i.e., the existence of a subjective element, is implicit in the very notion of the *opinio juris sive necessitas.*" (*I.C.J. Reports* 1969, p.44, para. 77.)

The Court has no jurisdiction to rule upon the conformity with international law of any conduct of States not parties to the present dispute, or of conduct of the parties unconnected with the dispute, nor has it authority to ascribe to States legal views which they do not themselves advance. The significance for the Court of cases of State conduct *prima facie* inconsistent with the principle of nonintervention lies in the nature of the ground offered as justification. Reliance by a State on a novel right or an unprecedented exception to the principle might, if shared in principle by other States, tend towards a modification of customary international law. In fact however the Court finds that States have not justified their conduct by reference to a new right of intervention or a new exception to the principle of its prohibition. The United States authorities have on some occasions clearly stated their grounds for intervening in the affairs of a foreign State for reasons connected with, for example, the domestic policies of that country, its ideology, the level of its armaments, or the direction of its foreign policy. But these were statements of international policy, and not an assertion of rules of existing international law.

208. In particular, as regards the conduct towards Nicaragua which is the subject of the present case, the United States has not claimed that its intervention, which it justified in this way on the political level, was also justified on the legal level, alleging the exercise of a new right of intervention regarded by the United States as existing in such circumstances. As mentioned above, the United States has, on the legal plane, justified its intervention expressly and solely by reference to the "classic" rules involved, namely, collective self-defence against an armed attack. Nicaragua, for its part, has often expressed its solidarity and sympathy with the opposition in various States, especially in El Salvador. But Nicaragua too has not argued that this was a legal basis for an intervention, let alone an intervention involving the use of force.

209. The Court therefore finds that no such general right of intervention, in support of an opposition within another State, exists in contemporary international law. The Court concludes that acts constituting a breach of the customary principle of nonintervention will also, if they directly or indirectly involve the use of force, constitute a breach of the principle of non-use of force in international relations.

*   *   *

257. The Court has noted above (paragraphs 169 and 170) the attitude of the United States, as expressed in the finding of the Congress of 29 July 1985, linking United States support to the *contras* with alleged breaches by the Government of Nicaragua of its "solemn commitments to the Nicaraguan people, the United States, and the Organization of American States." Those breaches were stated to involve questions such as the composition of the government, its political ideology and alignment, totalitarianism, human rights, militarization and aggression. So far as the question of "aggression in the form of armed subversion against its neighbours" is concerned, the Court has already dealt with the claimed justification of collective self-defence in response to armed attack, and will not return to that matter. It has also disposed of the suggestion of a right to collective counter-measures in face of an armed intervention. What is now in question is whether there is anything in the conduct of Nicaragua which might legally warrant counter-measures by the United States.

258. The questions as to which the Nicaraguan Government is said to have entered into a commitment are questions of domestic policy. The Court would not therefore normally consider it appropriate to engage in a verification of the truth of assertions of this kind, even assuming that it was in a position to do so. A State's domestic policy falls

within its exclusive jurisdiction, provided of course that it does not violate any obligation of international law. Every State possesses a fundamental right to choose and implement its own political, economic and social systems. Consequently, there would normally be no need to make any enquiries, in a matter outside the Court's jurisdiction, to ascertain in what sense and along what lines Nicaragua has actually exercised its right.

259. However, the assertion of a commitment raises the question of the possibility of a State binding itself by agreement in relation to a question of domestic policy, such as that relating to the holding of free elections on its territory. The Court cannot discover, within the range of subjects open to international agreement, any obstacle or provision to hinder a State from making a commitment of this kind. A State, which is free to decide upon the principle and methods of popular consultation within its domestic order, is sovereign for the purpose of accepting a limitation of its sovereignty in this field. This is a conceivable situation for a State which is bound by institutional links to a confederation of States, or indeed to an international organization. Both Nicaragua and the United States are members of the Organization of American States. The Charter of that Organization however goes no further in the direction of an agreed limitation on sovereignty of this kind than the provision in Article 3 (d) that

> "[t]he solidarity of the American States and the high aims which are sought through it require the political organization of those States on the basis of the effective exercise of representative democracy";

on the other hand, it provides for the right of every State "to organize itself as it sees fit" (Art. 12), and to "develop its cultural, political and economic life freely and naturally" (Art. 16).

260. The Court has set out above the facts as to the events of 1979, including the resolution of the XVIIth Meeting of Consultation of Ministers for Foreign Affairs of the Organization of American States, and the communications of 12 July 1979 from the Junta of the Government of National Reconstruction of Nicaragua to the Secretary-General of the Organization, accompanied by a "Plan to secure peace." The letter contained *inter alia* a list of the objectives of the Nicaraguan Junta and stated in particular its intention of installing the new regime by a peaceful, orderly transition and of respecting human rights under the supervision of the Inter-American Commission on Human Rights, which the Junta invited to visit Nicaragua "as soon as we are installed." In this way, before its installation in Managua, the new régime soothed apprehensions as desired and expressed its intention of governing the country democratically.

261. However, the Court is unable to find anything in these documents, whether the resolution or the communication accompanied by

the "Plan to secure peace," from which it can be inferred that any legal undertaking was intended to exist. Moreover, the Junta made it plain in one of these documents that its invitation to the Organization of American States to supervise Nicaragua's political life should not be allowed to obscure the fact that it was the Nicaraguans themselves who were to decide upon and conduct the country's domestic policy. The resolution of 23 June 1979 also declares that the solution of their problems is a matter "exclusively" for the Nicaraguan people, while stating that that solution was to be based (in Spanish, *debería inspirarse*) on certain foundations which were put forward merely as recommendations to the future government. This part of the resolution is a mere statement which does not comprise any formal offer which if accepted would constitute a promise in law, and hence a legal obligation. Nor can the Court take the view that Nicaragua actually undertook a commitment to organize free elections, and that this commitment was of a legal nature. The Nicaraguan Junta of National Reconstruction planned the holding of free elections as part of its political programme of government, following the recommendation of the XVIIth Meeting of Consultation of Foreign Ministers of the Organization of American States. This was an essentially political pledge, made not only to the Organization, but also to the people of Nicaragua, intended to be its first beneficiaries. But the Court cannot find an instrument with legal force, whether unilateral or synallagmatic, whereby Nicaragua has committed itself in respect of the principle or methods of holding elections. The Organization of American States Charter has already been mentioned, with its respect for the political independence of the member States; in the field of domestic policy, it goes no further than to list the social standards to the application of which the Members "agree to dedicate every effort," including:

> "[t]he incorporation and increasing participation of the marginal sectors of the population, in both rural and urban areas, in the economic, social, civic, cultural, and political life of the nation, in order to achieve the full integration of the national community, acceleration of the process of social mobility, and the consolidation of the democratic system." (Art. 43 (f).)

It is evident that provisions of this kind are far from being a commitment as to the use of particular political mechanisms.

262. Moreover, even supposing that such a political pledge had had the force of a legal commitment, it could not have justified the United States insisting on the fulfillment of a commitment made not directly towards the United States, but towards the Organization, the latter being alone empowered to monitor its implementation. The Court can see no legal basis for the "special responsibility regarding the implementation of the commitments made" by the Nicaraguan Government

which the United States considers itself to have assumed in view of "its role in the installation of the current Government of Nicaragua" (see paragraph 170 above). Moreover, even supposing that the United States were entitled to act in lieu of the Organization, it could hardly make use for the purpose of methods which the Organization could not use itself; in particular, it could not be authorized to use force in that event. Of its nature, a commitment like this is one of a category which, if violated, cannot justify the use of force against a sovereign State.

263. The finding of the United States Congress also expressed the view that the Nicaraguan Government had taken "significant steps towards establishing a totalitarian Communist dictatorship." However the regime in Nicaragua be defined, adherence by a State to any particular doctrine does not constitute a violation of customary international law; to hold otherwise would make nonsense of the fundamental principle of State sovereignty, on which the whole of international law rests, and the freedom of choice of the political, social, economic and cultural system of a State. Consequently, Nicaragua's domestic policy options, even assuming that they correspond to the description given of them by the Congress finding, cannot justify on the legal plane the various actions of the Respondent complained of. The Court cannot contemplate the creation of a new rule opening up a right of intervention by one State against another on the ground that the latter has opted for some particular ideology or political system.

264. The Court has also emphasized the importance to be attached, in other respects, to a text such as the Helsinki Final Act, or, on another level, to General Assembly resolution 2625 (XXV) which, as its name indicates, is a declaration on "Principles of International Law concerning Friendly Relations and Co-operation among States in accordance with the Charter of the United Nations." Texts like these, in relation to which the Court has pointed to the customary content of certain provisions such as the principles of the non-use of force and nonintervention, envisage the relations among States having different political, economic and social systems on the basis of coexistence among their various ideologies; the United States not only voiced no objection to their adoption, but took an active part in bringing it about.

265. Similar considerations apply to the criticisms expressed by the United States of the external policies and alliances of Nicaragua. Whatever the impact of individual alliances on regional or international political military balances, the Court is only competent to consider such questions from the standpoint of international law. From that aspect, it is sufficient to say that State sovereignty evidently extends to the area of its foreign policy, and that there is no rule of customary international law to prevent a State from choosing and conducting a foreign policy in co-ordination with that of another State.

266. The Court also notes that these justifications, advanced solely in a political context which it is naturally not for the Court to appraise, were not advanced as legal arguments. The respondent State has always confined itself to the classic argument of self-defence, and has not attempted to introduce a legal argument derived from a supposed rule of "ideological intervention," which would have been a striking innovation. The Court would recall that one of the accusations of the United States against Nicaragua is violation of "the 1965 General Assembly Declaration on Intervention" (paragraph 169 above), by its support for the armed opposition to the Government in El Salvador. It is not aware of the United States having officially abandoned reliance on this principle, substituting for it a new principle "of ideological intervention," the definition of which would be discretionary. As stated above (paragraph 29), the Court is not solely dependent for its decision on the argument of the Parties before it with respect to the applicable law: it is required to consider on its own initiative all rules of international law which may be relevant to the settlement of the dispute even if these rules have not been invoked by a party. The Court is however not entitled to ascribe to States legal views which they do not themselves formulate.

267. The Court also notes that Nicaragua is accused by the 1985 finding of the United States Congress of violating human rights. This particular point requires to be studied independently of the question of the existence of a "legal commitment" by Nicaragua towards the Organization of American States to respect these rights; the absence of such a commitment would not mean that Nicaragua could with impunity violate human rights. However, where human rights are protected by international conventions, that protection takes the form of such arrangements for monitoring or ensuring respect for human rights as are provided for in the conventions themselves. The political pledge by Nicaragua was made in the context of the Organization of American States, the organs of which were consequently entitled to monitor its observance. The Court has noted above (paragraph 168) that the Nicaraguan Government has since 1979 ratified a number of international instruments on human rights, and one of these was the American Convention on Human Rights (the Pact of San José, Costa Rica). The mechanisms provided for therein have functioned. The Inter-American Commission on Human Rights in fact took action and compiled two reports (OEA/Ser.L/V/11.53 and 62) following visits by the Commission to Nicaragua at the Government's invitation. Consequently, the Organization was in a position, if it so wished, to take a decision on the basis of these reports.

268. In any event, while the United States might form its own appraisal of the situation as to respect for human rights in Nicaragua,

the use of force could not be the appropriate method to monitor or ensure such respect. With regard to the steps actually taken, the protection of human rights, a strictly humanitarian objective, cannot be compatible with the mining of ports, the destruction of oil installations, or again with the training, arriving and equipping of the *contras*. The Court concludes that the argument derived from the preservation of human rights in Nicaragua cannot afford a legal justification for the conduct of the United States, and cannot in any event be reconciled with the legal strategy of the respondent State, which is based on the right of collective self-defence.

The International Reception Given United States
Economic Sanctions against Panama

NOTE ON THE REJECTION OF ECONOMIC COERCION BY
THE LATIN AMERICAN ECONOMIC SYSTEM

In early 1988 the United States imposed a trade embargo and other economic sanctions against Panama in an effort to restore the government of President Eric Arturo Delvalle to power after Delvalle was dismissed by the Panamanian National Assembly. Delvalle had attempted to dismiss General Noriega, and it is widely believed that in retaliation Noriega engineered Delvalle's dismissal.

In response to the imposition of these measures, SELA, the Latin American Economic System, held an extraordinary meeting in March 1988 to consider their validity under international law. With twenty-two Latin American nations attending the meeting, SELA on March 29 issued a decision condemning the U.S. measures as a coercive interference in the internal affairs of Panama in violation of the United Nations and OAS Charters and customary international law. SELA Decision No. 271 (March 29, 1988). Reiterating its previous condemnation of the imposition of coercive measures against any SELA member state, *see* Decision No. 112, it urged "the U.S. government to revoke immediately the enforcement measures which it has instituted against Panama" and reaffirmed "the sovereign right of all nations to choose their own economic, social and political destiny in peace and liberty, free from external pressure, aggression and threats." The decision further stated that SELA would consider, "in a spirit of solidarity," a Panamanian request for economic aid to counter the impact of the United States measures. We reprint the SELA decision.

Several years before, in May 1983, SELA had condemned the United States decision to cut imports of sugar from Nicaragua, which was then ruled by the Sandinista government, and member states then pledged to purchase the sugar which the United States had refused to import. Thereafter, in 1985, when the United States imposed a trade embargo against Nicaragua, SELA again condemned the United States action and promised to provide Nicaragua with economic aid to compensate for the losses caused by the United States measures. *See* SELA Decision Nos. 148, 188, 222.

ECONOMIC COERCIVE MEASURES AGAINST PANAMA
DECISION NUMBER 271 OF THE LATIN AMERICAN
ECONOMIC SYSTEM, MARCH 29, 1988

The Latin American Council,

Having seen:

Decision Nos. 112 and 113 adopted by the Latin American council concerning economic measures of a coercive nature;

The relevant provisions of the Charter of the United Nations and of the Charter of the Organization of American States;

The request submitted by the Government of Panama to the Permanent Secretariat of the Latin American Economic System on 18 March 1988, that, in compliance with Decision No 113, as a matter of urgency, a Special Meeting of the Latin American Council be convened at Ministerial level, and in which request that the country outlines the economic enforcement measures that have been employed against it, expressing its sovereign will to resolutely pursue the strengthening of its democratic system;

Decision Nos. 115, 189 and 269 concerning the 1977 Panama Canal Treaties;

Whereas:

Self-determination and nonintervention in the internal affairs of countries are fundamental principles of international relations;

The United States of America is imposing economic measures of a coercive nature on Panama which are causing serious harm to the Panamanian people;

These economic enforcement measures are contrary to International Law and are not in keeping with the Charter of the United Nations and the Charter of the Organization of American States;

Decision No 112 of the Latin American Council condemns the imposition of coercive measures and demands the elimination of economic embargoes and blockades, the freezing of funds, the suspension of credits and others;

Latin American and Caribbean solidarity is a fundamental condition for strengthening Latin American self-determination and sovereignty.

Decides;

Article 1. To reaffirm the sovereign right of all nations to choose their own economic, social and political destiny in peace and liberty, free from external pressures, aggressions and threats.

Article 2. To reiterate the condemnation expressed in Article 3 of Decision No. 112 of the imposition of coercive economic measures on any SELA Member State, since they jeopardize its sovereignty and economic security and undermine its right to independent development.

Article 3. To repudiate, therefore, the economic enforcement measures adopted by the Government of the United States of America against Panama affecting the autonomy and threatening the economic security of this Member State, and constituting a grave economic emergency such as foreseen in Article 1 of Decision No 113.

Article 4. To call upon the Government of the United States of America to revoke immediately the enforcement measures which it has instituted against Panama.

Article 5. To consider, in a spirit of solidarity, the request for assistance from the Government of Panama, outlined in the document "Economic Co-operation Requirements of the Republic of Panama" (CL/VI.E/DT No. 1, Corr 2) and to entrust the Permanent Secretariat of the Latin American Economic System with promoting and co-ordinating consultations with Member States as to the necessary actions and measures.

Article 6. To take note of the document CL/VI.E/DT No.1 placed before the VI Special Meeting of the Latin American Council of SELA by the Government of Panama, in which it reaffirms and places on record the commitment that it has assumed to pursue resolutely the strengthening of its democratic system.

Article 7. To reaffirm the need for strict observance of the 1977 Panama Canal Treaties and to exhort the Government of the United States of America to abide by their provisions.

The Views of the American States on the Promotion of Democracy in the Western Hemisphere

NOTE ON OAS RESOLUTION 1080

During 1991 and 1992 the countries of the Western Hemisphere gave increasing prominence to policies for promoting democracy in the region. This increased emphasis can be seen in the issuance of a number of declarations and communiques and in resolutions of the General Assembly of the OAS. It is also reflected in the OAS decision to impose collective sanctions against Haiti after its democratically elected government was overthrown. We reprint a number of documents which reflect this trend.

In these documents, there is repeated reaffirmation of the traditional nonintervention principle and no suggestion that states in the hemisphere have accepted a unilateral right of a state to coerce another state into adopting democratic institutions. In some instances, however, states have accepted the imposition of collective economic measures where a state has authorized such measures in advance in the event of an interruption of its democratic institutions.

In June 1991 the General Assembly of the OAS met in Santiago, Chile to consider means for promoting democracy in the region and approved "The Commitment of Santiago to Democracy and the Renewal of the Inter-American System." As part of this program, on June 5, 1991 the General Assembly adopted Resolution 1080, which was designed to protect and preserve existing democratic systems in the Western hemisphere. The resolution was passed unanimously by a vote of thirty-four to zero and calls upon the OAS to convene an emergency meeting within ten days of any "sudden or irregular interruption of the democratic political institutional process of the legitimate exercise of power by the democratically elected government in any of the Organization's member states." The purpose of such an emergency meeting "shall be to look into the events collectively and adopt any measures deemed appropriate, in accordance with the Charter and international law." It notes that "[u]nder the provisions of the Charter, one of the basic purposes of the Organization of American States is to promote and consolidate representative democracy, with due respect for the principle of nonintervention" and that there is a "widespread existence of democratic governments in the hemisphere."

It is noteworthy that the resolution was adopted by consensus and that it calls for the convocation of an emergency meeting only in cases where an existing democratic government is overthrown. Reference should also be made to a portion of the International Court of Justice's decision in the *Nicaragua* case excerpted *ante*. The Court accepted the proposition that a state may bind itself by agreement to maintain a democratic system and hold free elections. "The Court cannot discover, within the range of subjects open to international agreement, any obstacle or provision to hinder a State from making a commitment of this kind. A State, which is free to decide upon the principle and methods of popular consultation within its domestic order, is sovereign for the purpose of accepting a limitation of its sovereignty in this field." *Id.,* paragraph 259. Resolution 1080 had not been unanimously adopted by the time of the *Nicaragua* decision, and the Court expressly found that the OAS Charter did not constitute any such limitation on the sovereignty of member states. *Id.*

We reprint Resolution 1080 and the comments of the Mexican representative to the OAS made at the time of its adoption. His comments set forth the Mexican view of the relationship between OAS support for the preservation of existing democracies in member states and the principle of nonintervention. He notes that respect for the principle of nonintervention is an essential condition for the development of democracy which "must arise from the very essence of each one of our peoples" and for which there is "[n]o single model, no single scheme, no single normative-descriptive system," and he indicates that in applying the resolution, "we will be profoundly observant to see that there is no intervention and interference against other nations."

OAS GENERAL ASSEMBLY RESOLUTION 1080

(XXI-0/91), June 5, 1991

Whereas:

The Preamble of the Charter of the OAS establishes that representative democracy is an indispensable condition for the stability, peace and development of the region;

Under the provisions of the Charter, one of the basic purposes of the Organization of American States is to promote and consolidate representative democracy, with due respect for the principle of nonintervention;

Due respect must be observed for the policies of each member country in regard to the recognition of states and governments;

Bearing in mind the widespread existence of democratic governments in the hemisphere, the principle enshrined in the Charter, namely, that the solidarity of the American States and the high aims which it pursues require the political organization of those States to be based on effective exercise of representative democracy—must be made operative; the region faces serious political, social and economic problems that may threaten the stability of democratic governments;

The General Assembly Resolves:

1. To instruct the Secretary-General to call for the immediate convocation of a meeting of the Permanent Council in the case of any event giving rise to the sudden or irregular interruption of the democratic political institutional process of the legitimate exercise of power by the democratically elected government in any of the Organization's member states, in order, within the framework of the Charter, to examine the situation, decide on and convene an *ad hoc* meeting of the ministers of foreign affairs, or a special session of the General Assembly, all of which must take place within a ten-day period.

2. To determine that the purpose of the *ad hoc* meeting of ministers of foreign affairs or the special session of the General Assembly shall

be to look into the events collectively and adopt any measures deemed appropriate, in accordance with the Charter and international law.

3. To instruct the Permanent Council to devise a set of proposals that will serve as incentives to preserve and strengthen democratic systems, based on international solidarity and cooperation, and to apprise the General Assembly thereof at its twenty-second regular session.

STATEMENT OF THE MEXICAN REPRESENTATIVE
FOLLOWING ADOPTION OF OAS RESOLUTION 1080

(Twenty-First Sess. of the General Assembly of the OAS,
June 5, 1991, AG/DOC.2739/91) (Unofficial translation)

Mr. Chairman, now that this draft resolution has been approved, it is my Delegation's duty to express that we have voted in favor of this historic resolution, firstly, because we share the ideal—established as a norm in our Charter—of striving toward representative democracy as an indispensable condition for the region's stability, peace and development.

We also believe that there is a vocation within the Organization for adopting necessary measures, proposals providing incentives for the preservation and strengthening of democratic systems, because we consider that the fragility of democracies arises from complex factors of an economic and social nature; and that these causes and their eradication must constitute our Organization's central action priority in the field of preserving democracy.

We have also supported this resolution because the principle of nonintervention—understood in the original sense of the term—in no way constitutes an obstacle to the preservation of democracy because the principle of nonintervention is linked as sustenance and foundation for the construction of democratic systems.

Democracy must arise from the very essence of each one of our peoples: shaping itself to the rhythms and times, to the characteristics and modalities that each people impose upon it. No single model, no single scheme, no single normative-descriptive system exists that can be called the only democracy. Democracy contains a large number of principles articulated in time and space. It is also my Delegation's duty to point out that in the application of this resolution, in the analysis that is carried out, we will be profoundly observant to see that there is no intervention and interference against other nations. We shall also be alert to the policies upheld by each one of the countries with regard to the recognition of governments and, in particular, the Estrada Doctrine which governs our relations with governments and States.

Having made these clarifications, I thank you for giving me the floor to voice the reasons why we have supported this resolution and which we will observe in its implementation. Thank you, Mr. Chairman.

GUADALAJARA DECLARATION, JULY 19, 1991

(Unofficial translation)

[On July 18 and 19, 1991 Spain, Portugal and nineteen Latin American countries, including Cuba, met in Guadalajara, Mexico at the First Ibero-American Summit. At the conclusion of the summit, they issued the Guadalajara Declaration in which they proclaimed their common views on a number of significant international issues, including the promotion of democracy and respect for international law. Thus, for instance, they declared: "Our community rests on democracy, respect for human rights and fundamental freedoms. In this framework, the principles of sovereignty and nonintervention are reaffirmed and the right of each people to freely develop its political system and institutions in peace, stability and justice is recognized." They further agreed to "promote the strengthening of democracy and pluralism in international relations, with full respect for the sovereignty, territorial integrity and political independence of states, as well as the sovereign equality and self-determination of peoples." We reprint excerpts from the Guadalajara Declaration.]

We, the heads of state and government of Argentina, Bolivia, Brazil, Chile, Colombia, Costa Rica, Cuba, Dominican Republic, Ecuador, El Salvador, Guatemala, Honduras, Mexico, Nicaragua, Panama, Paraguay, Peru, Portugal, Spain, Uruguay and Venezuela, gathered in the city of Guadalajara, Mexico, on July 18 and 19, 1991, have resolved to issue the following declaration:

*   *   *

3. We recognize that this goal of convergence is based not just on our common cultural heritage but also on the richness of our origins and their plural nature. Our community rests on democracy, respect for human rights and fundamental freedoms. In this framework, the principles of sovereignty and nonintervention are reaffirmed and the right of each people to freely develop its political system and institutions in peace, stability and justice is recognized.

4. We find in the respectful approximation of our differences and in the multiple voice of our societies the bases of an Ibero-American cooperation project supported by dialogue, solidarity and the adoption of concerted actions.

5. We express our will to contribute together to a common future of peace, greater well-being and social equality. We are committed to the economic and social development of our peoples, full respect for human rights, the expansion of the democratic channels, the strengthening of our institutional systems and respect for the standards of international law.

*   *   *

7. We reaffirm that it is an obligation of the state to promote and guarantee the full respect of human rights. Based on our own efforts and on broad international, nonselective and nondiscriminatory cooperation, we are determined to strengthen Ibero-American values related to human rights, consolidating conducts of respect, freedom and harmony of a political, legal, economic and social nature.

*   *   *

I. *Enforcing International Law*

A) To direct the foreign affairs of our countries on the basis of international law and to act jointly and in a coordinated manner, in order to contribute to eliminating the use of, or the threat of the use of force.

*   *   *

C) To promote the right to develop and the establishment of fairer and more equitable economic relations.

CH) To participate actively in the restructuring of international forums, in particular the United Nations system, with the goal of achieving a fairer and more democratic international order which guarantees peace and promotes the peoples' welfare.

D) To promote the strengthening of democracy and pluralism in international relations, with full respect for the sovereignty, territorial integrity and political independence of states, as well as the sovereign equality and self-determination of peoples.

E) To facilitate consultations on development and the codification of international law on the basis of a consensual process oriented toward the themes which, because of their global nature, are of greatest urgency.

Deserving of priority attention are the strengthening of mechanisms for the peaceful solution of controversies; standards applicable in armed conflicts; promotion of the disarmament of conventional and nuclear weapons, as well as weapons of mass destruction; fortification of instruments to protect human rights; definition of the legal framework for environmental defense, fighting the drug trade, the law of the sea, laws on outer space and on technology transfer.

F) To strengthen cooperation among governments and entities within civil society with competent multilateral agencies on human rights; and to promote full adhesion to international instruments promoting and protecting those rights, on an international and regional level.

G) To commit ourselves to creating and/or consolidating national mechanisms in our respective countries for promoting, protecting and defending human rights, as well as establishing a close collaboration among them.

NOTE ON THE COUP IN HAITI AND OAS
MEASURES ADOPTED UNDER RESOLUTION 1080

On September 25, 1991 the President of Venezuela, Carlos Andres Perez, addressed the General Assembly of the United Nations and specifically stated the view that the United States measures against Cuba have lost "all justification and validity." His comments, the pertinent portions of which can be quoted in full, were made in the context of a review of the changing international situation:

> Let us move now from East-West confrontation to a North-South co-operation that will lead to a single united world.
>
> It is time to ask both the United States and Cuba to cease the confrontation which began in the context of the cold war. Let us have confidence that Cuba will open itself to the universal concept of democracy as we would all wish and that the United States will be open to a dialogue that puts an end to sanctions that have lost all justification and validity.

A/46/PV.8, p.3 (September 27, 1991). The approach of President Perez, consistent with Resolution 1080 and the Guadalajara Declaration, would thus appear to be one which emphasizes the importance of member states adopting democratic institutions but which respects the international prohibition on intervention in the internal affairs of states. Whether there may have been a recent subtle shift in Venezuela's position should be evaluated in light of the remarks of Venezuela's representative to the United Nations during the November 24, 1992 debate, *ante* Part I.

Only days after President Perez' speech, a military coup overthrew the democratically elected government of President Aristide in Haiti. Haiti had voted for Resolution 1080, and in conformity with that resolution, on September 30, 1991 the OAS Permanent Council adopted a resolution condemning the coup and convening an *ad hoc* Meeting of the Ministers of Foreign Affairs. Thereafter, on October 3, 1991 the Ministers of Foreign Affairs met and adopted Resolution MRE/RES. 1/91. OEA/Ser.F/V.1 corr.1 (October 3, 1991). That resolution, which is reprinted here, cited Resolution 1080 and reaffirmed that "one of the essential purposes of the Organization of American States is that of promoting and consolidating representative democracy subject to respect for the principle of nonintervention" and that "the solidarity of the American States and the high purposes thereof require the political organization of those states on a basis of the real exercise of representative democracy." The events in Haiti, the resolution declared, "constitute a sudden, violent and irregular interruption of the legitimate exercise of power by the democratic government of that country." It therefore resolved, among other things, to condemn the coup, to send a mission to Haiti to inform those who hold *de facto* power of the rejection by the OAS of the interruption of constitutional order, to recognize the representatives named by President Aristide as the only legitimate representatives of Haiti to organs of the Inter-American system, and to recommend that each member state take action to isolate the *de facto* regime diplomatically and suspend economic, financial, and commercial ties with Haiti.

On October 8, 1991 the Ministers of Foreign Affairs adopted a second resolution, MRE/RES. 2/91, which reaffirmed the previous resolution and elaborated on certain of its provisions. OEA/Ser.F/V.1 (October 8, 1991). The resolution urged "the Member states to proceed immediately to freeze the assets of the Haitian State and to impose a trade embargo on Haiti except for humanitarian aid." In addition, it directed that "a civilian mission be constituted to reestablish and strengthen constitutional democracy in Haiti, which should go to that country in order to facilitate the reestablishment and strengthening of democratic institutions, the full force and effect of the constitution, respect for the human rights of all Haitians, and to support the administration of justice and adequate functioning of all the institutions that will make it possible to achieve these objectives."

The OAS subsequently adopted two additional resolutions regarding the coup. The first established a variety of procedures for achieving greater compliance with the embargo and tightening the sanctions already in place by urging member states to deny vessels violating the embargo access to port facilities, to deny entry visas to, and freeze the assets of, perpetrators and supporters of the coup and to reduce their diplomatic missions in Haiti; and requesting member and observer states to seek the cooperation of multilateral financial institutions with the embargo. MRE /RES. 3/92, OEA/Ser.F/V.1 (May 17, 1992). The second OAS resolution urged greater compliance with the embargo, particularly regarding oil, arms and munitions supplies, and the freezing of the assets of the Haitian state. MRE/RES. 4/92, OEA/Ser.F/V.2 (December 13, 1992). In the meantime, after President Fujimora's "autocoup" in Peru in April 1992, the OAS, again meeting pursuant to Resolution 1080, adopted a resolution condemning the coup and calling for an immediate reestablishment of democratic institutions. In addition, the resolution asked all states to reassess their relations with Peru and the assistance which they provide it, taking into account the pace at which democracy is reestablished. MRE/RES. 1/92, OEA/Ser.F/V.2 (April 13, 1992). A further resolution on Peru was adopted a month later. MRE/RES. 2/92, OEA/Ser.F/V.2 (May 17, 1992). After each of two unsuccessful coup attempts in Venezuela in 1992, the OAS passed resolutions condemning the armed uprisings. Permanent Council Resolution of November 27, 1992, *reprinted in* Federal News Service (November 27, 1992); CP/RES. 576 (887/92) (February 4, 1992); AG/RES. 1189 (XXII-0/92) (May 18, 1992).

Since the Haitian coup the United Nations has unanimously adopted three resolutions supporting the approach of the OAS. Recognizing the Aristide government as the legitimate government of Haiti, it has appealed to member states to support the political and economic sanctions adopted by the OAS and affirmed that the *de facto* authorities will not be recognized by the United Nations. It has also instructed the Secretary-General of the United Nations to cooperate with the OAS in its efforts to achieve the reinstatement of democracy. G.A. Res. 7 (XLVI) (October 11, 1991); G.A. Res. 138 (XLVI) (December 17, 1991); G.A. Res. 20 (XLVII) (November 24, 1992).

SUPPORT TO THE DEMOCRATIC GOVERNMENT OF HAITI RESOLUTION OF THE MINISTERS OF FOREIGN AFFAIRS OF THE OAS 1/91, OCTOBER 2, 1991

The Ad Hoc Meeting Of Ministers Of Foreign Affairs

Having seen:

The Resolution of the Permanent Council of September 30 of this year convoking an ad hoc Meeting of Ministers of Foreign Affairs, pursuant to resolution AG/RES. 1080 (XXI-0/91), in response to the gravity of the events that have taken place in Haiti;

The Commitment of Santiago to Democracy and the Renewal of the Inter-American System, approved at the twenty-first regular session of the General Assembly, held at Santiago, Chile, in June of this year; and

Resolution AG/RES. 1117 (XXI-0/91) "Support for the Democratic Process in the Republic of Haiti";

Having heard:

The statement made to this meeting by the President of Haiti, Mr. Jean-Bertrand Aristide;

Reaffirming:

That the true meaning of American solidarity and good neighborliness can be none other than that of consolidating in this Hemisphere, in the framework of democratic institutions, a regime of individual liberty and social justice grounded in respect for the essential rights of man;

That one of the essential purposes of the Organization of American States is that of promoting and consolidating representative democracy subject to respect for the principle of nonintervention; and

That the solidarity of the American States and the high purposes thereof require the political organization of those states on a basis of the real exercise of representative democracy:

Considering:

That the grave events that have occurred in Haiti constitute a sudden, violent and irregular interruption of the legitimate exercise of power by the democratic government of that country;

That these events represent disregard for the legitimate Government of Haiti, which was constituted by the will of its people freely expressed in a free and democratic electoral process under international observation with the participation of this Organization;

That those events have compelled President Jean-Bertrand Aristide, against his will, to leave the soil of Haiti temporarily;

Resolves:

1. To reiterate the energetic condemnation voiced by the Permanent Council of the grave events taking place in Haiti, which hold in disregard the right of its people to self-determination, and demands full restoration of the rule of law and of the constitutional regime, and the immediate reinstatement of President Jean-Bertrand Aristide in the exercise of his legitimate authority.

2. To request the Secretary-General of the Organization, together with a group of Ministers of Foreign Affairs of Member States, to go to Haiti immediately and inform those who hold de facto power of the rejection by the American States of the interruption of constitutional order and of the decisions adopted in this Meeting.

3. To recognize the representatives designated by the constitutional Government of President Jean-Bertrand Aristide as the only legitimate representatives of the Government of Haiti to the organs, agencies and entities of the inter-American system.

4. To urge the Inter-American Commission on Human Rights, in response to President Jean-Bertrand Aristide's request, to take immediately all measures within its competence to protect and defend human rights in Haiti and to report thereon to the Permanent Council of the Organization.

5. To recommend, with due respect for the policy of each member State on the recognition of States and Governments, action to bring about the diplomatic isolation of those who hold de facto power in Haiti.

6. To recommend to all States that they suspend their economic, financial and commercial ties with Haiti and any aid and technical cooperation except that provided for strictly humanitarian purposes.

7. To request the Secretary-General of the Organization to pursue efforts to augment the Inter-American Fund for Priority Assistance to Haiti, but to abstain from using it so long as the present situation prevails.

8. To recommend to the General Secretariat of the Organization the suspension of all assistance to those who hold de facto power in Haiti and to request the regional organs and institutions, such as the Caribbean Community (CARICOM), the Inter-American Development Bank, the Inter-American Institute for Cooperation on Agriculture, and the Latin American Economic System (SELA), to adopt the same measure.

9. To urge all States to abstain from military, police or security assistance of any kind and from the delivery of arms, munitions or equipment to that country under any public or private arrangement.

10. To keep the ad hoc Meeting of Ministers of Foreign Affairs in session in order to receive, with the urgency that the situation requires, the report of the Mission referred to in operative paragraph 2, above, and to adopt all additional measures which may be necessary and appropriate in accordance with the Charter of the OAS and international law to bring about the immediate reinstatement of President Jean-Bertrand Aristide to the exercise of his legitimate authority.

11. To transmit this resolution to the United Nations Organization and its specialized agencies and to urge them to keep its spirit and objectives in mind.

NOTE ON THE DECLARATION OF THE PRESIDENTS
OF MEXICO, COLOMBIA AND VENEZUELA AND THE
DECLARATIONS OF THE RIO GROUP ON RELATIONS
WITH CUBA AND THE HAITIAN COUP

On October 23, 1991 the Presidents of Mexico, Venezuela, and Colombia, known as the Group of Three, met in Cozumel, Mexico. They invited President Castro to attend the meeting and the Cuban President gave a detailed account of the Fourth Congress of the Communist Party which had been held only a short time before in Cuba. In the communique which they issued at the conclusion of their discussions, the Declaration of Cozumel, the Group of Three expressed great interest in the political reforms introduced at the Fourth Congress and encouraged the expectations which they had created. They also announced a decision to work for reintegration of Cuba into the Latin American family of nations and offered to mediate between Cuba and the United States toward "a normalization of relations based on respect for each country's legitimate interests and strict adherence to international law." At the same time, they reaffirmed their support for the economic and diplomatic measures adopted by the OAS in response to the coup in Haiti.

The pertinent parts of the Declaration of Cozumel, as set forth in *Granma International,* p.9 (November 3, 1991), can be quoted in full:

> Colombian President Cesar Gaviria and Venezuelan President Carlos Andres Perez met with Mexican President Carlos Salinas de Gortari in Cozumel, Quintana Roo, Mexico, on October 23, 1991, at the latter's invitation, to discuss the advances made to date by the Group of Three.
>
> The presidents of the Group of Three made a general evaluation of the steps undertaken by the group, keeping in mind its fundamental objectives of economic integration and consolidation of economic, cultural and scientific and technical cooperation with the rest of Latin America and the Caribbean.

*   *   *

> The presidents also examined recent events affecting stability in the region. They reiterated their support for the OAS resolutions on Haiti and its condemnation of the military coup in that country. They urged the international community to apply the economic steps which had been agreed upon and called on the countries of the hemisphere to cooperate with the Secretary-General of the OAS so that the civilian mission agreed to by the foreign ministers can be assembled as quickly as possible.

*   *   *

> They later welcomed President Fidel Castro of Cuba, specially invited to this meeting by the Group of Three and who gave a detailed account of the Fourth Congress of the Communist Party of Cuba, held October 10-14, outlining the perspectives of the Congress with special emphasis on the possibilities for economic cooperation with Latin America.
>
> The three presidents recognized the invitation tendered by the Fourth Congress for Latin American capital to further Cuba's economic development and said it coincides with one of the fundamental objectives of the Group of Three, since it represents a uniting of efforts to promote cooperation with the Caribbean. It also integrally coincides in letter and spirit with the Declaration of Guadalajara, issued at the 1st Ibero-American Summit held last July.
>
> The three presidents took great interest in Fidel Castro's explanations of the implications and scope in regard to Cuba's institutional life of the reforms aimed at broadening political participation introduced by the Fourth Congress. They agreed that, based on President Castro's statements, these expectations should be encouraged, and decided to

work for the prompt and full reintegration of Cuba into the Latin American family and for true continental coexistence based on principles already guiding the region.

Cuba's integration into the Latin American context, they indicated, is without a doubt one of the requisites for making viable the collective goals of development and stability in the Caribbean.

In this context, Cuba's will to contribute to this effort is shown by its commitment to cooperate with the Group of Three in support of the pacification processes in Central America without the external interference of any country. It is equally demonstrated by Cuba's willingness to join the Tlatelolco Treaty for the Non-Proliferation of Nuclear Weapons in Latin America, as soon as it is signed by all the countries in the area, a step which would contribute significantly to the effectiveness of this international instrument in the short term.

Convinced that a negotiated solution to conflicts between nations is a fundamental principle in international affairs, the presidents expressed their political determination to contribute to a climate of understanding and cooperation in the region. They offered to mediate between the government of Cuba and the countries with which Cuba might have differences, in order to initiate a rapprochement tending toward a normalization of relations based on respect for each country's legitimate interests and strict adherence to international law.

In addition to issuing this declaration, the Group of Three presidents elaborated on their views at a press conference, also reprinted from *Granma International,* pp.8-9 (November 3, 1991). With regard to Cuba, President Salinas de Gortari of Mexico stated:

> Our conviction in Mexico is that the internal problems of Cuba are the exclusive responsibility of the Cuban people; but, at the same time, we realize that what happens in Cuba will have repercussions in our region, in our country and in the rest of the Caribbean bordering Latin America, as well as all of Latin America. That is why we are following the internal transformations being carried out by the Cubans themselves with great care and interest.

President Cesar Gaviria of Colombia also addressed his views on Cuba:

> Colombia, Venezuela and Mexico have been friends of Cuba, are friendly toward the Cuban people and the Cuban government. Naturally, we are interested in promoting changes that essentially correspond to the will of the Cuban people, as we have clearly defined in our declaration. We hope the changes occurring in Cuba are the will of the Cuban people.
>
> We are convinced that the United States will continue being as respectful as it has been up to the present of the policy that each one of us has regarding Cuba.

We understand the Cuba case as one of political pluralism in the hemisphere, and this meeting reiterates our belief that Cuba's case must be understood as a case of political pluralism on our continent.

President Carlos Andres Perez of Venezuela likewise spoke about Cuba and reiterated the message of his recent speech before the United Nations General Assembly previously quoted:

In my speech to the U.N. General Assembly this year, I made a special statement about the situation worrying all Latin American peoples, to the effect that while the cold war is fortunately now part of world history, it would seem that it still persists in the Americas and is expressed in the positions assumed by Cuba and the United States. And I made an appeal to Cuba so that its experienced leaders would undertake the reforms that they believe advisable within this universal concept of democracy, and that at the same time the United States abandon the blockade that neither seems relevant nor corresponds to the hemispheric realities that we want for a just and equitable treatment among all nations.

*   *   *

I have repeatedly stated that the most experienced government in Latin America is precisely that of President Castro and that we don't want to set ourselves up as advisers, but we have come to learn from his own lips the alternatives that are open to him in the new world reality, the decisions made at the Congress of the Communist Party and, naturally, to express our hope once again that Cuba, as a Latin American nation, as a Caribbean nation, will become fully incorporated into the life of the region, within the basic concept under which Latin American politics are unfolding.

President Perez also spoke about the Haitian coup and the sanctions imposed by the OAS:

The Haitian military coup troubled all of our America and the entire world, and we have seen how there has been repudiation throughout the world of President Aristide's overthrow. And why this time is there so much concern about a military coup in Latin America, when before they were almost always a constant in our history? Precisely because we believe that after Latin America has become democratized and the military has returned to its barracks, another military coup in our region sets a singular and dangerous precedent. And it's significant that for the first time the Organization of American States has adopted the measures that it adopted, not only politically condemning the coup, but also suspending relations with the Republic of Haiti and declaring economic sanctions.

Therefore I support the aspects of the declaration that the Group of Three just issued, exhorting all nations to maintain the measures, so that the economic sanctions can bear the fruits that we are hoping for, to convince those who defied established authority and the Haitian people, so that they return power to the legitimately elected president in Haiti, who is the first Haitian president clearly elected by the immense majority of his people. We trust that it will be that way.

The Rio Group, which includes thirteen leading Latin American and Caribbean nations, adopted a similar approach to Cuba and the Haitian coup at a summit meeting in December 1991 in Cartagena, Colombia. Virtually all Rio Group members maintain commercial relations with Cuba even though Cuba remains suspended from participation in the Organization of American States. At its December 1991 summit, the Rio Group issued a Declaration noting that it "earnestly desired" Cuba's reintegration into the Inter-American community and pledging to cooperate with Cuba so that it may achieve "peace, justice, liberty and democracy." At the same time, however, the Declaration conditioned Cuba's reintegration upon progress in democratic reform. *See Latin American Weekly Reports,* p.4 (December 19, 1991). In reference to the United States measures against Cuba, President Gaviria, as host of the summit, stated in summation of the meeting that "the confrontation between the United States and Cuba is an unnecessary holdover" and expressed regret that the two governments "should lack the will to dialogue." *Id.* Regarding Haiti, the Declaration condemned the coup as "illegal" and affirmed the Rio Group's support for the OAS sanctions. *Id.* The Rio Group states reaffirmed their stance on both issues at their December 1992 summit in Buenos Aires. *See* Declaration in Buenos Aires by the Heads of State and Government of the Rio Group (December 2, 1992).

NOTE ON THE UNITED STATES' RELIANCE ON
THE 1975 OAS RESOLUTION ON CUBA

In the past the United States has cited the 1975 resolution of the OAS on Cuba in support of its economic measures, in effect construing the resolution as an authorization for discretionary individual and collective sanctions against Cuba. In 1964 the Foreign Ministers, acting as the Organ of Consultation in Application of the Inter-American Treaty of Reciprocal Assistance ("Rio Treaty"), 62 Stat. 1681, TIAS 1838, 21 UNTS 77, a mutual defense agreement, had imposed a mandatory trade embargo against Cuba. OEA/Ser. C/II.9, Doc. 48, Rev.2 (1964). They did so as an act of collective self-defense in response to what the OAS member states believed were acts of subversion committed by

Cuba in other countries of the Western hemisphere. In 1975 the Foreign Ministers, again acting pursuant to the Rio Treaty, adopted a resolution granting each member state the "freedom to normalize or conduct their relations with the Republic of Cuba in accordance with their own national policy and interests, and at the level and in the manner which each State deems appropriate." OEA/Ser. F/II. Doc. 9/75 Rev.2 (July 29, 1975).

The 1964 resolution was expressly adopted pursuant to Articles 6 and 8 of the Rio Treaty. Article 6 is the only provision of the Rio Treaty under which the member states may consider collective action in response to threats to the security of one or more of the American states which arise from lesser forms of aggression than armed attack. It provided at that time:*

> If the inviolability or the integrity of the territory or the sovereignty or political independence of any American State should be affected by an aggression which is not an armed attack...the Organ of Consultation shall meet immediately in order to agree on the measures which must be taken in case of aggression to assist the victim of the aggression or, in any case, the measures which should be taken for the common defense and for the maintenance of the peace and security of the Continent.

Article 8, in turn, set forth the measures which the member states are permitted to adopt and provided at that time:

> For the purposes of this Treaty, the measures on which the Organ of Consultation may agree will comprise one or more of the following: recall of chiefs of diplomatic missions; breaking of diplomatic relations; breaking of consular relations; partial or complete interruption of economic relations or of rail, sea, air, postal, telegraphic, telephonic, and radiotelephonic or radiotelegraphic communications; and use of armed force.

After finding that Cuba's support for subversion in Venezuela constituted "an aggression and an intervention in the internal affairs of Venezuela," the resolution resolved to "apply, in accordance with the provisions of Articles 6 and 8 of the Inter-American Treaty of Reciprocal Assistance, the following measures:...b. That the governments of the American states suspend all their trade, whether direct or indirect, with Cuba, except in foodstuffs, medicines, and medical equipment that may be sent to Cuba for humanitarian reasons."

Under the Rio Treaty, the adoption of mandatory sanctions requires a vote of two-thirds of the member states, as did at that time the

---

*The Rio Treaty, including Articles 6 and 8, was, as noted *post,* subsequently amended, and Article 6 was renumbered Article 5. We quote the original provisions in effect at the time of the 1964 resolution. Except as noted, the amendments made no changes pertinent to the issue under consideration.

withdrawal of sanctions already imposed. By the mid-1970s a majority of member states did not support the continuance of sanctions against Cuba but were unable to obtain the required two-thirds support for withdrawal of the 1964 resolution. Instead, shortly before the vote on the 1975 resolution, the Rio Treaty was amended to permit the withdrawal of sanctions by majority vote. *See* AG/RES 178 (V-0/75), adopting a Protocol of Reforms to the Rio Treaty. Thereafter the 1975 resolution was adopted.

The United States contention that the 1975 resolution constituted an authorization for discretionary individual or collective sanctions against Cuba under Articles 6 and 8 of the Rio Treaty is not free of difficulty. As an immediate prelude to adopting the 1975 resolution, the member states amended the Rio Treaty to permit the lifting of sanctions by majority vote and then proceeded to adopt the resolution. This suggests that the resolution was not intended to constitute a new authorization of sanctions. The United States position therefore would have to depend on the view that the 1975 resolution constituted only a partial withdrawal of the 1964 sanctions, making sanctions discretionary rather than mandatory.

Whatever the proper construction of the resolution might be, however, the question may well be moot. Any remaining OAS authorization to impose individual or collective sanctions must perforce have been limited to sanctions imposed to counter Cuban support for subversion in the Western hemisphere. This was the stated concern of the 1964 OAS resolution and, in any event, the Rio Treaty itself provides no basis for the imposition of sanctions other than in response to aggression. Moreover, the statement of the Costa Rican representative, made at the closing of the 1975 Meeting of Foreign Ministers in his capacity as president of the Meeting, suggests as well this understanding of the resolution. As he explained, "what this has been all about is seeing to it that the few American governments that consider themselves to be directly or indirectly affected by the activities of the Cuban revolutionary regime no longer continue to block the maintenance of diplomatic, consular and commercial relations with the Government of Cuba on the part of the rest."

As set forth in Part III, the United States no longer makes reference to Cuban support for subversion or other aggression in explaining its economic measures. Indeed, at least since the United States stopped relying upon alleged Cuban threats to the security of any other country, it appears not to have cited the 1975 resolution, whereas previously it did.

We reprint here both the 1964 and 1975 resolutions and the Costa Rican representative's statement with respect to the latter.

RESOLUTION I OF THE NINTH MEETING OF CONSULTATION
OF MINISTERS OF FOREIGN AFFAIRS, SERVING AS ORGAN
OF CONSULTATION IN APPLICATION OF THE INTER-
AMERICAN TREATY OF RECIPROCAL ASSISTANCE

(OEA/Ser.C/II.9, Doc. 48, Rev.2 (August 10, 1964))

The Ninth Meeting of Consultation of Ministers of Foreign Affairs,
Serving as Organ of Consultation in Application of the Inter-American
Treaty of Reciprocal Assistance,

Having seen the report of the Investigating Committee designated
on December 3, 1963, by the Council of the Organization of American
States, acting provisionally as Organ of Consultation, and

Considering:

That the said report establishes among its conclusions that "the Republic of Venezuela has been the target of a series of actions sponsored
and directed by the Government of Cuba, openly intended to subvert
Venezuelan institutions and to overthrow the democratic Government
of Venezuela through terrorism, sabotage, assault, and guerrilla warfare"; and

That the aforementioned acts, like all acts of intervention and aggression, conflict with the principles and aims of the inter-American
system,

Resolves:

1. To declare that the acts verified by the Investigating Committee
constitute an aggression and an intervention on the part of the Government of Cuba in the internal affairs of Venezuela, which affects all
of the member states.

2. To condemn emphatically the present Government of Cuba for its
acts of aggression and of intervention against the territorial inviolability, the sovereignty, and the political independence of Venezuela.

3. To apply, in accordance with the provisions of Articles 6 and 8 of
the Inter-American Treaty of Reciprocal Assistance, the following measures:

a. That the governments of the American states not maintain diplomatic or consular relations with the Government of Cuba;

b. That the governments of the American states suspend all their
trade, whether direct or indirect, with Cuba, except in foodstuffs, medicines, and medical equipment that may be sent to Cuba for humanitarian reasons; and

c. That the governments of the American states suspend all sea transportation between their countries and Cuba, except for such transportation as may be necessary for reasons of a humanitarian nature.

4. To authorize the Council of the Organization of American States, by an affirmative vote of two-thirds of its members, to discontinue the measures adopted in the present resolution at such time as the Government of Cuba shall have ceased to constitute a danger to the peace and security of the hemisphere.

5. To warn the Government of Cuba that if it should persist in carrying out acts that possess characteristics of aggression and intervention against one or more of the member states of the Organization, the member states shall preserve their essential rights as sovereign states by the use of self-defense in either individual or collective form, which could go so far as resort to armed force, until such time as the Organ of Consultation takes measures to guarantee the peace and security of the hemisphere.

6. To urge those states not members of the Organization of American States that are animated by the same ideals as the Inter-American System to examine the possibility of effectively demonstrating their solidarity in achieving the purposes of this resolution.

7. To instruct the Secretary-General of the Organization of American States to transmit to the United Nations Security Council the text of the present resolution, in accordance with the provisions of Article 54 of the United Nations Charter.

FINAL ACT OF THE SIXTEENTH MEETING OF CONSULTATION
OF MINISTERS OF FOREIGN AFFAIRS, SERVING AS
ORGAN OF CONSULTATION IN APPLICATION OF THE
INTER-AMERICAN TREATY OF RECIPROCAL ASSISTANCE

(OEA/Ser.F/II. Doc. 16 9/75 Rev.2 (July 29, 1975))

The Sixteenth Meeting of Consultation of Ministers of Foreign Affairs,
Serving as the Organ of Consultation under the Inter-American
Treaty of Reciprocal Assistance (TIAR)

Considering:

That the States Parties to the TIAR have renewed their adherence to the principles of inter-American solidarity and co-operation, nonintervention and reciprocal assistance enunciated in the TIAR and the Charter of the Organization, and

Desiring:

To promote inter-American relations in the broadest possible way,

Resolves:

1. To reaffirm solemnly the principle of nonintervention and to urge States Parties to ensure that it is observed throughout the continent, in accordance with the Charter of the Organization, to which end they

once more proclaim their solidarity and reiterate their will to co-operate constantly with a view to fulfilling the purposes of a policy of peace,

2. To grant the States Parties to the TIAR freedom to normalize or conduct their relations with the Republic of Cuba in accordance with their own national policy and interests, and at the level and in the manner which each State deems appropriate, and

3. To transmit the text of this resolution to the Security Council of the United Nations.

CLOSING SPEECH BY THE MINISTER OF FOREIGN RELATIONS
OF COSTA RICA AND PRESIDENT OF THE SIXTEENTH
MEETING OF CONSULTATION OF THE MINISTERS OF
FOREIGN AFFAIRS, JULY 29, 1975

(OEA/Ser.F/II.16, Doc. 18/75 (July 29, 1975) (Unofficial translation))

Your Excellencies, Ministers of America; Distinguished Special Delegates; the Secretary-General of the Meeting; Ladies and Gentlemen:

A controversial chapter in the history of inter-American relations has been closed today, in San José: a chapter which also opened here in this city, 15 years ago, during the Seventh Consultative Meeting, held in August of 1960.

The convening of this Meeting, AG/RES. 193 (V-0/75), could not have been a surprise to any American government. The resolution approved by the General Assembly of the OAS at its Fifth Ordinary Session, which took place in May of this year, clearly announced the desirability—once the Protocol of Reforms to the TIAR (Inter-American Reciprocal Assistance Treaty) was approved in San José—of taking measures, already supported by a majority of the Member States, to void all resolutions adopted in accordance with Article 8 of the Rio Treaty. In addition, the case of Cuba has constituted a direct or indirect subject of debate in every single inter-American meeting held in recent years. The maintenance of sanctions against the regime of Prime Minister Castro cast itself like a noxious shadow over the work of the CEESI.

During the 15th Meeting of the Consultative Organ, held in Quito, it was evident that a majority of the American States wished to be at liberty to normalize their relations with the Government of Cuba. Approval of a resolution abrogating the one adopted against the Cuban regime during the 9th Consultative Meeting was not possible, but it was easy to predict that not much time would pass before the ingenuity of the Foreign Ministers and Ambassadors of the States belonging to the TIAR would come up with a formula that would make it possible to eliminate the issue of sanctions against Cuba from the inter-American agenda.

The formula which has been presented for consideration at the 16th Consultative Meeting met the aspirations of the vast majority. The draft resolution which was approved does not presume to extend a certificate of good behavior to the Cuban government. We continue to repudiate any action signifying intervention in the internal affairs of any American state and we will repudiate any such action committed in the future. The resolution that has been approved merely frees each American government—in accordance with its own sovereign interests—to decide what it wishes to do with respect to the normalization of its relations with the Cuban government.

It was not a matter of pronouncing ourselves here on the reincorporation of the Government of Doctor Castro in the OAS. No one has requested it and the affected government itself has made it clear in many ways—including the most offensive—that it does not wish to be part of the Inter-American System again. Nor has this been an attempt to impose on any government forming part of TIAR the obligation to normalize its relations with the Castroite Government. To the contrary, what this has been about is seeing to it that the few American governments that consider themselves to be directly or indirectly affected by the activities of the Cuban revolutionary regime, no longer continue to block the maintenance of diplomatic, consular and commercial relations with the Government of Cuba on the part of the rest.

The Government of Costa Rica hopes that, now that the sanctions have been eliminated, the Cuban regime will feel more sure of itself and will not feel it necessary to maintain many of the harsh restrictions which Cubans residing in their homeland must endure, whether they are friends or enemies of the government. This would facilitate the release of the political prisoners and the dialogue that some exiles have already begun, opening the possibility that Cubans inside and outside the island can become reconciled.

The sanctions against Cuba were a product of the Cold War, which today is well on the way toward its total end. When it was at its height, each bloc tried to widen its sphere of influence at the expense of its rival. Everything was permitted under the rules of the game—everything except frontal aggression which could lead to nuclear confrontation. Fanatical propaganda and support for subversion in countries of the opposing bloc were the primary arms employed in this peculiar worldwide contest. The establishment of the Castroite regime in Cuba opened a front of the Cold War in the Americas. From that moment onward, the tactics of propaganda and subversion tested in other continents were put into practice from Cuba and against Cuba.

In this climate of hostility, the Cuban regime openly expressed its support for the subversive movements in many Latin American countries, trained their leaders and supplied weapons to some of them. Nevertheless, all attempts to export the Cuban revolution roundly failed, just as all attempts made from outside to overthrow the Fidel Castro regime also roundly failed. Today we can say that while the Cuban government does provide rhetorical support to some of the dying subversive movements operating in Latin America, the truth is that it is no longer seriously trying to repeat its unsuccessful attempts at exporting revolution—the reproduction of whose model, moreover, is no longer of interest, even to the most radical left wing.

The maintenance of sanctions for more than 11 years has made them outmoded and turned them into a source of irritation within the inter-American family. It was necessary to eliminate the cause of irritation in order to attempt to find, in a harmonious atmosphere, the formulas needed to make the OAS more efficient and cooperation more fruitful between the developing nations and the only industrialized nation of the Hemisphere.

As His Excellency the President of the Republic said this afternoon, our Government reiterates its friendship and respect toward each and every one of the Governments represented here today, with which we maintain the most cordial relations. Our Government is hopeful that the decision adopted in this hall, in this our capital city, frees us of our obsession with fighting battles of the past, while the world is transforming itself all around us.

Our Government desires that we turn our attention away from the seeds of discord and that we focus, instead, on the fruits that could yield unity of action, based on respect for a diversity of criteria regarding the form of internal organization and the political philosophy of each one of the American States.

As I have said on several occasions, the inevitable delays arising from applying our energies to the peripheral topic of Cuba can be made up for through rapid decisions and actions in all the fields that truly affect our interests. Only in that way can we contribute with greater efficiency to improving the living conditions of the peoples of the Americas, something which they are demanding of us with more just fervor every day.

Excellencies, Special Delegates: Your presence in Costa Rica has filled us with satisfaction. Your participation in the 16th Consultative Meeting provokes our deep respect. We believe that the contribution made by each and every one of you, regardless of the position you upheld, has been constructive and from a high ground. For all of this I extend to you my deepest appreciation.

NOTE ON THE NATIONALIZATION OF
UNITED STATES-OWNED PROPERTY

In the General Assembly proceedings, the United States made brief reference to the Cuban nationalization of United States-owned property in explaining why it "chooses not to trade with Cuba" in the exercise of what the United States maintained was every sovereign's discretion to determine its own bilateral commercial relations. The United States representative additionally suggested, albeit without elaboration, that the United States economic sanctions could be justified under international law as countermeasures to Cuba's unlawful nationalization of United States-owned property.

As recounted in Part III, the United States had not relied on the nationalization issue when announcing the series of economic measures which began with the July 1960 elimination of the Cuban sugar quota and culminated in the July 1963 promulgation of the comprehensive commercial and financial prohibitions in effect today. It likewise did not rely on the nationalizations when defending its measures against charges of economic aggression at the Organization of American States and the United Nations. The emphasis then and thereafter was firmly on Cuba's alliance with the Soviet Union and Cuban support for subversion in the hemisphere and beyond. As the United States has intensified its measures over the last several years, the focus has shifted to the promotion of democracy in Cuba.

The Cuban Democracy Act of 1992 makes no mention of the nationalizations in its eleven point statement of the goals of United States policy toward Cuba. It makes no mention of the nationalizations in specifying the conditions under which the President may waive the additional sanctions imposed by the Act. Nor does it make any reference to the nationalizations in specifying the conditions which would *require* the President "to take steps to end the United States trade embargo of Cuba." Rather, the Cuban Democracy Act establishes as the only conditions for the relaxation and elimination of United States economic measures against Cuba certain specified changes in Cuba's political system and Cuba's moving toward a free market economic system.

On August 6, 1960 Cuba nationalized the holdings of twenty-eight United States or United States-owned corporations and nationalized the balance of large United States holdings in Cuba by the end of the year. An administrative commission of the United States later certified to the Secretary of State for possible espousal claims in the amount of $1.8 billion arising from these and related measures taken against United States property interests. Of the total amount, $1.021 billion represented the top ten corporate claims. The commission found that simple interest at the annual rate of 6 percent of the principal amount of the loss was required by international law. Foreign Claims Settlement Commission, 1972 Annual Report 412.

The Cuban decrees explained the nationalizations principally as a response to the United States elimination of the Cuban sugar quota on July 6, 1960, and the courts of the United States have found that this indeed was "a basic reason" for the nationalizations. *Banco Nacional de Cuba v. Sabbatino,* 307 F.2d 845, 865 (2d Cir. 1962), *rev'd on other grounds,* 376 U.S. 398 (1964).

In the *Sabbatino* litigation, the Cuban party maintained that the courts of the United States should not pass on the validity of the nationalizations under international law. The United States Supreme Court ultimately agreed, *Banco Nacional de Cuba v. Sabbatino,* 376 U.S. 398 (1964), emphasizing, *inter alia,* the lack of consensus in international law on the applicable principles. Before this ruling, however, the lower courts addressed the merits and found the nationalizations unlawful precisely because they were in retaliation for the United States elimination of the sugar quota. In doing so, they rejected the Cuban party's suggestion that the nationalizations were proper because, *inter alia,* the United States was the first offender against international law "by [its] attempt to coerce Cuba through the reduction of American purchases of the Cuban sugar." 307 F.2d at 866. This argument would have merit, the courts ruled, had the United States' elimination of the Cuban sugar quota been in violation of international law. However, the courts adopted the traditional United States view on economic coercion and found that such was not the case, *id.* at 866:

> But, whether she was wise or unwise, fair or unfair, in what she did, the United States did not breach a rule of international law in deciding, for whatever reasons she deemed sufficient, the sources from which she would buy her sugar. We cannot find any established principle of international jurisprudence that requires a nation to continue buying commodities from an unfriendly source.

On this analysis, the legality of the nationalizations itself rests on the question of economic coercion under international law.

In addition to the contention that the nationalizations were unlawful because they were retaliatory, the United States has maintained that they were unlawful because they failed to meet the standard of compensation required by international law, which is, in the view of the United States, "prompt, adequate and effective compensation." The nationalization decrees had provided for compensation in the form of Cuban government bonds having terms of not less than thirty years and bearing interest at less than two percent per annum. The interest was to be paid exclusively out of a fund consisting of 25 percent of the foreign exchange Cuba received from annual sales of sugar to the United States at a price of not less than 5.75 cents. The rate of amortization was left to future decision. The lower courts in the *Sabbatino* litigation found this offer of compensation illusory since, among other matters, the price of imported sugar had never before reached the stipulated price. Cuba offered in late 1960 to negotiate the question of compensation along with other issues; it publicly reiterated this position as recently as June 1992.

Whether there is any requirement under international law to provide compensation for the large-scale nationalizations of property, and whether there are circumstances excusing any such requirement and the measure of compensation required, if any, are highly controversial subjects well beyond the scope of this volume. Suffice it to note that in 1964, the Supreme Court of the United States found that "there are few if any issues in international law today on which opinion seems to be so divided as the limitations on a state's power to expropriate the property of aliens." *Banco Nacional de Cuba v. Sabbatino,* 376 U.S. 398, 428 (1964). In the intervening years, the General Assembly has addressed these questions in a number of resolutions adopted with the strong support of Latin American and other Third World states but over the equally strong objections of the United States and other developed Western states. *See, e.g.,* United Nations General Assembly Resolution on Permanent Sovereignty over Natural Resources, G.A. Res. 3171 (XXVII) (December 17, 1973), and the United Nations General Assembly Declaration on the Establishment of a New International Economic Order, G.A. Res. 3201 (S-VI) (April 9-May 2, 1974). The United States and the Western industrial states generally have rejected the view that there has been any change in the international law requirements as a result of these resolutions or contemporaneous state practice. One United States court has found that these resolutions and post–World War II state practice have modified the international law standard of compensation to one of "appropriate" compensation. *Banco Nacional de Cuba v. Chase Manhattan Bank,* 658 F.2d 875 (2d Cir. 1981). Cuba has maintained that these same General Assembly resolutions and state practice vindicate its position that, under international law, whether to pay compensation and how much for a large-scale program of nationalization of property are matters within its sovereign discretion.

If it is to justify its economic sanctions as a countermeasure to the nationalizations, the United States would have to demonstrate not only that the Cuban nationalizations violated international law but that the United States has observed the established requirements of proportionality and necessity as well. *See, e.g., Restatement, Third, Foreign Relations Law of the United States,* § 905 (1987). The requirement of "necessity" generally requires a state to avoid countermeasures as long as genuine negotiation or third-party settlement is available and offers some promise of resolving the matter. "Proportionality" requires that a countermeasure not be out of proportion to the violation and the injury suffered. Presumably, the extent of the United States measures and their intended impact upon Cuba described in this volume, together with the degree of consensus on the international law requirements pertaining to nationalizations, would be considered in evaluating whether the proportionality requirement could be met. It is perhaps notable in that connection that the United States has never sought to place the full weight of its economic measures against Cuba on the nationalization of United States-owned property.

NOTE ON UNITED STATES ALLEGATIONS OF CUBAN HUMAN RIGHTS VIOLATIONS

For most of the past thirty years, the United States sought to justify its economic measures against Cuba by reference to alleged acts of subversion in the Western hemisphere and elsewhere and to the threat Cuba's alliance with the Soviet Union was said to have posed to United States and hemispheric security. See Part III. That rationale no longer obtains, and as we have noted, in its place the United States now puts forward a desire to promote fundamental change in the nature of Cuba's political and economic system. In this connection, the United States has, on a number of occasions, charged that the Cuban government is responsible for serious human rights violations. Thus, for instance, in his May 20, 1991 Cuban Independence Day address, President Bush indicated that the United States measures would not be lifted until, *inter alia*, Cuba "holds fully free and fair elections under international supervision, [and] respects human rights..." The United States raised this issue as well in its remarks during the November 24, 1992 General Assembly debate on the United States economic measures. See Part I. We therefore consider whether these charges alter the international law analysis applicable to the United States economic measures.

The human rights violations with which the United States has charged Cuba primarily involve restrictions on the rights of free expression, political participation, and free association—rights which are closely associated with the broader right to electoral democracy. This is evident from a number of United States government public statements and documents, including the Cuban Democracy Act and Assistant Secretary of State Robert Gelbard's testimony before Congress on April 8, 1992. See Part III. The United States has expressed its most vehement condemnation of alleged incidents involving Cuban government arrests, imprisonment, intimidation and mistreatment of political dissidents engaging in peaceful political activities. Thus, for instance, the "Findings" of the Cuban Democracy Act charge the Cuban government with restricting "the Cuban people's exercise of freedom of speech, press, assembly, and other rights recognized by the Universal Declaration of Human Rights" and with suppressing "dissent through intimidation, imprisonment, and exile." Cuban Democracy Act of 1992, Title XVII, Pub.L. No. 102-484, § 1702; 106 Stat. 2575.

In recent years the United States has with increasing insistence brought charges of human rights violations to international forums. Most significantly, it has undertaken a major diplomatic effort to bring the matter before the United Nations, initially before the Human Rights Commission, and quite recently before the General Assembly. In response, the Human Rights Commission has expressed concern about the human rights situation in Cuba in a number of resolutions. Resolution 1992/61, adopted on March 3, 1992, is the most recent. Official Records of the Economic and Social Council, 1992, Supplement No. 2, E/1992/22. In 1988 the Commission sent a special delegation to Cuba to investigate the situation, and thereafter in 1991 appointed a Special Representative and then in 1992 a Special Rapporteur to monitor possible human rights violations and to prepare reports for the Commission. Based on the interim report of the Special Rapporteur, A/47/625 and Corr. 1 (November 19, 1992), which was prepared without the cooperation of the Cuban government, the General Assembly adopted a resolution expressing profound regrets about "the numerous uncontested reports of violations of basic human rights and fundamental freedoms that are described in the report of the Special Representative of the Secretary-General and in the interim report of the Special Rapporteur of the Commission on Human Rights." A/C.3/47/L.70 (December 2, 1992). It called upon Cuba "to cease the persecution and punishment of citizens for reasons related to freedom of expression and peaceful association; to permit legalization of independent groups; to respect guarantees of due process; to permit access to the prisons by national independent groups and international humanitarian agencies; to review sentences for crimes of a political nature; and to cease retaliatory measures towards those seeking permission to leave the country." This resolution was adopted only days after the General Assembly adopted its resolution on the United States economic measures against Cuba.

For its part Cuba strenuously disputes the claim that it violates the human rights of its citizens and argues that the United States is engaging in a politically motivated campaign to isolate Cuba in the international community through manipulation of the human rights issue. Although it cooperated with the Human Rights Commission's initial investigation of the human rights situation in Cuba in 1988 and 1989,

Cuba has refused to cooperate with the investigations of the Special Representative and thereafter the Special Rapporteur, both of whom were denied entry into Cuba. It charges that the United States is using its superpower status to coerce other member states into supporting its activities in the Human Rights Commission and thereby seriously abusing the human rights mechanisms of the United Nations to make unwarranted interventions into Cuba's internal affairs. Because of its refusal to cooperate with the Special Representative and the Special Rapporteur, the reports of human rights violations which the General Assembly noted were "uncontested." In its resolution the General Assembly called upon "the Government of Cuba to cooperate fully with the Special Rapporteur on Cuba by permitting full and free access by the Special Rapporteur in order to establish contact with the Government and the citizens of Cuba."

In his interim report, upon which the General Assembly relied, the Special Rapporteur recounted a number of incidents involving violations of the rights to free expression and association and related rights. A/47/625 (November 19, 1992). The concluding section of the report focuses on the relationship between the human rights situation in Cuba and the United States economic measures, including its efforts to isolate Cuba economically and politically.

The Special Rapporteur's observations in this connection, which we quote below, warrant serious consideration. He suggests the need to view the human rights issue in the broader context of the hostile external pressure which Cuba has faced for many years and its current state of near economic collapse resulting from the abrupt changes which have occurred in its trade and political relations with the Soviet Union and Eastern Europe. While nevertheless condemning the conduct of the Cuban government recounted in his report as "patently out of proportion," *id.*, p.22, and without referring to the United States by name, the Special Rapporteur questions the motivation for which international sanctions could be imposed given that such measures "are totally counterproductive if it is the international community's purpose to improve the human rights situation..." *Id.* Such measures, in his view, constitute the "surest way of prolonging an untenable internal situation, as the only remedy that would be left for not capitulating to external pressure would be to continue desperate efforts to stay anchored in the past." *Id.*, p.21. The collective memory of the Cuban people of the "traumatic experiences of their not-very-distant history and their fight for independence," *id.*, p.22, moreover, make sanctions against Cuba especially ineffective.

A number of considerations should be taken into account in evaluating the pertinence of possible human rights violations in Cuba to the legality of the United States economic measures under international law. First, as suggested by the Special Rapporteur, there are persuasive reasons to believe that the imposition of economic and political measures of the intensity of those imposed by the United States cannot be explained as an effort to improve the human rights situation in Cuba. Leaving aside the severe deprivations these measures cause the Cuban people and the doubtful impact they have in improving the human rights practices of the Cuban government, the United States measures should be seen as part of a thirty-year policy of isolating and punishing Cuba, for most of that period on security grounds and more recently as a means of coercing Cuba into adopting basic changes in its political and economic system. See Part III for an extended discussion of the current and historical purposes of the United States measures. Many states have poor records on human rights, including conduct far more serious than that with which Cuba is charged, such as torture, murder, pervasive racial and gender discrimination, deportation and other violations of fundamental rights, but few, if any, have been subject to measures of this kind. In this connection, the colloquy between State Department officials and Representative Solarz regarding the contrasting United States trade policies with Cuba and China should be recalled. See Part III. The only currently applicable explanation offered by the State Department to explain why China has been granted most favored nation status while Cuba is subject to a strict economic embargo among other measures is China's having adopted a free market system.

Furthermore, despite a vigorous diplomatic campaign to obtain international censure of Cuba for human rights violations, the United States has not placed primary reliance on the issue in seeking to justify its economic measures. In most of its public comments, it has rested the measures on their alleged effectiveness in promoting democratic change in Cuba and has often not even mentioned the human rights issue. Even when it has added charges of human rights violations as well, the emphasis has nevertheless been on the promotion of democracy, with human rights violations constituting only an aspect of what the United States views as a need for wholesale transformation of Cuba's political and economic system. This is particularly evident in the Cuban Democracy Act and in Assistant Secretary Gelbard's April 8, 1992 testimony before Congress, which, while raising human rights concerns, places great stress on the purpose to promote democratic change. Thus, even when the United States has placed reliance on human rights, it has recognized that the rights at issue are integrally related to the changes it seeks in Cuba's political and economic system and has not asserted these charges as an independent basis for its economic measures.

The United States' express policy, moreover, is to retain its economic measures until Cuba conducts internationally supervised elections and moves to a free market economy, irrespective of any changes in Cuba's human rights policies. President Bush expressly stated in his Cuban Independence Day address that the measures would not be lifted until Cuba holds internationally supervised elections *and* respects human rights. See Part III. The Cuban Democracy Act likewise requires Cuba to meet the following conditions before the President may waive the sanctions imposed by the Act. The President must certify that Cuba

(1) has held free and fair elections conducted under internationally recognized observers;

(2) has permitted opposition parties ample time to organize and campaign for such elections, and has permitted full access to the media to all candidates in the elections;

(3) is showing respect for the basic civil liberties and human rights of the citizens of Cuba;

(4) is moving toward establishing a free market economic system; and

(5) has committed itself to constitutional change that would ensure regular free and fair elections that meet the requirements of paragraph (2).

In any event, the kinds of human rights violations with which Cuba has been charged have not generally been viewed as providing a basis for the taking of countermeasures by other states. The *Restatement, Third, Foreign Relations Law of the United States* (1987), for instance, indicates that a state violates the customary international law of human rights, giving rise to a right in other states to take counter-measures,

when, as a matter of state policy, it practices, encourages, or condones

(a) genocide,

(b) slavery or slave trade,

(c) the murder or causing the disappearance of individuals,

(d) torture or other cruel, inhuman, or degrading treatment or punishment,

(e) prolonged arbitrary detention,

(f) systematic racial discrimination, or

(g) a consistent pattern of gross violations of internationally recognized human rights.

Id., § 702. There is no claim that Cuba has engaged in any of the kind of violations specified in subsections (a) to (f), and with regard to subsection (g) the *Restatement* further explains:

"Consistent pattern of gross violations" generally refers to violations of those rights that are universally accepted and that no government would admit to violating as state policy. They are generally civil and political rights such as those enumerated in Comment m [which include "systematic harassment, invasions of the privacy of the home, arbitrary arrest and detention (even if not prolonged); denial of freedom to leave a country; denial of the right to return to one's country; mass uprooting of a country's population; denial of freedom of conscience and religion; denial of personality before the law; denial of basic privacy such as the right to marry and raise a family; and invidious racial or religious discrimination"] or in the United States legislation quoted in this note [providing that no assistance may be provided "to the government of any country which engages in a consistent pattern of gross violations of internationally recognized human rights, including torture or cruel, inhuman, or degrading treatment or punishment, prolonged detention without charges, or other flagrant denial of the rights to life, liberty, and the security of person," 22 U.S.C. section 2151n(a)]. It would be difficult to claim a gross violation of a right whose definition and application are disputed. States differ, for example, as to whether a single party state provides "genuine elections" (Universal Declaration on Human Rights, Art. 21(3)) and affords every citizen the right "to vote and to be elected at genuine periodic elections which shall be by universal and equal suffrage and shall be held by secret ballot, guaranteeing the free expression of the will of the electors." (International Covenant on Civil and Political Rights, Art. 25(b)).

Id., Reporter's Note 10.

The violations of the rights of free expression and association and political participation with which Cuba is charged would not appear to fall within the *Restatement*'s definition of gross violations of internationally recognized human rights. Likewise, the reported violations recounted in the Special Rapporteur's interim report, and referred to in the General Assembly's December 1992 resolution, even if they could be considered gross violations, would not appear to meet the requirement that they be "consistent."

The *Restatement*'s view is supported by the decision of the International Court of Justice in the *Case Concerning the Barcelona Traction, Light and Power Company (Belgium v. Spain)*, 1970 I.C.J. Rep. 4. In considering whether Belgium could make an international claim against Spain on behalf of a corporation which the Court deemed to be a national of Canada, the Court drew a sharp distinction between violations of fundamental human rights which have become customary international law obligations and violations of other human rights which have not:

> In particular, an essential distinction should be drawn between the obligations of a State toward the international community as a whole, and those arising *vis-a-vis* another State in the field of diplomatic protection. By their very nature the former are the concern of all States. In

view of the importance of the rights involved, all States can be held to have a legal interest in their protection; they are obligations *erga omnes*.

Such obligations derive, for example, in contemporary international law, from the outlawing of acts of aggression, and of genocide, as also from the principles and rules concerning the basic rights of the human person, including protection from slavery and racial discrimination. Some of the corresponding rights of protection have entered into the body of general international law...; others are conferred by international instruments of a universal or quasi-universal character.

Obligations the performance of which is the subject of diplomatic protection are not of the same category. It cannot be held, when one such obligation in particular is in question, in a specific case, that all States have a legal interest in its observance.

Id. at 32.

Finally, it should be considered whether the United States economic measures can reasonably be expected to improve the human rights situation in Cuba and whether in light of their prolonged nature and the severe deprivations which they cause the Cuban people they can be viewed as a proportionate countermeasure to any human rights violations which have occurred. The observations of the Special Rapporteur on this subject and more generally on the relationship between the human rights situation in Cuba and the United States economic measures merit extended quotation, Interim Report, A/47/625, p.21–2:

60. While not overlooking the urgent need for specific measures [for the Cuban government to take], as proposed above, the Special Rapporteur nevertheless wishes to point out that any analysis concerning the situation and implementation of human rights in Cuba must, as a point of departure, accept the fact that the government is, and has for a long time been, surrounded by an international climate extremely hostile to many of its policies and, in some cases, even to its very existence. This hostile international climate does not seem to have been affected by the vast political, military and economic changes that have taken place in the world in the last few years. Similarly, the changes which have occurred in the previously socialist European countries as also in the policies of many third world countries, seem to have so far had an impact on Cuba's internal policy. On the other hand, the abrupt breakdown in the flow of aid previously received from abroad, as well as the almost total exclusion of Cuba as a beneficiary of the multilateral financing and technical assistance agencies, have not given the government much scope for maneuver in this field. A policy *vis-a-vis* Cuba based on economic sanctions and other measures designed to isolate the island constitute, in the opinion of the Special Rapporteur, at the present stage, the surest way of prolonging an untenable internal situation, as the only remedy that would be left for not capitulating to external pressure would be to continue desperate efforts to stay anchored in the

past. International sanctions, especially if accompanied by conditions implying the adoption of specific measures, be they political or economic, are totally counterproductive if it is the international community's intention to improve the human rights situation and, at the same time, to create conditions for a peaceful and gradual transition towards a genuinely pluralist and civil society. Any suggestion along the line that the future sovereignty of the Cuban people could be contingent on external powers or forces would, in the collective memory of the Cuban people, evoke traumatic experiences of their not-very-distant history and their fight for independence, and would be a very effective obstacle towards achieving changes which could be very welcome in other circumstances.

61. Cuba is going through one of the most difficult periods in its recent history so far as the economic situation is concerned. The reasons for this are obvious and they need no elaboration in this report. The level of living has deteriorated to a point where basic services such as public transport have reached levels close to a standstill. Given this situation, the public reaction can be none other than deception [sic] and despair. On the other hand, the government seems to be resorting to repressive measures for silencing any expression of discontent or independent opinion however moderate it may be. The persecution of individuals is being carried on, sometimes even at trifling levels, and with a callousness which, in the eyes of an impartial observer, would seem patently out of proportion. The cases referred to in this report give a clear picture of this situation.

62. The Cuban nation which, in adverse conditions, has managed to cast off much of the dead weight of underdevelopment and now has a literate and skilled population which, by applying measures such as those proposed, could take a step forward towards a productive and creative society in which the guarantees of human rights are respected in an environment of mutual confidence and social peace.

FREE TRADE: GATT AND THE NEW
INTERNATIONAL ECONOMIC ORDER

NOTE ON ECONOMIC EMBARGOES UNDER GATT

In the General Assembly proceedings Cuba contended that the United States trade embargo violates the provisions of the General Agreement on Tariffs and Trade ("GATT"), 61 Stat. Parts (5), (6), TIAS 1700, 4 Bevans 649, 55-61 UNTS, which prohibits the imposition of certain restrictions upon free trade. In addition, Cuba contended that the measures are contrary to more general principles subscribed to by the General Assembly which promote free trade and require developed countries to cooperate in furthering the economic development of developing countries. In this section we set forth materials which bear on these claims.

We first reprint the pertinent provisions of GATT, which is the most important multilateral treaty governing trade and to which both the United States and Cuba are contracting parties. Established in 1948, it is both a treaty and an international organization which administers the treaty and attempts to resolve disputes between contracting states as to its application. GATT's purpose is to facilitate international trade and to promote the free flow of commerce. In addition to Cuba's reliance on GATT in support of its position, the General Assembly, UNCTAD, SELA, and other international organizations and agencies have cited it in support of their resolutions, some of which are reprinted in this Part, condemning the use of coercive economic measures.

Article I of GATT requires that all contracting parties provide most favored nation status to the products of all other contracting parties. Article XI, moreover, provides that contracting parties may impose no "prohibition or restriction other than duties, taxes or other charges, whether made effective through quotas, import or export licenses or other measures" on the importation of products from any other contracting party or the exportation of products to any other contracting party. Likewise, Article XIII provides that no prohibitions or restrictions on imports from or exports to any other contracting party may be applied "unless the importation of the like product of all third countries or the exportation of the like product to all third countries is similarly prohibited or restricted."

There appears to be little or no dispute that trade embargoes contravene the requirements of Articles XI and XIII. Article XXI of GATT, however, creates a security exception which permits the imposition of otherwise prohibited measures which a contracting party "considers necessary for the protection of its essential security interests...taken in time of war or other emergency in international relations." In contrast, Article XXXV permits a state at the time it becomes a contracting party to GATT to refuse to apply the strictures of GATT to any other contracting party. It may do so for any reason without limitation. This provision, however, has no application in the present context because the United States did not avail itself of the right to exclude Cuba at the time it became a contracting party.

Both the use of trade embargoes and the invocation of the security exception of Article XXI have proved controversial. Contracting parties which have invoked the exception, including the United States, have sometimes contended that the determination of whether measures are necessary for the protection of a party's essential security interests is wholly subjective and is to be made unilaterally by the party which claims its security interests are threatened. This position receives some support in the language of Article XXI, which refers to measures which a contracting party "considers necessary for the protection" of its security interests, and in a brief reference to Article XXI made by the International Court of Justice in the *Nicaragua* case. *See* paragraph 222. It has also been strongly criticized, however, and the contracting parties have never defined more precisely the scope of the exemption. The matter was taken up at GATT's Thirty-Eighth Ministerial meeting in November 1982, but no substantive interpretation was made, only a decision recognizing that recourse to Article XXI can constitute "an element of disruption and uncertainty for international trade" and requiring contracting parties to inform other parties "to the fullest extent possible" of trade measures imposed pursuant to the security exception. *Decision of 30 November 1982, Concerning Article XXI of the General Agreement*, BISD, p.3 (29th Supp. 1983).

The issue was again raised after the United States imposed a trade embargo against Nicaragua in 1985. The President of the United States imposed the measures under the International Emergency Economic Powers Act ("IEEPA"), 50 U.S.C. § 1701, after declaring that Nicaragua's policies "constitute an unusual and extraordinary threat to the national security and foreign policy of the United States." Executive Order 12513, 50 Fed. Reg. 18629 (May 1, 1985). Nicaragua then brought the matter before GATT for resolution. The United States, however, refused to participate in the GATT dispute resolution procedure unless the GATT panel agreed in advance that it could not interfere with the right of the United States to impose its trade measures against Nicaragua and that it could not consider the validity of or motivation for the United States invocation of Article XXI. As a result, the GATT panel was not free to make an interpretation of the scope of the security exception, and its decision is inconclusive. 3 Int'l Trade Rep. (BNA) No. 45, p.1368-69 (November 12, 1985); Council—Trade Disputes, GATT Focus Newsletter, p.4 (November-December 1986); General Agreement on Tariffs and Trade, *GATT Activities* 1985, 47-48 (1986).

In considering whether the security exception may have application to the United States trade measures against Cuba, it should be recalled that the United States no longer asserts a security rationale in support of its measures, but relies, instead, upon its desire to promote democracy in Cuba. In addition, the United States measures against Cuba are not premised on a presidential declaration of a national emergency based on a threat to the national security of the United States, as was the case with its Nicaragua measures. Instead, the President certifies annually only that the continuation of the measures under the Trading With the Enemy Act, 50 U.S.C. App. § 5(b), are in "the national interest." *See, e.g.,* Presidential Determination No. 91-52, 56 Fed. Reg. 48415 (September 13, 1991). It should also be considered that in November 1982, at GATT's Thirty-Eighth Ministerial meeting, the contracting states considered a wide number of problems in international trade, including the imposition of trade measures for political purposes. In the Ministerial Declaration issued at the close of the meeting, the contracting parties, *inter alia,* undertook, "individually and jointly:...to abstain from taking restrictive trade measures, for reasons of a non-economic character, not consistent with the General Agreement." We reprint pertinent excerpts from the Declaration.

THE GENERAL AGREEMENT ON TARIFFS AND TRADE (AMENDED)

(61 Stat. Parts (5) and (6), TIAS 1700, 4 Bevans 639, 55-61 UNTS (1947))

* * *

Recognizing that their relations in the field of trade and economic endeavour should be conducted with a view to raising standards of living, ensuring full employment and a large and steadily growing volume of real income and effective demand, developing the full use of the resources of the world and expanding the production and exchange of goods,

Being desirous of contributing to these objectives by entering into reciprocal and mutually advantageous arrangements directed to the substantial reduction of tariffs and other barriers to trade and to the elimination of discriminatory treatment in international commerce,

Have through their Representatives agreed as follows:

Article I

General Most-Favoured-Nation Treatment

1. With respect to customs duties and charges of any kind imposed on or in connection with importation or exportation or imposed on the international transfer of payments for imports or exports, and with respect to the method of levying such duties and charges, and with respect to all rules and formalities in connection with importation and exportation, and with respect to all matters referred to in paragraphs 2 and 4 of Article III, any advantage, favour, privilege or immunity granted by any contracting party to any product originating in or destined for any other country shall be accorded immediately and unconditionally to the like product originating in or destined for the territories of all contracting parties.

* * *

Article XI

General Elimination of Quantitative Restrictions

1. No prohibitions or restrictions other than duties, taxes or other charges, whether made effective through quotas, import or export licenses or other measures, shall be instituted or maintained by any contracting party on the importation of any product of the territory of any other contracting party or on the exportation or sale for export of any product destined for the territory of any other contracting party.

* * *

Article XIII

Non-Discriminatory Administration of Quantitative Restrictions

1. No prohibition or restriction shall be applied by any contracting party on the importation of any product of the territory of any other contracting party or on the exportation of any product destined for the territory of any other contracting party, unless the importation of the like product of all third countries or the exportation of the like product to all third countries is similarly prohibited or restricted.

* * *

Article XXI

Security Exceptions

Nothing in this Agreement shall be construed

(a) to require any contracting party to furnish any information the disclosure of which it considers contrary to its essential security interests; or

(b) to prevent any contracting party from taking any action which it considers necessary for the protection of its essential security interests

(i) relating to fissionable materials or the materials from which they are derived;

(ii) relating to the traffic in arms, ammunition and implements of war and to such traffic in other goods and materials as is carried on directly or indirectly for the purpose of supplying a military establishment;

(iii) taken in time of war or other emergency in international relations; or

(c) to prevent any contracting party from taking any action in pursuance of its obligations under the United Nations Charter for the maintenance of international peace and security.

*   *   *

Article XXXV

Non-Application of the Agreement Between Particular Contracting Parties

1. This Agreement, or alternatively Article II of this Agreement, shall not apply as between any contracting party and any other contracting party if:

(a) the two contracting parties have not entered into tariff negotiations with each other, and

(b) either of the contracting parties, at the time either becomes a contracting party, does not consent to such application.

2. The contracting parties may review the operation of this Article in particular cases at the request of any contracting party and make appropriate recommendations.

GATT
THIRTY-EIGHTH SESSION AT MINISTERIAL LEVEL,
MINISTERIAL DECLARATION, NOVEMBER 29, 1982

1. The *Contracting Parties* to the General Agreement on Tariffs and Trade have met at Ministerial level on 24-29 November 1982. They recognize that the multilateral trading system, of which the General Agreement is the legal foundation, is seriously endangered. In the current crisis of the world economy, to which the lack of convergence in national economic policies has contributed, protectionist pressures on governments have multiplied, disregard of GATT disciplines has increased and certain shortcomings in the functioning of the GATT system have been accentuated. Conscious of the role of the GATT system in furthering economic well-being and an unprecedented expansion of world trade, and convinced of the lasting validity of the basic principles and objectives of the General Agreement in a world of increasing economic interdependence, the CONTRACTING PARTIES are resolved to overcome these threats to the system.

*   *   *

7. In drawing up the work programme and priorities for the 1980s, the contracting parties undertake, individually and jointly:

*   *   *

(iii) to abstain from taking restrictive trade measures, for reasons of a non-economic character, not consistent with the General Agreement....

NOTE ON THE NEW INTERNATIONAL ECONOMIC ORDER

Since at least the early 1960s the developing countries have advocated for the adoption of policies, programs, and legal obligations that would further economic growth through, among other things, international trade and that would require developed states to cooperate in various ways in promoting development. There have been, to name but a few of the efforts, numerous conferences adopting resolutions on the subject: the announcement of United Nations Development Decades; the establishment of a permanent organ of the General Assembly devoted to promoting trade and development, the United Nations Conference on Trade and Development ("UNCTAD"); and, perhaps most importantly, the adoption of a series of General Assembly resolutions as part of an effort to create a new international economic order.

The efforts of the developing countries in this area have frequently met with strong resistance on the part of the developed countries. Indeed, the adoption of the resolutions on the new international economic order were among the most controversial in the history of the United Nations. *See, e.g,* G.A. Res. 3016 (XXVII) (December 18, 1972) on Permanent Sovereignty Over Natural Resources of Developing Countries, which was supported by 102 countries, opposed by none, with twenty-two abstentions (including the United States and other developed countries); G.A. Res. 3171 (XXVIII) (December 17, 1973) on Permanent Sovereignty Over Natural Resources, which was supported by 108 countries, opposed by one (United Kingdom), with sixteen abstentions (including the United States and other developed countries); G.A. Res. 3201 (S-VI) (April 9-May 2, 1974) adopting the Declaration on the Establishment of a New International Economic Order and G.A. Res. 3202 (S-VI) (April 9-May 2, 1974) adopting a Program of Action on the Establishment of a New International Economic Order, both of which were adopted by consensus although with explicit and numerous reservations on the part of the United States and others; and G.A. Res. 3281 (XXIX) (December 17, 1974) adopting the Charter of Economic Rights and Duties of States, which was supported by 120 countries, opposed by six (including the United States and other Western European countries), with ten abstentions (also largely Western European countries). The contentious context in which these resolutions were adopted should be kept in mind in evaluating their import.

A consideration of the subject of development and free trade requires a volume of its own, and many have already been written. We can here provide only a brief summary of some of the most important General Assembly resolutions. The summary provides some basis for evaluating the consistency of the United States economic measures against Cuba with the principles of the new international economic order.

In 1964 the General Assembly decided to make UNCTAD a permanent organ of the General Assembly which would have regular meetings at intervals of not greater than three years. *See* Resolution on the Establishment of the United Nations Conference on Trade and Development as an organ of the General Assembly, G.A. Res. 1955 (XIX) (December 30, 1964). Indicating that "adequate and effectively functioning organizational arrangements are essential if the full contribution of international trade to the accelerated economic growth of the developing countries is to be successfully realized through the formulation and implementation of the necessary policies," the General Assembly declared the purposes of UNCTAD to be, *inter alia,* "[t]o promote international trade, especially with a view to accelerating economic development, particularly trade between countries at different stages of development, between developing countries and between countries with different systems of economic and social organization."

In 1974 the General Assembly adopted the Declaration on the Establishment of a New International Economic Order and the more detailed Program of Action on the Establishment of a New International Economic Order. Among other things, the Declaration recognized the right of "every country to adopt the economic and social system that it deems to be the most appropriate for its own development and not to be subjected to discrimination of any kind as a result" and the need for the international community to extend active assistance to developing countries "free of any political or military conditions," to provide "preferential and non-reciprocal treatment for developing countries, wherever feasible, in all fields of international economic co-operation whenever possible," to secure favorable "conditions for the transfer of financial resources to developing countries," and to provide "developing countries access to the achievements of modern science and technology."

Shortly after adoption of the Declaration, the General Assembly adopted the Charter of Economic Rights and Duties of States which further elaborated upon the rights and duties of states set forth in the Declaration. We reprint those articles of the Charter which are particularly relevant for purposes of evaluating the United States measures against Cuba.

CHARTER OF ECONOMIC RIGHTS AND DUTIES OF STATES

(G.A. Res. 3281 (XXIX) (April 9–May 2, 1974))

*   *   *

Article 1

Every State has the sovereign and inalienable right to choose its economic system as well as its political, social and cultural systems in accordance with the will of its people, without outside interference, coercion or threat in any form whatsoever.

*   *   *

Article 4

Every State has the right to engage in international trade and other forms of economic co-operation irrespective of any differences in political, economic and social systems. No State shall be subjected to discrimination of any kind based solely on such differences. In the pursuit of international trade and other forms of economic co-operation, every State is free to choose the forms of organization of its foreign economic relations and to enter into bilateral and multilateral arrangements consistent with its international obligations and with the needs of international economic co-operation.

*   *   *

Article 6

It is the duty of States to contribute to the development of international trade of goods, particularly by means of arrangements and by the conclusion of long-term multilateral commodity agreements, where appropriate, and taking into account the interests of producers and consumers. All States share the responsibility to promote the regular flow and access of all commercial goods traded at stable, remunerative and equitable prices, thus contributing to the equitable development of the world economy, taking into account, in particular, the interests of developing countries.

*   *   *

Article 9

All States have the responsibility to co-operate in the economic, social, cultural, scientific and technological fields for the promotion of economic and social progress throughout the world, especially that of the developing countries.

Article 10

All States are juridically equal and, as equal members of the international community, have the right to participate fully and effectively in the international decision-making process in the solution of world economic, financial and monetary problems, *inter alia,* through the appropriate international organizations in accordance with their existing and evolving rules, and to share equitably in the benefits resulting therefrom.

*   *   *

Article 13

1. Every State has the right to benefit from the advances and developments in science and technology for the acceleration of its economic and social development.

2. All States should promote international scientific and technological co-operation and the transfer of technology, with proper regard for all legitimate interests including, *inter alia,* the rights and duties of holders, suppliers and recipients of technology. In particular, all States should facilitate the access of developing countries to the achievements of modern science and technology, the transfer of technology and the creation of indigenous technology for the benefit of the developing countries in forms and in accordance with procedures which are suited to their economies and their needs.

3. Accordingly, developed countries should co-operate with the developing countries in the establishment, strengthening and development of their scientific and technological infrastructures and their scientific research and technological activities so as to help to expand and transform the economies of developing countries.

4. All States should co-operate in research with a view to evolving further internationally accepted guidelines or regulations for the transfer of technology, taking fully into account the interests of developing countries.

Article 14

Every State has the duty to co-operate in promoting a steady and increasing expansion and liberalization of world trade and an improvement in the welfare and living standards of all peoples, in particular those of developing countries. Accordingly, all States should co-operate, *inter alia,* towards the progressive dismantling of obstacles to trade and the improvement of the international framework for the conduct of world trade and, to these ends, co-ordinated efforts shall be made to solve in an equitable way the trade problems of all countries, taking into account the specific trade problems of the developing countries. In this connexion, States shall take measures aimed at securing additional benefits for the international trade of developing countries so as to achieve a substantial increase in their foreign exchange earnings, the diversification of their exports, the acceleration of the rate of growth of their trade, taking into account their development needs, an improvement in the possibilities for these countries to participate in the expansion of world trade and a balance more favourable to developing countries in the sharing of the advantages resulting from this expansion, through, in the largest possible measure, a substantial improvement in the conditions of access for the products of interest to the developing countries and, wherever appropriate, measures designed to attain stable, equitable and remunerative prices for primary products.

*   *   *

Article 17

International co-operation for development is the shared goal and common duty of all States. Every State should co-operate with the efforts of developing countries to accelerate their economic and social development by providing favourable external conditions and by extending active assistance to them, consistent with their development needs and objectives, with strict respect for the sovereign equality of States and free of any conditions derogating from their sovereignty.

Article 18

Developed countries should extend, improve and enlarge the system of generalized non-reciprocal and non-discriminatory tariff preferences to the developing countries consistent with the relevant agreed conclusions and relevant decisions as adopted on this subject, in the framework of the competent international organizations. Developed countries should also give serious consideration to the adoption of other differential measures, in areas where this is feasible and appropriate and in ways which will provide special and more favourable treatment, in order to meet the trade and development needs of the developing countries. In the conduct of international economic relations the developed countries should endeavour to avoid measures having a negative effect on the development of the national economies of the developing countries, as promoted by generalized tariff preferences and other generally agreed differential measures in their favour.

Article 19

With a view to accelerating the economic growth of developing countries and bridging the economic gap between developed and developing countries, developed countries should grant generalized preferential, non-reciprocal and non-discriminatory treatment to developing countries in those fields of international economic co-operation where it may be feasible.

*   *   *

Article 22

1. All States should respond to the generally recognized or mutually agreed development needs and objectives of developing countries by promoting increased net flows of real resources to the developing countries from all sources, taking into account any obligations and commitments undertaken by the States concerned, in order to reinforce the efforts of developing countries to accelerate their economic and social development.

2. In this context, consistent with the aims and objectives mentioned above and taking into account any obligations and commitments undertaken in this regard, it should be their endeavour to increase the net amount of financial flows from official sources to developing countries and to improve the terms and conditions thereof.

3. The flow of development assistance resources should include economic and technical assistance.

*   *   *

Article 24

All States have the duty to conduct their mutual economic relations in a manner which takes into account the interests of other countries. In particular, all States should avoid prejudicing the interests of developing countries.

*   *   *

Article 26

All States have the duty to coexist in tolerance and live together in peace, irrespective of differences in political, economic, social and cultural systems, and to facilitate trade between States having different economic and social systems. International trade should be conducted without prejudice to generalized non-discriminatory and non-reciprocal preferences in favour of developing countries, on the basis of mutual advantage, equitable benefits and the exchange of most-favoured-nation treatment.

APPENDIX

ADDITIONAL GENERAL ASSEMBLY MATERIALS

A1. RESOLUTION OF THE LATIN AMERICAN PARLIAMENT

(A/46/193/Add.1, August 27, 1991)

[Established by treaty in 1987, the Latin American Parliament is a "permanent unicameral regional organ." Treaty of Institutionalization of the Latin-American Parliament, November 16, 1987, *reprinted in* 27 I.L.M. 430 (1988). Among its stated principles are the "defense of democracy," "nonintervention," "self-determination of peoples to obtain, in their internal regime, the political, economic and social system they freely decide," "political and ideological plurality as basis of a democratically organized Latin-American community" and "juridical equality of States." The Parliament's members are "democratically constituted" legislative bodies, which are represented in the Parliament by plurally constituted delegations. The original signatories to the 1987 treaty were Argentina, Bolivia, Brazil, Colombia, Costa Rica, Cuba, Ecuador, El Salvador, Guatemala, Honduras, Mexico, Nicaragua, Panama, Paraguay, Peru, Dominican Republic, Uruguay, and Venezuela. There are now twenty-three members. The Parliament was first established in 1964 without any official status.]

The 13th Regular General Assembly of the Latin American Parliament, meeting in Cartagena, Colombia, from 31 July to 3 August 1991, has agreed on the following:

Resolution

1. Noting with concern that for the last 30 years the sister people of Cuba have been suffering under a rigid economic and trade blockade, which even applies to food and medicine;

2. Deeply concerned by the fact that the blockade of Cuba has caused serious difficulties for that nation's economy, consequently detrimental to the entire population;

3. Considering that this kind of practice, in addition to violating international law, goes against the spirit that prevails in today's world, characterized by *détente*, the relaxing of cold war tensions and greater understanding between the great Powers, which propitiates the process of democratization in all regions of the globe;

We resolve

1. To express our solidarity with the people of Cuba, in the face of the serious economic situation that they are now facing.

2. To ask for an end to the economic and trade blockade imposed on that island for 30 years.

The Regular Assembly of the Latin American Parliament, Cartagena, 2 August 1991.

A2. STATEMENTS OF SUPPORT BY RELIGIOUS BODIES

(A/46/193/Adds. 2-6, September 12, 1991)

Regional Committee of the Christian Peace Conference in Latin America and the Caribbean

Letter Dated 5 September 1991 from the Executive Board

We Christians of various denominations in Latin America and the Caribbean who make up the Executive Board of the Christian Peace Conference in Latin America and the Caribbean (CCP-LAC), meeting in the city of Havana, Cuba, from 3 to 6 September 1991, wish to say the following to you, Mr. Pérez de Cuéllar, Secretary-General of the United Nations.

We have seen how children, old people, women and other citizens of Cuba have suffered because they lacked medicines and other elements essential to the full life praised in the Gospel.

We have noted the shortage of raw materials which affects the working population in the production of consumer goods and the manifold consequences this has for agriculture and the work of the population, primarily as a result of the blockade imposed on Cuba.

We emphasize the injustice, irrationality and illegality of this prolonged embargo. There is no logical reason to justify it under any type of law whether natural, constitutional or international.

Today our world demands sane coexistence among nations, and this embargo is not conducive to establishing an order that will bring stability to the region.

For these reasons we request that an item concerning the lifting of the embargo imposed on the Republic of Cuba by the United States Government be included in the agenda of the forthcoming session of the General Assembly. This would be a genuine sign that we have

taken a first, viable step along a road leading to sane political coexistence in this continent, as was forcefully stated by the Presidents who
gathered at the Ibero-American summit in Guadalajara, Mexico.

We pray to the Lord that those whose task it is to take decisions on
so important an issue may assume their responsibility nobly. We are
hopeful that we will achieve a just and humane situation in accordance
with the teachings of the One who came that we might have everlast-
ing life.

O.A. Romero Study and Solidarity Group

Letter Dated 5 September 1991 from the Coordinator
to the Secretary-General

In view of the forthcoming session of the General Assembly of the United
Nations, we request that an item concerning the unjust economic em-
bargo and blockade against Cuba by the Government of the United
States of America be included in the agenda of that session.

We are requesting this as members of the Catholic Church in Cuba,
for we are concerned about our brothers and about being true to the
Spirit and are in communion with our bishops; the latter protested
against the embargo in April 1969, stating that it was an attack on life,
God's greatest gift. It is also a violation of the wish of the Holy Father,
John Paul II, who has insistently called for peace among peoples and
for frontiers to be open arms to reconciliation rather than areas of
tension. Moreover, we have noted that our peoples have a deep longing
for peace.

We renew our efforts and our prayers for that peace which comes
from God and we pray that an end may be put to the very inhuman
and unchristian embargo which has been making life difficult for millions of children and old people, women and men, for more than 30
years.

May God guide you and bless your efforts, for "blessed are the peacemakers" (Matthew 5:9).

Bishop of the Methodist Church of Cuba

Letter Dated 30 August 1991 from the
Bishop of the Methodist Church of Cuba Addressed
to the Secretary-General

We were pleased and heartened to hear that the representative of our
people and Government to the United Nations, H.E. Mr. Ricardo Alarcón,
will request the General Assembly of that Organization, over which
you preside, to include an item on the embargo against Cuba and the
total elimination thereof.

*   *   *

We pray that the prophetic voices echoing in both the North and the South may be heard in the United Nations General Assembly, so that truth and justice may triumph and our Cuban people may shape their destiny without interference, embargoes or impositions of any type.

We take this opportunity to convey to you the renewed assurances of our highest consideration and we pray that God may guide you in your mission.

Methodist Church of Cuba

Statement of the Position of the Methodist Church
with Respect to the Blockade against Cuba

(Havana, 15 June 1991)

The Assembly of the Annual Conference of the Methodist Church of Cuba, meeting at the premises located at 25 and K, Vedado, Havana, from 12 to 16 June 1991, and having been consulted on the question of the commercial blockade against Cuba, has resolved to issue the following declaration expressing its position in principle with regard to this matter. Jesus Christ was sacrificed on the cross to redeem and save man from his sinful condition and to raise him to the full stature of a human being. The Methodist Church of Cuba advocates the total elimination of the North American trade embargo against our country.

The reasons for our rejection of the blockade are as follows:

(1) The blockade has a degrading effect on the people of our country, since it denies them the possibility of survival, health and development.

(2) It affects children, the elderly and society as a whole, which is being subjected to economic strangulation.

(3) Our Methodist social doctrine holds that any act which tends to reduce man to a subhuman condition is an act against the Creator.

Council of Methodist Churches in Latin America and the Caribbean

Declaration Issued by the Council of Bishops and
Heads of Churches of the Council of Methodist Churches
in Latin America and the Caribbean

(Antigua, Guatemala, 15 August 1991)

Solidarity with the Republic of Cuba

WHEREAS:

1. The economic marginality of Latin America is a sign of repression;

2. The economic blockade of Cuba, led by the United States, is a cruel means of causing death;

3. The Methodist Church of Cuba is committed to the struggle to suspend the economic blockade;

4. As Methodist Evangelical Churches, we form a united continental ecclesiastical body, and solidarity is built through concrete action;

5. The General Conference of the United Methodist Church of the United States has voted in favour of the request to lift the blockade;

The Council of Bishops and Heads of Churches of the Council of Methodist Churches in Latin America and the Caribbean resolves:

I. To pledge to fight, through the efforts of its national churches at various levels, to secure the lifting of the economic blockade against Cuba;

II. To propose that the Council of Methodist Churches in Latin America, as the continental ecumenical body, make a similar pledge to support the Methodist Church of Cuba in its efforts to secure the lifting of the economic blockade against Cuba;

III. To submit this proposal for cooperation to the Methodist Church of Cuba for its information;

IV. To invite the Council of Bishops of the United Methodist Church, the United States Board of International Ministries and the United Church of Canada to join in this effort;

V. To affirm and defend the sovereign right of the Cuban people to decide their own destiny without foreign interference.

Document approved in special session by the Council of Bishops, done at Antigua, Guatemala, on 15 August 1991.

(Signed)	(Signed)	(Signed)
Secundino Morales	Raul Ruiz Avila	Aldo M. Etchepoyen
Secretary	Vice-President	President

Public Declaration of the Meeting of Methodist Churches

(Antigua, Guatemala, 16 August 1991)

On 14 August 1991, in Antigua, Guatemala, the Council of Bishops of the Council of Methodist Churches in Latin America and the Caribbean signed a declaration in support of the people of Cuba.

In solidarity with the Cuban people, and endorsing the terms of the above-mentioned declaration, the Meeting of Methodist Churches held in Antigua, Guatemala

CALLS FOR:

1. An end to the unjust and prolonged blockade against Cuba, promoted by the United States of America, which is affecting the lives of our Cuban brothers.

2. The support of all the countries of the Americas and the Caribbean for the people of Cuba, so that they may freely and wisely determine their destiny, without pressure or threats of intervention.

Bishop Aldo Etchegoyen
Council of Methodist Churches in
Latin America and the Caribbean

Mrs. Rosemary Waas
Methodist Church of
Great Britain

Rev. C. Evans Bailey
Methodist Church in the
Caribbean and the Americas

Rev. Tom Edmonds
United Church of Canada

Bishop Melvin Talvert
United Methodist Church of
the United States

Dr. Martin Luther King, Jr. Memorial Centre

Letter Dated 29 August 1991 from the Director
Addressed to the Secretary-General

Considering the sacred mission entrusted to the United Nations by all peace- and justice-loving peoples, and that the Organization constitutes an international forum which can make possible a world of fraternal relations between nations, I am addressing you in my capacity as Director of the Dr. Martin Luther King Jr. Memorial Centre.

For more than three decades, our people have suffered the consequences of the economic, commercial and financial embargo imposed by various Administrations of the United States Government. These measures, and the constant pressures which are exerted in order to impose a particular political point of view, offend our Christian conscience and the ethical convictions which we hold as followers of Jesus Christ, Our Lord. There is no moral reason which justifies the violation of the rights of a country, however small it may be, because it has a different political system.

Expressing the general feeling of our evangelical people, we request that the question of these discriminatory measures should be considered by the General Assembly at its forty-sixth session and that the requisite steps should be taken to put an end to them.

Cuban Ecumenical Council

Letter Dated 4 September 1991 from the President
Addressed to the Secretary-General

Blessed are the peacemakers: For they shall be called the children of God.
Matthew 5:9

We Christians have been discovering the hand of God in the origins of time; He is guiding individuals, peoples and institutions towards the realization of His will, and God's will is that we should all take part in His Kingdom, which is justice, love and peace.

The Cuban Ecumenical Council, an organization uniting churches and institutions which are working for peace and love among men, cannot remain detached when injustice and enmity are violating the life of peoples.

For these reasons, as Christians who belong to the Cuban people, we note with great satisfaction that our Government's representative to the United Nations, Mr. Rafael Alarcón de Quesada, has proposed that the question of the embargo against Cuba be considered by the General Assembly at this session.

We cannot be indifferent to the unjust economic embargo against Cuba, since it has meant that the people have had to pay a high price for these past 30 years and more.

Because it disregards the supreme dignity of man, because of its degrading implications for health, well-being and development and because it violates the right of every human being to life itself, we have decided to address ourselves to you, asking you to heed our plea, as Christians and as Cubans, in order that we may be allowed to determine our future freely and in a sovereign manner.

We believe that there are inviolable principles which identify us as Christians, compelling us to reject the commercial embargo imposed on our country; we know that God will place in your mind and heart the will to ensure that justice shines forth for the good of all our people, and we hope that this question will be considered at the forthcoming session of the General Assembly.

We ask God to give you wisdom in your efforts and we ask you, Sir, to accept the assurances of our highest consideration.

Sincerely,   (Signed)
(Signed)   Rita Olivia Valdes
Rev. Orestes Gonzalez Cruz   Executive Secretary Cuban
President   Ecumenical Council

A3. STATEMENT BY AMBASSADOR ALARCÓN BEFORE
THE GENERAL COMMITTEE OF THE 46TH SESSION OF
THE GENERAL ASSEMBLY ON SEPTEMBER 18, 1991

(Unofficial transcript and translation)

The Government of the United States wants to prevent a public discussion on the criminal blockade it has imposed on Cuba for more than thirty years. As stated by the State Department last August 21st, the analysis of this item by the United Nations would be "inappropriate."

If we were to believe the text of the American declaration, it would seem that, by asking to include this item for discussion, Cuba is seeking to damage the sovereignty of the United States, a poor country that has the right to make its own decision as to with whom it wishes to have diplomatic or economic relations. Apparently, Cuba is the one threatening the capacity of the United States to self-determination and is even trying to mobilize the international community to exert an illegitimate and arbitrary pressure.

If someone were to believe those who wrote the document of August 21st, he or she could imagine them as the representatives of a small harassed country whose sovereign decisions others try to interfere, forcing it to adopt behavioral patterns opposed to its national interest.

Furthermore, they claim that the request to introduce the item is out of the question since it is not a blockade but merely an embargo. The United States have no relations with Cuba but, as they suggest, they do nothing to prevent others from having them.

The statement by the State Department, in an attempt to justify the policy of the United States, faces an insurmountable difficulty. It takes for granted—and so it would need in order to be effective—a total degree of ignorance, an absolute lack of knowledge about the facts by the international community as a whole. Nevertheless, I am convinced that, outside Washington, it is very difficult to find such an immoderate cult to misinformation. The fact that the authors of the statement believe, albeit partially, in whatever was said in that text should not be discarded. They would need, nevertheless, to be exceedingly naive to imagine that anyone else would believe it.

No one could seriously question the relevance or need to have this item examined by the General Assembly, which should not only examine it, but also demand from the United States to immediately, totally, and unconditionally put an end to a policy contradictory with the basic principles of the Charter, affecting international relations and ignoring not only legal standards but also the most basic ethical considerations.

The Government of the United States totally prohibits any economic, commercial or financial relation between Cuba and any enterprise, institution or individual under Washington's jurisdiction. Thus it not only violated bilateral agreements in force at the moment of imposing its arbitrary sanctions but it has been also ignoring and contravening the General Agreement on Tariffs and Trade and several GATT decisions as well as a number of resolutions of the General Assembly. Suffice it to read these documents only once to clearly perceive that the United Nations is fully competent to discuss the Yankee blockade against Cuba—even the embargo, as they call it with ofidian-like slyness.

The aim of that policy, since it was instituted more than thirty years ago, was to impose the U.S. will on Cuba through coercion and by force.

Therefore, and also because that policy openly violates the principles of nonintervention and sovereign equality of States—even restricted to what Washington with hypocritical pretense calls an "embargo"—it should be rejected by the General Assembly.

That policy, among other things, totally prevents Cuba from purchasing medicines in the American market and also implies many other restrictions to communications and contacts between both countries which seriously affect all Cubans causing great sufferings to its people. Therefore, that policy as it constitutes the most open, systematic and permanent violation of the human rights of the people of Cuba—even that which the Yankee rulers cunningly describe as an "embargo"—must be resolutely condemned by the General Assembly.

The violation of the rights of American citizens themselves imposed by the blockade against Cuba—or "embargo" as they like to call it with pretended naiveté—would deserve further consideration. I will only mention two examples. The poor in the United States also suffer from meningitis type B but they are prevented from vaccination against it as, so far, the only vaccine is manufactured in Cuba and is obviously banned from the American market. Mr. Dan Snow was condemned to 90 days imprisonment, 5 years of probation and fined $5,000 because he participated in fishing activities in Cuban waters.

But there is more, much more, Mr. President: NO ONE better than Washington knows that what they impose on Cuba is not only the "embargo"—which is equally unjustified and should be condemned—but the most strict and illegal blockade which has no boundaries, and has no limit and no respect for the sovereignty of other countries. Never before has humankind known similar arrogance to that of the American rulers, never before has any government been so prepotent in its attempts to spread its laws, rules and regulations all over the world as if they were the only Government on Earth; there has never been such a rageful persecution of the economic activities of a small underdeveloped country throughout the planet. History is yet to witness such a stubborn hatred and implacable and cruel persecution, undertaken for such a long time, against a poor and small country in order to have its people surrender by hunger.

In order not to prolong my statement, I have requested the Secretary-General to distribute among all members a document which briefly outlines some of the provisions currently applied—and enforced for many years now—by the Government of the United States. All of them clearly show how the American authorities extend their aggressive measures against Cuba beyond their territory, interfere in the internal affairs of other States and arbitrarily and illegally impose their laws, rules and regulations on third countries and compel enterprises, institutions and individuals which are not under the United States jurisdiction to accept American diktats.

Thus, the United States expands the measures of blockade to American enterprises overseas, to foreign enterprises based in other countries whose capital is shared by American interests; it prevents Cuba from buying products manufactured in third countries, by third countries enterprises, if they contain any American component, including elements which could supply technological information in different stages of its design or manufacture; it bans the sale of products manufactured by third countries to the United States if they have any Cuban component, even if totally transformed.

Those and other restrictions, as stated in public and official documents, are currently imposed by the United States. They not only seriously affect Cuba and create numerous and continued obstacles to the development of our economic and commercial links with third countries, but they also affect the legitimate interests of enterprises, institutions and individuals in those countries. The long arm of the new Yankee inquisitors, in their obsession to harm Cuba, interferes anywhere, tramples upon international legislation, mocks the sovereignty of others and disrespects their rights.

As an example the aforementioned document, which all of you have received, outlines several cases in which the Yankee Department of the Treasury impeded Cuba's purchase of medical equipment manufactured outside the United States by non-American enterprises.

Of course, for Washington it is not enough to try to apply its law beyond its borders. It also exerts every kind of pressure and threats, and punishes foreign enterprises which, nevertheless, maintain commercial and economic ties with Cuba.

Not fully satisfied, the U.S. Senate has recently adopted several amendments with the aim of tightening the blockade, of grossly ignoring the sovereignty of other countries and of conditioning U.S. assistance to certain countries to their breaking of economic relations with Cuba.

Mr. President, United States imperialism has been waging economic warfare against the people of Cuba for more than thirty years. It tries to destroy its economy, to hinder its development, to force Cubans to return to a past of slavery and exploitation, for which they resort to the most cruel means.

In an attempt to justify its repugnant and illegal behavior, Washington has tried different excuses through the years, all of them having a common denominator: to make Cuba submit and decide upon its destiny.

The American rulers, rejoicing from the failure of the European Socialist experience, have intensified the economic blockade and increased pressure and threats.

They forget that Cubans did not import the Revolution from elsewhere, that it was, and still is, the result of a century of struggle and of our own efforts and sacrifices. For us, the Revolution means not only social justice and the attainment of the most profound aspirations of the large masses which were exploited in the past, but also the attainment of the independence successive generations of Cubans have heroically fought for. For us, Homeland and Revolution, Independence and Socialism are one and the same. Therefore, there is no room in Cuba for equivocation.

We Cubans have enough courage, determination and profound patriotic and moral reasons to continue resisting the blockade, the threats, the pressures and all aggressive actions of our obstinate and stubborn enemies.

But in Cuba, not only is the future of Cubans at stake. If imperialists are allowed to do as they please, if they are allowed to impose their will beyond their borders, if they are allowed to violate the rule of law, to ignore the sovereignty of others, we would be allowing them to act as if they were the owners of the world and expand their eagerness of domination everywhere. And all peoples, not only Cubans, will suffer the consequences of their hegemonic dreams and excessive arrogance and will be witnesses of another barbaric era. And it is because all of these elements, Mr. President, that my delegation requests that the General Assembly examines, in Plenary and as a priority issue, the need to put an end to the economic, commercial and financial blockade imposed by the United States against Cuba.

A4. SUMMARY RECORD OF THE FIRST MEETING OF THE
GENERAL COMMITTEE, HELD ON SEPTEMBER 18, 1991

(A/BUR/46/SR. 1, September 24, 1991)

*   *   *

Item 144

48. The *Chairman* said that the inclusion of item 144 had been requested by Cuba (A/46/193 and addenda 1 to 7). The representative of Cuba had asked to participate in the discussion of the item under rule 43 of the rules of procedure.

49. *At the invitation of the Chairman, Mr. Alarcón de Quesada (Cuba) took a place at the Committee table.*

*   *   *

56. Mr. Rosenstock (United States of America) said that his country took pride in being one of the earliest advocates of a liberal policy with

regard to the inclusion of items in the agenda. The values of that policy did not diminish with the passage of time but he regretted that other countries no longer adhered to those values and were unable to resist name-calling. The United States had no objection to the inclusion of the item on the agenda and would express its views at the appropriate time.

57. *The Committee decided to recommend that the General Assembly should include item 144 in the agenda.*

58. *Mr. Alarcón de Quesada (Cuba) withdrew.*

A5. ADDITIONAL UNITED STATES COMMUNICATIONS WITH MEMBER STATES, FALL 1991

U.S. relations with Cuba is not an appropriate issue for discussion at the UN. Every government has a right and a responsibility to choose with whom it wishes to have relations. We consider this a bilateral matter between the U.S. and Cuba.

The United States regards any UNGA consideration of this issue as an interference in its internal affairs. The UNGA is not an appropriate forum for consideration of this issue.

The United States does not have full diplomatic or commercial relations with Cuba as a result of Cuba's support for insurgency abroad, policies of internal repression, and lack of democratic institutions.

The embargo was established in an effort to influence Cuban behavior. We seek to limit the flow of hard currency that can be used by the Cuban government to support insurgency in El Salvador and to repress its own people. Cuba has supplied arms, including advanced anti-aircraft missiles, to the FMLN. Cuba has denied a UNHRC envoy access to the Cuban people, in open disregard of a UN mandate.

It is an absurd assertion that this is a "blockade." The embargo is consistent with international law.

We note that on May 17, 1991, President Bush stated in a radio address from the Oval Office: "If Cuba holds fully free and fair elections under international supervision, respects basic human rights, and stops subverting its neighbors, we can expect relations between our two countries to improve significantly."

U.S. embargo regulations allow for licensing of humanitarian donations to private institutions in Cuba. Items under this provision may include food, medicine and medical supplies, clothes, educational materials and other goods which are required to meet basic human needs.

Embargo regulations allow Cuba to purchase directly from the United States any medicines unavailable elsewhere.

We understand that many other UN members within the Latin American and Caribbean Group [GRULAC] will not support the Cuban resolution.

II.

The Cuban delegation at this year's UN General Assembly has inscribed a new issue on the agenda: "The Necessity of Ending the Economic, Commercial, and Financial Embargo Imposed by the United States of America Against Cuba."

The Cuban initiative is totally unacceptable. The U.S. embargo is consistent with international law.

Furthermore, the U.S. relationship with Cuba is not an appropriate issue for discussion at the UN. Every government is free to choose with whom it wishes to have relations.

The Cuban initiative is designed to resurrect old superpower antagonisms at a time when a new spirit of international cooperation has taken root in the UN.

The United States does not have full diplomatic or commercial relations with Cuba because the Government of Cuba supports insurgency abroad, engages in internal repression, and lacks democratic institutions.

The embargo was established in an effort to influence Cuban behavior. We seek to limit the flow of hard currency which can be used by the Cuban Government to support insurgency in El Salvador and to repress its own people.

The United States supports peaceful democratic change in Cuba. It is the Cuban people who should decide the future of Cuba.

President Bush said last May that if Cuba held free and fair elections, under international supervision, respected human rights and ended support for insurgencies, relations with the United States could improve significantly.

Cuba's recent Fourth Party Congress failed to make any significant reforms in either the economic or political spheres.

In recent weeks, Cuban authorities have stepped up repression of dissident activity. Twelve activists who signed a document urging free elections were arrested prior to the Party Congress, and are being charged with making "clandestine publications" and "abetting crime."

Despite successful efforts to remain a member of the UN Human Rights Commission, Cuba has continued to flaunt UNHRC actions, refusing to cooperate with that organization's special envoy.

We urge the Government of [deleted] to instruct its UN mission to approach the Cubans in an effort to have the resolution withdrawn, or to vote against the resolution should the Cubans insist on submitting it to the plenary.

We do not wish to see a bitter fight develop over this agenda item. We will, however, defend our legitimate interests. At any rate, a debate of the issue will only create tensions and will not result in the U.S. lifting the embargo.

A6. CUBA'S DRAFT RESOLUTION, FORTY-SIXTH SESSION

(A/46/L.20, November 11, 1991)

The General Assembly,

Reaffirming the purpose of the United Nations to develop friendly relations among nations based on respect for the principle of equal rights and self-determination of peoples, and to take other appropriate measures to strengthen universal peace,

Recalling its resolution 2131 (XX) of 21 December 1965, the annex to which contains the Declaration on the Inadmissibility of Intervention in the Domestic Affairs of States and the Protection of Their Independence and Sovereignty, which established, *inter alia,* that no State may use or encourage the use of economic, political or any other type of measures to coerce another State in order to obtain from it the subordination of the exercise of its sovereign rights,

Recalling also its resolution 2625 (XXV) of 24 October 1970, the annex to which contains the Declaration on the Principles of International Law concerning Friendly Relations and Cooperation among States in accordance with the Charter of the United Nations, which reaffirms, *inter alia,* the duty of States to refrain in their international relations from military, political, economic or any other form of coercion aimed against the political independence or territorial integrity of any State,

Recalling further its resolution 36/103 of 9 December 1981, the annex to which contains the Declaration on the Inadmissibility of Intervention and Interference in the Internal Affairs of States, which sets forth, *inter alia,* the duty of a State, in the conduct of its international relations, to refrain from measures which would constitute interference or intervention in the internal or external Affairs of another State, including any multilateral or unilateral economic reprisal or blockade, as instruments of political pressure or coercion against another State, in violation of the Charter of the United Nations,

Considering that for more than 30 years, a series of economic, commercial and financial measures and actions has been applied against Cuba, causing serious harm to the Cuban people and infringing the sovereignty of that country,

Considering, in particular that the implementation of those measures and actions is being extraterritorially extended, constituting a blockade against Cuba which not only affects the normal development of international relations but also impairs the inalienable right of the affected countries to exercise freely the prerogatives deriving from their national sovereignty,

Reaffirming the right of every country freely to choose its economic, commercial and financial partners, in exercise of its national sovereignty, without any constraint or interference,

1. *Declares* that policy contradicts the principles embodied in the Charter of the United Nations and in international law;

2. *Affirms* the necessity of ending that policy and, to that effect, *calls for* an immediate end to the measures and actions comprising it;

3. *Invites* the international community to extend to Cuba the necessary cooperation to mitigate the consequences of that policy;

4. *Requests* the Secretary-General to report to the General Assembly at its forty-seventh session on the implementation of the present resolution;

5. *Decides* to include the item entitled "necessity of ending the economic, commercial and financial embargo imposed by the United States of America against Cuba" in the provisional agenda of the forty-seventh session of the General Assembly.

A7. AMBASSADOR ALARCÓN'S ADDRESS TO THE GENERAL ASSEMBLY PLENARY MEETING, NOVEMBER 13, 1991

(A/46/PV.46, November 15, 1991, Unofficial translation)

Mr. President,

The fact that at the outset my statement deals with certain special circumstances with which this item has been surrounded certainly will surprise no one.

Allow me, firstly, to say that it has not been and it is not our intention to present to you a bilateral quarrel—even if, incidentally, more than one appears in the agenda of this Assembly—and that it is very far from our mind to try to lead this Assembly to intervene in issues which are of the exclusive competence of the sovereignty of any State. We would not allow ourselves the boldness of unnecessarily bothering your very busy schedules with an issue that did not deserve it.

The item we are now considering is of vital importance for my people. It has directly to do, no more and no less, with the right to life, with the survival of a whole nation. It is also a problem affecting, also directly, the purposes and principles enshrined in the Charter, and which impedes the normal development of international relations and is seriously detrimental to the legitimate interests of many States, institutions and persons worldwide.

Everyone in this room knows it, and millions outside this room also know it.

Everyone is also aware of the causes that explain the very peculiar situation confronted by this Assembly in dealing with this issue. Everyone, once and again, here and in the capitals, orally and in writing, has been told why, with a language so crude that it cannot escape anyone's perception. I have here a collection of the different communications that the Government of the United States has disseminated through the ministries of foreign affairs of many countries in which the most fallacious arguments go hand in hand with the most transparent threats. All those communications bear a clear message: Washington does not only have the intention of persisting in its illegal and criminal blockade against Cuba, but also aims to block its discussion by the General Assembly.

In those documents and in the statement by the State Department of 21 August it is said that it is not a blockade, but simply an embargo. But, to the surprise of anyone reading them, it is asserted that: "A blockade implies that the United States is taking action to prevent other countries from trading with Cuba. This is clearly not the case."

In document A/46/193/Add.7 of 12 September 1991, we clearly demonstrated that the blockade is precisely that, a blockade being carried out by Washington worldwide, extending its anti-Cuban laws and regulations beyond its territory. In that document, received by delegations two months ago, we quoted specifically a number of U.S. provisions which have been in force for years demonstrating the extraterritorial extension of Washington's jurisdiction. Sixty days have passed since the distribution of document A/46/193/Add.7 and nobody has up to now questioned the accuracy of the information it contains. Of course, anyone has still the opportunity to do so during the debate of this item.

The said document is a mere compilation taken from the Code of Federal Regulations of the United States. Allow me now to present to you some examples showing how the extraterritorial implementation of those provisions not only seriously damages Cuba but also affects the interests of third countries and is a continuous source of international conflicts.

In a number of recent cases, legitimate commercial operations between Cuban and non-U.S. enterprises, which are, thus, not under the jurisdiction of the United States, could not be carried out as a consequence of express prohibitions from Washington. Official entities of the third countries involved participated in some of those operations. I have here the relevant documents pertaining to each case. I will limit myself to mentioning the items whose export to Cuba was prohibited: ophthalmic eye-drops, tires, hydraulic components, "V" transmission belts, kitchen-kits for aircraft, electrical controls and regulators, materials for electric installations, electric accessories, heater components, wood-cutting tools, metal-cutting tools, iron connectors for electric installations, light-bulbs, electric fuses, commercial kitchens, electric switches, shipping related products, plastic resins, cellophane paper, water-treatment resins, materials for the production of telephone cables, glue for motor couplings, filters, medical literature and soft drinks. As you can see, these are not at all "strategic materials." I will limit myself to dwell upon some of the most recent cases.

The Editorial Interamericana S.A. of Spain had been for years an important supplier of medical books to Cuba until 1991 when it was acquired by the U.S. enterprise McGraw-Hill, which prohibited all sales to our country and even the participation of its now Spanish subsidiary in Cuba's Book Fair. This transatlantic imposition of decisions taken in Washington makes the access by Cubans to medical literature even more difficult, but also certainly leaves jobless a number of Spanish workers.

On instructions from its headquarters in the United States, the Pepsi-Cola company in Montreal decided in mid-May this year not to abide by a contract it has subscribed for the sale of 28,000 boxes of soft-drinks to Cuba. The political implications of this act were correctly interpreted by the Canadian authorities. In a communication addressed by Mr. R. H. Davidson, Director General for Latin America and the Caribbean of the Canadian Ministry of Foreign Affairs to the said Company, he expressed: "Canadian Government Trade Policy, which we would expect to be supported by companies incorporated in Canada favours trade in non-strategic goods with Cuba. The Canadian Government has also consistently opposed the extraterritorial application of U.S. trade policy towards Cuba, either directly by the U.S. Government or through U.S. parent corporations since the adoption of the U.S. Cuban Assets Control Regulations in 1963."

Cuba and the Swedish company Alfa-Laval have had traditional commercial links. Nevertheless, on May this year, that corporation canceled a sale contract it had subscribed with MEDICUBA. This operation was related to Swedish equipment, manufactured in Sweden by Alfa-Laval, that Cuba had been purchasing for years until the inquisitors in Washington found that a single part of that equipment, a filtering membrane, was of U.S. origin.

In document A/46/193/Add.7 we listed a number of commercial operations for the purchase of medical and laboratory equipment and their spare-parts, all of them manufactured out of the United States by non U.S. companies, that could not be carried out on account of prohibitions of the Treasury Department of the United States.

I do not intend to read this other document I am showing, but the least I can do is to mention it in this room where the Children's Summit met scarcely a year ago. Do you all remember promises made on that occasion to the children of the world? Did somebody say, then, that Cuban children were excluded from that promise? This document contains a list of spare-parts, some of them very small and not at all costly. They have no "strategic" value and serve no military purpose whatsoever. Their only use is in children's hospitals. We are not speaking about toys, but of parts indispensable to equipment for the treatment of children with cardiac conditions. These spare-parts have only one defect: they are of U.S. origin. I am certain that all U.S. Embassies have a copy of this list and that is the reason for the increasing difficulties we are confronting in purchasing these products almost worldwide. Some of our colleagues have stated that this item now being considered by the General Assembly is very sensitive. Can anyone doubt it? Among other things it puts to the test the sensitivity of all and everyone of us in face of the right of children to life.

Cuban children have other experiences with the blockade. In 1981 an epidemic of hemorrhagic "dengue" erupted in Cuba in circumstances which allow us to suspect its introduction from abroad. The U.S. authorities, then, hindered our efforts to acquire the necessary products for the elimination of the agent of that epidemic which we could only find, after enormous effort and at a very steep cost, and in a distant market, notwithstanding the démarches made in Washington by the World Health Organization. Cuban children paid the price of one hundred lives to that episode of abominable cruelty.

In its efforts to illegally impose its policy of blockade in other countries beyond its jurisdiction, Washington has practiced pressure and interference through several means. Early in 1983 the State Department received a note from the Canadian Ministry of Foreign Affairs stating, *inter alia:* "We can not accept...that U.S. officials take steps in Canada in support of the application of U.S. Law to inhibit Canadian firms from pursuing express Canadian Government policies of promoting trade with Cuba in non-strategic goods...if they are indeed long-standing U.S. practice they should be discontinued."

These activities of interference by Washington are being generalized in all countries and multiplied in recent months. Abundant testimony of this fact has been reflected in the press, especially in Latin America.

The savage persecution against the Cuban nickel exports deserves special attention. In this war of thirty years against one of the main products of a poor and underdeveloped country, the Government of the United States has achieved its main goals and has closed our traditional markets one after the other. This has even implied the cancellation of duly subscribed contracts, some of them even being already fulfilled by private and public corporations of the largest consumers of this mineral. To achieve this the United States has used all methods, from the embargo of stainless steel shipments "suspicious" of containing Cuban nickel, the imposition of a very strict control machinery in consuming countries, the demand of guarantees that no product exported to the United States would contain Cuban nickel, to the threat and the extortion carried out by Yankee diplomats visiting one by one the nickel consuming companies in several countries.

Now Washington is also demanding those exporting sugar to the United States to guarantee that the shipments sold to the U.S. market contain no Cuban sugar.

Another example of extraterritoriality is the U.S. attempt to completely proscribe the use of the dollar in any transaction regarding Cuba, even when it has no link whatsoever with persons or entities in the United States. By so doing Washington is interfering in the functioning of banks and financial institutions in third countries and restricting their activities even if they have no relation at all with the United States.

Mr. President:

What I have just described is the result of the extraterritorial application of the blockade provisions against Cuba presently in force. Obviously, this policy violates the Charter of San Francisco, the General Agreement of Tariffs and Trade and a number of resolutions of this General Assembly; it runs counter to international law and not only constitutes a criminal aggression against Cuba, but also its practical application goes against the sovereignty of other States and is, thus, a constant source of international conflict, as well as ignores the most basic rights of the Cuban people and harms the legitimate interests of others.

All this is valid regarding what is in existence today. But, as if it were not more than enough, since last year the U.S. Congress is considering legislative proposals geared at intensifying and extending its economic, commercial and financial blockade against Cuba. Some of them have already been integrated into legislation waiting for executive sanction. Their aim is to totally eliminate trade with Cuba by subsidiaries of U.S. corporations in and under the jurisdiction of third countries. Almost all Cuban imports that would thus be prohibited are foodstuffs and medicines, as has been recognized in this document I am now showing to you of the office that the U.S. Government has entrusted with implementing the blockade. To achieve that aim, the United States would illegally and arbitrarily increase the extension of its laws to territories beyond its jurisdiction and would violate the sovereignty of other countries.

For that reason the Embassy of Ireland in Washington, on behalf of the States members of the European Communities, presented last year this note to the State Department, which I am now showing, objecting to the proposed legislation.

One of its paragraphs reads: "The Community is still of the view that the United States have no basis in international law to claim the right to license non-U.S. transactions with Cuba by companies incorporated outside the U.S.A., whatever their ownership or control."

We also recognize the value of the statement by the Secretary of Commerce of the United Kingdom of last September, which I take the liberty of quoting: "It is for the British Government, not the U.S. Congress, to determine the U.K.'s policy on trade with Cuba. We will not accept any attempt to superimpose U.S. law on U.K. companies. I hope the Congress will think long and hard before seeking to interfere with legitimate civil trade between this country and Cuba."

Mr. President:

I have put before you a series of very concrete details, all of them based on documents and incontestable proof clearly showing how the Government of the United States is carrying out an illegal economic, commercial and financial blockade against Cuba. I have quoted official statements of friends and allies of the United States that demonstrate how the actions and measures constituting this blockade are contrary to international law and not only affect Cuba, but third countries as well. In so doing it has not been my intention to upset anyone and even less those Governments which my own Government dutifully respects and considers. I hope that they understand that it was my obligation to demonstrate the total falsehood of the U.S. allegations that this item is restricted to a bilateral difference between the two countries and also to reject the astounding absurdity of those who see in the debate of this issue an interference in the internal affairs of the United States.

I think that no one can harbour doubts that this blockade is an international problem and that its consideration by the General Assembly is entirely legitimate. This Assembly has also the unavoidable moral and political obligation to contribute to putting to an immediate end a policy that, apart from being illegal, causes serious damage to a whole people. To this end we have tabled the draft resolution contained in document A/46/L.20. In drafting it we have taken into account the observations and suggestions presented to us by a number of delegations. We highly appreciate their interest and spirit of cooperation.

It goes without saying that our intention in proposing this draft is not to put delegations in an uncomfortable position. But to put it in simple terms, it is our duty to demand justice for Cuba and for its people and the necessary solidarity to achieve it, and we will carry out that duty in this Assembly and in other international fora.

We all know the exact nature of the obstacles impeding this Assembly from taking a just decision on this issue. It has nothing to do with legal interpretations or semantic disquisitions.

The true "argument," the only "argument" of the Government of the United States is in this paper that I am now showing to you with which many of you are acquainted. I have a number of versions coming from different capitals. Allow me to read the paragraph that contains the only and true Yankee "argument": "In view of your relations with them, we would appreciate your going to the Cubans in an effort to have the resolution withdrawn. The Cubans should understand that their insistence that you support them threatens your good relationships with the U.S. The American Congress and people will be watching this important issue very carefully."

We know to what places on this planet this clear and direct threat, showing the total lack of respect by Washington for the dignity and sovereignty of other nations, has been conveyed. We know what certain special envoys have said in a number of capitals. We know of the gross impertinences they have used in a number of meetings, even with Heads of State of independent republics that they attempt to treat as if they were colonial possessions. We also know that in more than one case, the threatening language has been compounded by suspensions of credits, interruption of bilateral projects and other measures of pressure and reprisal. On all of this we also have perfectly documented proof that we prefer to keep to ourselves for the time being.

But what more do we need?

"The Cubans should understand that their insistence that you support them threatens your good relations with the U.S. The American Congress and people will be watching this important issue very carefully."

In its effort to hinder the international community from taking the necessary action, the Government of the United States has launched a frantic and inordinate campaign of intimidation, threats and pressure. In these circumstance the Assembly would find it very difficult to fully exercise its responsibilities, to objectively consider the draft resolution before it and to allow each and everyone to assume, in all freedom and without fear of reprisal, the most appropriate position.

Cuba firmly believes in international solidarity. Cuba demands it for its people because it needs it at present. But those sentiments, even in these times fraught with risks for our country, compel us to solidarily understand the difficulties that others would unjustly be confronted with in maintaining a dignified position regarding this item.

Thus, Mr. President, I would like to officially communicate that my delegation has decided not to insist in putting to the vote the draft resolution contained in document A/46/L.20 during the present session of the General Assembly and that action on it be postponed for the next session.

Many Governments, institutions and individuals worldwide have demanded that an end be put to the economic, commercial and financial blockade imposed against Cuba. We put our trust in their solidarity. We trust that their efforts will be multiplied and become even more powerful, helping to create the appropriate conditions that would allow the General Assembly to make a just decision next year.

Mr. President:

I cannot conclude my statement without clarifying an issue on which confusion has been sown. Attempts have been made to explain the blockade as a result of the cold war and the confrontation that prevailed between the two formerly antagonistic blocks.

But the true historical facts can very easily be found. Suffice it to read the autobiographies of former Presidents Eisenhower and Nixon to understand that since the first few weeks after the triumph of the Cuban Revolution, the Government of the United States instituted its hostility against my country. The adoption of the Agrarian Reform Law on 17 May 1959 was confronted with Washington's stubborn and inadmissible opposition embodied in the implementation of the first acts of the economic warfare that it still wages against Cuba. This happened months, many months before the adoption of the first measures of a socialist orientation in Cuba and much before our re-establishment of relations with the Soviet Union.

Any high school student knows the true motivations of the United States regarding Cuba.

In 1808, ten years before the birth of Karl Marx, the United States tried to obtain from Spain the sale of its then Cuban colony.

In 1823, twenty-five years before the first publishing of the "Communist Manifesto," the United States invented the so-called theory of the "ripe fruit" according to which Cuba, when separated from Spain, would be necessarily incorporated to North America.

In 1898, five years before the founding of the Bolshevik Party, the United States intervened in our war for independence, frustrating it and imposing upon us four years of military rule.

In 1901, sixteen years before the triumph of the Socialist October Revolution in Russia, and while militarily occupying our island, the United States imposed an amendment to the Cuban Constitution through which it stripped Cuba of part of its territory which it still usurps in Guantanamo and assumed the "right" of intervening in Cuba.

Several decades prior to the commencement of the so-called Cold War, the United States intervened in more than one occasion with its occupation troops, ousting and imposing Governments and intervening in all possible manners in the internal affairs of the country until 1 January 1959, when Cuba achieved its full and definitive independence.

Cubans did not import their Revolution from elsewhere. It is the fruit of a struggle lasting for more than a century.

Circumstances facing those who, in the 19th Century, started the long struggle of our people for independence, were even more difficult. They chose the flag with a lone star as the highest symbol of the nation they were striving to build. This star represented the solitude of a small country that had to struggle against colonialism by itself, without allies, in a small island, for thirty consecutive years. But it also represented the indomitable will of a people that would never give up, that would never renounce its independence, that would never betray its principles.

Let no one be confused. Present day Cubans are hoisting that same flag and will know how to defend it with the same impassioned firmness as their forefathers. In defending our Revolution, Cubans defend not only the dignified and just society that we will continue to build in spite of all difficulties, we are not only defending our society without beggars, without illiterates, without anyone forsaken, our society with schools and hospitals and justice and dignity for all, we are also defending the definitively and finally liberated Motherland, the Motherland of which no one, ever, will be able to deprive us.

Thank you.

A8. GENERAL ASSEMBLY PLENARY MEETING, NOVEMBER 13, 1991

(A/46/PV.46, November 15, 1991)

The President (interpretation from Arabic):

The representative of Cuba proposed in his statement that the Assembly defer action on draft resolution A/46/L.20 to the forty-seventh session of the General Assembly.

This proposal would entail the inscription of the item on the provisional agenda of the forty-seventh session of the General Assembly and the carrying over of the draft resolution to that session.

May I therefore take it that the Assembly decides to defer further consideration of this item to the forty-seventh session of the General Assembly, to inscribe this item on the provisional agenda of the forty-seventh session of the General Assembly and to carry over the draft resolution referred to above?

I see no objection.

It was so decided.

The President (interpretation from Arabic):

We have thus concluded our consideration of agenda item 142.

A9. SUMMARY OF PRESS CONFERENCE HELD BY AMBASSADOR ALARCÓN, NOVEMBER 14, 1991

(Unofficial document)

At a press conference held today at Headquarters, Ricardo Alarcón de Quesada, Permanent Representative of Cuba to the United Nations, spoke of the economic, commercial and financial embargo imposed against his country by the United States.

The United States, he said, had accused Cuba of lying, and he wondered why it had failed to express that view in the General Assembly. He imagined that had to do with the fact that, by accusing Cuba of lying, the United States would also be accusing some of its main partners and allies of lying.

He said European and other States which were well known to have close links with the United States were saying that the blockade against Cuba violated international law. The United States, as recently as yesterday, continued to maintain that discussion of the matter at the United Nations would not be appropriate on the grounds that it was an internal decision but, "unfortunately for them," the General Assembly had reiterated that it was a valid item, and decided to continue consideration of the matter next year. In a decision that was, as far as he knew, without precedent, the Assembly had also decided that the draft resolution should be carried over to its next session. In other words, the item would be very much discussed at the United Nations as long as the blockade existed.

It was the United States that was lying, he continued, and was at the same time projecting a very weak position. It was curious to see the remaining super-Power in this new world order protesting of interference in its internal affairs, but not being able to persuade the majority of the Assembly to accept its view, and having to accept the continuation of the debate. He said he would make available to correspondents copies of documentation he had presented to the General Assembly yesterday to back up his statement.

A correspondent asked whether Cuba had decided not to have the Assembly discuss the issue because it had anticipated lack of cooperation among Latin American countries. Mr. Alarcón de Quesada said the only reason why Cuba took that decision was because the United States had put "very serious pressure" on many countries. Cuba knew that United States officials had said that was the highest priority for them at this session of the General Assembly, and that they would very carefully watch everybody's attitude on the matter. They had threatened many countries and Cuba had thought it would not be proper to put its friends and supporters at risk of paying the very high price the United States was imposing.

He said Cuba had not—and would not—withdraw the draft resolution, and would not abandon the question. Many people and institutions around the world were watching the process, and it was hoped they would continue adding pressure for an open debate at the General Assembly. By postponing it to next year, Cuba was trying to create a large movement throughout the world for its cause.

He said Cuba could not suspend credit, punish small countries with economic sanctions, threaten the national security of countries, insult Heads of State and threaten them as if they were colonies. But Cuba could mobilize support, and counted on the support of masses of people. Next year would prove whose position was the stronger. Cuba believed in international solidarity, and had to show understanding of its supporters and trust in their solidarity.

Asked for comment on the fact that the Mack amendment had not been passed, and that foreign subsidiaries could therefore continue to trade with Cuba, he said the amendment was pending Presidential approval. He said the United States had been violating international law, and quoted from a statement by Canada to the effect that that country had been opposed to attempts by the United States to impose its legislation on Canada since the adoption in 1963 of the Cuban Assets Control Regulations. The Mack amendment, he continued, was aimed at preventing any kind of trade through so-called subsidiaries outside United States territory.

Mr. Alarcón de Quesada also quoted from an official note presented to the United States State Department by the Irish Embassy in Washington on behalf of the States members of the European Community, stating that: "The Community is still of the view that the United States have no basis in international law to claim the right to license non-United States transactions with Cuba by companies incorporated outside the U.S.A., whatever their ownership or control."

Senator Mack, he continued, wanted to prohibit the Treasury and Commerce Departments from giving licenses to foreign subsidiaries for trade with Cuba, but the United States had no right to attribute to itself the right to decide whether a foreign company could trade with another country or not. Senator Mack was "a very original guy," and wanted to go even beyond that, and to dictate how trade should be conducted in Britain, in Canada, in Switzerland and throughout the world. He believed this attempt would fail.

A correspondent asked a question in Spanish, which was translated by Mr. Alarcón de Quesada, concerning the attitude of the Rio Group, and Latin American countries in general, on that issue. She asked whether the Rio Group had tried to persuade Cuba not to put the resolution to a vote, and how the Latin Americans could contribute to facilitating a solution.

He replied that the reason had been explained in his address to the General Assembly, and that was the only basis for the decision. The General Assembly had taken a unanimous decision, which would indicate that the Latin American countries were in favour of the proposal. In a wider context, Cuba had very good relations at the moment with the "vast majority of Latin American countries," including the Rio Group. Their actions had proved that they were not supporting the blockade, and some had expressed themselves openly against it. The so-called Group of Three—Mexico, Colombia and Venezuela—had issued a statement in which they expressed their intention to help solve "the problems Cuba experienced with some countries."

Cuba had always been prepared to discuss with the United States any outstanding legitimate bilateral issue, he said, but on the clear understanding and condition that such discussions be held on an equal basis, with respect for the sovereignty of both States. That implied that, as the very first step, the United States had to withdraw its policy of blockade against Cuba. However, immediately after the statement by the Presidents of the Group of Three, a United States State Department spokesman had reiterated the opposition of the United States to any effort of that kind. That clearly reflected the official United States position.

Asked how, if there was a blockade against Cuba, the country had managed to accumulate a debt of $7 billion, and how it was possible to do business with, for example, Spain, Britain, Japan, Venezuela, Brazil and Mexico, Mr. Alarcón de Quesada said not everybody abided by the blockade, which proved that it was not one hundred percent successful, and that the United States had not succeeded in forcing everybody to violate international law, or to accept the imposition of its will. But there was a blockade, as there was a policy to punish those who traded and were interested in having links with Cuba. There was an effort to isolate Cuba economically. To what extent it was successful was another question. It had never been completely successful.

If the resolution had been put to a vote, how many votes would Cuba have received, a correspondent asked. Mr. Alarcón de Quesada said he would not assist the United States in punishing other countries, and would withhold the names of the countries that would definitely have voted in favour of the resolution. Very few countries would have opposed the resolution, and probably a rather large number would have abstained. There had often been reference to the fact that only six or seven countries had appeared on the list of speakers to speak in Cuba's favour. But why, with the exception of Panama, had nobody else inscribed their names to speak in favour of the United States, he asked.

A correspondent quoted the United States as saying the question of the embargo against Cuba was a bilateral matter, and it was not appropriate for discussion in the United Nations, and asked whether Cuba would attempt to enter into bilateral discussions with the United States.

There were a number of bilateral problems in the world that were discussed by the United Nations, he replied. However, this was not a bilateral problem. It was an attempt by the United States to interfere in the sovereign decisions of other countries. No serious Government would accept that argument and that was why the United States— despite the fact that it was not one of the weaker Members of the General Assembly—could still not get the Assembly to drop the item. The item would continue to be the top priority at the United Nations as long as the blockade existed.

Document Distributed At Ambassador Alarcón's Press Conference:
Points Regarding The U.S. Policy Of Blockade Against Cuba

Cuba does not attempt to elucidate within the context of the United
Nations issues regarding the bilateral differences between Cuba and
the United States. Cuba's only intention is to defend its right as a
country to carry out freely its international economic and commercial
relations without any type of interference.

The U.S. has indicated that the debate of this issue by the United
Nations will not result in changes in their policies. This illustrates the
true appreciation by the U.S. of the role of this Organization. Cuba, on
the other hand, is confident that an action by the United Nations which
would favour the cessation of the blockade would be truly conducive to
a more normal development of international relations and would
strengthen the rights of other States in face of measures of this nature.

The policy of blockade against Cuba constitutes a remnant of the
cold war. It is contrary to the general aspiration of achieving a new
spirit of international cooperation and keeps latent a hotbed of tension
without any practical results. Any serious intention by the United States
for the elimination of this hotbed of tension should be necessarily preceded by the lifting of the blockade as an encompassment of a change
in policy.

The blockade is legally structured to influence not only economic
and trade relations between Cuba and the United States, but also attempts to regulate Cuba's relations with other nations as well. For
example, the blockade imposes limitations on the export to Cuba by
third countries of products containing components or materials origi-
nated in the U.S. (even when these have been totally transformed into
a new product or have been produced in that third country), as well as
the export to the United States of products containing Cuban commodities, as sugar and nickel, for example.

Cuba defends the right of each country to choose freely with whom it
wishes to have relations, but not to interfere in the political, economic
and trade relations of third countries, as is the case with the U.S.
policy of blockade against Cuba.

The Government of the United States has exercised strong pressures on the Governments and the entrepreneurial sectors of countries
having commercial relations with Cuba with the aim of hindering those
relations and preventing their development. The United States has
requested those Governments to "carefully examine their economic relations with Cuba and alert local companies against involving themselves with the said country." In other cases it has even indicated to
foreign business sectors that if they ignore the U.S. interest of not
trading with Cuba, Washington would block all commercial and financial operations by their companies in the U.S. territory.

The blockade has consistently been losing credibility and, at present, it constitutes a policy solely defended by the most backward segment of the Cuban emigration in the United States and those politicians committed with it. In fact, within the United States, there are already entrepreneurial, academic, political and religious sectors as well as many in the Cuban community and others, which are already advocating for changes in the present U.S. policy towards Cuba. President Bush in one of his recent statements in Miami was compelled to recognize that he had received many requests in that direction.

The policy of blockade constitutes a serious violation of the human rights of the Cuban people; it deprives it of elements essential to life as foodstuffs and medicines, which do not constitute exceptions from the commercial restrictions as it has been claimed. Since May 1964, the Department of Commerce of the United States amended the regulations for the control of exports, revoking the emission of general licenses for shipments of foodstuffs and pharmaceutical products to Cuba.

The possibility of exporting to Cuba—as final destination subjected to an embargo—goods donated with the aim of satisfying basic human needs, as provided by the law of amendments to exports which went into effect in March 1986, was virtually annulled in August of that year with the Presidential Proclamation No. 5517 which established stricter controls on the organizations promoting trips and the transfer of money and goods to Cuba. This possibility, in short, has never materialized.

One of the arguments with which the U.S. has tried to justify the preservation of its policy of blockade against Cuba is the alleged need to check the "threat posed by Cuba in the Western Hemisphere." (This argument has been used for more than 30 years.)

The relations existing at present between Cuba and the other countries in the Hemisphere, as well as the increasing trend in favour of Cuba's reinsertion in the Intermerican System, clearly and evidently demonstrate the obsolete and anachronistic nature of this policy.

By sustaining the need to maintain and reinforce its policy of blockade against Cuba as a means of preventing "democratically elected governments in Latin America from being subverted," the United States, in order to justify its actions, is invoking the defense of countries that are precisely among our closest friends and with which we maintain the best relations and contacts, without it being a source of concern for them.

Document Distributed At Ambassador Alarcón's Press
Conference: Notes and Messages Received from Various
Organizations, Institutions, and Persons Condemning
the United States Blockade Against Cuba
(Unofficial Translation)

Latin Association for Human Rights. Declaration. La Paz, Bolivia. 12/
12/91

International Socialist Committee for Latin America and the Caribbean. Resolution. Aruba. 11/4/91

Permanent Conference of Latin American Political Parties (COPPAL).
Resolution. Chile. 24/6/91

Latin American Parliament. Cartagena de Indias Declaration. Colombia. 2/8/91

Inter American Meeting on Labor Law and Social Security. Declaration. Havana. 23-25/1/89

Spanish American Political Association. Miami, Florida. 29/9/91

SWAPO Youth League of Namibia. Windhoek. 12/9/91

National Autonomous University of Mexico. Mexico City. 11/9/91

Metropolitan Autonomous University of Mexico. Mexico City. 11/9/91

Permanent Seminar on Chicano and Border Studies. 11/9/91

Mexican journalists, intellectuals, and deputies. 11/9/91

Brazil-Cuba Cultural Association

Mario Mauede, leader of the Workers Party of Brazil. 17/9/91

Silvio Mota, Federal Magistrate.

Mayor National University of San Marcos. Peru. 13/9/91

Senate and Chamber of Deputies. Peru. 18/9/91

Student Federation of Peru. 15/9/91

Minas Gerais Federation. Brazil. 17/9/91

Union of Municipal Public Servants of Belo Horizonte. Brazil.

Mato Grosso Federal University. Brazil. (Environmental Studies Department.)

World Trade Union Federation.

American Association of Jurists.

Popular Socialist Youth. Mexico.

Patriotic Union, Santa Fe de Bogota. Colombia.

International Relations Commission of the United Left of Peru.

Popular Socialist Party of Mexico.

National Federation of the Law School of Peru.

Angola People's Assembly.

Spelman College, Georgia.

Popular Socialist Youth, Durango State Committee. Mexico.

Middle and High School Teachers Association of Buenos Aires.

Cuban Movement for the Peace and Sovereignty of Peoples.

Christian Meditation Group "Solidarity with Latin America."

Fraternity of Baptist Churches of Cuba.

National Technological University. Buenos Aires.

Brazilian Socialist Party.

National Ecumenical Movement of Puerto Rico.

President of the Democratic Labor Party, Mato Grosso. Brazil.

Dante Martins de Oliveira, former Minister of Agrarian Reform and Development. Brazil.

Leader of the Democratic Labor Party in the Senate of the Federative Republic of Brazil.

Anti-Imperialist Tribunal of Our America President Guillermo Torriello.

Evangelical Methodist Church of Panama.

Center for Social Training of Panama.

Employee Association of the University of Panama.

Federation of Associations and Organizations of Public Employees of Panama.

General Confederation of Workers. Peru.

Center for Cuban Studies, New York.

Ecuadoran Parliament.

Mexican Congress.

Peruvian Socialist Movement.

World Council of Churches.

Parliamentarians from Ontario, Canada.

Parliamentarians from Brazil.

Chamber of Deputies of Bolivia.

Latin American Association of Jurists.

Andean Parliament.

Council of Protestant Churches of Latin America and the Caribbean.

Methodist Church of the Caribbean and the Americas.

United Methodist Church of the United States.

Methodist Church of Great Britain.

United Church of Canada.

Ramsey Clark, former Justice Secretary. United States.

80 Philosophers of various U.S. Universities who visited Cuba in June 1991.

Italian Artists.

Spanish Artists.

62 Deputies of the European Parliament representing the following groups: Socialist, Rainbow, Left Coalition, Greens, and Unitarian Left.

Cardinal Angel Suquia, President of the Episcopal Conference of Spain and Madrid Archbishop.

Cuauhtémoc Cárdenas, President of the Revolutionary Democratic Party. Mexico.

Carlos Andres Perez, President of Venezuela.
Chilean Socialist Party.
Popular Intransigence Party. Argentina.
Clifford Durand, Philosophy Professor, Morgan State University, Baltimore.
José Francisco Gómez, Vice President of the Socialist International for Latin America.
Yoruba Religious Society. Cuba.
Lisa Brock, Professor, Chicago Art Institute.
Caribbean Federation of Youth.
Caribbean Conference of Churches.
Association of Workers of the Cuban Community, Miami.
Antonio Maceo Brigade, Miami.
National Coordinator of the struggle for land and housing in Paraguay.
Association of Cuban residents in Germany, Berlin.

A10. CUBA'S INITIAL RESPONSE TO UNITED STATES
RESTRICTIONS ON THIRD-COUNTRY SHIPPING

(A/47/179, April 27, 1992)

Letter dated 24 April 1992 from the Permanent Representative of
Cuba to the United Nations addressed to the Secretary-General

I have the honour to transmit herewith a statement issued by the Ministry of Foreign Affairs of the Republic of Cuba in response to a statement made by the President of the United States on 18 April 1992 concerning my country (see annex).

I request you to arrange for this letter and its annex to be circulated as an official document of the General Assembly, under item 39 of the preliminary list, and of the Security Council.

(signed)
Ricardo Alarcón de Quesada
Ambassador
Permanent Representative of Cuba
to the United Nations

Annex

Statement issued on 22 April 1992 by the Ministry
of Foreign Affairs of the Republic of Cuba

On 18 April 1992 George Bush made a statement in which he reaffirmed his intention to tighten even further the economic, commercial and financial embargo against Cuba.

The statement comes at a time when criticism of this hostile policy is becoming more pronounced than ever among broad sectors of world public opinion, one of the main purposes of the statement being to hamper the efforts of those who oppose that policy.

It is odd that, at a time when opposition to the United States embargo against Cuba is gathering force among men, women and official and nongovernmental organizations representing the most diverse currents of opinion, the President of the United States should make a statement in which he takes so opposite a position.

The facts are so obvious that even officials of the Washington Government have admitted to them in their public remarks.

A recent example is the statement made by a representative of the State Department, Mr. Robert Gelbard, at a hearing conducted in the United States Congress on 8 April.

On that occasion, Gelbard told the legislators that "some Governments" agreed that Cuba should not receive any aid, but that "very few" favoured the imposition of what he called an embargo on that island.

The growing attention paid by world public opinion to this matter was also highlighted towards the end of 1991, when the United Nations General Assembly decided at its forty-sixth session to include in its agenda an item entitled, "Necessity of ending the economic, commercial and financial embargo imposed by the United States of America against Cuba."

As everyone is aware, this item will be open for discussion at the meetings of the General Assembly's session this year.

One of the arguments advanced last year by the United States delegation to the United Nations in its attempt to prevent inclusion of the item in the agenda was that the issue was one of a bilateral embargo—consistent with the provisions of international law—and not a blockade.

Even though there are numerous United States provisions currently in force and from years past which demonstrate conclusively how the White House has been trying to extend its jurisdiction beyond its territory in order to impose its laws, orders and regulations on Cuba, Bush's most recent pronouncement on the subject is of singular significance in this context.

The President makes no attempt to conceal his intention of imposing on Cuba a political, economic and social order which is consistent with Washington's interests, while, without shrinking from hinting at reprisals against countries which do not toe this line, he casts himself in the role of leader of a crusade in which "my administration will continue to stress to the Governments of the entire world" the necessity of isolating the island economically.

In this context and without the slightest moral—or diplomatic, for that matter—hesitation, Bush proclaimed his intention of violating the recognized principle of freedom of the seas when he stated that he had instructed the Department of the Treasury to issue regulations prohibiting vessels engaging in trade with Cuba from entering United States ports.

The United States chief executive has thus openly violated the internationally recognized rules of law in accordance with which no State may employ pressure, coercion or any other actions in restraint of free merchant shipping and freedom of navigation.

This aggressive stance, together with other foreign policy actions in the early years of the 1990s, is a further indication of how the United States Government understands the so-called new world order, while at the same time it sounds a warning that Washington may be seeking to mount a naval blockade against Cuba which would have incalculable consequences.

And this is happening precisely at a time when in many places around the world in a massive, fraternal joining together of people of all races and beliefs, people are pledging their willingness to stand by Cuba's side to send—as the promoters have said—an oil tanker or a ship carrying medicines or powdered milk to our people who are stoically bearing the brunt of a double embargo, especially the embargo which Bush is seeking to tighten further in the name of opening a channel between us and the so-called "peaceful transition to democracy."

The United States President knows that the ships which he is trying to prevent from reaching Cuba are carrying foodstuffs and medicines for the Cuban people and supplies needed, *inter alia,* to provide electric lighting in our homes, to harvest the sugar crop or to keep the school system functioning.

The Ministry of Foreign Affairs of Cuba believes that the statement by the President of the United States in which the ideas described above were put forward has undoubtedly performed the service of highlighting the brutal reality of the economic, trade and financial embargo against our country, and at the same time it has shown the President to be a public instigator of illegal actions violating time-honoured legal norms observed by civilized Governments and nations.

A11. CUBA'S DRAFT RESOLUTION

(A/47/L. 20, November 18, 1992)

The General Assembly,

Determined to encourage strict compliance with the purposes and principles enshrined in the Charter of the United Nations,

Reaffirming, among other principles, the sovereign equality of States, nonintervention and non-interference in their internal affairs, freedom of trade and international navigation, which are also enshrined in many international legal instruments,

Concerned by the promulgation and application by Member States of laws and regulations whose extra-territorial effects affect the sovereignty of other States and the legitimate interests of entities or persons under their jurisdiction, and the freedom of trade and navigation,

Having learned of the recent promulgation by the Government of the United States of America of measures of that nature aimed at strengthening and extending the economic, commercial and financial embargo against Cuba,

1. *Calls upon* all States to refrain from promulgating and applying laws and measures of the kind referred to in the preamble to this resolution in conformity with their obligations under the Charter of the United Nations and international law, and with the commitments which they have freely entered into in acceding to international legal instruments which, *inter alia,* reaffirm the freedom of trade and navigation;

2. *Urges* States which have such laws or measures to take the necessary steps to repeal or invalidate them as soon as possible in accordance with their legal regime;

3. *Requests* the Secretary-General to prepare a report on the implementation of this resolution and to submit it for consideration by the General Assembly at its forty-eighth session;

4. *Decides* to include in the provisional agenda of the forty-eighth session the item entitled "Necessity of ending the economic, commercial and financial embargo imposed by the United States of America against Cuba."

A12. ADDITIONAL REMARKS AT THE GENERAL ASSEMBLY PLENARY MEETING, NOVEMBER 24, 1992

(A/47/PV.70, November 24, 1992)

Mr. Pak (Democratic People's Republic of Korea): On 23 October 1992, in defiance of the strong opposition of the international community, the President of the United States signed into law the so-called Torricelli Amendment against Cuba.

As is well known, for over 30 years the United States has imposed an economic, commercial and financial embargo on Cuba and has sought to coerce it into adopting the political and economic system imposed by the United States.

However, upset by the firm confidence and will of the Cuban people, which has become even more unshakable following the end of the cold war, the United States this time took further measures to tighten the economic blockade imposed on Cuba in order to stifle it and break the Cuban people's confidence in socialism.

The so-called Torricelli Amendment covers a number of measures that have an adverse effect not only on the main sectors of the Cuban economy but also on many social aspects, including medical care and food supply, which are essential to human life.

In adopting that amendment the United States has exceeded the limitations of its national jurisdiction under international law and has also violated the sovereignty of other States.

The so-called Torricelli Amendment is structured not only to influence economic and commercial relations between Cuba and the United States but also to regulate Cuba's relations with other countries by envisaging punitive measures against its corporations and other Governments that maintain commercial relations with Cuba and applying sanctions against those nations that provide any type of assistance to Cuba, while at the same time prohibiting subsidiaries of United States corporations in third countries from embarking upon any commercial transactions with Cuba and prohibiting all vessels that have entered Cuban ports from operating in United States ports for 180 days.

The so-called Torricelli Amendment, given its nature and aims, constitutes a flagrant violation of the fundamental principles enshrined in the Charter of the United Nations, which stipulates the development of friendly relations among nations based on respect for the principles of equal rights and self-determination of peoples.

The Amendment also contravenes General Assembly resolution 2132 (XX), which prohibits the use of economic, political or any other type of measure to coerce another State in order to obtain from it the subordination of the exercise of its sovereign rights, and resolution 2625 (XXV), which recalled the duty of States to refrain in their international relations from military, political, economic or any other form of coercion aimed against the independence or territorial integrity of any State. It is also in violation of General Assembly resolution 36/103, which declares that it is the duty of a State in the conduct of its international relations to refrain from measures which would constitute interference or intervention in the internal affairs of another State, including any multilateral or unilateral economic reprisal or blockade as an instrument of political pressure or coercion against another State.

The elimination of coercive economic measures would contribute to strengthening friendly relations and cooperation between nations and to ensuring world peace and security. We are of the view that for the elimination of coercive measures all nations, and in particular big Powers, should first of all carry out their obligations under the Charter of the United Nations and international law. They should also respect the rights of Member States freely to determine their political and economic systems and should refrain from interference in the internal affairs of other States.

In this regard we welcome the final document of the Tenth Summit Conference of non-aligned countries, held at Jakarta last September, which once again called for the termination of the economic, commercial and financial measures and actions imposed on Cuba for over three decades.

The delegation of the Democratic People's Republic of Korea maintains that the illegal blockade imposed by the United States on Cuba must end immediately and that the so-called Torricelli Amendment, which affects the sovereignty of both Cuba and of third countries that have economic and commercial ties with it, must be repealed without delay.

The Democratic People's Republic of Korea strongly rejects the so-called Torricelli Amendment, considering it to be a piratical one aimed at strangling Cuba and infringing upon the inviolable, sovereign rights of other States and a flagrant violation of international legal instruments that reaffirm freedom of trade and navigation as well as human rights. We urge the United States to take the necessary steps under the Charter of the United Nations to stop such arrogant acts as attempting to force its will upon other nations.

The delegation of the Democratic People's Republic of Korea would also like to take this opportunity to reiterate its support for and solidarity with the Cuban people in their struggle for the sovereignty of their country against interference and blockade.

Mr. Malik (Iraq): (interpretation from Arabic): While we value the efforts that have succeeded in bringing this vital issue to the General Assembly for debate and decision, we feel that, if the norms of international law and the provisions of the United Nations Charter had been complied with, this issue should have been dealt with by the General Assembly a very long time ago. The American embargo against Cuba has been in place for over 30 years. During that time, three aspects have become highlighted. The first relates to the long suffering of the Cuban people and its patience; the second relates to the failure of the American policy; and the third relates to the manner in which this tragic situation and other similar situations have been dealt with at the international level as well as to the role played by the United States in such situations.

In discussing these three aspects, the most important point that takes precedence over all else is that this Assembly should be able to adopt the bold decision of calling for the lifting of the blockade against Cuba, the abandonment of the policy of imposing hegemony on peoples by means of terrorism, war and starvation and for adherence to the real principles enshrined in the United Nations Charter, international law and the Universal Declaration of Human Rights.

I do not think that the international community needs to be presented with statistics, figures and the details of events in order for it to assess the enormous damage that has been inflicted and continues to be inflicted on the Cuban people through the American blockade that has lasted for over 30 years. Undoubtedly the agencies of the United States Administration have a great wealth of information on the extent of the Cuban people's suffering and a very accurate assessment of the economic, social, psychological and other effects of the blockade.

Such detailed information is a must for those agencies in the assessment of the results achieved by the blockade in the all-out effort to make the Cuban people submit to the American will. The long drawn-out embargo and the resultant economic conditions of the Cuban people underscore the blatant trampling by the United States of every value and of all the norms that govern relations between countries and peoples.

The United States has used a variety of methods in fighting the Cuban people. It has not confined itself to the economic embargo but has waged mass-media and psychological war on the Cuban people in addition to threats of direct military intervention. Not content with forcing its own institutions, corporations, companies and citizens to implement the embargo procedures against Cuba, the United States has resorted to various types of pressure, blackmail and threats in forcing other countries and their corporations to refrain from trading with Cuba.

Such a policy cannot be considered as anything other than an act of aggression that falls under the definition of aggression in General Assembly Resolution 3314 (XXIX) of 1974 and that runs counter to the declaration on Principles of International Law concerning Friendly Relations and Cooperation among States in accordance with the Charter of the United Nations contained in General Assembly resolution 2625 (XXV) of 1970. It also contradicts the Declaration on the Preparation of Societies for Life in Peace, contained in General Assembly resolution 33/73 and runs counter to the Charter of Economic Rights and Duties of States, contained in General Assembly Resolution 3281 (XXIX).

The huge losses sustained by the Cuban people as a result of the continued American embargo highlight the fundamental humanitarian dimension that should guide any consideration of the way to deal with such inhuman policies which entail great suffering and hardship for civilian populations, especially children, women and the elderly. The damage done leaves much deeper effects on the following generations and deprives those generations of the right to live in peace and tranquility. Obviously, this is a flagrant and stark violation of the fundamental principles of human rights, as well as the principles of democracy and of equal opportunities.

There is no doubt that all these factors make the discussion of this item at this crucial stage in international relations a matter of very special importance as it embodies all the elements that propel it to the foreground as a case in point that refutes the claims made by the United States and its Western allies when they take to the high ground and declaim about the humanitarian motives of their campaigns in defense of freedom, democracy, international legality, the rule of law and human rights while the United States doggedly pursues the policy of starving those peoples who reject its hegemony and of depriving such peoples of the right to freedom and progress.

In the course of the general debate, at the beginning of this session of the General Assembly, several third world delegations voiced their rejection of the policy of double standards and of monopolization by certain strong Powers of the process of international decision-making at the expense of the smaller and weaker countries. Those delegations have called for a new world order that would embrace all on a basis of justice, equality and uniform, single standards.

The United States' posture against Cuba is not limited to Cuba. It is an aspect of a consistent policy and a permanent approach in dealing with the peoples of other countries.

I do not want to repeat what I said earlier, but I would remind you of what is happening at present to the Iraqi people as a result of the inhuman total United States embargo against Iraq that has been in place for over two years now, through the domination by the United States of the Security Council. The continued embargo against Iraq has no logical, legal or humanitarian justification. Iraq is committed to all the Security Council's resolutions. The letter from the Minister of Foreign Affairs of Iraq to the Secretary-General, dated 19 January 1992, as well as the statement delivered yesterday (23 November 1992) in the Security Council by Tariq Aziz, Deputy Prime Minister of Iraq, in which he expressed Iraq's full commitment to and implementation of Security Council resolution 687 (1991) and its cooperation with the United Nations bodies show that the realities of the situation make it incumbent upon the Security Council to discharge its obligations towards Iraq in accordance with the provisions of the same resolution and to lift the embargo and end the suffering of Iraqi people. The circumstances which were contrived as the pretext for plotting against Iraq, launching aggression against Iraq and imposing the embargo against its people no longer exist. In this connection, I should like to refer to the report of the mission headed by Prince Sadruddin Agha Khan which states that every month that passes brings a huge number of the Iraqi populace to the brink of disaster, and that the first victims, as usual, are the poor, the children, the widows and the elderly, i.e., the most vulnerable sectors of any society. The same report refers to the fact that the effects of the war and the economic sanctions will lead to the exhaustion of the reserves of food and basic commodities included among the subsidized food rations.

We can also refer to the numerous reports of the international humanitarian organizations, both governmental and non-governmental, which have visited Iraq and seen at first hand the critical humanitarian situation and the great shortages of medicines and food supplies, services and commodities which have resulted in exposing thousands of people to death, particularly children under five years of age. This situation makes it quite clear that the United States of America is depriving the Iraqi people as a whole of the right to life, which is the basic and most fundamental of human rights.

The Security Council resolutions which were drafted by experts in the United States Administration themselves have been exceeded by several stages. Those resolutions did not include originally the perpetuation of the embargo with the aim of killing 20 million Iraqi citizens.

If the new international situation has made it possible for the United States of America to hand down its resolutions against Iraq and impose them on the Security Council, its embargo against the Cuban people has not been imposed through the adoption of resolutions by the Security Council. Obversely, the United States lifts the embargo against the racist regime in South Africa, regardless of the existence of binding international resolutions.

These contradictions in the American position are neither erratic nor accidental. They are simply symptoms of the policy of aggression pursued by the United States against peoples, and a reflection of its double standards in dealing with international issues. It is this posture that exposes the vacuity of all the hollow declamations about a new world order. That new world "order" cannot be an order, because it is not based on uniform stable rules: it is fluid and governed by double standards and colonial interests. Neither can it be a "world" order, because it is not universal, it is one country's "order," in alliance with its friends. And it certainly cannot be called "new," as it is a throwback to the hated age of colonialism.

We call upon the international community and, in particular, we call upon the peoples of the Third World, to unite in defence of the legitimate interests of their peoples, the principles of peace, prosperity, stability and in the search for a really new and truly international order that takes its point of departure from the precepts of true universality, justice and democracy.

Proceeding from this, my delegation believes that the international community should take the required and just step to resolve this matter by calling upon the United States of America to end its embargo against Cuba and against other peoples.

Mr. Ndong (Equatorial Guinea) (interpretation from Spanish): The Head of our Delegation, the Minister of Foreign and Francophone Affairs of Equatorial Guinea spoke in the general debate at the forty-seventh session of the General Assembly and now I, on behalf of the delegation of Equatorial Guinea, wish to take this opportunity to say to Ambassador Ganev of Bulgaria and the Bureau how pleased it is at the outstanding manner in which they are guiding our deliberations.

I wish to reiterate my country's and my Government's total commitment to and trust in the San Francisco Charter in general and more specifically the preambular paragraphs and Articles 1, 2, 33 and 41, setting forth clearly the purposes and principles, the pacific settlement of disputes, and actions to be taken with respect to threats to the peace, breaches of the peace, and acts of aggression. It is my delegation's understanding that we should consider the substance of agenda item 39 against the background of those concepts. Each of us here as sovereign States Members of the Organization should become fully aware of our responsibilities and reconsider our old positions so that we can cooperate with this our Organization so that it can fully discharge its mandate to find solutions ensuring peaceful coexistence and international security for all.

As members are aware, the Republic of Equatorial Guinea is a small country but it holds dear peace and tranquility. We are one of the poorest countries of the world but we feel very proud, rich and important because of our ideals, our convictions, our faith in justice, sovereign equality, mutual respect, nonintervention in internal affairs and in the self-determination of peoples. We believe that these principles continue to be basic and valid and are the pillars underlying the construction of the true road to peace.

It is our unwavering conviction that it is the rejection of these principles, or attempt to discredit, devalue or invalidate any of these principles, that leads to current tension on the planet and could also suddenly lead to self-destruction, in other words, a third world war.

This issue, the necessity of ending the economic, commercial and financial embargo against Cuba, is in the view of my delegation rather arbitrary and unfair. Mankind has no colour, name or face. In my statement in the general debate at the forty-sixth session of the General Assembly, on 10 October 1991, when speaking on the item that is now before us for our consideration today, I said

". . . we urge the United States of America and the Republic of Cuba to open the doors to negotiations in order to arrive at solutions acceptable to the peoples on both sides, innocent victims of their rigid positions. That is an urgent requirement of the new era in which we find ourselves. The international community and history will praise and thank them for it." *(A / 46 / PV. 30, p. 70)*

In supporting the initiative at this session of the General Assembly and the efforts being made to unblock the situation we also appeal to all other sovereign States Members to support the decision which will be taken by the Assembly.

The Republic of Equatorial Guinea, consistent with its political beliefs and decisions and in keeping with international principles, is currently carrying out a democratization process and adopting a multi-party system, regardless of egoistical pressures and interests by third countries and false friends. Against this background of our convictions and in order to contribute to international peace we will vote in favour of draft resolution A/47/L. 20/Rev.1.

His Holiness Pope John XXIII, of sainted memory, in a sincere desire to bring together the entire community of believers, said when he opened Vatican II on 12 October 1962:

> "We are not trying to establish who is right and who is not. There is only one thing that we will say to all of you. Let us reunite."

In the political sense, reuniting means searching for peace. The international community and the development of the poorest and most disadvantaged countries require this; it is an imperative.

Mr. Elhouderi (Libyan Arab Jamahiriya) (interpretation from Arabic): My country's delegation supports what was stated by Indonesia on behalf of the non-aligned countries.

The economic, trade and financial embargo imposed by certain States on other States are factors which cause tension in international relations, for, in addition to the extremely harmful effects of this type of blockade, coercive measures in any shape or form run counter to the principles of international law and contravene the resolutions of the United Nations. Article 32 of the Charter of Economic Rights and Duties of States, adopted by the General Assembly at its twenty-ninth session, stipulates that

> "no State should use or encourage the use of economic, political or other measures to coerce another State so as to obtain from it the subordination of the exercise of its sovereign rights." *(3281 (XXIX), art. 32)*

This clear principle which emanates from the Charter of the United Nations has been reiterated in several General Assembly resolutions, such as 38/197, 39/210, 40/185 and 44/215 in which the General Assembly calls upon all developed States to refrain from the threat of imposing trade restrictions, blockades or embargoes or any other economic sanctions against developing countries, as such practices run counter to the Charter of the United Nations and to multilateral and bilateral commitments and constitute a form of political and economic coercion that has negative effects on the economic development of the countries subjected to them.

In this context, we would recall that the ministerial conference of the Group of 77 last year called upon the international community to adopt urgent and effective measures to put an end to the use of economic coercion measures, especially against developing countries as a means of imposing the will of any one country on another. The non-aligned countries also have taken the same stance in the declaration agreed to by the Ministers of Foreign Affairs of the Movement last May wherein they voiced their regret regarding the continued use of coercive economic measures against developing countries.

The world-wide consensus embodied in these international instruments, resolutions and declarations clearly underscores the international community's rejection of this coercive approach in international relations. Regardless of the fact, however, that the international community has expressed the undeniable desire that all countries in the world should seek to settle their differences and disputes in keeping with the United Nations Charter and the principles of international law, the policies of pressure, boycott and embargo continue to be pursued by developed countries against developing countries, as can be seen from the issue before us for consideration today.

The economic, financial and trade embargo that has been in place against Cuba for more than three decades has had extremely serious effects on the Cuban people, a people that is small in number and whose resources are limited. It is not at all difficult to assess the additional burdens and hardships that will ensue from the continued imposition of this siege, in the light of the information contained in the statement by the Minister of Foreign Affairs of Cuba in the General Assembly last September. In that statement, it was made clear that the intention continues to be to expand and intensify the economic embargo against Cuba, by various means which include the imposition of restrictions on merchant ships trading with Cuba, the obstruction of international trade with Cuba in general and the prevention of that country from purchasing such essentials as medicines, food and oil products.

The building of an international community in which justice, equality and respect for human dignity may prevail in a climate of harmony and constructive international cooperation will be feasible only when the way of life of the past is renounced and the residues of the cold war are swept away. The emergence of such an equitable international community depends on respect for the sovereignty of States, the promotion of dialogue, the renunciation of policies of confrontation and the encouragement of States to settle their differences by peaceful means in line with international covenants. My delegation is of the view that such tendencies which consolidate the effects of current international changes should apply to all aspects of international relations and should result in ending pressures, lifting blockades, embargoes, boycotts, and reversing the freezing of assets by certain developed countries against a number of developing countries, including my own, which has been a victim of such measures for about a decade now. If the States concerned should choose to listen to this call, they will not only promote overall world economic growth but will also consolidate the foundations of constructive international cooperation and pave the way towards friendly relations which would certainly promote international peace and security and create a climate of trust, harmony and cooperation between all peoples.

Mr. Al-Haddad (Yemen) (interpretation from Arabic): The representative of Indonesia spoke on behalf of the Movement of Non-Aligned Countries, and we associate ourselves with what he said with regard to the economic blockade against Cuba. The international community, which continues to experience profound changes in the course of this period of transition, looks forward to the achievement of the goals of the United Nations Charter and hopes that all states will respect the Charter and the rules of international law governing relations between States.

All countries—large and small, rich and poor—hope to strengthen all kinds of economic and social cooperation amongst them and aspire after the emergence of a world order of justice and peace. The achievement of such goals require that the States Members of the United Nations show respect for the principles of national sovereignty, non-interference in the internal affairs of other countries and respect for the economic, social and political choices of other States.

Under the agenda item now before the General Assembly, the question is not merely the economic and trade blockade against Cuba and the need to lift it. Rather, it is that States Members of the Organization should not enact laws that infringe the sovereignty of other States and that lead, *inter alia,* to restricting the freedom of trade and navigation or to impose economic, trade or financial blockades against those other States.

The international community's efforts which aim at strengthening international multilateral and bilateral cooperation in all fields, require that all States should honour their commitments, particularly those contained in international instruments, as this would serve to enhance stability and prosperity and ensure the maintenance of international peace and security.

Mr. Hadid (Algeria) (interpretation from French): The end of the cold war gave rise to great hopes that dialogue and cooperation in the interest of peace and development would prevail in international relations.

Those same notions of peace, cooperation and development that have already been debated at length in this Hall also form the basis of our consideration of agenda item 39. The state of the relations between Cuba and the United States of America leads us to reaffirm our view that misunderstandings and bilateral disputes between States Members of the Organization should be addressed through dialogue and through efforts made by each party, in keeping with the new constructive spirit that should prevail in today's world. Such an approach, based on mutual respect for the principles of the United Nations and of international law, would, in our view, contribute to the maintenance of international peace and security and the strengthening of international cooperation for development.

Our debate today also raises the issue of the repercussions on developing countries of recent changes in the countries of Eastern Europe and the former Soviet Union. Those repercussions must be borne in mind as we examine the issue before us. Indeed, the case of Cuba is a particularly eloquent example of their negative effect on a number of developing countries. Linked as it was to the countries of the former socialist group by very close economic ties, 85 percent of its trade having been with those countries. Cuba's economy has been seriously affected.

This situation highlights once again the need to give due attention to the strengthening of all aspects of international cooperation so that the changes in Eastern Europe can become a positive factor in the evolution of the world economy. That surely calls for mechanisms and measures that will benefit the developing countries.

We hope that today's debate will promote dialogue and cooperation in the settlement of disputes and the renewal of development for the benefit of all.

Mr. Mumbengegwi (Zimbabwe): Allow me to begin by welcoming the statement made by the Ambassador of Indonesia on behalf of the Non-Aligned Movement. The Zimbabwe delegation fully supports his statement.

The end of the cold war brought with it many possibilities hitherto unimaginable. One of the most significant possibilities was that of former adversaries around the world that had previously stood on opposite sides of the ideological divide coming together to resolve their differences through negotiation and dialogue, as called for in the Charter of the United Nations. Zimbabwe would have hoped that, whatever differences might have existed in the past, this global easing of tensions between States would have generated sufficient momentum to render the current debate unnecessary.

Of particular concern to the international community is the fact that what could have been regarded as bilateral differences have assumed an international dimension because of measures that have extraterritorial elements impacting negatively on the sovereign right of every State to engage freely in international trade and other forms of international cooperation, irrespective of any differences in political, economic and social systems, as provided for in the basic principles of the United Nations and of international law.

My delegation believes that negotiation and dialogue constitute the best method of settling differences between States Members of our Organization in the post–cold war era. This is consistent with the call in the Charter for all peoples and nations to practise tolerance and live together in peace as good neighbours, so as to promote the economic and social advance of all peoples, leading to social progress and better standards of life in larger freedom.

Mrs. George (Trinidad and Tobago): My delegation abstained in the vote on draft resolution A/47/L. 20/Rev. 1. However, while Trinidad and Tobago accepts that States are free to enact legislation governing their trading relations with other States, my delegation wishes to record its objection to the extraterritorial application of such regulations as can affect the sovereignty of third States.

My delegation also wishes to associate itself with the statement made earlier today by the representative of Indonesia on behalf of the non-aligned States.